A clear survey and analysis of Wesleyan missions and mission studies, written by thirty-one authors in five continents. I wholeheartedly welcome this scholarly work as an excellent tool to reflect on world mission in today's context.

—**Jan A. B. Jongeneel**
Utrecht University

Even a single good essay on "World Mission in the Wesleyan Spirit" would be welcome. That the editors have here assembled thirty-one outstanding essays on the subject is a great tribute to them, an enormous gift to readers, and an enduring legacy for the world Church. John and Charles Wesley would be pleased. I predict that this book will serve a vital role in every corner of the world parish for years to come.

—**Jonathan J. Bonk**
Executive Director
Overseas Ministries Study Center

This volume is a veritable 'Who's Who' of Wesleyan missiologists which promises to be one of the most important books in Protestant missiology to be published during this decade. It will be a classic text read by pastors, missionaries, mission executives, and students of mission the world over. It will be required reading in my missions courses.

—**Charles Van Engen**
School of Intercultural Studies
Fuller Theological Seminary

This volume represents a significant milestone in mission studies and fills a void in the scholarly literature in missiology. The editors have assembled an impressive list of international contributors. This tour de force makes *World Mission in the Wesleyan Spirit* a veritable goldmine. It is a magnificent service to world Christianity!

—**Tite Tiénou**
Dean and Professor of Theology of Mission
Trinity Evangelical Divinity School

The American Society of Missiology Series seeks to publish scholarly work of high merit and wide interest on numerous aspects of missiology—the study of Christian mission in its historical, social, and theological dimensions. Able proposals on new and creative approaches to the practice and understanding of mission will receive close attention from the ASM Series Committee.

American Society of Missiology Series, No. 44

World Mission
IN THE WESLEYAN SPIRIT

Edited by
DARRELL L. WHITEMAN and GERALD H. ANDERSON
Foreword by DAVID B. BARRETT

Providence House Publishers
WWW.PROVIDENCEHOUSE.COM
FRANKLIN, TENNESSEE

Library of Congress Control Number: 2009932813

ISBN: 978-1-57736-424-5

Cover illustration of "John Wesley Preaching on His Father's Grave" *provided through the courtesy of the Watkinson Library, Trinity College, Hartford, Connecticut.*

Cover design by LeAnna Massingille

All scripture quotations, unless otherwise indicated, are taken from the Holy Bible: New Revised Standard Version/Division of Christian Education of the National Council of Churches of Christ in the United States of America.—Nashville: Thomas Nelson Publishers, c 1989. Used by permission. All rights reserved.

Scripture quotations marked GNT are from the Good News Translation in Today's English Version-Second Edition Copyright © 1992 by American Bible Society. Used by Permission.

Scripture quotations marked NIV are taken from HOLY BIBLE, NEW INTERNATIONAL VERSION®. Copyright © 1973, 1978, 1984 by International Bible Society. Used by permission of Zondervan Publishing House.

Scripture quotations marked RSV are taken from the Revised Standard Version of the Bible, copyright 1952 [2nd edition, 1971] by the Division of Christian Education of the National Council of the Churches of Christ in the United States of America. Used by permission. All rights reserved.

Scripture quotations marked NKJV™ are taken from the New King James Version®. Copyright © 1982 by Thomas Nelson, Inc. Used by permission. All rights reserved.

Scripture quotations marked KJV are taken from the Holy Bible, King James Version, Cambridge, 1796.

Scripture quotations marked ESV are taken from the Holy Bible: English Standard Version, copyright © 2001, Wheaton: Good News Publishers. Used by permission. All rights reserved.

Scripture quotations from The Message Copyright © by Eugene H. Peterson 1993, 1994, 1995, 1996, 2000, 2001, 2002. Used by permission of NavPress Publishing Group.

PROVIDENCE HOUSE PUBLISHERS
238 Seaboard Lane • Franklin, Tennessee 37067
www.providencehouse.com
800-321-5692

CONTENTS

PREFACE TO THE SERIES

The purpose of the American Society of Missiology Series is to publish—without regard for disciplinary, national, or denominational boundaries—scholarly works on missiological themes from the entire spectrum of scholarly pursuits relevant to Christian mission, which is always the focus of books in the Series.

By "mission" is meant the effort to effect passage over the boundary between faith in Jesus Christ and its absence. In this understanding of mission, the basic functions of Christian proclamation, dialogue, witness, service, worship, liberation, and nurture are of special concern. And in that context questions arise, including: How does the transition from one cultural context to another influence the shape and interaction between these dynamic functions, especially in regard to the cultural and religious plurality that comprises the global context of Christian life and mission?

The promotion of scholarly dialogue among missiologists, and among missiologists and scholars in other fields of inquiry, may involve the publication of views that some missiologists cannot accept, and with which members of the Editorial Committee themselves do not agree. Manuscripts published in the Series, accordingly, reflect the opinions of their authors and are not understood to represent the position of the American Society of Missiology or of the Editorial Committee. Selection is guided by such criteria as intrinsic worth, readability, coherence, and accessibility to a range of interested persons and not merely to experts or specialists.

The ASM Series seeks to publish scholarly works of high merit and wide interest on numerous aspects of missiology—the scholarly study of mission. Able presentations on new and creative approaches to the practice and understanding of mission will receive close attention.

THE ASM SERIES COMMITTEE
Jonathan J. Bonk
Angelyn Dries, O.S.F.
Scott W. Sunquist

FOREWORD

One gloomy morning in the year 1904, my Taid (Welsh for grand-father) Richard Davies crossed the road and entered his tiny Calvinistic Methodist chapel in Barmouth, Wales. Things looked dreary as he began his sermon. Suddenly, three people in the small congregation stood up and then fell flat on the floor. Three more followed suit. Most of the congregation followed likewise, shouting and singing in what would later be called "being slain in the Spirit." Rushing to a phone, Davies called his Wesleyan ministerial colleagues across Wales. Astounded and amazed, he heard that all were at that moment experiencing the same phenomena. Thus began the noted Welsh Revival. During the next six months, there were 100,000 new converts to Christ, sometimes amounting to thousands every day. Several hundred became foreign missionaries to Asia, Africa, Europe, and South America. Then one gloomy day in 1905, the Revival suddenly stopped and the phenomena never returned.

RECORDING THE EVIDENCE

Some eighty years later, the Mission Society for United Methodists was launched in Dallas, Texas, in 1985, and I was privileged to preach the inaugural sermon. The search for data and explanations goes on. The Welsh Revival is recorded today by Wesleyan Methodists in nine publica-tions in Welsh and many others in English. The whole course of Methodism and the Wesleyan movement worldwide can thus be followed from the shelves of the world's fifty thousand biggest libraries. There we find a total of 6,330 distinct Wesleyan publications in English, 440 of which are books or tracts written by Wesley himself and other ministers. Every publication has now been catalogued and documented—books, booklets, letters, gospels, Scriptures, journals, dissertations, maps, videos, CDs, DVDs, musical scores, sound recordings, archives, reports, and surveys. We now add the 31 ground-breaking essays in this volume, *World Mission in the Wesleyan Spirit,* bringing the total to 6,361.

REACHING TWO HUNDRED FIFTY LANGUAGES

The contributing authors are familiar in great detail with some aspect and culture of the Wesleyan world. They are multilingualists, which is essential to such study. In fact, study of the progress on this worldwide movement is greatly assisted by the publishing of Wesleyan materials, listing their publications from the year 1738 to the present. In addition to the works written in English, Wesleyan materials have been published in the following languages.

In the German language we find 143 Wesleyan books and other publications; Korean 78 publications; French 53; Spanish 49; Japanese 28; Swedish 26; Dutch 20; Portuguese 16; Chinese 14; Welsh 9; Norwegian 7; Italian 6; Russian 4; Bulgarian 4; Latin 4 (one written by Wesley himself); Hindi 3 (one being *Life of Wesley* in 2003); and Greek 3. There are 40 languages with only two publications, and another 100 languages with only one publication—a total of more than 150 languages, not including those languages which have not yet been recorded.

LANGUAGES WITH NO REVIVAL PHENOMENA

One puzzling observation is that of the world's 407 lingua francas (each with over a million speakers), the majority have no Wesleyan materials: there are at least 50 more very large languages with no Wesleyan materials—Arabic, Swahili, Hausa, Bengali, Marathi, Punjabi, Urdu, Somali, Javanese, Dari, Persian, Amharic, Sinhalese, and more than 30 others.

The underlying reason for this situation is primarily the absence of strong Protestant missions, Methodists in particular, in these areas. In many such cases, we find strong Roman Catholic missions, most of which center on and parallel Wesley's counterparts—Francis of Assisi, Dominic, Loyola, Xavier, Thomas à Kempis, Las Casas, Teresa, and innumerable other Wesley-types. It should also be noted that Wesley materials are well known in several Roman Catholic circles. Catholic libraries invariably have surprising numbers on these subjects.

STRATEGIZING FOR WESLEYAN WORLD MISSION

This analysis poses a major problem for the Wesleyan approach to world mission. The total Wesleyan influence of all kinds—laity, clergy, missions, publications, Scriptures, finance, *et alia*—touches around 30 percent of the task of world mission. Catholics, Orthodox, and their own influence is around 30 percent as well, and has extensive influence in another 30 percent, often sympathetic to the Wesleyan 30 percent. This means in fact that both 30 percent (60 percent together) should be cooperating rather than ignoring the 40 percent remaining unreached or unevangelized areas and peoples who currently have no access to Christianity, Christ, or the Gospel.

PAST, PRESENT, AND FUTURE IN GLOBAL MISSION

A very abbreviated statement on the subject of our 31 new essays will now be made. This takes the form of a tiny modification of a diagram of the whole extent of Christian history which has been published in my book, *World Christian Trends* (2001), on page 88. That diagram portrays the relative size of the Christian mission throughout the two thousand years of Christian history. We modify the changes bringing the expansion of Christianity up to date during the last one hundred fifty years. The purpose of the diagram is to utilize the detailed statistics produced by all churches. The whole purpose of such statistics is not to indulge in triumphalism, but to illustrate the progress of the three-fold graphic depiction: 1) to describe the historical past of the Christian movement; 2) to describe the numerical requirements of the present, such as publicity and arrangement for the many major current conferences; and 3) to present the churches and agencies as they plan for the future.

The modification of the contemporary Christian scene shows the central parts of Protestantism and Catholicism separated by a band illustrating Christian outreach with a broken line—Catholicism above the line, Protestants below. This illustrates the endeavour of one side to convert or at least to recognize the existence of the other. The situation depicts the Wesleyan world's relation with the Catholics—as outlined above the roughly 30 percent of the resources for Wesleyan world mission, 30 percent for Catholic resources, leaving 40 percent unreached by either bloc. It is a shockingly similar situation to the global situation of that of 105 years ago in the year 1904.

A DETAILED LOOK AT WESLEYAN RESOURCES

The table on page xv sets out a major component of one aspect of this global mission—the deployment of church members. There is a startling number of new developments, especially the huge numbers since 1965 of Catholic and Protestant Charismatics. One line therefore has been described at this point—the Catholic Charismatics, now numbering 120 million. They penetrate communions and are active with their Protestant counterparts, so that in any statement of global influence they are close to sharing in the Wesleyan model.

UNDERSTANDING TOTALS

The table ends with five different statements on the number of Wesleyans in the world. These are not contradictory, but arise from differing meanings. Thus "doubly-counted" is not a statement of incompetence: it can also mean "doubly-committed." The reader is thus invited to examine the exact meaning of the words as derived.

SUMMARY

These 31 essays are not only absorbing reading, they illuminate the current worldwide situation and its call to new kinds of collaboration.

David B. Barrett
Richmond, Virginia
April 2009

WESLEYAN INFLUENCE AND AFFILIATION TODAY
(with tentative or estimated figures)

Rank a	Organization b	Initials c	Members d	% Wesleyan e	Wesleyans f
1.	World Methodist Council	WMC	70,226,000	100.0	70,226,000
2.	Independent Methodist Churches	IMC	3,000,000	100.0	3,000,000
3.	Christian Holiness Association	CHA	5,000,000	92.0	4,600,000
4.	International Moravian Unity of Brethren	IMUB	1,042,000	90.0	900,000
5.	Global Network of Mission Structures	GNMS	7,700,000	70.0	5,390,000
6.	Protestant Charismatics	ICO	100,000,000	60.0	60,000,000
7.	World Evangelical Alliance	WEA	420,000,000	30.0	126,000,000
8.	Pentecostal World Fellowship	PWF	52,821,000	14.0	7,390,000
9.	World Council of Churches	WCC	560,000,000	12.5	70,000,000
10.	Catholic Charismatic Renewal	ICCRS	120,000,000	10.0	12,000,000
11.	Christian World Communions	CCWC	2,149,000,000	3.5	75,228,000
12.	Global Christian Forum	GCF	2,200,000,000	3.4	75,228,000
	Total Wesleyans including doubly-counted or doubly-committed				509,962,000
	Doubly-counted Wesleyans in Western countries (Europe, Northern America)				214,088,000
	Doubly-counted African, Amerindian, Asian Wesleyan-type				80,000,000
	Total of Wesleyans and Wesleyan-types in all lands				215,874,000
	Total Wesleyans			1.9	**130,000,000**
	Global population				**6,828,157,000**

Legend:
- a. rank (shown in column e in descending order of commitment to Wesleyanism)
- b. organization
- c. initials of b
- d. members of b whether Wesleyan or not
- e. percent Wesleyan in b
- f. Wesleyans in the world (including doubly-counted where stated)

INTRODUCTION

In 1984, the Mission Society for United Methodists was founded by a group of United Methodist pastors and lay leaders in the United States. This mission-sending organization was created as an alternative to the official General Board of Global Ministries of The United Methodist Church, and therefore did not have the formal endorsement of The United Methodist Church. From those humble beginnings, God has blessed the growth of this organization so that twenty-five years later, there are 215 missionaries serving in thirty-five countries around the world, supported by 322 churches and 5,334 individuals. The Mission Society has become a global entity responding to spiritual and material needs throughout the world. While retaining its Wesleyan ethos and heritage, The Mission Society has expanded beyond its initial United Methodist orbit. Today, it is working with fourteen different denominations and independent churches, and its missionaries come from many denominational traditions. Therefore, in 2005 the "for United Methodists" part of the original name was dropped in favor of simply The Mission Society.

This collection of essays commemorates the twenty-fifth anniversary of The Mission Society. On this occasion, we want to take a look at world mission in the past and the present, with anticipation of future directions and opportunities. God's mission in the world can be understood through several perspectives, each of which is needed to understand God's mission in its fullness. Therefore, we have organized these essays into the following categories: biblical, theological, historical, cultural, and strategic perspectives.

What does it mean to do and to understand world mission in the Wesleyan spirit? These essays will fill out in both broad strokes and considerable detail how a Wesleyan theological orientation shapes our practice of mission. For example, woven through the fabric of these essays is John Wesley's concept of prevenient grace, the notion that God is at work in every people group revealing something of God's self and nature, preparing them for saving grace and eventually sanctifying grace. The

Wesleyan spirit in world mission is also seen in the integration of evangelism with social ministries in what is frequently called holistic mission. In practical everyday activity, this means that we hold together both the Great Commission and the Great Commandment. Jesus did not divorce calling people to repentance and eternal life from responding to their daily needs, to their broken bodies, and to their damaged spirits. Mission in the Wesleyan spirit has held these two dimensions of the Gospel together in creative tension, and continues to do so today. This is the legacy, empowered by the Holy Spirit, that motivates The Mission Society in all it does.

In his inaugural sermon at the dedication of the Mission Society for United Methodists on May 6, 1985, David B. Barrett said it was "like being present, in New Testament days, on that occasion in A.D. 45 when the church in Antioch met to commission and send out Barnabas and Saul on their first missionary journey . . . with its sense of excitement, its sense of expectancy, its sense of being in the direct line of God's will."

Time magazine described Dr. Barrett's *World Christian Encyclopedia* as "a miracle." Once again, Dr. Barrett is party to "a miracle"—this time to celebrate what God has done with The Mission Society. Joining with him in this celebration, thirty-one scholars and church leaders from Asia, Africa, Latin America, North America, and the United Kingdom have contributed to this anniversary volume which marks a milestone in the endeavor of an agency that seeks to advance the mission of Jesus Christ "so that the world may believe" (John 17:23) and "for the healing of the nations" (Rev. 22:2). There is still a sense of excitement, a sense of expectancy, and a sense of being in the direct line of God's will.

Darrell L. Whiteman
Gerald H. Anderson

PART ONE
Biblical Perspectives

IN THIS SECTION, WE RECEIVE INSIGHTS FROM SCRIPTURE that help us understand God's mission in the world. Daniel Arichea reminds us that the way Jesus lived and interacted with people and his culture is the best model for Asians to understand how to become followers of Jesus. As a model, Jesus reminds us of the importance of identifying with the poor, how to both embrace and critique culture, and how to interact with people from other religious traditions. Arichea reminds us that theological Christology is of less importance to Asians than is practical Christology, for "explaining the human and divine nature of Christ is not as important as discovering how Jesus himself is pertinent to the actual situations of Asians."

Dean Flemming helps us see that the Jerusalem Council debate in Acts 15, which laid down guidelines concluding that Gentiles don't have to become Jews in order to follow Jesus, is an excellent paradigm for doing contextualization today in a Wesleyan spirit. Wesley's emphasis on Scripture and experience, for example, as seen in the Jerusalem Council debate, reminds us that "our theology does little good unless it is demonstrated in the everyday lives of God's people." The many parallels between Wesleyan theology and the debate and conclusions of the Jerusalem Council give us good guidelines for contextualizing theology in diverse cultural and religious contexts.

We turn to the Old Testament story of Jonah for the final chapter in this section. Here we see Jonah portrayed as a reluctant missionary, but more important, as Sandra Richter notes, we see that God, "as the lord of the cosmos, cares about every man, woman, and child on this planet."

World mission informed by Scripture is fundamental to a Wesleyan understanding of mission, and in this section we see this clearly expressed in the person of Jesus, the debate of the Jerusalem Council, and in the story of Jonah.

1

JESUS AS PARADIGM

AN ASIAN PERSPECTIVE

Daniel C. Arichea, Jr.

INTRODUCTION

Theology in Asia has been primarily patterned after the theology of the West. This is so because, with very few exceptions, Christianity came to Asia from the West, and theological education in Asia has been modeled after that of the West. For one thing, Asian theologians were sent for training to the countries of the colonizers.[1] For another thing, theological schools in Asia were patterned after theological schools in the West, with most of the teachers coming from the West as well.

THE "PERSON" OF JESUS

This background is necessary in order to understand the development of Christological concerns in the Asian church. Three things can be mentioned. First, there was great interest in the "person" of Christ, especially as the second person in the Trinity. Is Jesus human or divine, and how is he related to the whole issue of the Trinity? This focus on the person of Christ has influenced Christology so much that even in addressing the relationship between Christianity and other religions, a great deal of attention is given to the relationship of Christ with religious personalities who are prominent in the living faiths of Asia.[2]

JESUS AS SAVIOR

Second, the role of Jesus Christ that was considered as primary and most important is that of Savior, that is, one who saves people from sin and guarantees them a place in the eternal heavens. The Gospel that came to Asia was primarily addressed to individuals, urging them to make decisions for Jesus, which means accepting him as personal Savior and Lord. This focus on individual salvation made the Gospel otherworldly; it became a message of hope and comfort to people whose earthly existence was characterized by suffering and hopelessness. The Gospel message enabled them to endure all of life's trials and tribulations, and assured them glory and honor beyond this life. This world is, after all, not their final home; there is a world "somewhere beyond the blue" that is waiting for them.

JESUS AS JUDGE OF CULTURE

Finally, a third observation: the Christian faith was understood as a judgment against receptor cultures.[3] The primary stance of the Western missionary movement was that of Christ against culture. More often than not, the receptor culture was regarded as anti-Christ and anti-Christian, and therefore part of the darkness that needed to be overcome by the light of Christ. People and communities who came to Christ must necessarily reject their own culture.

Culture in the Asian context is quite broad in its scope. In many countries, culture includes religion; in fact, culture and religion are so closely intertwined that it is impossible to separate them.[4] If the receptor culture was not acceptable as a vehicle of the Gospel, then what happened? Since the Gospel never comes disembodied, the result in most cases was for the Gospel to be proclaimed with the use of Western cultural categories; in many instances, the Gospel message and its Western garb were so closely intertwined that it was not possible to distinguish one from the other. And what happened to Asians who accepted the Gospel message? They also accepted the vehicle through which the Gospel came to them, and that vehicle was Western culture in one form or another. So Asians who became Christians became something that they were not: they became believers of a Western message and began to live within a Western cultural framework. The end result of all this was that Christ was regarded as a foreigner, and the Christian faith was regarded as alien to Asia as well. As Phillips says, "It is one of the ironies of history that Christianity, which was born in Asia, has become 'alien' in its own home."[5]

JESUS AS PARADIGM

In the light of all of this, how should we do Christology in Asia today? There is a need to capture and put emphasis on the Jesus of the Gospels as paradigm for Asian Christian communities both collectively and individually. We Christians in Asia should be able to go beyond theoretical discussions and theological affirmations about Jesus Christ, and move toward a posture of *imitatio Christi* in both our attitude and behavior. It is not Christology per se, but "Christopraxis." In the words of an Indonesian scholar, "Christopraxis is a Christology of action where truth is done and applied by mirroring the ministry and humanity of Christ."[6] More accurately, it is "Jesu-praxis," imitating Jesus, or in the words of 1 Peter, to "follow in his steps" (1 Pet. 2:21 GNT).

To achieve this, there needs to be a serious attempt to focus on the life and ministry of Jesus, which receives very little attention in the New Testament other than in the Gospels. For example, the main focus of Paul in his letters is the death, resurrection, and return of Christ.[7] While these are important especially for their salvific value, yet in the context of Asia, the life of Jesus has more meaning and significance. Jesus is revealed much more in his words and deeds while on earth than by his death, resurrection, and return. It is not that the role of Jesus as Savior from sin and as the giver of eternal life is discarded altogether. It is simply that for Jesus to be Savior from sin and the giver of eternal life, he must first of all be Savior for the present life.

Therefore, when we talk of Jesus as paradigm, we mean that his words and actions provide us with guidelines on what we should do as his followers in the distinct contexts in which we find ourselves in various parts of Asia.

RELATION WITH THE MARGINALIZED

There are at least three areas in which this concept of Jesus as paradigm can be applied: marginalized people, culture, and religious plurality. So first we ask, can Jesus be a paradigm for us as we consider the Asian situation in which so many people live in the margins and are regarded by society as secondary and insignificant? What can we glean from the Gospels?

One reason why the Jesus of the Gospels is so attractive to Asians is because he paid attention to people with whom Asians can identify: the poor, the sick, the forgotten, the outcasts, women, and children. He fed the hungry; he healed the sick; he raised the dead; he comforted the sorrowing. When John the Baptist sent people to ask Jesus whether he was the Messiah or not, his answer was, "Go back and tell John what you are hearing and seeing: the blind can see, the lame can walk, those who suffer from dreaded skin diseases are made clean, the deaf hear, the dead are brought back to life, and the Good News is preached to the poor" (Matt. 11:4–5 GNT). In the Beatitudes (Matt. 5:3–12 and Luke 6:20–26), God promises blessings to those who would be considered by society as undeserving of praise. Included among them are the poor. In Luke, Jesus is quoted as saying "Blessed are you poor." In Matthew, this is rendered as "Blessed are the poor in spirit." This does not spiritualize the problem of poverty but relates material poverty to spiritual poverty. People are "poor in spirit" because first of all they are materially poor. Because of their poverty, they find it extremely difficult or even impossible to fulfill the requirements of the Jewish religion.[8] But no matter. Jesus includes them among the blessed ones.

When we read the Gospels, we get the distinct impression that Jesus was always on the side of those who were despised and rejected by society as well as by organized religion; he identifies with them and works for their liberation. This is clearly seen both in his actions and his teachings. The Gospels present a Jesus who was with the *ochloi*, the crowds, and who interacted with all kinds of people in society, including those who were hated and despised, such as Zealots, tax collectors, prostitutes, and people afflicted with leprosy and other sicknesses.

Jesus' identification with the poor and the oppressed has resulted in the development of various kinds of theologies that address the concern of the marginalized in society. Examples of these are the Minjung theology in Korea, Dalit theology in India, and the theology of struggle in the Philippines.[9] It is here where we see the importance of theological developments in Asia, where Asian values are taken seriously and where the Gospel is interpreted through Asian eyes and

Asian hearts. While there is a great deal of diversity in Asia, there is at least one common element in all the endeavors of doing theology in Asia, namely, the emphasis on the importance of people who are generally not given much importance by society. Jesus thus becomes the model for Christian life, and his teachings become the law of the faith community. It is this aspect of Christology that many Asian theologians are rediscovering.[10]

The one major problem in Asia, and in a real sense the root of all other problems, is poverty. In a document[11] circulated at the 2008 General Conference of The United Methodist Church, it was noted that "half of the world's population—nearly 3 billion people—live on less than $2 a day."[12] Half of the 3 billion are Asians! Asia is rich in natural resources, but its people are poor. And the church in Asia is poor. If Christianity has to have an impact, it must address more vigorously this problem of poverty. Since the church is poor, it cannot simply have a ministry to the poor, but more appropriately, it must discover how to work with and among the poor. It must follow Jesus, who became poor for the sake of the world.

We Asians, particularly those in the Wesleyan tradition, need to remind ourselves not only of our New Testament roots, but of our Wesleyan roots. Once again we must have a serious conversation with John Wesley, who was truly concerned for the poor and throughout his entire ministry paid attention to the "least of these" in society.[13]

RELATION WITH CULTURE

Second, how should Jesus be a paradigm for Asians as they live in the midst of diversity of cultures? Asia is a cultural minefield. One cannot move from one country to another without realizing the rich diversity that is Asia itself. For example, of the six thousand or so living languages in the world, more than half are in Asia. And of course, most of the religions of the world originated in Asia and continue to thrive in Asia.

In our endeavor to take Asian culture seriously and use it as a worthy and effective vehicle of the Gospel as it is proclaimed and lived out in Asia today, the Jesus of the Gospels once again becomes a model for us. Jesus took seriously Jewish culture and its demands. He regularly attended synagogue meetings. As a faithful Jew, he went regularly to Jerusalem to attend the required religious festivals.[14] Jesus' sensitivity to culture is also shown

in his message, which he conveyed often with the use of cultural categories
with which his Jewish audiences could identify. He used parables, many of
which were taken from agricultural settings and very appropriate for rural
Palestine. He talked about shepherds and sheep, landlords and tenants,
the birds of the air, the grass of the fields, the mustard seed. Certainly one
cannot read the Gospels without getting the impression that Jesus was at
home in his own culture.

But Jesus did not observe cultural requirements blindly. In fact he
subordinated culture to human need. When culture (even religious
culture) conflicts with the fulfillment of human need, culture should be
sacrificed, for after all, culture is secondary to human concerns. This is
shown clearly in Jesus' attitude toward the Sabbath. In many cases he
broke the rules of the Sabbath in order to respond to human need.[15]

Jesus' attitude toward culture has something important to say to us
Asians. We need to believe and affirm that there is no such thing as
Christian or un-Christian cultures. All cultures, including our own, have
the potential of being used as vehicles and instruments of the Gospel.
Nevertheless, in any culture there are elements that don't measure up
to the standards of the Gospel and may prevent people from being
faithful to the Gospel message. It is because of this that there is a need
for a critical attitude toward culture in relation to the Gospel, and when
necessary certain elements in culture must be either rejected or transformed to make sure that they conform to the Gospel's demands.

Jesus' attitude toward culture is therefore a good model for us Asians
as we are confronted with the diversity of cultures and as we endeavor to
use Asian categories to express our faith, whether these be in theological
affirmations, church structures, art, music, or other avenues.[16]

It is inevitable however that questions related to these endeavors
would arise. How far can we go in the utilization of nonbiblical cultures
and still be faithful to the Gospel message? How far can we talk of an Asian
Christ without compromising the real Christ as revealed in the
Scriptures? Is it legitimate at all to put an Asian face to the Gospel?

Here Asians need to be in conversation with the Gospel of John: "The
Word became a human being, . . . and lived among us" (John 1:14 GNT).
Jesus, the Incarnate Word, became a Jew, a product of his day and time.
His involvement in a specific language, a specific culture, and a specific
geographical setting has the effect of sanctifying language, culture, and
geography, and giving these earthly factors the potential of becoming

worthy vehicles of the Gospel message. The Word becoming incarnate in Galilee does not make Galilee special, but makes every place in the world a potential Galilee, that is, a scene of the Incarnation of the Word. The Word becoming incarnate within the Aramaic language does not make Aramaic special, but makes every language in the world a potential Aramaic, that is, a language that is worthy as a means of proclaiming the Gospel. The Word becoming incarnate within Jewish culture does not make Jewish culture special, but makes every culture in the world potentially worthy as an instrument of the Gospel.

Here Asians also need to be in conversation with the apostle Paul. In his message to the Athenians on Mars Hill (as recorded in Acts 17:22–31), he includes this quotation: "In him we live and move and have our being." (NIV) This has become part of many prayers in the church. In its original setting, however, this saying is part of a poem to Zeus attributed to Epimenides the Cretan (about 600 B.C.E.):

> They fashioned a tomb for thee, O holy and high one—
> The Cretans, always liars, evil beasts, idle bellies!
> But thou art not dead, thou livest and abidest for ever,
> For in thee, we live and move and have our being.

Paul takes this hymn to Zeus and uses it to refer to the God revealed in Jesus Christ. Since he was speaking to Athenian scholars, he quoted from their own literature.

Can Paul be a model for us? Are we brave enough to take our religious folklore and other traditional literature and apply them to the Christian God in much the same way that Paul did with Greek literature? Are we willing to locate within our culture literary types that are equivalent to the literary types in the Bible, use them in Bible translation, and utilize them as vehicles in the effective proclamation of the Gospel?

RELATION WITH OTHER COMMUNITIES OF FAITH

Finally, a third point. How can Jesus be a paradigm for us Asian Christians in our dealings with people who belong to other religious traditions? Our concern is not primarily how Jesus should be proclaimed relevantly in the midst of religious diversity, but what Jesus can teach us

Asians as we live out our faith as a minority group among peoples belonging to various religious traditions.

This is no easy matter, especially considering the fact that Jesus was never directly confronted with other religious movements. Jesus was a Jew, and the only religion he had dealings with was Judaism. So then how can he become a paradigm for Asian Christians?

In the Gospel of Mark, Jesus begins his ministry with a one-sentence sermon: "The right time has come . . . and the Kingdom of God is near! Turn away from your sins and believe the Good News!" (Mark 1:15 GNT). Except for chapter 4, there is no record in Mark's gospel of any lengthy teaching of Jesus about the kingdom of God. Instead of teaching about it, Jesus demonstrates it by his actions and in his interaction with other people. The tone is set in the first chapter of Mark, verse 38: "We must go to the other villages around here. I have to preach in them also, because that is why I came" (GNT). And Mark makes clear that the "other villages" do include Gentile territories. It is an accepted fact that while the majority of the people in Palestine during Jesus' time were Jews, there were non-Jews among them. In fact, there were even Gentile territories, that is, areas where the majority of the people were Gentiles.

In Mark's gospel, Jesus seemed to habitually cross over into non-Jewish territory! As he did, he encountered Gentiles and responded to their pleas for healing and help. In Gadara, obviously a Gentile territory because of the pigs, Jesus healed a man by sending the demons to a herd of pigs (Mark 5:1–20). Chapter 7 records three of these visits to Gentile territories. In the city of Tyre, Jesus had a confrontation with a Canaanite woman, and at the end of the encounter, Jesus pronounced her as a woman of great faith (Mark 7:24–30). Then Jesus visits the Decapolis and heals a deaf-mute (Mark 7:31–37). And finally, Jesus takes his disciples to the Gentile city of Caesarea Philippi, and it was there where Jesus asked his disciples the question about who he was to them (Mark 8:27ff).

All these visits to Gentile territory seem to indicate Jesus' attitude toward Gentiles. By going to Gentile territory and by including in his ministry the healing of Gentiles, Jesus goes against the exclusive tendencies of his time, and opens up the possibilities for the establishment of a more inclusive community that would include not only Jews but Gentiles as well. Here again, we see that Jesus does not say anything about accepting Gentiles into the fellowship of the church. What he does, so many times, is to enact living parables that truly demonstrate the nature of the community that he wants to establish, namely, a community that knows no racial or national barriers.

Jesus also becomes a paradigm by what he taught. A relevant passage here is Matthew 5:43–48, where Jesus exhorts his followers to love their enemies. Doing good to enemies is not a new idea. In the book of Proverbs, there is such an exhortation, which Paul quotes in Romans 12:20, "If your enemies are hungry, feed them; if they are thirsty, give them a drink; for by doing this you will make them burn with shame" (GNT).

In the above passage, doing good to enemies is motivated by self-interest: you do good to them not because it is the right thing to do, but because it is a good strategy for putting them in their proper place.

Jesus, on the other hand, has no such motivation. In fact, his use of the word "love" in relation to enemies is something that is new. We are told to love our neighbors. But to love our enemies? That is humanly impossible; in fact, that is being completely irrational and irresponsible! But Jesus anchors loving the enemy on a very important tenet of faith, that is, the very doctrine of creation: all of us, that is, all humankind, are created by the one God. This would mean then we are all sisters and brothers, regardless of the faith community to which we belong.

How does all of this apply to us Asian Christians, especially in the context of religious plurality? Through the example of Jesus, we are being challenged to live out the ethical implications of our faith in our relationship with those who belong to other faith communities. One regrettable fact is that we Christians sometimes (and often!) exhibit the exact opposite attitude of what Jesus taught and exemplified in his actions. Our relationship with our non-Christian neighbors has been characterized more often than not by arrogance rather than by humility, by hatred rather than by love, by rejection rather than by acceptance. In short, we have not been very good neighbors to the non-Christians around us.

It is inevitable that questions would arise related to these endeavors.[17] One of the most serious issues is how to deal with the exclusive claims of the Christian faith, as represented for example by John 14:6 ("I am the way, the truth and the life") and Acts 4:12 ("no other name"). This is connected to the whole issue of truth and revelation: is there truth in other faiths, or is the truth only revealed by God through the Christian faith?

In this regard, Asian Christians need to be in conversation with the apostle Paul. In the Acts 17 passages that we have already referred to,

Paul tells the Athenians, "I see that in every way you Athenians are very religious. For as I walked through your city and looked at the places where you worship, I found an altar on which is written, 'To an Unknown God.' *That which you worship, then, even though you do not know it, is what I now proclaim to you*" (Acts 17:22–23 GNT, emphasis added).

In a sense then, Paul acknowledged that the Athenians were worshiping the true God although they were not aware of it. Can we at least try to see the "Unknown God" in other religious movements?

Here Asian Christians, especially those in the Wesleyan tradition, need to be in conversation with John Wesley. He had, for instance, quite a positive attitude toward other religions, claiming that some people who belong to other religions may have been given the experience of "true religion" through "God's inward voice." Further, while he does recognize and affirm the distinctiveness of Christ and the experience of forgiveness through him, he does not condemn to hell all others who have no faith in Christ. Maddox writes: "He repeatedly prefaced claims about the qualifications for eternal salvation with an exemption from consideration of those who received only initial revelation. He argued that Scripture gave no authority for anyone to make definite claims about them. Their fate must be left to the mercy of God, who is the God of heathens as well as of Christians."[18]

CONCLUSION

In conclusion, then, it is apparent that in the context of Asia today, theoretical or systematic Christology has much less relevance than practical Christology. Another way of putting it is that the matter of explaining the human and divine nature of Christ is not as important as discovering how Jesus himself is pertinent to the actual situations of Asians. We should continue to proclaim his death and resurrection. We should recover the meaning of his ascension as the means by which he now fills the whole universe (Eph. 4:10). But most important, in the context of Asia today, we must discover and rediscover again and again the relevance of his earthly life and his teachings. Christology must become Christopraxis.

NOTES

1. Thus, Indonesian church leaders found their way to theological schools in the Netherlands, church leaders from the Philippines got their theological education in the United States, and most Indian theologians found their way to Great Britain. Asian theologians were also trained along denominational lines, with Lutherans going to Lutheran theological schools in Germany and other parts of the world. This was also true with Methodists and Presbyterians and other denominations.

2. This is illustrated in many publications. For instance, in *Asian Faces of Jesus* (ed. R. S. Sugirtharajah, Maryknoll, N.Y.: Orbis Books, 1993), the articles include "Jesus and Krishna," "Christ and Buddha," and "Confessing Christ in the Islamic Context," which includes discussion on the relationship of Jesus and the prophet Muhammad. I still remember the religious debates in the 1950s and 1960s centering on the issue of whether Jesus was divine; these debates were triggered by the resurgence of a religious group known as Iglesia ni Cristo (Church of Christ) that denied the divinity of Christ. The Iglesia ni Cristo has since grown into quite a large religious group with more than two million adherents.

3. Using the categories of H. Richard Niebuhr, *Christ and Culture* (San Francisco: HarperCollins, 2001).

4. Thus in Thailand, being Thai and being Buddhist are one and the same; in Malaysia, a Malay is by definition a Muslim.

5. T. V. Phillips, *East of the Euphrates: Early Christianity in Asia* (Delhi: CSS and ISPCK, 1998), p. ix.

6. Daniel Lucas Lukito, *Making Christology Relevant to the Third World* (Bern, Switz.: Peter Lang, 1998), p. 23. The subtitle of Lukito's book is "Applying Christopraxis to Local Struggle."

7. These aspects of Christ are also emphasized in the liturgy of Holy Communion, where the mystery of faith is proclaimed as "Christ has died; Christ is risen; Christ will come again."

8. During the time of Jesus, wealth was needed in order to fulfill the requirements of religion. Thus the wealthier one was, the closer that person was to God. Wealth and prosperity were considered signs of God's blessings. No wonder the disciples reacted very strongly to Jesus' statement that it is very difficult, in fact, impossible for a rich person to enter the kingdom of God: "Who then can be saved?" Such a reaction made sense. If the rich can't be saved despite all their wealth, then how can poor people be saved when they have no wealth at all! But Jesus turns this around. It is in fact those people who are considered poor in spirit who are blessed by God.

9. Some recent publications include: *Dalit and Minjung Theologies: a Dialogue*, Dalit-Minjung Theological Conference (2005), Serampore, India (Bangalore: BTESSC, SATHRI, c2006). Manohar Chandra Prasad, *The Book of Exodus and Dalit Liberation, with Reference to Minjung Theology* (Bangalore: Asian Trading Corp., 2005). Eleazar Fernandez, *Toward a Theology of Struggle* (Maryknoll, N.Y.: Orbis Books, 1994).

10. An example of this is represented by Carlos Abesamis, *A Third Look at Jesus* (Quezon City, Philippines: Claretian Publications, 2000). He says that his emphasis is more on telling the story of Jesus rather than "drafting formulas about Jesus and his nature" (p. 3). See also *Asian Faces of Jesus*, ed. R. S. Sugirtharajah, (Maryknoll, N.Y.: Orbis Books, 2001).

11. "The Poor in a Global Church: What Is at Stake for United Methodists?" report presented by the General Board of Higher Education and Ministry at the 2008 General Conference of The United Methodist Church.

12. The report cited in the previous note also includes the following facts:

- The gross domestic product of the poorest 48 nations (i.e., a quarter of the world's countries) is less than the wealth of the world's three richest people combined.
- The world's richest 500 individuals have a combined income greater than that of the poorest 416 million people.
- A staggering 1 billion children live in poverty (1 in 2 children in the world); 640 million live without adequate shelter; 400 million have no access to safe water; and 270 million lack access to health services.
- Each day 30,000 children die due to poverty and preventable diseases.
- The United States, the richest nation in the world, reported an official poverty rate of 12.6 percent in 2005, representing 37 million Americans.
- In 2001, the poverty rate for minors in the United States was the highest in the industrialized world; and in the same year, this country had the highest relative poverty and deep poverty among 11 industrialized countries.

13. The best book so far on this subject is *The Poor and the People Called Methodists*, edited by Richard P. Heitzenrater (Nashville: Kingswood Books, 2002). When one reads Wesley's *Journal* and *Sermons*, one gets the impression that many members of the Methodist societies during Wesley's time were poor. Accordingly Wesley conducted his ministry in such a way that he and the societies would maximize their help to and concern for the poor.

14. The reference for this is the Gospel of John, in which Jesus travels back and forth from Galilee to Jerusalem. In the Synoptic Gospels, Jesus stays most of the time in Galilee and only spends the last week of his earthly life in Jerusalem.

15. In Mark 2:23–28, we are informed that while walking through some wheat fields on a Sabbath morning, the disciples began to pick the heads of wheat, an act

that was legal on ordinary days but illegal on the Sabbath. Now obviously the disciples had a purpose in what they did; Matthew in fact specifies that the disciples were hungry (Matt. 12:1). Jesus knew that the disciples were doing something against the law, but he justified their action with these words: "The Sabbath was made for the good of human beings; they were not made for the Sabbath. So the Son of Man is Lord even of the Sabbath" (Mark 2:27–28 GNT).

In Mark 3:1–6, Jesus comes in direct conflict with religious authorities. Confronted with a man whose hand was paralyzed, Jesus asked the people, "What does our Law allow us to do on the Sabbath? To help or to harm? To save someone's life or to destroy it?" (Mark 3:4 GNT). It is worthy of note that right after this incident, the religious authorities began to make plans to kill Jesus.

16. Already there are attempts to produce Asian liturgy and Asian music. This obviously was the motivation behind the establishment of The Asian Institute of Liturgy and Music (AILM) in Quezon City, Philippines.

17. It is well known that there are three positions in the relationship of the Christian faith with other faiths: the exclusive (one against all), the inclusive (one above all), and the pluralist (one with and among all). For a brief discussion of this, see Hope Antone, "Living with Pluralities," in *The Asian Church in the New Millennium: Reflections on Faith and Life* (ed. Raul Fernandez-Calienes, Delhi: ISPCK, 2000), pp. 20*ff*.

18. Randy Maddox, "Wesley as Theological Mentor: The Question of Truth or Salvation Through Other Religions," *Wesleyan Theological Journal* 27 (1992): pp. 7–29. Maddox cites for support John Wesley's Sermon 91, "On Charity," Sermon 127, "On the Wedding Garment," and Sermon 130, "On Living Without God." The other pieces of information in the above paragraph are all taken from Maddox's article.

BIBLIOGRAPHY

Abesamis, Carlos. *A Third Look at Jesus*. Quezon City, Philippines: Claretian Publications, 2000.

Abogunrin, S. O., et al., (eds). *Christology in African Context*. Nigerian Association for Biblical Studies. Nairobi: Philarem Corporate Printers, 2003.

Alangaram, A. *Christ of the Asian People: Towards an Asian Contextual Christology*. Bangalore: Asian Trading Corporation, 1999.

Bediako, Kwame. *Jesus and the Gospel in Africa: History and Experience*. Maryknoll, N.Y.: Orbis Books, 2004.

Chediath, G. *Christology*. Kottayam, India: Oriental Institute of Religious Studies, 2002.

Christianand, M. P. *The Mystery of Christ*. New Delhi: Indian Society for Promoting Christian Knowledge, 2001.

Dalit-Minjung Theological Conference 2005, Serampore, India. *Dalit and Minjung Theologies: A Dialogue*. Bangalore: BTESSC, SATHRI, c2006.

De la Torre, Miguel A. *The Quest for the Cuban Christ*. Gainesville: University Press of Florida, 2002.

Fernandez, Eeleazar. *Toward a Theology of Struggle*. Maryknoll, N.Y.: Orbis Books, 1994.

Fernandez-Calienes, Raul, ed. *The Asian Church in the New Millennium: Reflections on Faith and Life*. Delhi: ISPCK, 2000.

Gavin D'Costa, ed. *Christian Uniqueness Reconsidered*. Maryknoll, N.Y.: Orbis Books, 1990.

Griffith, Paul J. *Christianity Through Non-Christian Eyes*. Maryknoll, N.Y.: Orbis Books, 1990.

Heitzenrater, Richard P., ed. *The Poor and the People Called Methodists*. Nashville: Kingswood Books, 2002.

———. *Wesley and the People Called Methodists*. Nashville: Abingdon Press, 1995.

Kuster, Volker. *The Many Faces of Jesus Christ*. Maryknoll, N.Y.: Orbis Books, 1999.

Lalpekhlua, L. H. *Contextual Christology: A Tribal Perspective*. Delhi: ISPCK, 2007.

Lukito, Daniel Lucas. *Making Christology Relevant to the Third World: Applying Christopraxis to Local Struggle*. Berne, Switz.: Peter Lang, 1998.

Maddox, Randy. "Wesley as Theological Mentor: The Question of Truth or Salvation Through Other Religions." *Wesleyan Theological Journal* 27 (1992): 7–29.

Miguez Bonino, Jose. *Faces of Jesus: Latin American Christologies*. Maryknoll, N.Y.: Orbis Books, 1984.

Mugambi, J. N. K., and Laurenti Magesa, eds. *Jesus in African Christianity: Experimentation and Diversity in African Christology*. Nairobi, Kenya: Initiatives Publishers, 1989.

Niebuhr, H. Richard. *Christ and Culture*. San Francisco: HarperCollins, 2001.

Pedraja, Luis G. *Jesus Is My Uncle: Christology from a Hispanic Perspective*. Nashville: Abingdon Press, 1999.

Phillips, T. V. *East of the Euphrates: Early Christianity in Asia*. Delhi: CSS and ISPCK, 1998.

Prasad, Manohar Chandra. *The Book of Exodus and Dalit Liberation, with Reference to Minjung Theology*. Bangalore: Asian Trading Corp., 2005.

Schreiter, Robert J., ed. *Faces of Jesus in Africa*. Maryknoll, N.Y.: Orbis Books, 1991.

Stinton, Diane B. *Jesus of Africa: Voices of Contemporary African Christology*. Maryknoll, N.Y.: Orbis Books, 2004.

Sugirtharajah, R. S. *Asian Faces of Jesus*. Maryknoll, N.Y.: Orbis Books, 1993.

Tangonan, Wilfredo H. *Social Transformation in the Philippines: Three Methodist Contributions*. UMI Microfilm, 2007.

2

CONTEXTUALIZATION IN A WESLEYAN SPIRIT

A Case Study of Acts 15

Dean Flemming

Contextualizing the Gospel well has never been easy. Today Christians in a variety of global settings struggle with how to tell and live the Gospel in culturally appropriate ways, without giving away too much of the Gospel in the process. Some resist contextualization in the name of preserving a "pure" Gospel. Others pursue local relevance to the point that the Gospel itself becomes all but unrecognizable. Are there scriptural resources that can help us steer via media between these two pitfalls?

I believe there are. The biblical writers not only give us theological and ethical content; they also model a process of doing theology in authentic and context-sensitive ways. The New Testament is brimming with "case studies" in contextualizing the Gospel of Christ. Among the most instructive is Luke's narrative of the Jerusalem Council in Acts 15. This essay, then, has a three-fold aim:

- to show how Acts 15 models a process of doing theology in light of new and challenging circumstances;
- to note points of coherence between the Jerusalem Council story and the perspective of Wesleyan theology; and
- to consider ways in which this narrative might inform the church's task of contextualizing the Gospel today.

DOING THEOLOGY IN ACTS 15

The Council of Jerusalem is a watershed event in Luke's story of the Gospel's progress from its Jewish beginnings to becoming a word for all people. It is also perhaps the most comprehensive account in the New Testament of the church doing contextual theology. Acts 15 illustrates how the unchanging Gospel can speak a fresh word to changing circumstances.[1]

The need for theological reflection is triggered by a crisis in the young, multicultural church. Certain Jewish believers from the mother church in Jerusalem insist that Gentile converts be circumcised and keep the Jewish law, like Jewish proselytes. Only then can they have "a place at the table" in the messianic community (vv. 1, 5). The key issue is not whether the Gentiles can be included in the people of God, but rather the conditions of their membership.

The young church faces sharp theological disagreement, involving two competing interpretations of the Gospel. For the conservative Jewish Christians, circumcision was not simply an optional cultural form. It was an indispensable symbol of the covenant relationship with God—a matter of spiritual life and death. Representatives of both the mother Jerusalem church and the younger culturally mixed community in Antioch debate the issue extensively (vv. 6–7).

The theological crisis is resolved by three speeches: from Peter (vv. 7–11), Paul and Barnabas (v. 12), and James, the spokesperson for the Jerusalem church (vv. 13–21). Crucially, James redefines the idea of the "people of God" to include non-Jews (v. 14). Together these speeches present a unified case: Gentiles do not have to become Jewish—culturally, nationally, or religiously—in order to be full-fledged followers of Christ.

At the same time, the Council asks Gentile converts to make four concessions—the so-called decree (vv. 20–21, 28–29). Scholars debate the precise significance of these restrictions.[2] Some see them as prohibitions against practices associated with idolatry and pagan temples.[3] More likely, they represent the kind of elementary purity taboos found in Leviticus 17–18, which relate to Gentiles who live as "foreigners" among Jews (so argue most commentators). The main purpose of these prohibitions is to enable Gentile Christians to maintain fellowship with Jewish believers within a "mixed" church. The Council thus forges "the double principle of no needful circumcision on the one hand and no needless offense on the other."[4]

A MODEL FOR CONTEXTUALIZATION?

Can this story serve as a pattern for contextualizing the Gospel today? Some are skeptical. Timothy Wiarda, for example, argues that the process we see in Acts 15 and what happens now are not analogous. The Jerusalem Council, he notes, occurred at a critical turning point in the history of salvation. What is more, it involved the decision-making of the early apostles and elders, which cannot be repeated today.[5] Wiarda concludes that any paradigmatic value of Acts 15 is minimal.[6]

Granted, the unique role of the Council in the early progress of the Gospel means that it cannot serve as a prescriptive blueprint. Nor can we take the details of the church's decision, such as specific stipulations from the decree, as normative for all time. Nevertheless, within the book of Acts, this narrative has an exemplary function. Part of the goal of Acts is to call its readers to be involved in God's plan to bring salvation to the ends of the earth.[7] The stories Luke tells—the preaching of the apostles, the church's Spirit-led witness to Jews and Gentiles, the church's theological response to new circumstances—provide models for his audience as they explore how to live out God's mission in their own settings.

That is especially true of the extended and pivotal narrative of the Jerusalem Council. Apparently, Luke is not only interested in the theological outcomes of the Council; he is also concerned with the theological process within the story. This narrative carries profound implications for the church, both in Luke's day and our own.[8] Acts invites us to read ourselves into the Jerusalem Council story. We can learn from the journey it describes as we articulate and embody the Gospel within demanding circumstances today.

ACTS 15 IN A WESLEYAN CONTEXT

While reflecting on Acts 15, I have been struck by the number of points at which this narrative resonates with classic Wesleyan concerns. This story seems well suited to inform the task of contextualizing the Gospel in a Wesleyan spirit. Consider the following elements.

The Spirit's Work As The Context For Creative Theologizing

Acts 15 bristles with references to the activity of God or the Holy Spirit. God's recent work among the Gentiles guides the church in rethinking its theology. The basis for the church's theological insight is that "it seemed good to the Holy Spirit and to us" (v. 28 NIV). This suggests both divine and human participation in the theological process. But the order of words implies that the will of the Spirit is paramount.[9] The Spirit brings discernment to a Christian community in theological dialogue. Presumably, this guidance involves recognizing God's genuine activity in the lives of others (vv. 7–14), as well as grasping how Scripture speaks to the situation (vv. 15–20).

This attention to the work of the Spirit is consistent with a Wesleyan approach to Scripture and doing theology. Wesley believed that the will of God revealed in Scripture could only be grasped through the Spirit's ongoing illumination.[10] Furthermore, Wesley emphasized "the immanent work of the Holy Spirit in the people's lives and in the task of theology."[11]

There is a dimension of contextualization that goes beyond pragmatic methods. All of our efforts to do context-sensitive theology flounder if the Holy Spirit does not inspire, guide, and enable the church. Like the Council, we especially need the Spirit's discernment in order to recognize when our theological and ethical reflections are in accordance with Scripture and God's working. At the same time, we must be open to the Spirit's check on our theological innovations.

The Decisive Role Of Scripture

Scripture plays a vital and authoritative role in the church's theological reflection. James clinches his argument before the Council with an appeal to Amos 9:11–12 (Acts 15:15–18). Scripture shows that the incorporation of the Gentiles into the people of God was prophesied long ago. This is entirely fitting. For a Jewish Christian audience, questions about observing the law needed to be resolved on the basis of Scripture.[12]

But notice how James uses Scripture here. He does not say that Peter's story of God's inclusion of the Gentiles agrees with Scripture. Rather, he declares that the words of Scripture agree with "this" action of God (v. 15). This implies that what God is doing in the church leads to a fuller understanding of Amos's prophecy.

Using familiar Jewish exegetical strategies, James brings out the significance of Scripture for the setting at hand.[13] For example, he selects the Greek translation (LXX) of Amos 9:11–12, rather than the Hebrew Masoretic text. This is crucial, since the Greek text affirms that all of humanity will seek the Lord when God restores David's reign

(Acts 15:17a). Moreover, James adapts Amos's prophecy to the context. By omitting phrases and varying the translation of the main verbs, James clarifies that Amos speaks of the rebuilding of the eschatological temple of the messianic age. Amos, then, rightly interpreted, provides a scriptural basis for the inclusion of the Gentiles in the end-time people of God.

Immediately, James applies this fresh interpretation of Scripture to the situation: Gentiles are freed from the requirements of circumcision and observing the law (v. 19). Furthermore, Scripture is apparently the source for the stipulations placed on Gentile believers to ensure fellowship within an intercultural church. In Acts 15, then, "the authoritative role of Scripture is intertwined with the experience and concrete needs of the community."[14]

Contextualization in a Wesleyan spirit will recognize the primacy of Scripture in the theological process.[15] Authentic contextualization is never context-driven. It must be grounded in the normative Gospel revealed in Scripture. This is especially important when deciding among different theological visions and cultural concerns.[16]

At the same time, Wesley did not craft his theology in light of Scripture alone. Scripture guides our theological reflection in conversation with other witnesses: reason, the traditions of a faithful community, and the life experience and context of God's people.[17] This dynamic interplay enables Wesleyan contextualization to be open to new insights and to speak a fresh word to changing circumstances.

Likewise, a Wesleyan approach to contextualization will not treat the biblical text in a static, wooden fashion. We cannot slavishly limit ourselves to language and thought forms that were meaningful to people in the first-century Greco-Roman world. Under the Spirit's guidance, we must find ways to unpack the meaning of Scripture that make sense to people where they are.

The Place Of Experience

The experience of God's work among the Gentiles is critical to the Acts 15 narrative. Initially, Gentile conversions spark the theological crisis that leads to the Council (14:27–15:1; cf. 15:4–5). Later, the narratives of that experience help to liberate the church for an unfettered Gentile mission. Peter retells the story of the breakthrough in Caesarea and then interprets it theologically (vv. 7–11). Paul and Barnabas recount God's mighty acts and the assembly is silenced (v. 12). James appeals to Peter's story as a reason for coming to a new understanding of who makes up the people of God (vv. 13–14). Ultimately, these particular stories become the community's story.

This resonates with a Wesleyan openness to the role of experience in the theological process. Wesley believed that the truth of Scripture and Christian doctrine was confirmed by the corporate experience of the Christian community.[18] Put differently, our theology does little good unless it is demonstrated in the everyday lives of God's people.

An experiential component to contextualization might be especially important for churches ministering in postmodern or majority world contexts. In many settings today, living stories of faith and transformed lives carry a greater impact than tightly reasoned arguments.

The Role Of The Community And Its Leadership

The Acts 15 story has striking *communal* character. The community as a whole, including its leaders, is involved from beginning to end. The "apostles and elders" in Jerusalem ultimately debate (v. 7), decide (v. 25), and dispatch representatives to Antioch, bearing an authoritative letter (vv. 22–23). James, who represents continuity with Jesus and the church's Jewish roots, plays the leading role.

But the Council does not simply make a "top-down" decision. Luke takes great pains to emphasize the participation of the wider community, in terms of:

- sending and receiving delegates (vv. 3–4);
- listening to and evaluating the testimonies of God's work in the lives of his people (v. 12);
- confirming the decision of its leaders (v. 22); and
- receiving and endorsing the exhortation of the Council (v. 31).[19]

Not only the leaders, but also the collective mind of the church recognizes how the Spirit's wind is blowing: "It seemed good to the Holy Spirit *and to us*" (v. 28, emphasis added). The whole church acts as an intercultural hermeneutical community, resulting in a new and fuller understanding of the Spirit's work.

This communal factor coheres with a Wesleyan approach to interpreting Scripture and doing theology. To be Wesleyan involves a willingness to identify with "the universal church and Christian teachings through the centuries" (tradition).[20] It also includes openness to the insights and experiences of the wider community of faith.

Today that will mean doing local theology in light of the global church. We must learn to think, not just contextually, but also *transcontextually*. This requires truly listening to one another in a spirit of humility. It means enabling our various contextual insights to contribute toward a richer, fuller grasp of God's word and its implications. Are we willing to allow our cherished interpretations and theologies to be challenged—even corrected—by the insights of fellow believers in Lagos, London, or Lima?

To cite a personal example, it was only while teaching in the Middle East that I discovered how incomplete was my grasp of New Testament passages about persecution. My hermeneutical perspective changed when I listened to students for whom persecution was a reality of everyday life. In the ethos of Acts 15, we must learn to function as a global interpretive community, based on our shared participation in the one story of Christ.[21]

The Necessity Of Compromise For The Sake Of Unity

There are some things worth contending for. In Acts 15, the Pharisees' contextualization of the Gospel may be sincere. But it goes beyond the boundaries of acceptable theological diversity (cf. 15:1, 5, 10, 24). It threatens to subvert the Gospel of salvation by grace through faith for everyone and God's redeeming plan for the Gentiles (vv. 9, 11). The church firmly rejects imposing on Gentiles such national or religious "add-ons" as circumcision and law keeping.

Nonessential issues, however, are a different matter. The decree of the Council (15:20, 29; 21:25) shows a church creatively wrestling with the dynamics of an intercultural community. Although the Council's restrictions on Gentiles have scriptural precedent, it seems best to understand them as temporary and context-specific measures, intended to keep an open door to table fellowship between Jewish and Gentile Christians.[22] Gentiles should abstain from these things out of respect for the sensitivities of their Jewish sisters and brothers in Christ. It is on this basis that the decree is a "necessary" (15:28) compromise for a culturally mixed setting.

The Jewish Christians had to make concessions as well. They needed to relax the traditional interpretation of purity laws, which would have excluded them from fellowship with Gentiles. At the same time, the decree would avoid erecting needless obstacles for Jewish Christians in their mission to unbelieving Jews.

Wesleyans would see the decree as evidence of a "catholic spirit," which transcends differences in culture or opinion.[23] Flexibility in nonessential matters for the sake of others is a vital aspect of contextualization. Christians in the Philippines, for instance, might decide to abstain from eating popular dishes made from pork blood when they live near Muslims or Muslim converts who have strong sensitivities against it.[24] The Jerusalem Council models the importance of surrendering our personal preferences for the sake of oneness in Christ, whatever the setting.

The Goal Of Transformation

Authentic contextualization bears fruit in transforming individuals and communities of disciples. When the Gospel speaks afresh to new circumstances, then attitudes and actions change. In Acts 15, the apostles' witness capsizes the ethnocentric perspective of those who thought they had a permanent "most favored nation" status. The unanimous decision of the Council (vv. 22, 25) implies that even the believing Pharisees came to a new understanding of the Gospel and its implications. In the end, God uses the theological process to bring joy (v. 31) and the reconciling of a divided church (v. 33).

For Wesley, Scripture interpretation and the theology resulting from it have a soteriological goal.[25] Scripture, well interpreted, should lead people to experience salvation and to live holy and loving lives. Furthermore, the test of authentic contextualization is less in the output of sound doctrinal statements than in the embodiment of the faith in our particular settings. Our reflections on the Gospel should draw us toward a growing conformity to the crucified Christ in our attitudes, thinking, and living. Otherwise, our efforts at contextualization become like the Tin Man in *The Wizard of Oz*—without a beating heart.

Contextualization And Mission

The context-sensitive reflection of the Council leads to the furthering of God's mission in the world. James and the others affirm decisively that Gentiles can be evangelized *as Gentiles*, without prior conditions. The result is further proclamation of the word (v. 35) and a clear path for the Gentile mission described in the rest of Acts. As David Seccombe observes, "One of the great strengths of Christianity . . . in every age has been its adaptability to any culture, the basis of which was hammered out at the Jerusalem Council."[26] Contextualization in a Wesleyan spirit seeks both the *advancement* of the Gospel and the *embodiment* of the Gospel.

CONCLUSION

I began by noting that authentic contextualization is difficult work. But there are resources to help us. Wesleyan ways of interpreting Scripture and doing theology can positively inform the task of contextualizing the Gospel in our diverse settings. And we have seen that a Wesleyan approach dovetails at numerous points with the process of theological reflection we discover in Acts 15. Contextualization in a Wesleyan spirit— and in the spirit of the Jerusalem Council—aspires to be:

- Spirit-guided;
- scripturally grounded;
- confirmed by experience;
- embraced by the faith community;
- practiced with humility;
- both contextual and transcontextual;
- committed to the Gospel;
- flexible in nonessentials;
- catholic in spirit;
- transforming; and
- mission-oriented.

If such a list seems daunting, we can draw hope from this knowledge: the same Spirit who inspired the church in Acts to find fresh ways of appropriating the Gospel for its world continues to guide the church in mission today. May we listen to Scripture, to the Spirit, and to one another, as we tell and live the Gospel within the many challenging circumstances of our world.

NOTES

1. For a fuller treatment of the Jerusalem Council and its significance for the task of contextualization, see Dean Flemming, *Contextualization in the New Testament: Patterns for Theology and Mission* (Downers Grove, Ill./Leicester: InterVarsity Press/Apollos, 2005), pp. 43–53. The following discussion draws from this previous study.

2. For a survey of the options, see Eckhard J. Schnabel, *Early Christian Mission: Paul and the Early Church*, vol. 2 (Downers Grove, Ill.: InterVarsity Press, 2004), pp. 1016–17.

3. See, for example, Ben Witherington III, *The Acts of the Apostles: A Socio-Rhetorical Commentary* (Grand Rapids: Eerdmans, 1998), pp. 461–67.

4. N. T. Wright, *Acts for Everyone: Part 2* (London: SPCK, 2008), p. 45.

5. Timothy Wiarda, "The Jerusalem Council and the Theological Task," *Journal of the Evangelical Theological Society* 46 (June 2003): pp. 234–35, 237–39.

6. See Ibid., pp. 243–48; *cf.* The more cautious assessment of David K. Strong and Cynthia A. Strong, "The Globalizing Hermeneutic of the Jerusalem Council," in *Globalizing Theology: Belief and Practice in an Era of World Christianity*, ed. Craig Ott and Harold A. Netland (Grand Rapids: Baker, 2006), pp. 127–28.

7. Joel B. Green, "Acts of the Apostles," in *Dictionary of the Later New Testament and its Developments*, ed. R. P. Martin and P. H. Davids (Downers Grove, Ill.: InterVarsity Press, 1997), p. 17.

8. See Luke T. Johnson, *Decision Making in the Church: A Biblical Model* (Philadelphia: Fortress, 1983), pp. 56–57; see also Hilary Mbachu, *Inculturation Theology of the Jerusalem Council in Acts 15: An Inspiration for the Igbo Church Today* (Frankfurt: Peter Lang, 1995), pp. 73–75.

9. Brian Rapske, "Opposition to the Plan of God and Persecution," in *Witness to the Gospel: The Theology of Acts*, ed. I. H. Marshall and D. Peterson (Grand Rapids: Eerdmans, 1998), p. 243.

10. "We need the same Spirit," Wesley writes, "to understand the Scripture which enabled the holy men of old to write it." From "A Letter to the Right Reverend the Lord Bishop of Gloucester," in *The Bicentennial Edition of the Works of John Wesley* (Nashville: Abingdon Press, 1976–), vol. 11, p. 509.

11. Donald A. D. Thorsen, *The Wesleyan Quadrilateral: Scripture, Tradition, Reason and Experience as a Model of Evangelical Theology* (Nappanee, Ind.: Francis Asbury Press, 1990), p. 226.

12. Richard Bauckham, "James and the Jerusalem Church," in *The Book of Acts in Its First Century Setting*, vol. 4, *Palestinian Setting*, ed. R. Bauckham (Grand Rapids: Eerdmans, 1995), p. 452.

13. See Ibid., pp. 453–56.

14. Flemming, *Contextualization*, p. 49.

15. Thorsen, *Wesleyan Quadrilateral*, pp. 127–30.

16. Strong and Strong, "Globalizing Hermeneutic," p. 132.

17. See Scott J. Jones, *John Wesley's Conception and Use of Scripture* (Nashville: Kingswood, 1995), 62–103; Thorsen, *Wesleyan Quadrilateral*, pp. 125–27.

18. See, for example, Thorsen, *Wesleyan Quadrilateral*, pp. 201–25; Jones, *John Wesley's Conception*, pp. 176–83.

19. See John Christopher Thomas, "Reading the Bible from within Our Traditions: A Pentecostal Hermeneutic as Test Case," in *Between Two Horizons: Spanning New Testament Studies and Systematic Theology*, ed. Joel B. Green and Max Turner (Grand Rapids: Eerdmans, 2000), p. 117.

20. Richard P. Thompson, "Community in Conversation: Multiple Readings of Scripture and a Wesleyan Understanding of the Church," in *Reading the Bible in Wesleyan Ways: Some Constructive Proposals*, ed. B. L. Callen and R. P. Thompson (Kansas City, Mo.: Beacon Hill, 2004), p. 182.

21. See Paul G. Hiebert, "Critical Contextualization," *International Bulletin of Missionary Research* 11 (July 1987): pp. 110–11.

22. The prohibition against "sexual immorality" (*porneia*) appears to be the one exception; it is consistently forbidden in Scripture. Perhaps because it was such a common practice in the Greco-Roman world and a particular barrier to fellowship between Jews and Gentiles, the Council thought it necessary to single it out. See Ajith Fernando, *Acts, The NIV Application Commentary* (Grand Rapids: Zondervan, 1998), pp. 419, 421.

23. See Wesley, Sermon 39, "Catholic Spirit," *Works* (Bicentennial ed.), vol. 2, pp. 79–95.

24 See David K. Strong, "The Jerusalem Council: Some Implications for Contextualization. Acts 15:1–35," in *Mission in Acts: Ancient Narrative in Contemporary Contextualization*, ed. R. H. Gallagher and P. Hertig (Maryknoll, N.Y.: Orbis Books, 2004), p. 205.

25. Wesley's soteriological hermeneutic is widely recognized. See, e.g., Joel B. Green, "Reading the Bible as Wesleyans: A Response to Robert Wall," *Wesleyan Theological Journal 33*, no. 2 (Fall 1998): pp. 124–27; Jones, *John Wesley's Conception*, pp. 104–27.

26. David Seccombe, "The New People of God," in *Witness to the Gospel: The Theology of Acts*, ed. I. H. Marshall and D. Peterson (Grand Rapids: Eerdmans, 1998), p. 366.

BIBLIOGRAPHY

Bauckham, Richard. "James and the Jerusalem Church." In *The Book of Acts in Its First Century Setting*. Vol. 4, *Palestinian Setting*, ed. R. Bauckham. Grand Rapids: Eerdmans, 1995, pp. 415–80.

Flemming, Dean. "The Third Horizon: A Wesleyan Contribution to the Contextualization Debate." *Wesleyan Theological Journal 30*, no. 2 (Fall 1995): pp. 139–63.

———. *Contextualization in the New Testament: Patterns for Theology and Mission*. Downers Grove, Ill./Leicester: InterVarsity Press/Apollos, 2005.

Johnson, Luke T. *Decision Making in the Church: A Biblical Model*. Philadelphia: Fortress Press, 1983.

Jones, Scott J. *John Wesley's Conception of and Use of Scripture*. Nashville: Kingswood Books, 1995.

Mbachu, Hilary. *Inculturation Theology of the Jerusalem Council in Acts 15: An Inspiration for the Igbo Church Today*. Frankfurt: Peter Lang, 1995.

Schnabel, Eckhard J. *Early Christian Mission*. Vol. 2, *Paul and the Early Church*. Downers Grove, Ill.: InterVarsity Press, 2004.

Strong, David K. "The Jerusalem Council: Some Implications for Contextualization. Acts 15:1–35." In *Mission in Acts: Ancient Narratives in Contemporary Context*, ed. Robert L. Gallagher and Paul Hertig, 196–208. Maryknoll, N.Y.: Orbis, 2004.

Strong, David K. and Cynthia A. Strong. "The Globalizing Hermeneutic of the Jerusalem Council." In *Globalizing Theology: Belief and Practice in an Era of World Christianity*, ed. Craig Ott and

Harold A. Netland, 127–39. Grand Rapids: Baker, 2006.

Thomas, John Christopher. "Reading the Bible from within Our Traditions: A Pentecostal Hermeneutic as Test Case." In *Between Two Horizons: Spanning New Testament Studies and Systematic Theology*, ed. Joel B. Green and Max Turner, pp. 108–22. Grand Rapids: Eerdmans, 2000.

Thorsen, Donald A. D. *The Wesleyan Quadrilateral: Scripture, Tradition, Reason and Experience as a Model of Evangelical Theology*. Nappanee, Ind.: Francis Asbury Press, 1990.

Wesley, John. *The Bicentennial Edition of the Works of John Wesley*. Gen. eds. Frank Baker and Richard P. Heitzenrater. Nashville: Abingdon Press, 1976–.

Wiarda, Timothy. "The Jerusalem Council and the Theological Task." *Journal of the Evangelical Theological Society*. 46, no. 2 (June 2003): pp. 233–48.

3

WHEN GOD SENDS A MISSIONARY

THE PROPHET JONAH

Sandra Richter

WHEN GOD SENDS A MISSIONARY

The Old Testament contains a story with which we are all quite familiar—the story of a prophet who was called to announce the judgment and grace of God to a people his own nation named "enemy." It is a story of courage and cowardice, prejudice and repentance, sailors, ships, and one very large fish. It is also the story of a missionary.

WHO WAS JONAH?

The Book of Jonah opens with the call of the prophet to Nineveh:

> The word of the Lord came to Jonah the son of Amittai saying: "Arise and go to Nineveh, the great city, and proclaim against it for their wickedness has come up before me" (Jon. 1:1–2, author's translation).

Beyond this brief biographical note, the only information we have regarding this man is found in 2 Kings 14:25. Here during the days of Israel's divided monarchy we are told of a certain Jonah, the son of Amittai of Gath-hepher, who prophesied regarding the future military successes of Jeroboam II, a king of Israel's northern kingdom. This note places Jonah somewhere in the eighth century B.C.E., and it speaks of him in relationship to both the northern and southern kingdoms of Israel. This indicates that Jonah had a well-known ministry throughout the country. The fact that he hailed from Gath-hepher, an obscure little village in the far north (see Josh. 19:13), further indicates that this man's ministry must have won him significant notoriety in his day. Yet the only story we have regarding his life and ministry is his call to Nineveh. It would seem that this must be an important story indeed.

WHAT WAS NINEVEH?

Whereas Jonah was the citizen of a relatively small and insignificant country, and an even smaller and less significant village, Nineveh was a major urban center in the most powerful body politic of the day, the Assyrian Empire (see Fig. 1). In fact, because of its strategic location and resources, Nineveh would soon become the capital of the Assyrian Empire.

The historians tell us that Assyria was the first true empire of the ancient Near East. Having faded in and out of world history since the third millennium B.C.E., this nation experienced a great resurgence in the ninth century B.C.E. The result was the *Neo*-Assyrian Empire—a nation whose goals of expansion were facilitated by what appears to have been a complete lack of scruples. The first to boast a fully professional army (both war chariots and a mounted cavalry), the Assyrians delighted in their reputation for brutality, terrorism, and economic oppression. The inscriptions of these great kings of Aššur brag of flaying princes alive, decimating agricultural support systems, terrifying their opponents, and causing rivers to run with blood. It was the Assyrians who conceived the idea of exile—that horrific military protocol in which whole populations were stripped of their patrimony and forcefully relocated, effectively divesting entire communities of the ability to recover their identity or the will to ever rebel again. The declared objective of this empire? To utilize these strategies to subjugate and assimilate the lands of the ancient Near East.

JONAH'S WORLD

As a result, Israel had many opportunities to experience the wrath of the Neo-Assyrian Empire. The campaigns of Shalmaneser III (858–824 B.C.E.)

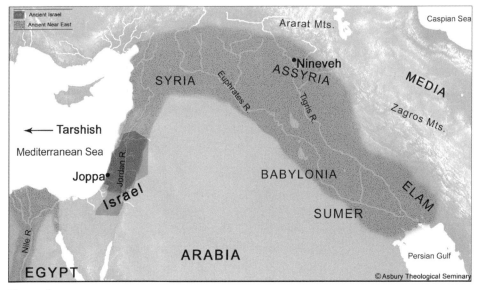

Figure 1

brutalized the western states of the ancient Near East and, in the process, the northern kingdom of Israel. In fact, King Jehu of Israel is named and pictured groveling for mercy in Shalmaneser's famous Black Obelisk victory monument. In 734–732 B.C.E. Assyria's Tiglath Pileser III campaigned to the west, crushing the northern kingdom's allied resistance and deposing Israel's king (2 Kings 15:29–30). In 722 B.C.E., Shalmaneser V brought Israel's northern kingdom to an end and exiled her citizenry—the "ten lost tribes" of Israel. A few years later Assyria furthered its western ambitions by bringing the southern kingdom of Judah to her knees under Hezekiah (2 Kings 18–19). When the Israelite prophet Nahum at long last announces Assyria's demise in 612 B.C.E., he speaks of Nineveh as "the bloody city . . . whose prey never departs" (Nah. 3:1). This was the empire of Assyria and this was her royal city, Nineveh. Jonah was right to fear these people. And it would be difficult to fault him for hating them.

Perhaps even more pertinent to our understanding of Jonah's calling is the fact that for Jonah to go to Nineveh to preach the religion of Israel was equivalent to Jonah signing his own death warrant. The Assyrians would not take kindly to some outlander from Palestine recounting their failures, or even worse, threatening them with what the citizens of Nineveh would have perceived as a "Podunk" national deity. Assyria was the land of the great gods—Shamash, Aššur, Sin, An, and Adu. Who was this god, Yahweh? So the missionary call, although succinctly stated in the first passage of our text, is huge. The journey alone would have taken weeks, the only logical end of this mission being Jonah's martyrdom at the hands of a hated and brutal enemy. So Jonah did what most of us would have done . . . he ran.

CHAPTER ONE: "HURL"

So Jonah rose up to flee to Tarshish from the presence of Yahweh. He went down to Joppa, found a ship that was going to Tarshish, paid the fare, and went down into it to go with them to Tarshish from the presence of Yahweh (Jon. 1:3).

The city of Tarshish is most likely Tartessos, a city and emporium of the Phoenicians in the south of Spain. And whereas Nineveh was 660 miles east of Israel, Tarshish was more than two thousand miles west of Israel! To get to Tarshish one would need to go nearly as far west as a seafaring man in Jonah's day could. Past Greece, past Italy, and on to the confluence of the Mediterranean and the Atlantic Ocean. This was Jonah's plan—to go as far in the other direction as he could. So our prophet gets on a boat, heavily loaded for trade, thinking that somehow he could hide himself "from the presence of Yahweh" in the hold of a ship. But Yahweh knows where his servant is and where he is going. Thus, Yahweh hurls (Hebrew *tûl*) a wind at Jonah's ship (1:4).

The storm that results is so formidable that these career seamen are terrified. Forced to turn to desperate measures, the sailors throw the cargo (their livelihood) overboard. They are hoping as any sailor would that by lightening the ship they might be able to survive the storm by running ahead of it. And considering the short draft and small size of these ancient vessels, running ahead of the storm really was their only option.[1] We can be assured that every able man was on deck, and as the text emphasizes, every man was urgently calling upon his god for rescue (1:5).

When the captain finds Jonah asleep in the hold, he is angry (1:6). When he learns that Jonah worships a god of both earth and sea, and that Jonah is running from that god, he and his crew are horrified: "How could you do this to us?! . . . What can we do to save ourselves?!" (1:10–11). Jonah, who knows the import of his sin, responds: "*Hurl* (Hebrew *tûl*) me into the sea" (1:12).

It is interesting to me that these sailors who do not share Jonah's faith (or his value system) are not willing to kill Jonah. Rather, they "dug their oars into the water" and desperately rowed for shore, even though they knew that Jonah was the reason for their mortal peril. But there is nothing to be done—the sailors cannot make headway against this storm. So at last they hurl Jonah into the sea, and the sea "ceased its raging" (1:15). As a result, Jonah's first missionary act is accomplished. For when these pagan sailors saw that the waves and the wind stopped, they "feared Yahweh greatly and they offered a sacrifice to Yahweh and made vows" (1:16). Thus, we learn from this first chapter that God will secure his witness from his missionary however he must. And we leave chapter one with our hero adrift in the open sea. As a Hebrew he probably does not know how to swim. But even if he does, he has no real chance of survival. Jonah will die. And this missionary who feared martyrdom now faces execution at the hand of his own God.

CHAPTER TWO: "APPOINT"

But with chapter two a new theme emerges, this one marked by the Hebrew term *mānâ* "to appoint." God "appoints" a great fish to swallow Jonah. Most of us have understood this to be the prophet's greatest moment of crisis, and certainly in the course of normal events to be swallowed by a "great fish" would be a crisis. But in truth Jonah's greatest moment of crisis was when he found himself abandoned to the sea. And this fish, who we tend to view as the great antagonist of the tale, is actually the hero. For the whale is used by God to save Jonah's life. This unexpected turn of events is particularly apparent in Jonah's song of deliverance:

> I called out of my distress to Yahweh, and he answered me. I cried for help from the depth of Sheol, and you heard my voice. For you had cast me into the deep, into the heart of the seas, and the current engulfed me . . . Water encompassed me to the soul, the great deep surrounded me. . . . But you brought up my life from the pit, oh Yahweh my God! (2:2–6)

Thus, although surely not Jonah's ideal plan of rescue, the prophet recognizes the hand of God in the undisciplined foraging habits of the "great fish."

Years ago, as a budding PhD student in Hebrew Bible at Harvard University, I was asked to present on the Book of Jonah at the *L'Abri* Study Center in Southborough, Massachusetts. The question on everyone's mind? Is there a "great fish" out there capable of swallowing a human . . . whole? And is there any possibility of that human surviving the process?

After reading an array of literature on aquatic creatures and interviewing several whale experts from the Boston area,[2] I learned to my surprise that there are several ocean-dwelling creatures that are capable of swallowing a man whole. And there are even a few that are capable of swallowing a man without necessarily killing him. Of these, the most likely candidate is the sperm whale. The male of this species reaches up to 60 feet in length (35–45 tons), has an esophagus measuring 17 to 20 inches in diameter, and possesses a three-part stomach—the first of which is used to squeeze out sea water and store swallowed food. This whale is known for gulping down its prey whole, and its primary diet includes the giant squid (*Architeuthidae dux*)—a mollusk which typically reaches 33 feet in length and can weigh up to 440 pounds. Moreover, this whale is known for swallowing bizzare items (including rocks), and then ridding itself of these inedibles by belching or regurgitation.[3] Thus, swallowing and regurgitating a man would present little challenge to this "great fish." In fact, as the sperm whale has historically been the leading commercial species for the whaling industry, and is apparently a particularly aggressive whale, there are actually a number of reports of sperm whales attacking and/or swallowing humans.

One spectacular (and debated) report from February 1891,[4] which was published in several journals and newspapers, involves one James Bartley who was reportedly swallowed in the course of hunting a large sperm whale off the Falkland Islands. When the whale was finally captured, and the crew began dismembering the unfortunate creature, they found trapped inside its stomach the missing sailor, doubled up and unconscious: "He remained two weeks a raving lunatic . . . [but] at the end of the third week he had entirely recovered from the shock and resumed his duties."[5] A similar report comes from Sir John Bland Sutton and was published in the *Massachusetts Gazette Boston Post Boy and Advertiser* (no. 738) on October 14, 1771. Here an Edgartown, Massachusetts whaling vessel was attacked by a sperm whale and one Marshall Jenkins was taken into the whale's mouth, dragged under the surface, and then spit out on the wreckage of the boat—injured, but alive. The magazine

Natural History recorded another such account with a more unhappy ending in June 1947. Here, Egerton Y. Davis, Jr. tells of a young whaler who was swallowed by a huge sperm whale. The animal was fatally wounded and retrieved the next day. In the slaughtering process, the whalers discovered their comrade in the whale's stomach with visible injuries to his chest (the apparent cause of death) and the exposed parts of his body semidigested. The lice on the seaman's head were still alive.[6]

In sum, yes, it is completely possible that a human could be swallowed by a sperm whale, swallowed whole, and even regurgitated. The challenge, of course, would be for the human to survive the process.

Returning to our story, Yahweh next *appoints* the great fish to vomit Jonah up on dry land (the very place to which the sailors were trying to row). Again, this was not an ideal way to travel, but it worked. And as a result, Jonah, the great man of God, who had intentionally and willfully defied the command of his God, is given a second chance.

CHAPTER THREE: JONAH GOES TO NINEVEH

If you are a VeggieTales fan, or if like our family your toddler is a VeggieTales fan, then you know all about Archibald Asparagus and the city of the fish-slappers. As the Jonah character, Archibald was instructed to bring a message of repentance and potential redemption to the city of Nineveh. But Archibald responds to this instruction with what scholars would call "cognitive dissonance"—a dissonance he sets to music.

> *No, it cannot be*
> *your messages are meant for me*
> *and my brothers.*
> *We are your chosen people,*
> *but Nineveh,*
> *they're not!*
> *There must be some mistake*
> *a big misunderstanding,*
> *it's really hard to take*
> *how could you be so demanding!*
>   (Big Idea, Inc., *Jonah: A VeggieTales Movie*)

Archibald did not want to go to Nineveh because he thought the gifts of God were only for the people of God. This is an understandable mistake considering that the Mosaic Covenant identifies Israel and the biological offspring of Abraham as the only ones to whom God had specifically addressed his blessing of redemption. Yet in the story of Jonah we see that the specifics of the Mosaic Covenant are not all there is to God's larger plan. And we learn right along with Jonah that God's vision for the *world* is not actually new with the New Covenant. Rather, in this story we find that God has been concerned for the lost of all the world since the dawn of time. Archibald and Jonah, however, even at this point in the story, do not quite get it. Jonah has been disciplined, and he will obey; but he still must be educated in the heart and character of his missionary God.

In this state of cognitive dissonance, Jonah arrives at Nineveh and begins to preach. And the people of the bloody city (to his great consternation) repent. The king of Nineveh proclaims that the entire city will fast: "Who knows? Perhaps God may turn and relent and withdraw his burning anger so that we may not perish" (3:9). It is significant that the king speaks exactly what the unbelieving sailors declared on the boat (1:6). And God, as is his character, relents.

Now if I were Jonah—giving my testimony on furlough and raising funds for next year—this would be the climax of my story, the point at which I would shout "hallelujah" and call for an "amen" from the crowd. But this is not the climax of Jonah's book. In fact, in many ways this very desirable outcome is merely a sidebar. Moreover, unlike the other prophetic books, we are not offered one of Jonah's highly effective sermons to Nineveh. We get only one quote: "Yet forty days and Nineveh will be overthrown!" (3:4). Hardly memorable in today's market. Why is this? I believe it is because this book is not actually about Nineveh or about Jonah's ministry to them. Rather, this book is about the character of the God whom Jonah serves.

CHAPTER FOUR: TO "APPOINT"

So Nineveh repents, God relents, and Jonah is angry . . . very angry. Is he angry because his preaching has not been confirmed? Perhaps. Or is he angry because his enemy has been forgiven? This is more likely (4:2–3). In his irritation, Jonah goes out to the east side of Nineveh,

hoping to watch the wrath of God fall upon the city. The text tells us that
Jonah builds a shelter against the raging desert sun and God "appoints"
a plant to grow up to shade him. Now Jonah is happy, very happy. But
then God "appoints" a worm to eat the plant, and the plant withers.
Then God "appoints" a strong east wind so that Jonah is not only without
shelter from the sun, now he is buffeted by a dry, scorching wind as well.
And now Jonah is angry again . . . so angry that he "begged with all his
soul to die saying, 'Death is better to me than life!'" (4:8). This is very
angry indeed.

This leads us finally to the climax and central message of the book.
Then God said to Jonah: "Do you have good reason to be angry about the
plant?" And Jonah said, "I have good reason to be angry, even to death!"
Then Yahweh said, "You had compassion on the plant for which you did
not labor and which you did not nurture, which came up overnight and
perished overnight. Should I not have compassion on Nineveh, the great
city in which there are more than 120,000 humans who do not know their
right hand from their left as well as many animals?" (Jon. 4:9–11).

CONCLUSION

Remembering that this book is not actually about Nineveh, but about
the character of Jonah's God, what is the message to its ancient audience
and to us?

The first message here is that Yahweh is truly the Lord of the cosmos.
He can *hurl* wind. He can *appoint* a whale, a plant, a worm, the wind.

A second is that God's messengers are in his hand. If he sees the need,
God will cast those messengers into the sea. But he is equally capable of
rescuing them, even if that rescue requires the most unusual lifeguard of
all time.

The third and most central message is that Yahweh, as the Lord of the
cosmos, cares about every man, woman, and child on this planet. Every
son of Adam, every daughter of Eve, every exile of Eden falls within the
purview of his concern. This holds true even if that son of Adam or
daughter of Eve is as wicked, violent, or dangerous as the citizens of the
Neo-Assyrian Empire.

In sum, to contradict Archibald Asparagus, there has been no
mistake, no misunderstanding. The word of God is not just for the

people of God. It is for the lost. It is even for the enemies of the kingdom of God. Jonah is delivered from the consequences of his own sin. He ran, and he nearly died as a result. Yet when Jonah cried out to God, God saved him. The message of Jonah's book is that God will do no less for the citizens of Nineveh.

Come ye weary, heavy laden, bruised and broken by the fall.
If you tarry till you're better, you will never come at all.

(Joseph Hart, from *A Collection of Hymns for the Use of the People Called Methodists*)

NOTES

1. See Dan L. Davis, "Sailing the Open Seas: Recent Deepwater Archaeological Finds Disprove Conventional Wisdom that Ancient Mariners were Timid Shore-Huggers," *Archaeology Odyssey*, 6/1 (January/February 2003).

2. Greg Early of the Edgerton Research Laboratory at the New England Aquarium in Boston; David Morin of the Cetacean Research Unit of Gloucester, Massachusetts; and Douglas Beach of the National Marine Fishery in Gloucester, Massachusetts.

3. See A. A. Berzin, *The Sperm Whale,* ed. A. V. Yablokov, Pacific Scientific Research Institute of Fisheries and Oceanography (Jerusalem: Israel Program for Scientific Translations, 1972), pp. 95–101, pp. 186–209. For images of the giant squid, see the National Geographic Web site [cited 25 October 2008]:

http://animals.nationalgeographic.com/animals/invertebrates/giant-squid.html.

4. See "Man in Whale" in the "Letters" section of *Natural History* (April 1947), pp. 145, 199, and Edward B. Davis, "A Whale of a Tale: Fundamentalist Fish Stories" *Perspectives* 43 (Dec 1991): pp. 224–37.

5. Sir Francis Fox, *Sixty-Three Years of Engineering, Scientific and Social Work* (London: J. Murray, 1927), pp. 298–300, quoted from Ambrose John Wilson, "The sign of the Prophet Jonah and Its Modern Confirmations," *The Princeton Theological Review* (1927): p. 636.

6. Op. cit.; *cf.* Carl Keil and Franz Delitzsch, *Commentary on the Old Testament: Minor Prophets,* trans. James Martin, (Peabody, Mass.: Hendrickson Publishers, 1989), p. 398, n. 1.

PART TWO
Theological Perspectives

JOHN WESLEY WAS NO DESK THEOLOGIAN. HIS THEOLOGY was created on the move and emerged from his practice of mission and ministry. His theology of mission is found in his sermons, letters, and journals. Perhaps, because of the practical nature of his theology of mission, it has greatly influenced how we understand and practice mission today. In this section, written from a theological perspective, we explore many of his theological ideas and principles. For example, one of the dominant themes in Wesley's theology of mission is his understanding of prevenient grace, which we will see is woven through the fabric of the essays in this section, as well as through the entire book. The eight chapters represented will explore various aspects of a Wesleyan theology of mission.

We begin with Gerald Anderson's study of "Prevenient Grace in World Mission," where he points out that a proper understanding of this concept does not lead to the slippery slope of syncretism or to the blind alley of universalism. Rather, prevenient grace gives missionaries great hope and positive motivation for mission, because we go expecting to discover where God is already at work in the lives and cultures of people different from ourselves.

Bishop Robert Aboagye-Mensah from Ghana, West Africa, documents how Wesleyan theology has shaped the founding and growth of the Methodist Church Ghana from its inception in 1835 to the present. Wesley's high view of Scripture, his emphasis on an evangelical conversion, and his commitment to social ministries have all been instrumental in enabling the church in this African context to grow significantly and to substantially influence Ghanaian society.

"Wesley's theology was fundamentally and in essence a theology of mission," states Howard Snyder in his chapter. Wesley was constantly engaged in the practice of mission, and Snyder lifts up five biblical themes in Wesley's theology: the image of God in human beings, prevenient grace, salvation as healing from the disease of sin, perfecting Christian character, and the restoration of all things.

Billy Abraham draws on his Irish Methodist background that awakened his interest in mission at an early age, but then as he witnessed the decline of Christianity in Europe and in the mainline churches in the U.S., he argues that the paradigm of humanitarian and charitable work that governed the work of mission in United Methodism has been totally inadequate. He demonstrates how the reduction of mission to humanitarian work kills the church because it ignores the need for personal evangelism and church planting. As globalization and rapid communication cause the nice, neat boundaries of nation states to give way to the market state, new forms of mission theology and practice are multiplying within United Methodism and bringing renewal to mission activity.

We turn our attention next to Latin America, where Luís Wesley de Souza looks at two Methodist Church traditions in Chile as paradigmatic of two themes in Wesleyan theology that must be held in tension. He argues that the church must be concerned with and relevant for the poor, and at the same time have a prophetic voice in society. This balancing act is Wesleyan to the core and most appropriate for the Latin American context. He notes that too often we have forgotten the poor and neglected the laity. He notes that the church—a community of believers empowered by the Spirit and sent on a mission—in Latin America, must develop a mission ecclesiology that is lay based and led under the guidance of the Holy Spirit.

Terry Muck looks at John Wesley's contribution to today's theology of religions, examines three areas of Wesley's thought, and concludes that, "If we believe all people we meet are children of God, with access to God's grace, indeed, already have God's grace active in their lives, then people of other religions are just a short step away from salvation." The three areas examined are that we as Christians need to live more like Christians to send a positive message, we must have respect for all of God's creatures, and we must have a more loving attitude toward people who are not yet Christians.

Timothy Tennent develops insights from Wesley's "Catholic Spirit" to discuss three key features of Wesley's understanding of ecumenism: unity in the essentials with diversity in the nonessentials, an experiential and practical theology, and the idea of the "world is my parish" anticipating today's global Christianity. Wesley's approach to ecumenism gives us guidelines on how to engage the increasingly diverse global Christian community and to interact with those from other faith traditions.

   In the final chapter in this section, Robert Tuttle writes, "Once John Wesley recognized that evangelism was bearing witness to a God already at work, ministry became less of a chore and more of an opportunity." In his essay on "God at Work in the World," Tuttle argues that the Gospel affirms the world and its cultures, as well as the universal work of the Holy Spirit, but this does not lead to universalism and does not undercut the motivation for mission. In fact, just the opposite, for God simply uses existing culture to reveal something about God's self, and to draw people to God.

4

PREVENIENT GRACE IN WORLD MISSION

Gerald H. Anderson

INTRODUCTION

A distinctive feature of John Wesley's theology was his teaching about prevenient grace (sometimes referred to as preventing grace, meaning that which precedes, comes before). This was not new in Christian doctrine—having its roots in Scripture and some of the early church fathers, as well as in Anglican doctrine—but it was newly emphasized by Wesley and became a defining part of his teaching, partly because of his opposition to the doctrine of unconditional predestination and his convictions about human free will. Charles Allen Rogers writes, "Wesley's understanding of prevenient grace is a central and decisive element in his theology"; it is "one of his distinctive contributions to Christian theology."[1] Mark Royster, in his study of Wesley, concludes that "prevenient grace is crucial to the integrity of Wesley's rigorous biblical theology."[2]

WESLEY'S POSITION

Wesley wrote, "Natural free-will, in the present state of mankind, I do not understand. I only assert, that there is a measure of free-will supernaturally restored to every man, together with that supernatural light which 'enlightens every man that comes into the world.'"[3] In his view, "There is no man, unless he has quenched the Spirit, that is wholly void of the grace of God. No man living is entirely destitute of what is vulgarly called 'natural conscience.' But this is not natural; it is more properly termed 'preventing grace.' Every man has a greater or less measure of this, which waiteth not for the call of man. . . . Everyone has some measure of that light, some faint glimmering ray, which sooner or later, more or less, enlightenens every man that commeth into the world. . . . So that no man sins because he has not grace, but because he does not use the grace which he hath."[4] According to Wesley, "Salvation begins with what is usually termed (and very properly) 'preventing grace'; including the first wish to please God, the first dawn of light concerning his will, and the first slight transient conviction of having sinned against him. All these imply some tendency toward life, some degree of salvation, the beginning of a deliverance from a blind, unfeeling heart, quite insensible of God and the things of God."[5]

According to Randy L. Maddox, "Wesley invoked the prevenience of grace to affirm that *every* salutary human action or virtue . . . is grounded in the prior empowering of God's grace. This affirmation permeates his writings . . ."[6]

Describing Wesley's position, Robert G. Tuttle, Jr., says, "Prevenient grace is the Holy Spirit at work in everyone between conception and conversion. The Holy Spirit woos or *prevents* us from moving so far toward disobedience, that when we finally understand the claims of the Gospel upon our lives, we are guaranteed the freedom to say yes."[7]

Scott J. Jones summarizes, "We are saved by grace alone. At the same time, humanity is given the ability, by grace, to respond or not respond. Because God loves us, God does not coerce us. This pattern of human response being given to God's prevenient grace is crucial to Wesley's idea of salvation. It is God who saves, but humans must cooperate. Yet even their ability to cooperate, the faith that responds, is made possible by God's grace."[8]

Karl Rahner once complained, "Theology has been led astray for too long already by the tacit assumption that grace would no longer be grace if God became too free with it."[9] That is not the case here.

Prevenient grace affirms the universal salvific will of God, meaning that God wants everyone to be saved, and God's providence continuously takes the initiative in extending grace to everyone everywhere, through the power of the Holy Spirit. From the moment of creation the pre-incarnate Logos was present (John 1:1–18). This graceful initiative is a preparation for the Gospel, which enables persons both to accept or to resist God's gracious gift. God's initiative is an invitation to accept the gift and follow the Giver. It is a preparation for evangelism. A response of acceptance marks the beginning of an individual's pilgrimage of faith in the work of Christ in whom the salvation of humanity is accomplished, and we are assured that God "rewards those who seek him" (Heb. 11:6). We cannot limit or know all the ways in which Christ works in the world, but we can witness to what we do know and to what he has done for us.

D. T. Niles, the Methodist evangelist from Sri Lanka, once said, "This previousness of Jesus in the lives of men and women is the fact of central importance in understanding how He ministers to persons. He comes, He arrives—at His own time, in His own way, by His own initiative."[10]

In *The United Methodist Hymnal* (1989), a whole section of hymns (pp. 337–59), under the heading "Prevenient Grace," affirms this witness. Included among them are:

I sought the Lord, and afterward I knew
he moved my soul to seek him, seeking me.
It was not I that found, O Savior true;
no, I was found of thee.
   (No. 341, "I Sought the Lord")

Softly and tenderly Jesus is calling,
calling for you and for me;
see, on the portals
he's waiting and watching,
watching for you
and for me.
Come home, come home;
you who are weary,
Come home;
earnestly, tenderly, Jesus is calling,
calling, O sinner, come home.
   (No. 348, "Softly and Tenderly Jesus Is Calling")

In 1986 the United Methodist General Board of Global Ministries adopted a "Theology of Mission Statement" titled *Partnership in God's Mission*. In a closing section it says, "United Methodist mission partners engaged in witness with persons of other religious faiths draw upon the assurance of the prevenient grace of God, remembering that the saving work of God is within the church and beyond. . . . In a new and uncertain age, the most fervent prayer of mission partners is that we will be led by the Holy Spirit into the unfolding future of God's mission."

In 1988 the United Methodist General Conference adopted a biblical and theological statement on mission titled *Grace Upon Grace: God's Mission and Ours*. It states, "God is preveniently present to all people. As our evangelical vocation, United Methodists witness to all persons about the Lordship of Jesus Christ. Our faith requires that we present our commitment with integrity; our faith requires that we respect the integrity of others. As religious traditions interact, we are called to listen with sensitivity to those of differing faith while presenting Christ in the spirit of Christ."

Wesley's famous words, "I look upon the world as my parish," reveal a motivation that has constrained his followers to go to new frontiers, at home and abroad, to proclaim the Gospel, because God was already there and calling them. God's grace goes ahead of the church and the missionary. God is present before the missionary arrives, preparing people for the Gospel message.

Knowing that God is already present before they arrive does not diminish the incentive or motivation for those who go in mission. Instead, it is an encouragement to know that God is there, preparing the way, waiting for them, ready to welcome them, lead them, and bless them. God's prevenient grace provides a point of contact for the missionary, so the work of Gospel witness builds on what God has already done.

PEOPLE OF OTHER FAITHS

Discussions about prevenient grace inevitably lead to questions about the relationship between God's redemptive activity in Jesus Christ and people of other faiths. We have already affirmed that God's prevenient grace is present with everyone. The more difficult question is whether God's grace is present in other religions. This remains one of the most difficult and divisive issues for a Christian theology of religions.

In 1968, at a consultation on mission studies in Birmingham, England, there was a debate over "Presence and Proclamation" between Max Warren, the longtime general secretary of the Church Missionary

Society of the Anglican Church, and Donald McGavran, the dean of the
School of World Mission at Fuller Theological Seminary in Pasadena,
California. Their contrasting views set forth some of the basic issues and
differing positions.

Warren (from the same church tradition as Wesley) said, "I find
God at work everywhere, often working very strangely by my limited
human understanding, but working nevertheless. . . . In our mission to
the great world outside the Covenant people, we have strong biblical
support for a spirit of expectancy as we go to discover in those of other
faiths the prevenient grace of the uncovenanted Christ."[11]

Warren then quoted from Raymond Panikkar's book, *The Unknown
Christ of Hinduism* (1964),

> The Christian attitude is not ultimately one of bringing Christ *in*, but of
> bringing him *forth*, of discovering Christ; not one of command but of
> service. Or, in other words, Christ died and rose for all men—before and
> after him—his redemption is universal and unique. . . . The Christian
> instinctively falls in love with the positive aspects of other religions . . .
> because he believes that he discovers there the footprints of God's
> redemption, and some veiled sometimes disfigured grace which he
> believes he must unveil and reformulate, out of love for his neighbor and
> a sense of responsibility for the faith God has given him.[12]

Warren comments:

> Such a view is not the vestibule to the temple of syncretism. It is the
> unequivocable unambiguous assertion of the universal Saviorhood and
> Lordship of Jesus Christ. There is indeed "no salvation in anyone else at
> all, for there is no other name under heaven granted to men, by which
> we may receive salvation." . . . Along some such lines as these, I submit,
> we can discover a Christology which will equip us for our mission in the
> religiously pluralistic world in which our task is set. For it is in this kind
> of world that we have to proclaim the Christ who is "present." [13]

Warren continues:

> When I go to meet the man of another faith I do not, in any sense what-
> ever, precede Christ. He is there before me. He has been at work in that
> other man, as He has been at work in me. . . . Always He is the Way, the

Truth, and the Life. There is no other way, no other truth, no other life but He. This follows, surely, from our deep conviction about the sovereignty of Christ.[14]

In response, Donald McGavran argued that much of the talk about "presence" and "proclamation" in mission at that time was theologically flawed when these activities became ends rather than means toward the classic goal of mission which is "to make Jesus Christ known as Lord and Savior and to persuade [people] to become His disciples and responsible members of His Church."[15] McGavran warned about the tendency toward theological compromise and relativism when evangelistic witness to the Gospel is replaced by vague meanings about Christian "presence," that become programs of interfaith "dialogue," which lead to advocacy for religious coexistence in place of mission. "Presence," he said, "is not a biblical concept," therefore it should "not be a self-conscious mode of mission."[16]

Both papers by Warren and McGavran deserve careful study and serious consideration. Warren was probing the potential of understanding prevenient grace for new paradigms of mission in a post-colonial context of resurgent religious pluralism. McGavran was pointing to the problems this caused when it deviated from biblical norms of mission goals and strategy. Forty years later the issues and tensions remain.

CONTINUITY AND DISCONTINUITY

Even for those who agree that God's prevenient grace is present among all people and who take seriously the Lordship of Jesus Christ, there are difficulties and differences in describing the implications of this for people of other faiths.

In Scripture and in the history of Christian doctrine, there are two major streams or traditions regarding the relationship of God's redemptive activity in Jesus Christ and God's activity among people of other faiths.[17] One tradition, while recognizing the uniqueness and universality of Jesus Christ, emphasizes the *continuity* of God's revealing and redeeming activity in Christ with God's activity among all people everywhere. It views Christian faith as the climax of a divine revelation, says F. C. Grant, that began long before human history ("he chose us in Christ before the foundation of the world," Eph. 1:4) and has been available to everyone, thus emphasizing the initiative of prevenient grace.[18] Jesus Christ in this view is crucial, normative, and definitive, but not exclusive. What is true of Jesus Christ in a focal way is pervasively true of the whole cosmos. He is the key or clue to the rest of God's activity.

But the Word of God is not limited to and did not end with the historic person of Jesus, yet it is not apart from Christ in the Spirit. There is much biblical and patristic testimony to support this tradition. John's Gospel affirms that the same light which was in Jesus enlightens everyone (John. 1:1–9), for "Christ is all and in all" (Col. 3:11). Paul said that a thousand years before the birth of Jesus, "Christ" was with the Israelites in their wanderings in Sinai (1 Cor. 10:4 RSV). And Acts 14 assures us that God "did not leave himself without a witness" among all the nations, even among those who had no knowledge of the biblical revelation (Acts 14:16–17). In this view, the *logos spermatikos* is active everywhere, sowing seeds of truth, and preparing the way for the Gospel, "For the grace of God has appeared, bringing salvation to all" (Titus 2:11).

The other tradition emphasizes a radical *discontinuity* between the realm of Christian revelation, beginning with God's prevenient grace, and the whole range of non-Christian religious experience. In this view the non-Christian religions are the various efforts of human beings to apprehend their existence, whereas Christianity is the result of the self-disclosure of God in Jesus Christ. God has spoken to humanity only in the person of Jesus Christ and "there is salvation in no one else" (Acts 4:12). This tradition—emphasizing Christ's saying in John 14:6 that "no one comes to the Father but by me," (RSV)—is the narrow, exclusivist tradition, which is equally, if not more strongly represented in Scripture and in the history of Christian doctrine.

These two streams of teaching and tradition are hard to reconcile; they seem almost contradictory. Yet they are often found almost side-by-side in the New Testament, as Lesslie Newbigin pointed out in my conversations with him. For instance, in John's Gospel, we are told that Jesus was "the true light that enlightens every man" (1:4, 9 RSV). Yet in the same passage we are told that "the light shines in the darkness" (not everything was light!), and it was only to those "who believed in his name, he gave power to become children of God" (1:12 RSV). John 3 tells us that God sent his only Son into the world "that the world might be saved through him. He who believes in him is not condemned; he who does not believe is condemned" (RSV). In John 10 Jesus says, "I am the door, if

anyone enters by me, he will be saved," (v. 9) but there are "other sheep,
that are not of this fold; I must bring them also. . . . So there shall be one
flock, one shepherd" (v. 16 RSV). In John 14:2, Jesus says, "In my Father's
house are many mansions," (NKJV) which some pluralists quote to suggest
that there are many religions of salvific value in the kingdom of God. But
in that same chapter Jesus also said, "I am the way, and the truth, and the
life; no one comes to the Father, but by me" (John 14:6 RSV).

Similarly, in Acts we find Peter telling some Gentiles, "Truly I perceive
that God shows no partiality, but in every nation anyone who fears him and
does what is right is acceptable to him" (10:34–35 RSV). Then Peter tells them
that every one who believes in Jesus receives forgiveness of sins, whereupon
"the Holy Spirit fell on all who heard the word" (v. 44 RSV) and Peter
"commanded them to be baptized in the name of Jesus Christ" (10:48 RSV).

My point is that both these streams are part of the Christian tradition.
Both have support in Scripture and patristic tradition. Both affirm God's
prevenient grace among all people. Both have been well represented in
the history of Christian missions. The problem is that the church tends to
swing its emphasis in different periods from one extreme to the other,
and thereby distorts its message and mission, presenting only a partial
Gospel. Unfortunately, it is easier to present a partial, simplistic Gospel
than to present the full Gospel, which is seldom simple. It is imperative
that both of these traditions in Christian thought be maintained in some
sort of balanced tension. This is difficult to do when those from one tradition offer continuity with doubtful uniqueness, and those from the other
side offer uniqueness without continuity. What is needed in our theological
understanding about mission and religious pluralism is uniqueness with
continuity,[19] which prevenient grace provides.

As mentioned earlier, it is generally recognized that God's prevenient
grace is present and active among non-Christians, but the more difficult
question is whether Christ is present in non-Christian religions as such,
and whether they may thereby be considered ways of salvation. It is one
thing to recognize that Christ is present with people of other faiths; it is
quite another to say that this provides salvific efficacy to other faiths, and
that people of other faiths may be saved *in* their religions or even *through*
their religions, without an affirmation of faith in Jesus Christ.

I recall many years ago asking D. T. Niles whether non-Christians
could be saved in and through their own religions without explicit faith
in Christ. His reply was, "*If* they are saved, they are saved because of what
Christ has done for them." He elaborates on this in his book *The Preacher's*

Task and the Stone of Stumbling, where he writes, "It is outside the preacher's competence or commission to pass judgment on what others claim to be their experience of salvation; his business is only to invite them to acknowledge Jesus Christ as their Savior."[20]

CONCLUSION

The place and implication of prevenient grace for world mission in the Wesleyan spirit is consistent with the position of Orthodox and Catholic mission theology. Pope John Paul II expressed such views in his general audience on February 4, 1998, when he said, "Apart from Christ there are no other autonomous sources or ways of salvation. . . . Therefore, in the great religions, which the church views with respect and esteem, . . . Christians recognize the presence of salvific elements that operate dependent on the influence of Christ's grace. . . . These religions can thus contribute, by virtue of the Holy Spirit who 'blows where he wills,' to help men along the path to eternal happiness." But, such activity, he said, is always "the result of Christ's redeeming action."[21]

This was also officially stated in 2000 by Cardinal Joseph Ratzinger (now Pope Benedict XVI) in his theological declaration, endorsed by John Paul II, titled *"Dominus Iesus,* On the Unicity and Salvific Universality of Jesus Christ and the Church," in which he emphasized that "the universal salvific will of the one and triune God is offered and accomplished once for all in the mystery of the incarnation, death and resurrection of the Son of God," and any suggestions "that propose a salvific action of God beyond the unique mediation of Christ would be contrary to Christian and Catholic faith" (par. 14). Other religions, he said, may have positive elements and rays of truth, but they are not salvific in and of themselves. Rather, they serve "as a preparation for the Gospel and can only be understood in reference to Christ" (par. 12, quoting from the 1990 Encyclical Letter of John Paul II, *Redemptoris Missio* [Mission of the Redeemer], par. 29). These positive elements and other religious experiences, said Ratzinger, "acquire meaning and value only from Christ's own mediation, and they cannot be understood as parallel or complementary to his [mediation]" (par. 14, quoting *RM* 5).

Thus prevenient grace is in the mainstream of historic Christian teaching, grounded in Scripture, and incorporated by the major Christian traditions in their mission theology.

NOTES

1. Charles Allen Rogers, "The Concept of Prevenient Grace in the Theology of John Wesley." (PhD diss., Duke Univ., 1967, pp. ix, 291). Rogers says, "Prevenient grace, for Wesley, is a scriptural teaching," however, "The primary source for Wesley's concept of prevenient grace was the substantial tradition of sixteenth and seventeenth century British theology, particularly the theologians of the Church of England" (pp. 25, 28).

2. Mark Royster, "John Wesley's Doctrine of Prevenient Grace in Missiological Perspective." (D. Miss. diss., Asbury Theological Seminary, 1989, p. 71).

3. John Wesley, ed. Albert C. Outler, *The Bicentennial Edition of the Works of John Wesley*, (Nashville: Abingdon Press, 1976–), vol. 10, p. 230. Hereafter cited as Wesley's *Works*.

4. Wesley's *Works*, vol. 3: p. 207.

5. Ibid., pp. 203–4.

6. Randy L. Maddox, *Responsible Grace: John Wesley's Practical Theology* (Nashville: Kingswood Books, 1994), p. 84.

7. Robert G. Tuttle, Jr., *Sanctity without Starch: A Layperson's Guide to a Wesleyan Theology of Grace* (Anderson, Ind.: Bristol Books, 1992), pp. 12–13.

8. Scott J. Jones, *United Methodist Doctrine: The Extreme Center* (Nashville: Abingdon Press, 2002), p. 158.

9. Quoted by Eugene Hillman, *The Wider Ecumenism* (London: Burns & Oates, 1968), p. 34.

10. D. T. Niles, *Upon the Earth: The Mission of God and the Missionary Enterprise of the Churches* (New York: McGraw-Hill, 1962), p. 46. See also Christopher L. Furtado, *The Contribution of D. T. Niles to the Church Universal and Local* (Madras: Christian Literature Society, 1978), pp. 168–73, for a discussion of Niles's views on "the previousness of Jesus," which suggests

that Niles may have been influenced by the thought of E. Stanley Jones, as found in his book *The Christ of the Indian Road* (Nashville: Abingdon Press, 1925).

11. Max Warren, "Presence and Proclamation," in *The Conciliar-Evangelical Debate: The Crucial Documents, 1964–1976*, ed. Donald McGavran, (South Pasadena, Calif.: William Carey Library, 1977), pp. 192, 197.

12. Warren, "Presence and Proclamation," p. 197.

13. Ibid., pp. 197–98.

14. Ibid., p. 203.

15. Donald McGavran, "Presence and Proclamation in Christian Mission," in *The Conciliar-Evangelical Debate*, pp. 205–18.

16. Ibid., pp. 216–17.

17. I have written about this in other articles, for example, "Theology of Religions and Missiology: A Time of Testing," in *The Good News of the Kingdom: Mission Theology for the Third Millennium*, eds. Charles Van Engen, Dean S. Gilliland, and Paul Pierson (Maryknoll, N.Y.: Orbis Books, 1993), pp. 205ff.

18. See the response by F. C. Grant to the "Dogmatic Constitution on Divine Revelation," in *The Documents of Vatican II*, ed. Walter M. Abbott (New York: Herder & Herder/Association Press, 1966), p. 129.

19. This formulation was first suggested by Edmund Soper, a former Methodist missionary and professor of missions, in his book *The Philosophy of the Christian World Mission* (Nashville: Abingdon-Cokesbury Press, 1943), pp. 225–27.

20. D. T. Niles, *The Preacher's Task and the Stone of Stumbling* (New York: Harper, 1958), p. 33.

21. See text in *L'Osservatore Romano* (Vatican City), English language edition, February 1998.

5

"THE WORLD OUR PARISH"

CHRISTIAN MISSION AND THE WESLEYAN HERITAGE IN A GHANAIAN CONTEXT

Robert Aboagye-Mensah

EARLY HISTORY OF THE METHODIST CHURCH GHANA

On January 1, 1835, a young man sent by the Wesleyan Mission Society of Great Britain landed on the shores of Cape Coast in the then Gold Coast (renamed Ghana after independence in March 1957). That historic entry inaugurated a Christian mission that has grown to be the present Methodist Church Ghana, which has now become part of the global family of the people called Methodists. The mission was actually initiated by a group of Ghanaian young Christians led by one William de Graft who requested Bibles from a ship captain named Potter. When Captain Potter returned home he informed the Missionary Society of the Wesleyan Methodist Church of Great Britain of the need for Bibles and the Society decided to send a missionary with the Bibles to the Gold Coast. The name of the twenty-seven-year-old missionary was Joseph Dunwell.

In 1932 the three Methodist Churches, the Wesleyan Methodist Church, the Primitive Methodist Church, and The United Methodist Church in Great Britain, were united under the name The Methodist Church, and assisted in establishing and administering churches overseas with the sole aim of partnering with the nationals to spread "the Faith in their own countries and among their own kindred."[1] The Methodist Church Ghana then came under this arrangement which lasted until July 28, 1961, when it was granted "the ultimate authority of the

Conference of the Methodist Church" in Great Britain to be "constituted and recognized as an equal and autonomous community of Christian believers, in no way subordinate to the Methodist Church, though joining with the Methodist Church in their common faith and heritage."[2]

The Methodist Church Ghana celebrated its 170 years of existence in 2005. Over almost two centuries of existence, the church has functioned within the Wesleyan heritage in which it firmly believes and to which it has remained true. The Methodist Church Ghana has spread throughout the country. It is found in both urban and rural areas, and its Societies are administered by about one thousand ordained ministers of the Gospel.

Since its establishment in 1835 the Methodist Church Ghana has been a missionary church, penetrating countries in the West African subregion with the Gospel by spreading Methodism. The Methodist Churches in Nigeria and La Cote d'Ivoire were both established by Methodist Church Ghana. It has also assisted the Methodist Churches in Gambia and in Togo in many ways and continues to do so. Today, Methodist Church Ghana congregations can be found among immigrants living in Great Britain, Italy, Germany, Holland, the United States of America, and Canada under different forms of arrangements, partnerships, and fellowships. The world has indeed become our parish.

Since its inception in 1835 the Methodist Church Ghana has been deeply influenced by John Wesley's holistic understanding of and practice of mission. For John Wesley there was no sharp dichotomy between evangelism and mission. He understood evangelism to be an essential aspect of the biblical understanding of Christian mission. And Christian mission is a committed participation of God's people who have been invited and commanded by the triune God to be his witnesses within the history of God's world for the redemption of God's creation, which includes human beings themselves. The implication is that for John Wesley, Christian mission is derived from and shares in the mission of God that challenges the church to be God's witnesses in bringing people to personal faith in Christ, transformation of society, culture, economy, and politics including the establishment of formal education. With this great influence of Wesley's holistic perspective on mission, the Methodist Church Ghana has been able to hold in creative tension the verbal proclamation of the Gospel where people from all levels of society are challenged to know and have a personal experience of the living triune God. This has been combined with engagement in the social, cultural, and political transformation of peoples and communities, particularly in the most deprived areas of Ghana. What continues to inspire the Methodist Church Ghana in its engagement in mission is the belief that the church does not have a mission for God, but rather God has a mission for the church. Essentially the church is in the world to carry out God's mission.

HOLY SCRIPTURES—THE INSPIRED WORD OF GOD

The first means by which mission has been pursued by the Methodist Church Ghana has been to take seriously the importance that Wesley places on Scripture in his understanding of Christian mission. For Wesley what distinguishes Methodists, and for that matter Christians from non-Christians, is the value they place on the Bible. In his article, "The Character of a Methodist," he writes:

> We believe, indeed, that "all Scripture is given by the inspiration of God"; and herein we are distinguished from Jews, Turks, and the Infidels. *We believe the written word of God to be the only and sufficient rule both of Christian faith and practice.* . . . We believe Christ to be the eternal, supreme God; and herein we are distinguished from the Socinians and Arians.[3]

In a letter to a friend Wesley expressed the same high regard for Scripture in matters of faith and Christian living when he noted: "I allow no other rule, whether of faith or practice, than of the Holy Scriptures."[4]

There is no book other than the Bible that spells out for us what Christian mission is all about. To put it differently and more emphatically: "Mission is what the Bible is all about."[5] In Luke 24 Jesus makes it clear to the disciples that he is the focus of the whole canon of the Old Testament and that revelation forms the basis of their mission to Israel and the nations. So the Bible and Christian mission are intricately woven together. Through the Bible the disciples of Jesus will know that the Christ will suffer and rise from the dead on the third day and repentance and forgiveness of sins must be preached in his name to all nations, beginning at Jerusalem (Luke 24:27, 44–47). It is interesting to observe from the above quotation of John Wesley how his high esteem of Scripture is closely linked with his affirmation of Jesus as the Christ, the eternal Supreme God. This Christ-focused affirmation derived from Wesley's

understanding of the Holy Scripture as the Word inspired by God consti-
tutes the ground and the content of his engagement in the mission of
preaching and teaching; and that also informs his personal and social
involvement and commitment to the poor and needy.

John Wesley's high view of Holy Scripture forms the basis of
Methodist Church Ghana's understanding of its mission to the world. The
Deed of Foundation of our church states this position unambiguously:

> The Doctrines of the Evangelical Faith that Methodism has held from the
> beginning and still holds are based upon the divine revelation recorded
> in the Holy Scriptures. The Methodist Church acknowledges this revela-
> tion as the supreme rule of faith and practice. These Evangelical
> doctrines to which the Preachers of the Methodist Church both Ministers
> and Laymen are pledged are contained in Wesley's *Notes on the New
> Testament* and the first four volumes of his sermons.[6]

The growth of the Methodist Church Ghana is largely attributed to
the central place it gives the Holy Bible as an inspired Word of God. To
this end, the preaching of the Word remains the central focus of our
worship services and the class meetings remain a place for the study of
the Scriptures. It has been observed that whenever Christians acknowledge the Holy Scriptures as the revealed Word of God, and commit
themselves to the mission of proclaiming Christ to the world as the Lord
of every aspect of life and all human endeavors, the church experiences
tremendous growth. It is equally true that whenever the Bible is treated
like any other book and it is pushed to the peripheries of the church's
faith and practice, and Christians fail to proclaim Christ to the world,
that church gradually dies.

SAVED FROM FIRE AND EVANGELICAL CONVERSION

Two experiences in Wesley's life have had deep influence on the mission
of the Methodist Church Ghana. The first is Wesley's rescue from the
fire set to the Epworth rectory when he was only six years old and his
miraculous escape. This narrow escape from fire had a profound impact
on Wesley's family and his own life and mission. Susanna Wesley's
prayer two years after her son had been saved from fire indicated her

promise to God that she would be "more particularly careful of the soul of this child, that Thou hast so mercifully provided for, than ever I have been, that I may do my endeavors to instill into his mind the disciplines of true religion and virtue."[7] John Wesley described himself using the biblical phrase "a brand plucked from the burning" to indicate God's "providential deliverance from the fire and also a divine dispensation pointing to some extraordinary mission for him."[8]

The second experience is Wesley's Aldersgate Street encounter with Christ on May 24, 1738, when he heard someone reading Luther's "Preface" to the Epistle to the Romans. As he expressed it:

> About a quarter before nine, while he was describing the change which God works in the heart through faith in Christ I felt my heart strangely warmed. I felt that I did trust in Christ, Christ alone for salvation, and an assurance was given me, that he had taken away my sins, even mine, and saved me from the law of sin and death.[9]

This experience of Wesley's is often described as his evangelical conversion. In the Methodist Church Ghana these two experiences of Wesley are rehearsed every year during a week's celebration of his conversion and mission. All Dioceses and Circuits use the period to do outdoor evangelism and engage in activities for the renewal of the church. Many people have come to know Christ as personal Savior and Lord through those celebrations. The period is also used to help church members understand such important Wesleyan teachings as justification and sanctification. Christians are reminded of Wesley's saying that the supreme duty of a Methodist is to save as many souls as he/she possibly can. Every year the occasion is also used to remind members "that in the Providence of God Methodism was raised up to spread Scriptural holiness through the land by the proclamation of the Evangelical Faith and declares its unfaltering resolve to be true to its divinely appointed mission."[10]

SOCIAL INVOLVEMENT

John Wesley's involvement in social issues covers a wide spectrum of concerns. It flows out of his understanding of spreading Scriptural holiness across the land. He fought against injustices in the court systems, spoke against corrupt election practices, and showed deep concern about government policies that adversely affected the nation, especially the poor. He personally visited the prisons and called for reforms of the prisons and an end to inhumane treatment of prisoners. Not only did Wesley strongly support the abolition of slavery and the slave trade, he spoke vehemently against racial discrimination. In his letter to William Wilberforce dated February 26, 1791, he encouraged him to carry on with the "glorious enterprise" of opposing:

> that execrable villany, which is the scandal of religion, of England, and of human nature. Unless God has raised you up for this very thing, you will be worn out by the opposition of men and devils. . . . Go on, in the name of God and in the power of his might, till even American slavery (the vilest that ever saw the sun) shall vanish away before it. Reading this morning a tract, wrote by a poor African, I was particularly struck by the circum-stances—that a man who has a black skin, being wronged or outraged by a white man, can have no redress; it being a law, in all our colonies, that the oath of black against a white goes for nothing. What villany is this![11]

What is remarkable about Wesley is that his commitment to social transformation is derived from his evangelical faith in the redemptive work of Christ and creation. He was able to see within the poor person covered with dirt and rags an immortal spirit capable of knowing God, loving him, and dwelling with him in eternity. Wesley could see through the rags and dirt of a human being "purpled over with the blood of Christ"; and Wesley loved that poor man for the sake of his Redeemer. When he sees the poor, however degraded and disreputable, Wesley is convinced that he must show that person respect, honor, and love because that person is "the offspring of God; the purchase of his Son's blood, and the candidate for immortality. This courtesy let us feel and show toward all and we shall please all men to their edification."[12]

Wesley's social concern has had a profound impact on the Methodist Church Ghana. Following Wesley's biblical and theological understanding as expressed above, the church has, during its more than 170 years in mission in the Gold Coast and Ghana, involved itself in providing quality education and health care, particularly among the poor in the rural areas. The church has played a significant role in the creation of political leaders, some of whom were at the forefront of the fight for the independence of Ghana.

CONCLUSION

Methodism grew out of two Bible bands led by Joseph Smith and William de Graft seeking to study the Scriptures carefully in the latter half of 1831. Through the instrumentality of William de Graft, the Wesleyan Methodist Missionary Society in London sent their first missionary, Joseph Dunwell, to Ghana, then called Gold Coast. He landed in Ghana on January 1, 1835. A fortnight after his arrival, Dunwell introduced Methodism in the south western half of Ghana.[13] The first Methodist class of twelve members out of Smith's group, called the "Meeting," was formed on Sunday, January 4.

Out of this nucleus, Methodism began to exert its influence in Ghana as more missionaries responded to the call to replace those who lost their lives and those who were recalled. According to Richard Foli, "the period 1852–1900 was one that saw rapid expansion of Methodism in Ghana, the main reason being a good use of indigenous converts and evangelists. In 1885 for example, there were only three European missionaries as against 15 African ministers and 126 local catechists and evangelists."[14] By 1918, Methodism could boast of 12 missionaries, 42 African ministers, and 665 catechists and teachers. The total number of congregations increased to 261 with a total Christian community of 78,252. A hundred years after its establishment, the church recorded an estimated number of about 125,225 members with 767 chapels, 47 African ministers, 24 European missionaries and 335 catechists.[15]

In 1961, the Methodist Church Ghana (MCG) had its autonomy with 69 African ministers and a total Christian community of 153,052. By 1985, the MCG celebrated its 150th anniversary with a total Christian community of 335,749. Though this rose to about 507,422 in 1988, it needs to be mentioned that there were decreases in membership between 1988 and 1990, apparently due to a leadership crisis which rocked the church.[16] Pragmatic evangelistic programs were adopted by the church in 1995 (dubbed "5 in 1995") and further strengthened thereafter by similar drives, which has kept the spirit alive. Since 2005 the MCG has been focusing on "doubling our membership." The total number of ministers in active service as of 2007 was 754 with a total Christian community of 584,969 in 3,203 Societies and 611 preaching posts. While 10 missionaries from The Mission Society work in Ghana, MCG has sent out about 17 ministers for missionary outreach in North America, Canada, the

United Kingdom, Germany, Holland, and Italy, among others and in Sierra Leone in Africa.

The social ministry of the church has also seen significant gains. From a modest number of 31 schools in 1856, the MCG now has about 865 primary and middle schools which the church was managing in 1960. In 2007 the MCG recorded 744 kindergartens, 1,042 primary schools, 519 junior high schools, 26 senior high schools (including 5 private ones), 22 second cycle vocational and technical institutions, 3 teacher training colleges, and one university college. The church also has 2 hospitals and 16 clinics.[17] In terms of theological education, the MCG is one of the sponsoring churches of Trinity Theological Seminary, Legon, established in 1942 where most of its ministers are trained and others through Theological Education by Extension. The MCG also trains its lay evangelists, deacons, preachers, and leaders at the Freeman Centre for Missions and Leadership Development, Kumasi.

In this essay we have demonstrated that the Wesleyan spirit of mission is holistic in nature, and it is inspired by Wesley's high esteem of Scripture, his experience of the mercy and love of God, and his belief in the creation and the redemptive work of Christ. We have also shown that the Methodist Church Ghana, following a similar pattern in biblical and theological convictions, has demonstrated that the Christian mission is holistic in its impact on human beings and their communities.

NOTES

1. *The Constitution and Standing Orders of The Methodist Church Ghana,* 2000 Revised Edition, published by authority of the Conference of the Methodist Church Ghana, reprinted 2008, p. 9.

2. Ibid.

3. John Wesley, *The Works of John Wesley,* 3rd ed., Complete and Unabridged, vol. 8, *Addresses, Essays, Letters* (Grand Rapids: Baker Book House, reprinted 1984), p. 340. Italics added for emphasis.

4. Cited in "Themes in Wesley's Theological Understanding," Echol Lee Nix, Jr., 2000, Boston Collaborative Encyclopedia of Western Theology: John Wesley, http://people.bu.edu/wwildman/bce/Wesley.htm.

5. Christopher J. H. Wright, *The Mission of God, Unlocking the Bible's Grand Narrative* (Downers Grove, Ill.: Inter-Varsity Press, 2007), p. 29.

6. *The Constitution and Standing Orders of The Methodist Church Ghana*, p. 10. Wesley's *Notes on the New Testament* and his sermons are not intended to impose a system of formal or speculative theology on Methodist preachers, but to set up standards of preaching and belief that should secure loyalty to the fundamental

truths of the Gospel of Redemption and ensure the continued witness of the church to the realities of the Christian experience of salvation.

7. Cited in Roy Hattersley, *A Brand from the Burning: The Life of John Wesley* (London: Little, Brown, 2002), p. 27.

8. http://people.bu.edu/wwildman/bce/Wesley.htm.

9. Ibid.

10. *The Constitution and Standing Orders of The Methodist Church Ghana*, p. 10.

11. John Wesley, *The Works of John Wesley*, 3rd ed., Complete and Unabridged, vol. 13, *Letters*, (Grand Rapids: Baker Book House, reprinted 1984), p. 153.

12. Ibid., vol. 7, pp. 145–46.

13. F. L. Bartels, *The Roots of Ghana Methodism* (Cambridge: Cambridge University Press, 1965), p. 6.

14. Richard Foli, *Christianity in Ghana: A Comparative Church Growth Study* (Accra: Trust Publications, 2006), p. 23.

15. Bartels, *The Roots of Ghana Methodism*, p. 205.

16. Foli, *Christianity in Ghana*, pp. 156–57.

17. Methodist Church Ghana, 5th Biennial/43rd Conference Agenda, Winneba, Ghana, August 2008, BOA 42.

6

THE MISSIONAL FLAVOR OF JOHN WESLEY'S THEOLOGY

Howard A. Snyder

INTRODUCTION

John Wesley's theological significance and contribution are increasingly recognized globally.[1] Less recognized is that Wesley was fundamentally a theologian of *mission*; that his teaching was a theology of the mission of God, *missio Dei* (to use today's terms).

Similarly, it is recognized today that Wesley wed theology and praxis (living out one's faith). Less recognized is the fact that in Wesley the underlying impulse of both theology and praxis was mission.

If we look at Wesley through a contemporary missiological lens, we see missional themes that perhaps were less obvious in prior periods. However we must take care to approach Wesley inductively, not deductively, understanding him on his own terms and within his own context.

Viewed inductively, I argue, Wesley's theology was *fundamentally* and in *essence* a theology of mission, and to miss this fact is to misunderstand Wesley. Granted, Wesley did not use the term "missional," or even "mission" or "mission of God" in the contemporary sense. He used the language of his day—often innovatively. But his fundamental theology, including his theological terminology, had a missiological flavor. In fact, viewing Wesley's theology missiologically prompts a kind of paradigm shift through which the coherence and potency of Wesley's thought and action emerge more clearly.

Wesley was constantly engaged in the *practice* of mission—preaching the Gospel to the poor and all who would hear; forming Methodist classes and societies; writing letters, sermons, and pamphlets; counseling and sending out preachers—and constantly reflecting theologically on what he was doing. Though deeply involved in the lives of the Methodist people, Wesley kept remarkably well informed about the intellectual, philosophical, and scientific issues of his day.

Wesley had a remarkable capacity to step outside his own tradition theologically. This was due in part to his personality and temperament and the nature of his intellect; in part to the hybrid Anglican tradition with its *via media* and the "Anglican triad" of Scripture, reason, and tradition; in part to the revival in patristic studies at Oxford during his student days; and probably also to his crosscultural experiences in America (1735–1738). It certainly owed much also to Wesley's willingness to step outside his own social class to minister to and with the poor.

Wesley emphasized five *biblical* themes that together constitute a dynamic theology of mission: image of God, prevenient (or preceding) grace, salvation as healing, the "perfecting" of Christian character, and the restoration of all things. Though interwoven throughout Wesley's writings, each of these themes has its own distinctiveness and missiological significance.

THE IMAGE OF GOD

Man and woman are created in God's image. For Wesley, this was more than an affirmation of human worth or dignity (as it is often taken today). It had key redemptive and eschatological implications. Since human beings bear God's image, even though marred by sin, they can be redeemed, healed, and restored. Created in the divine image, men and women are "capable of God."[2] They have an inherent capacity for deep communion and companionship with God if the effects of sin can be overcome.

Among other implications, this means that the first word in evangelistic witness is not bad news but good news—not, "You are a sinner," but "You bear God's image." Evangelism starts with good news. But Wesley does not lose his balance here, as some contemporary theology does; there is no compromise with the sinfulness of sin and the alienation, guilt, and judgment that result from sin. "All have sinned and fall short of the glory of God" (Rom. 3:23). For Wesley, that is neither the last *nor the first word*. Sin is the defacing, but not the total loss, of God's image. In every person there is something worth saving and something that can be restored.

In a secondary sense, the whole created order bears God's stamp and image. Here Wesley's worldview is more Hebraic and biblical than Greek or Platonic; more ecological, "both/and," than is most Reformed theology and most contemporary evangelical theology. In his mature thought, especially, Wesley did not make a sharp break between the physical and the spiritual realms. It was no theological embarrassment to him to see the interpenetration of the material and the spiritual worlds and to affirm the working of God's Spirit in both, interactively. This provides (in part) the theological basis for recognizing that salvation concerns not only human experience but also the whole created order.

PREVENIENT (PRECEDING) GRACE

In Wesley's view, all creation is infused or suffused with God's grace as an unconditional benefit of Christ's atonement. There is nowhere one can go where God's grace is not found, though people (and people corporately, as cultures and societies) can and do close their hearts and minds to God's grace.[3]

Based on the Latin *praevenire* ("to come before, anticipate, get the start of"), Wesley called this gracious dynamic "preventing grace"—because that's what "prevent" meant in his day. Since "prevent" has almost the opposite sense today, the more common term has become "prevenient grace." We might more accurately call it *preceding grace*—that gracious, loving, drawing action or influence of God that is always at work seeking to bring people and cultures to God.

This has several key implications. The first and most basic one is that in Christ by the Holy Spirit, God has gone ahead of us (ahead of every person), preceding us, counteracting the effects of sin so that people can respond to God's grace. God's preceding grace is not in itself saving grace; its function is to draw us to salvation in Christ.[4]

Wesley spoke of *preventing* (preceding), *justifying* (or converting), and *sanctifying* grace.[5] These are not three different kinds of grace. Grace is one; it is the gracious, loving, self-giving activity and influence of the one triune God. The threefold distinction refers not so much to the nature of grace itself but to the way people *experience* that grace. By God's prior grace people are drawn to God (or they resist that grace). If they respond in faith, grace becomes justifying grace, leading directly into sanctifying grace if people continue to open their lives to the work of God's Spirit. Or, put differently, the loving grace of God precedes us, draws us to Christ, converts us, and progressively sanctifies us, leading finally to "glorification" in the new creation.

One missiological implication of preceding grace is that God's Spirit is the missionary. God is already active in all persons, cultures, societies, and to a degree in many (not all) religions.[6] God works for good, limiting the effects of evil and seeking to bring people to himself. While some people, responding to preceding grace, may find their way to God, the role of the church and Christian mission is essential so that more people may know and respond to Christ and be saved from their sins and that vital, outreaching churches may be formed in all societies. The work of Christian mission is to cooperate with God's preceding grace so that people may experience God's convicting, justifying, and sanctifying grace.

Preceding or prevenient grace can be pressed too far, so that the distinction between *preceding* and *justifying* grace is lost. The danger would be to distort Wesley's balance—to so emphasize that we are saved by grace, not by works, that the necessity of knowing and responding to God's grace in Jesus Christ in faith and obedience is eclipsed. The whole point of prevenient grace is that it *precedes* in order that there might be response of repentance, faith, love, and good works.

SALVATION AS HEALING

Wesley viewed salvation as healing from the disease of sin. People are guilty for their acts of sin, but actual sin betrays the deeper problem of the moral disease that alienates people from God, from themselves and each other, and from the earth. So Charles Wesley prayed,

> *The seed of sin's disease*
> *Spirit of health, remove,*
> *Spirit of finished holiness,*
> *Spirit of perfect love.*[7]

John Wesley preached that God's love in Christ is "the medicine of life, the never-failing remedy, for all the evils of a disordered world, for all the miseries and vices" of men and women.[8] The true "religion of Jesus Christ" is "God's method of *healing a soul*" that is diseased by sin. "Hereby the great Physician of souls applies medicines to heal this sickness, to restore human nature, totally corrupted in all its faculties."[9] Wesley said, "This is the religion we long to see established in the world, a religion of love and joy and peace, having its seat in the heart, . . . but ever showing itself by its fruits, continually springing forth . . . in every kind of beneficence, in spreading virtue and happiness all around it."[10] "According to Scripture," Wesley said, "the Christian religion was designed 'for the healing of the nations.'"[11] As he grew older, Wesley increasingly emphasized salvation as the healing of the whole created order.

Reformed theology uses primarily the law court model of salvation, stressing the Book of Romans. Jesus' atonement cancels the penalty for sin so that we can be forgiven, justified. Wesley affirmed this, but for Wesley the deeper issue was the moral disease that needed healing by God's grace.

Randy Maddox notes Wesley's "distinctive integration" of Eastern and Western conceptions of God's grace. "Given their juridical focus, Western theologians have identified God's grace predominately as *pardon*, or the unmerited forgiveness of our guilt through Christ. By contrast, Eastern theologians construe grace primarily in terms of the power to heal our infirm nature that comes through participation in God."[12] Wesley weds the two streams. His sermons combine in almost equal measure the accents of *pardon* and *power* in presenting God's grace.

For instance Wesley, in "The Witness of Our Own Spirit" says, "As soon as ever the grace of God (in the former sense, his pardoning love) is manifested to our soul, the grace of God (in the latter sense, the power of his Spirit) takes place therein. And now we can perform through God, what to [ourselves] was impossible . . . a recovery of the image of God, a renewal of soul after his likeness."[13]

Maddox notes:

> Wesley's integration of the two dimensions of grace was not merely a
> conjunctive one. The emphasis on pardon was incorporated into the

larger theme of empowerment for healing. Thereby, God's unmerited forgiveness became instrumental to the healing of our corrupt
nature, in keeping with Wesley's deep sympathy with a therapeutic
emphasis like that characteristic of Eastern Christianity. At the same
time, the Christological basis of grace was made more evident than is
typical in the East, integrating the legitimate concern emphasized by
the West.[14]

Today "therapeutic" models of salvation are anathema to many
evangelicals because they are thought to undercut the biblical emphasis
on the guilt of sin and justification by grace alone. To use healing
language for salvation is seen as capitulation to popular humanistic
psychology, an over-emphasis on subjective "feeling," and today's moral
relativism. But Wesley means something deeper. Pardon for sin through
the atoning death of Jesus Christ is essential. But the point of Christ's
atonement is that human beings, and by extension their societies,
cultures, and environments, may be healed from the disease and
alienation of sin.

This has multiple implications for mission. The healing model
underscores the personal and relational nature of salvation. It has the
potential for "healing" the divisions between our understandings of
spiritual, physical, social-relational, environmental, and cosmic health.
God's salvation intends and entails healing in all dimensions.
Salvation-as-healing makes it clear that God is intimately concerned
with every aspect of our lives. Yet biblically understood, it also makes
clear that the healing we most fundamentally need is spiritual: our
relationship to God.[15] Biblically grounded (and as Wesley understood
it), salvation as healing is no concession to pop psychology; it is an
affirmation of who God is, what it means to be created in God's image,
and what it takes for that image to be restored in Jesus Christ by the
Holy Spirit.

This healing paradigm is often especially powerful in mission
contexts. As Philip Jenkins notes in *The Next Christendom*, many African
and other independent churches "stress Jesus' role as prophet and
healer, as Great Physician. Although this approach is not so familiar in
the modern West, this is one of many areas in which the independents
are very much in tune with the Mediterranean Christianity of the
earliest centuries."[16]

"PERFECTING" CHRISTIAN CHARACTER

Reflecting his eighteenth-century Anglican context, Wesley used the language of "Christian perfection." In our relation to God and other people, the goal is perfection—that is, the maturing of Christian character after the image of Jesus Christ.

Today the word "perfection" is easily misunderstood to mean a completed absolute rectitude, even flawlessness, rather than the process of perfecting (though the word can mean both). It is actually closer to Wesley's meaning to speak of "Christian perfecting" or "the perfecting (or maturing) of Christian character" than to speak of "Christian perfection."[17]

Wesley, of course, was attempting to be biblical in his terminology. It is clear from his writings that by Christian perfection Wesley meant the Spirit-given ability to love God with all our heart, soul, strength, and mind and our neighbors as ourselves. The central issue is the work of the Spirit in transforming us (personally and communally, as the church) into the image of Christ; of forming in us the character of Christ, which is equivalent to the fruit of the Spirit. Christian perfection is having and living out "the fullness of Christ" or "the fullness of the Spirit."[18]

We are called to holiness, which means (as Wesley often said) having the mind that was in Christ Jesus, being conformed to his image, and walking as he walked. This is where salvation-healing leads, if we walk in the Spirit. This healing makes the church a sign and agent of the larger, broader healing that God is bringing in Christ through the Spirit.

Wesley sometimes called this experience of the perfecting of character "social holiness." By "social holiness" Wesley meant the experience and demonstration of the character of Jesus Christ *in Christian community*, the church. In Wesley, "social holiness" does *not* mean social justice or the social witness of the church. That witness grows out of the "social holiness" that is the character of the church itself and might better be called "kingdom witness" or something similar. Wesley was making a very specific and essential (and often neglected) point in using the term "social holiness": Holiness (the character of Christ) is not solitary or lone or individualistic sanctity but a social (i.e., relational) experience based on our relationship with God the Trinity and experienced, refined, and lived out jointly in Christian community. Wesley was very clear on this, and it is a disservice to Wesleyan theology to use the term "social holiness" as equivalent to "social witness" without at least acknowledging that we mean something different than Wesley did. [19]

The Wesleyan emphasis on Christian perfecting has two fundamental aspects that are key for effective witness: First, we emphasize (and incarnate) the fact that the *goal* (the *telos*) is always growth into the fullness of the character of Jesus Christ as the corporate experience of the church and the experience of each Jesus-follower. Second, we stress (and help Christians experience) the fullness of the Spirit. Normally, Wesley taught, this deeper work of the Spirit comes as a distinct experience subsequent to conversion, though (as Wesley acknowledged) it may be experienced more gradually or less perceptibly and thus, no doubt, through multiple fresh fillings (or deeper workings) of the Spirit. Effective mission means giving believers opportunities to enter into that deeper life—to confront the dividedness of their own hearts and enter into that fullness, wholeness, and integration in *Christian community* that is our inheritance in Jesus Christ and a foretaste of that communion we will enjoy in the heavenly kingdom.

THE RESTORATION OF ALL THINGS

God's promise to "restore everything" (Matt. 17:11, Mark 9:12, Acts 3:21) was a key element of John Wesley's theology. Wesley's hopeful certainty was based not on a few scattered biblical references but on the whole thrust of the biblical story, beginning to end. His sermons "The New Creation," "The General Deliverance," and "The General Spread of the Gospel" highlight key Scriptures: Romans 8:19–22 on the liberation of the whole creation from its "bondage to decay," Isaiah 11:9 on the earth being full of the knowledge of the Lord, and Revelation 21:5, "See, I am making all things new." Another favorite Wesley text was 1 John 3:8, "The Son of God was revealed for this purpose, to destroy the works of the devil," the text for Sermon 62, "The End of Christ's Coming." For Wesley, salvation was all about *restoration* and healing.

Wesley was clear, however, that the restoration of all things does not come without suffering. Romans 8:17–24 speaks of our "groanings" and "sufferings," saying that as we wait and work in hope, we are called to "share in [Jesus'] sufferings in order that we may also share in his glory" (Rom. 8:17 NIV). In fact the whole creation, now in "bondage to decay," is "groaning as in the pains of childbirth right up to the present time" (Rom. 8:22 NIV).

Wesley saw suffering as a mystery, but a necessary one in order that God's glory may be fully revealed. God achieves the world's redemption through suffering—the suffering of Jesus Christ above all, but we become sharers, partakers, in Jesus' sufferings—and God weaves those (and eventually all suffering, Wesley believed) into his redemptive, restorative purposes.

Wesley saw suffering however not just as private virtue, or simply as part of compassionate service. Wesley frankly admitted the suffering of all creation—viewing that suffering within the larger framework of the restoration of all things (referring to Romans 8). In a remarkable passage in his sermon "The New Creation" Wesley writes:

> How many millions of creatures in the sea, in the air, and on every part of the earth, can now no otherwise preserve their own lives than by taking away the lives of others; by tearing in pieces and devouring their poor, innocent, unresisting fellow-creatures! Miserable lot of such innumerable multitudes, who, insignificant as they seem, are the offspring of one common Father, the creatures of the same God of love! . . . But it shall not always be so. He that sitteth upon the throne will soon change the face of all things, and give a demonstrative proof to all his creatures that "his mercy is over all his works" [Ps. 145:9]. The horrid state of things which at present obtains will soon be at an end. On the new earth no creature will kill or hurt or give pain to another. . . . "The wolf shall dwell with the lamb" (the words may be literally as well as figuratively understood) "and the leopard shall lie down with the kid" [Isa. 11:6]. "They shall not hurt or destroy" [Isa. 11:9] from the rising up of the sun to the going down of the same. [20]

Perhaps the most remarkable thing here (bypassing all the scientific questions we might raise) is that Wesley sees this restoration, this new creation, as literal and physical, not exclusively spiritual. Passages such as Isaiah 11 are to be taken "literally as well as figuratively."

Wesley lived in the hope of the restoration of all creation—and understanding that our present sufferings somehow play a necessary part in our own contribution to the kingdom of God in its fullness.

CONCLUSION

Clearly these five central themes in Wesley—the image of God, preceding grace, salvation as healing, the maturing of Christian character, and universal restoration—are all *missional*. Together they clarify the mission of the church. By the Holy Spirit they empower and impel the church into mission, into redemptive kingdom witness.

NOTES

1. For example, Charles Yrigoyen, ed., *The Global Impact of the Wesleyan Traditions and Their Related Movements* (Lanham, Md.: Scarecrow Press, 2002).

2. Here as elsewhere Wesley is emphasizing and reintroducing themes from early Eastern Christian theology and spirituality.

3. "For allowing that all the souls of men are dead in sin by nature, this excuses none, seeing there is no man that is in a state of mere nature; there is no man, unless he has quenched the Spirit, that is wholly void of the grace of God. No man living is entirely destitute of what is vulgarly called natural conscience. But this is not natural: It is more properly termed, preventing grace." John Wesley, Sermon 85, "On Working Out Our Own Salvation," in *Sermons III*, ed. Albert C. Outler, vol. 3 of *The Bicentennial Edition of the Works of John Wesley* (Nashville: Abingdon Press, 1976–), p. 199. Hereafter cited as *Works*.

4. There is a sense in which preceding grace may become salvific, Wesley taught, in the case of individuals who have never had opportunity to hear of Jesus but who respond in obedience to the (preceding) grace they have received. Thus Cornelius before Peter's preaching, though "in the Christian sense . . . then an unbeliever," was not outside God's favor. "[W]hat is not exactly according to the divine rule must stand in need of divine favour and indulgence." Wesley, *Explanatory Notes Upon the New Testament*, Acts 10:4. Anyone thus saved, however, is saved by Christ's atonement, even though they are unaware of it. In these cases, then, preceding grace becomes (in effect) saving grace. See Randy Maddox, *Responsible Grace: John Wesley's Practical Theology* (Nashville: Kingswood 1994), pp. 32–34.

5. "By 'means of grace' I understand outward signs, words, or actions, ordained of God, and appointed for this end, to be the ordinary channels whereby

he might convey to men, preventing, justifying, or sanctifying grace." Wesley, *Works*, vol. 1, Sermon 16, "The Means of Grace," p. 1.

6. Non-Christian religions are not in themselves *means* of grace, but God's grace to some degree works in them—if in no other way, at least to restrain evil. Presumably most religions are a mixture of good and evil (as Christianity itself can be when it becomes religion). A pagan religion, like an individual person or a culture, may become totally corrupt, but even there God's grace is at work, to some degree restraining evil, or finally bringing judgment.

7. Charles Wesley, "Glorious Liberty," Hymn No. 442 in *The Hymn Book of the Free Methodist Church*, 1883 (Chicago: Free Methodist Publishing House, 1906).

8. Wesley, *An Earnest Appeal to Men of Reason and Religion*, in *Works*, vol. 11, ed. Gerald R. Cragg, p. 45.

9. Wesley, Sermon 44, "Original Sin," in *Works*, vol. 2, p. 3.

10. Wesley, *Earnest Appeal*, in *Works*, vol. 11, p. 46.

11. Wesley, Sermon 61, "The Mystery of Iniquity," in *Works*, vol. 2, par. 31; (Rev. 22:2).

12. Maddox, *Responsible Grace*, pp. 84–85. Maddox cites the dissertation of Robert Hillman, which found that in 463 references to grace in 140 of Wesley's sermons, 147 construe grace as pardon

(mercy) and 176 as power, and 140 references combine the two dimensions. This "two-dimensional understanding of grace" is found also in Charles Wesley's hymns (p. 297).

13. Wesley, Sermon 12, "The Witness of Our Own Spirit," in *Works*, vol. 1, p. 15.

14. Maddox, *Responsible Grace*, p. 85.

15. See for example Luke 5:20–26, where Jesus both heals and forgives the paralytic.

16. Philip Jenkins, *The Next Christendom: The Coming of Global Christianity* (New York: Oxford University Press, 2002), p. 16.

17. Terms such as "Christian perfection," "entire sanctification," and even "holiness" have always been problematic in the Wesleyan tradition, even for many who wish to maintain, with no dilution or compromise, what Wesley taught.

18. Key passages are Ephesians 3:19, 4:13, Colossians 2:10, among others, and those that speak of being filled with the Spirit, such as Ephesians 5:18.

19. "Christianity is essentially a social religion, and . . . to turn it into a solitary religion is indeed to destroy it. . . . it cannot subsist, without living and conversing with other people." Wesley, Sermon 24, "Upon Our Lord's Sermon on the Mount, Discourse the Fourth," in *The Works of John Wesley*, vol. 1 (Nashville: Abingdon Press, 1984), 533–34.

20. Wesley, Sermon 64, "The New Creation," in *Works*, vol. 2, par. 17.

BIBLIOGRAPHY

Chilcote, Paul W., ed. *The Wesleyan Tradition: A Paradigm for Renewal*. Nashville: Abingdon Press, 2002.

Hempton, David. *Methodism: Empire of the Spirit*. New Haven: Yale Univ. Press, 2005.

Henderson, D. Michael. *John Wesley's Class Meeting: A Model for Making Disciples*. Nappanee, Ind: Evangel Publishing House, 1997.

Jennings, Theodore W., Jr., *Good News to the Poor: John Wesley's Evangelical*

Economics. Nashville: Abingdon Press, 1990.

Maddox, Randy L. "Anticipating the New Creation: Wesleyan Foundations for Holistic Mission." *Asbury Journal* 62:1 (Spring 2007): pp. 49–66.

———. *Responsible Grace: John Wesley's Practical Theology.* Nashville: Abingdon Kingswood, 1994.

Meeks, M. Douglas, ed. *The Portion of the Poor: Good News to the Poor in the Wesleyan Tradition.* Nashville: Abingdon Kingswood, 1995.

Runyon, Theodore. *The New Creation: John Wesley's Theology Today.* Nashville: Abingdon Press, 1998.

Snyder, Howard A., ed. *Global Good News: Mission in a New Context.* Nashville: Abingdon Press, 2001.

———. *The Radical Wesley and Patterns for Church Renewal.* Downers Grove, Ill.: InterVarsity Press, 1980.

———. "Salvation Means Creation Healed: Creation, Cross, Kingdom, and Mission." *Asbury Journal* 62:1 (Spring 2007): pp. 9–47.

Yrigoyen, Charles, Jr., ed. *The Global Impact of the Wesleyan Traditions and Their Related Movements.* Lanham, Md: Scarecrow Press, 2002.

7

METHODISM, MISSION, AND THE MARKET STATE

William J. Abraham

Despite the grandeur of its title this paper is intentionally written more as a narrative in mission than as a conventional academic paper. I shall write from the bottom up, charting my own journey in the theology and practice of mission and within that touching on the relevant theological and sociopolitical issues that arise. I shall suggest in conclusion that this journey in mission highlights in the end the missional significance of a wider cultural shift that is represented in the move from a nation state to market state.

My first interest in mission as a serious enterprise was evoked by exposure to the stories of missionaries that were transmitted in Methodist circles in Ireland. Mission, understood as the spread of the Gospel in word and deed, was simply part of the air we breathed in Irish Methodism. I remember vividly taking part in a presentation at a young people's convention that reenacted the heroic story of Gladys Alyward. I can recall the names of veteran missionaries that served overseas. Many of these were regular visitors at the Irish Methodist Missionary Summer School that met annually in a boarding school outside Kilkeel. The participants at this event were relatively young; the week was packed with Bible studies, hiking, talks on mission, and informal activities. The speakers were invariably outstanding (one year we had Philip Potter from the West Indies). Such was the bonding that we met in regional groups through the winter. This meeting also featured missionaries who had been abroad but had come home for the education of their children. It was clear that the gifts they brought back to Irish Methodism were pivotal to its health and survival. There was an irenic enthusiasm that was contagious.

During my education at university, my interest in mission waned. My priorities were directed to my studies in philosophy and theology. However, when I came to Perkins School of Theology to teach, I took up the study and teaching of evangelism alongside work in philosophy of religion. My interest in mission was reignited. The focus of my work very naturally centered on the mission situation in the West.

In this work I became convinced that the paradigm of humanitarian and charitable work that governed the work of mission in United Methodism was totally inadequate. The decline of Christianity in Europe and in the mainline in the United States exposed this paradigm as passé. Moreover, I grew restless with the way in which the challenge of mission was conceptualized in terms of personal evangelism plus social action. *De facto* this remains the operational vision of mission in United Methodism, despite the fact that the mission statement focuses "on the making of disciples of Jesus Christ for the transformation of the world."

My unease is both theological and practical. On the theological level, this way of thinking gives no attention to Christian initiation in evangelism nor to establishing local churches in mission. On the practical level, this mission statement is a dead letter; there is no real commitment to implementing it. Even if United Methodists nominally believe in making disciples, they do not know how to do so. The addition of the final qualifying phrase ("for the transformation of the world") in 2008 will reinforce the mantra that mission is personal evangelism plus social action. Given that we have no clue about personal evangelism, we are left with social action. This is sometimes upgraded to the ministry of peace and justice, an inflated and illusory description of charitable work. However we frame the description, the problem of the reduction of mission to humanitarian work remains intact.

Yet we have not hit bottom in our analysis. There is also the problem of our mode of missionary work. The work of overseas mission has been outsourced to general agencies with a life of their own. In all of my time of ministry, I have heard next to nothing about the work of the general church in mission. I can get information if I really want it; but the default position is that we have handed the work of mission to agencies and let them do the work on our behalf. Beyond the odd blip, the work of missions overseas has disappeared off the radar screen of the local church. No doubt this has been done with the best of intentions; however, I find it bizarre. We have become the victims of radical centralization, and the gifts and energy of laity have been ignored.

The intersection of these two problems (the reduction of mission to humanitarian work and its centralization in general agencies) initially came to a head for me serendipitously. In my work in evangelism I had developed with a group of laity in Uvalde, Texas, a contemporary catechumenate that would take seriously the initiation of new believers into the kingdom of God in local churches. When we first began our work, we were promised financial help from the Annual Conference Office; this was abruptly withdrawn when we ran afoul of the politically correct censorship that was in place. As we shared the program with other local churches, somehow the material made its way into a Russian translation and ended up in Karaganda, Kazakhstan. After being used there, I was invited to visit Karaganda. Knowing that one of my heroes, Alexander Solzhenitsyn, had written *One Day in the Life of Ivan Denisovich* while in the gulag in the region, I agreed.

I have often told the friend who engineered this trip that he had wrecked my life. Long exposure to the brutal history of the Soviet Union was of little help in coming to terms with the devastation that I witnessed. I had to keep a diary; otherwise the suffering I encountered involved a meltdown that wiped out the memories of the previous day. In the midst of this I taught a network of new believers who were on fire with faith, filled with curiosity, and facing a host of challenges in the creation of an indigenous Kazakh church. I also met a team of extraordinary United Methodist missionaries from The Mission Society who had sacrificially given their lives to the work in Kazakhstan. Since then, one has died and been buried with honor among those he served. It is a matter of shame that next to nobody in our church knows of his sterling, humble service. I came back deeply disoriented and found myself forced to revisit the challenge of mission. It was abundantly clear to me that the reduction of mission to humanitarian work was a travesty in that it ignored the crying need for ministry directed explicitly to personal salvation and church planting.

On my second visit I found myself waking up in the middle of the night wondering how I could be of help. It was not enough to show up from time to time; something more structured was needed. Turning to the general agencies of the church would likely be useless. There would be too much red tape to overcome, and the commitment to conversion and church planting would fall on deaf ears. Moreover, working formally with The Mission Society (the other option) would mean taking on political battles for which I had no inclination. With a small group of friends, I decided to set up a skeleton organization that would provide the mechanisms needed. We gave ourselves a name (Oasis), formed a board, secured legal standing, and began fundraising. We also educated ourselves as best we could about the history and culture of Kazakhstan. Over time, board members traveled to Karaganda; on return they were hooked for life. We developed an informal theology of mission, worked out a philosophy of ministry, became creative in fundraising, and did what we could from a distance. All those involved have stayed the course; despite the heavy demands of work and family life they are committed for life to the work of mission overseas. What has clearly emerged from this experience is this: ordinary lay people are thirsting to be involved in missionary work in a fitting manner.

Through another set of providences, we now find ourselves working elsewhere in Asia. This started when a generous gift for the work there, which was to be channeled through her local church, was sent back to the donor. Startled by this response, the donor contacted me to see if Oasis could help. Happily, we had the expertise to run the traps and make sure everything was in order. The decision to help meant that we were now opening a second front, for our policy is to build a lasting relationship with those we seek to serve. In this instance the needs are extraordinary. The primary work is the hard, grinding task of sharing the Gospel, forming new believers, and establishing new churches. On one end, this means supporting the formation of a mission school that trains evangelists and church planters; on another end, it entails the full range of humanitarian service that comes in a situation of extreme poverty. We envisage a lifelong relationship where we work together in mutual affection for the glory of God.

As I write this, we are now prayerfully considering a less taxing relationship with a church planter in Rumania. This, too, began serendipitously when I met a former musician in a satanic rock band while teaching in San José, Costa Rica. He had come from Rumania but was converted while on tour in Central America. After seminary training, he was called by God to return home and start a Methodist church. He is now already hard at work there; the plan to connect him to a lively United Methodist Church is already in play.

What is the significance of this informal journey in mission?

First, we have been driven to come to terms with the place of evangelism and church planting in the theology of mission. While uneasy with the current theology and philosophy of mission in United Methodism, we have not been driven by a desire to rock the boat, to play the judgmental prophet, or to make a name for ourselves in mission. Given the radical imbalance and the incompetence in robust forms of evangelism, it would be easy to get hot and bothered. However, we have too much on our plate to waste time on polemics. We want to see evangelism and church planting put back on the missionary table, but we have no desire to harm in any way the humanitarian work that must be done. We have simply found ourselves confronted with a need and have set about meeting it in a careful and systematic manner. In time we can expect that the formal theology of mission in United Methodism will be adjusted and corrected.

Second, we have discovered that others have found themselves driven by their experience to undertake similar sorts of missionary work either through their local churches or through parachurch organizations. They have had to go around or beyond the structures and practices currently in place. In my local church in Dallas, Vision Africa, created and led by a former student who is now a bishop, is now a thriving missionary organization engaged in church planting and other ministries in Nigeria. Back in my home town of Enniskillen in Ireland, a friend I knew in university, now retired from a distinguished career in teaching, is working informally in Sudan. I am aware of a significant number of laity, churches, and United Methodist clergy who are working in mission outside the system. Some are tempted to declare war on institutionalism, but this is a minority report; most recognize the necessity of institutional structures and are creating their own in an ad hoc fashion.

Third, we have rediscovered in this work the critical significance of Wesley's catholic spirit, where the first priority is to support the work of the Gospel wherever it exists rather than confine ourselves parochially to The United Methodist Church. We have had to repent of our sectarianism and offer assistance to believers who do not belong to our denominational tribe. To be sure, it is vital to have systems of accountability if we are to be good stewards of the money entrusted to us; but too often this has been a cover for bigotry and an exclusionary attitude toward other Christians.

Fourth, we have had to work on a philosophy of ministry. There are two aspects to this—one relates to the overall approach, the other to the role of laity. First, we reject two traditional paradigms. On the one hand, we have no interest in returning to an era where the Western churches sent missionaries and financial resources and then demanded to control everything on the ground. On the other hand, we reject the Nevius plan in which local churches overseas are to be left alone to fend for themselves. While this strategy has its virtues, it does not deal with the extreme poverty we have encountered. Our philosophy is to form a relationship with indigenous Christians, work with them on the ground, and provide substantial financial resources with no strings attached. Second, we believe that there is a place for informal missionary work on the part of laity. This is not mission tourism; it is a long-haul commitment that is costly and deeply life-changing. We are well aware that our work will have its own temptations and vices; sincerity and energy are not enough. We are sensitive to the challenges of cross-cultural communication and the pitfalls of dependence; however, we also know that God works through broken and earthen vessels.

One way to describe what we have done is to say that we have become a mission broker that connects local churches and laity with missionary work overseas. We have been learning of late not to speak of what we do in Oasis but to highlight the work done by those with whom we are yoked in the providence of God. We are operating from the bottom up, developing our theory and practices as we proceed. Yet this is not the whole story. The emergence of these informal missionary practices represent a straw in the wind; they reflect a sociopolitical shift that mirrors the change from a nation state to a market state. At the risk of being grandiose, I think that this fifth and final comment is pivotal for future reflection on mission in United Methodism.

Whatever the ecclesiology in play at any particular time in history, the actual ethos and practices of the church mirror what is happening in the surrounding culture. This is natural, for Christians are initiated in their everyday lives into modes of thinking and acting that they inevitably bring into their service in the church. The missionary practices of the last generation have mirrored the ethos and practice of the nation state. In the nation state the following are crucial: the protection of a generic cultural and national identity, civil peace through law, independence in the international order, bureaucratic competence, the monopoly of the legitimate use of violence, clear and secure boundaries, control of the economy and currency, centralization, heavily reliant on professional experts, secularization, and the provision of maximal welfare from the cradle to the grave. It is surely obvious that many of these elements show up in the mission theology and practice of United Methodism since its creation in 1968. Thus we have witnessed the following: the secularization of mission, the concentration of a monopoly of power in central bureaucracies run by experts, a generic and contested identity in the theology of mission, the sharp rejection if not demonization of alternatives as a threat to peace in the church, and an ethos of paternalism in which laity are treated as secondary agents who are tolerated because they provide funding but not as agents in their own right. Clearly the twin concerns of the reduction of mission to humanitarian service and the exclusion of laity fit snugly into this bigger picture.

It is clear, however, that the nation state is now being displaced by the market state. Nations can no longer control their borders, their cultural and national identity, and their economies. They cannot stand aside from the international order, monopolize the use of violence, keep spiritual interests out of the public order, ignore noncentralized initiatives, and provide welfare from the cradle to the grave. Globalization, the revolution in communications, terrorism, massive natural disasters, the revival of radical religious commitment, and the like are systematically reordering the life of nations. The state continues to exist but its mode is that of the market: while it will still provide indispensable, institutionalized services, it has shifted to an ethos in which personal initiative and the provision of opportunity are given privileged status.[1]

This is precisely what is emerging in the new forms and practices of missionary theology and practice that are multiplying within United Methodism. We can be sure that these changes will bring with them their own virtues and vices. For the moment it is imperative that we come to terms with the changes that are afoot and find better ways to service the Gospel in this radically changed environment.

NOTES

1. For a brilliant but contested account of the move to the market state see Philip Bobbitt, *The Shield of Achilles* (New York: Anchor, 2002).

8

THE CHALLENGES OF JOHN WESLEY'S THEOLOGY IN LATIN AMERICAN MISSION CONTEXTS

Luís Wesley de Souza

For a long time, since my adolescence, I had heard about the Wesleyan family in Chile—its stories, uniqueness, and challenges. I recently went to Santiago with some of my Candler students, where I spoke at two very distinctive churches of unquestionable Wesleyan origins. One is the First Methodist Church of Santiago, where about forty people, including my twelve students, gathered for worship and fellowship. On the same day I also visited and spoke at the cathedral of the Methodist Pentecostal Church of Chile (MPCC). In stark contrast with the first visit, I found several thousands of people gathered for worship and fellowship in the cathedral.[1]

MAKING A CASE FOR JUSTICE AND PROPHETIC VOICE

At the First Methodist Church of Santiago, I had the honor to meet Bishop Isaías Gutiérrez Vallejos, who told me how the Methodist Church of Chile (MCC), under his leadership, stood up and exercised an unusually courageous prophetic voice while the country was run by one of the most oppressive and violent military dictatorships in the history of South America.

Bishop Gutiérrez, along with others, understood that doing mission in such a context required putting their own lives at risk. Unfortunately, this was the constant reality as they decided not to remain in obsequious silence but to explicitly and publically cry out for justice, confronting

Augusto Pinochet's power. They knew that Pinochet had implemented harsh measures against his political opponents, which included systematic violations of civil liberties and human rights. Gutiérrez also understood that being a people called Methodists in the midst of that kind of political and ideological mess would require, from the church as a whole, to be prophetically present and evangelistically committed to life abundant "in [our] Chile where we live and witness."[2] Because of its responsible, engaged and yet extremely vulnerable prophetic voice and presence, the Methodist Church in Chile paid the price. It soon became unpopular, ideologically marginalized and expelled from the array of support of the regime and society at large.

MAKING A CASE FOR RELEVANCE AND CONNECTION

The Methodist Pentecostal Church of Chile is a church that stemmed from mainline Methodism in 1909 when a revival broke out within the Methodist Church, which led to a split and the formation of the MPCC and, later on, other Pentecostal churches. The emergence of Chilean Pentecostalism, particularly the MPCC, was also an affirmation of an authentic, Chilean expression of non-Catholic Christianity over foreign mainline missionary models that implicitly denied freedom and spontaneity in worship and condemned miracles, healings, tears, and visions.[3] The MPCC soon realized that leadership and ministry should be exercised under the Holy Spirit's guidance through simple and open Christian believers, not just clergy.

I had also heard about some of the criticisms toward the MPCC, notably of its former leaders' support of the right-wing dictatorship in the late 1970s and 1980s, which was obviously a historical, embarrassing mistake of great magnitude.[4] Nevertheless, at the MPCC I learned what it takes for a church to exercise a contextualized Wesleyan practice of mission that highly adapts to local circumstances, connects to the poor in their very struggles of life, and translates it into other forms of concrete relevance. As José Míguez Bonino observed:

> The Chilean Wesleyan Pentecostal churches . . . have strongly engaged their culture—in songs, methods of expansion, language, and so on— while retaining the connectional organization, ministerial order, and the sacramental life (including infant baptism) of the Methodist tradition.[5]

The MPCC did not grow because of its alleged support for the regime. It grew because it was capable of drinking from and of being inspired by its Wesleyan missional heritage at the same time that it coped with the context and became a popular religion, a true church *of* the poor. As far as I know, it is one of the very few churches of Wesleyan origins that seriously considered the *modus vivendi* of John Wesley's missional ecclesiology: plenty of room for the laity to exercise their talents and gifts, itinerant evangelists, religious societies, class meetings, bands, and so on.

In addition, as the Chilean Pentecostal theologian Juan Sepúlveda indicates in his article "Pentecostalism as Popular Religiosity" (1989), Pentecostalism's attraction lies in its ability to reach vast numbers of people through its spirituality. As a researcher in popular subjectivity and religiosity among the poor, Sepúlveda asserts that, "a theology which begins with experience will have a language and methodology distinct from those of classical, conceptual theology."[6]

Touching on the conclusions I have drawn from my research on classical Pentecostalism in Latin America, I soon realized that MPCC follows the pattern of other Pentecostal churches in many ways. From a historical viewpoint, one observes that classical Pentecostalism has drunk from Wesleyan wells and grew out of the Holiness revival during the second half of the nineteenth century.[7] Cuban historian and theologian Justo L. González, for example, is incisive in affirming that Pentecostalism in general and, more specifically, the Latin American classical Pentecostal movement is an inheritor of John Wesley.[8]

Essentially, in the process of developing its Wesleyan theology and practices of mission, the MPCC saw the importance given by John Wesley to *experience* and opened up people's minds to develop a theology of experience and an experiential reading of the Bible from the underside of history, which created avenues for the "laity" to reflect on their own spiritual daily journeys as they engaged in mission. In doing so, the MPCC became indigenous in Chile and developed an ability to (1) contextualize its language and methods, (2) become culturally, spiritually, and emotionally relevant to the Chilean people, (3) generate a Christian identity closely connected with the Chilean cultural forms and meanings, and (4) respond to the needs of a people in the midst of social and economic struggles.[9]

TWO VISITS, MANY LESSONS

As a missiologist shaped by both the Wesleyan rich spirituality of social sanctity and a progressive evangelicalism (Brazil's movement of *missão integral* [holistic mission]) that seeks not to dichotomize evangelism and social transformation, besides being highly concerned about social justice and solidarity with the poor, I see both churches, the MCC and the MPCC, being effective in their own terms as they claim their Wesleyan heritage and mission practice. Most of all, I see that they remind each other of those key aspects of mission practice that are eventually missed by the other, and reflect on the essentials of being church in context. It is vital to exercise a prophetic voice against the oppressor, but it is also vital for the mission of the church to be socially, culturally, spiritually, and emotionally relevant, and to connect with the forms and meanings of the culture of those who suffer.

What follows, then, are reflections on some of the challenges of Latin American Wesleyanism and propositions for its practice of mission. These challenges are based on the fact that the people called Methodists in Latin American contexts must be mission driven, situated in time and space, in many given cultures and conjunctures. In doing so, I will focus on (1) how the Wesleyan theology of mission challenges the church in its prophetic, relevant, and transforming presence in Latin America, and (2) how the context informs the Wesleyan movement in its missionary nature.

Challenge One: Practicing A Mission Theology That Is Both Holistic And Liberating

Wesley's theology speaks loudly and relevantly to a context that cries out for justice, solidarity, reconciliation, and social transformation. The Wesleyan dynamic of religion of the heart is combined with social religion or social holiness. It points out that doing *mission work that is transformative* requires the churches of Wesleyan origins in Latin America to be nothing less than liberating communities. However, being a transforming movement is nobler than simply embracing liberation theology. Before anything else, it is re-claiming, re-visiting, and re-envisioning our own Wesleyan theology, which is holistic in its core, essence, and practice of mission among the poor, the oppressed, the excluded, the marginalized, and the exploited. That is to say, that even before liberation theology came about in our continent we already had a liberating Methodism and, ultimately, a liberating Christianity.

A liberating church that carries out a holistic message and practice would have a *mission ethics that is socially engaged*. The tough socioeconomic situations of Latin America challenge the church in a broader sense and churches of Wesleyan origins in particular for a serious and committed engagement. In other words, the social ethics and dimension of Wesley must be noted, reflected, and practiced in Latin America more than in many other parts of the world, which would generate an engaged, incarnate church that is truly Wesleyan.

Such a reflection and praxis must lead the church to own a *mission voice that is prophetic*. Because of the nature of Wesleyan social ethics, Latin American Wesleyans do need to do contextual exegeses and, in doing so, take the context of where they live and minister seriously, and translate it into a *mission service that is in solidarity with the poor* and a *mission proclamation that aims for justice, reconciliation, and liberation*.

Practicing a mission theology that is both holistic and liberating is an enormous challenge, and it requires the Latin American Wesleyan family to nourish a mission motive that owns a kingdom consciousness. A faithful Wesleyan organized expression of the church would have this kind of consciousness as the driving force of mission. It would develop a *mission structure that is kingdom driven*, enabling the church to focus on people's participation in the *Missio Dei*, instead of draining energy in maintaining and preserving the structure as an end in itself. The structure serves the church, not the other way around. Howard A. Snyder reminds us that, "It is critically important, especially in a globalized, multicultural situation such as the church faces today, to be clear that the essence of the church is people, not organization; that it is a community, not an institution. This is a critical distinction, and the failure to make it often creates great confusion."[10]

Challenge Two: Developing A Mission Presence
That Is Both Fully Incarnational And Indigenous

As the Wesleyan missiologist George G. Hunter III puts it, "the church is called to be an extension of its Lord's incarnation, compassionately responsive to the needs of hurting people."[11] Hunter also reminds us that another Wesleyan missiologist, Darrell Whiteman, often affirms that "the Incarnation is the model; indigenization is the method."[12] There is no other option but to follow Jesus' model—incarnation—and it is not different for the Wesleyan practice of mission needed in Latin America. It requires a *mission practice that is entirely relevant*. That is why it is not enough for the proclamations of the Gospel and the ministry of the church to be socially and politically relevant. Message and ministry have also to be culturally, spiritually, and emotionally adapted and incarnated.

As it was with Wesley's ministry in England, notably the kind of mission he established in Bristol, developing a *mission method that is indigenous* is the only way to become fully relevant to any given Latin American sociocultural context. There are different levels of sociocultural relevance that the Latin American Wesleyan communities can represent to the people, but it would surely begin by developing and exercising methods that are proper to the very ground upon which the Christian mission is developed.

Pan-Wesleyan mission initiatives in Latin America must model a *mission presence that is incarnational* in its very nature. Here again, the church must have a clear, indigenous understanding of local realities in order to address the cultural, emotional, and spiritual needs of the people. It will obviously require the church to study the context, but more important is the need for exercising a *mission connection that accepts the challenge of living together with people*. The church's theology and mission practice must generate an indigenous way of touching the Latin American people.

It is also vital for the church to exercise a *mission language that is understandable*. In the process of indigenizing Christianity, language and methodology are determined and shaped by the lay participants of a given context. It is crucial that, from the beginning, the Gospel be communicated in a simple and culturally relevant way, both methodologically and linguistically. Foreign formulations of theological terminologies and/or strategic models, even those translations and interpretations of the Wesleyan theological richness made by outsiders, are to be submitted to and evaluated by the insiders, right from the early stage of mission enterprises.

**Challenge Three: Being A Mission People,
Both Spirit-filled And Laity Led**

As it happened with classical Pentecostalism in Latin America, the Wesleyan movement in England and North America had a special concern "of providing leadership that was spiritually alive, doctrinally sound, and missiologically active,"[13] as Richard P. Heitzenrater notes. More than any other Christian movement in history before the rise of Pentecostalism, Methodism "relied more and more heavily upon lay persons without theological education or training in religious leadership."[14] Leaders were raised up among the laity. It was through and because of the laity that

Methodists went out to the people, not waiting for them to come to the church. The essence of the church—the community of believers empowered by the Spirit and sent on a mission—gives no room for any attempt to make distinctions between clergy and laity, except when and where the priestly roles become purely contextual and functional.

Pan-Wesleyan churches, mission initiatives, and movements in Latin America should not be afraid of giving up their pretense of institutional control over the Holy Spirit's work. Wesley understood "the explicit role of the Holy Spirit as central"[15] both individually and collectively, not only as the basis for claiming assurance and the source of spiritual fruits, but also for witnessing the Gospel message creatively, ministering to God's people, and serving God in the world.

The roots we have in John Wesley's theology tell us that being a church in context requires the church to be a *mission movement that is open to and enriching of creativity*. Affirming the past—especially when we try to reaffirm the mistaken, wrong, and misleading pasts—is a way of subverting the present and damaging the future of the church. It may close minds to new contextual forms, languages, methods, styles, aesthetics, and experiences in mission. Wesley's movement was rooted in the Christian tradition and, at the same time, was remarkably creative and innovative. Reasoning, experiencing, revisiting, and reexamining the Scripture were exercises of creativity and sensitivity to the Holy Spirit. It was not arrested by narrow and closed minds or by any deceptive institutional suppression of people's initiatives.

It was a movement of the people and, as such, it trusted the Holy Spirit to inspire people as they exercised their ministry in the world. The Wesleyan movement developed itself by recognizing the fundamental importance of the laity. Methodists used to trust entirely in the explicit role of the Holy Spirit as the source of knowledge and spiritual fruits, as well as the gifts of the Spirit for the ministry of the lay people, entrusting them to work freely and creatively.[16]

That is why we cannot be honest with Wesley's ecclesiology without considering his unique ways of giving unlimited room to the laity. It says to the Latin American pan-Wesleyan community that it must develop a contextualized *mission ecclesiology that is lay based and led*. The essence of the formation of an indigenous church that lives out Christianity in context is its radical confidence that, under the Holy Spirit's guidance and empowerment, lay people are capable of carrying out the work. As it was with the

Methodist movement, clericalism should not be an emphasis or a priority at all, although strong leadership is needed in order to facilitate the ministry of the church. The most important of all is that lay initiatives be encouraged, welcomed, and supported.

As "lay" people are entrusted, church leadership must be capable of allowing them to elaborate their content of faith from their own experience and with their own cultural features. As Howard Snyder reminds us, the major limits for church growth are not financial resources or viable physical facilities. Rather, "it is more likely to depend on the availability of people—either expatriate or indigenous—who are open to the Spirit and ready to exercise their gifts in witness and ministry."[17]

Challenge Four: Reclaiming A Mission Heritage That Is Soundly And Practically Concerned For The Poor

The Wesleyan movement also developed itself in the midst of poverty. Differently from what concerned the Methodists for a long time, however, we somehow have forgotten the poor and neglected the laity. This is why today's Latin American Wesleyanism must recall and be inspired by the ideals of the church as experienced by early Methodism under John Wesley.

Now and then, *the church is a place for the poor to feel at home*. Richard P. Heitzenrater reminds us that "at the very early stages in their development, the societies began to demonstrate a special interest in the needs of the poor and disadvantaged, giving food and money to the needy, visiting the sick and imprisoned, and teaching the children of the unfortunate . . . to improve their life in a spiritual and moral sense."[18] This kind of concern for the poor and disadvantaged was "especially noteworthy in the light of later Methodism."[19] This is why "Early Methodists were known for their concern and care for the poor, the stratum of society from which so many of them came."[20]

Poverty is not to be ignored or neglected at all. Instead, the church is the very community that lives together with those who suffer economically and socially. Moreover, unless the church has compassion for the poor, upon whom the community must be built, it will never reflect God's love and mercy. "Of all peoples and classes, God especially has compassion on the poor, and his acts in history confirm this," Snyder notes.[21] The way by which Wesley's theology and practice of mission embraced an evangelistic faith by the poor teaches us that no Wesleyan-rooted church in Latin America or elsewhere should forget God's transforming power in the lives of individuals and society.

"From the beginning and throughout history," says Snyder, "the most rapid, enduring and society-transforming church growth has normally occurred among the poor."[22] Snyder's perception correlates with the MPCC. What really matters here, however, is not the measure of growth the church has performed, although it is one of the many signs of vitality of the MPCC, but its true nature as *an indigenous church* that is able to take the initiative of providing relevant responses to the needs of those who face social and economic struggles. A true indigenous church in Latin America must have compassion on the poor, for this is one of the very bases upon which the church must be built to reflect God's love and mercy.

Wesley's practice of mission tells us that we are supposed to be a *mission community that reconstructs people's dignity*. The church in Latin America, particularly the churches with Wesleyan origins, has to rethink its concept of a "preferential option for the poor," and must become the home *of* the poor. In fact, doing this will require from the Latin American Wesleyan family a true conversion to the poor. There must be an *in loco* understanding of the reality of the poor. In other words, the church is not supposed to simply go where the poor live, but to participate within their very own reality. It means to take hold and grow among the poor and the oppressed.[23] The church in its mission enterprises must develop an overt, all-encompassing relationship with poverty that may enable the community of faith to act naturally and intuitively toward people who live and face daily socioeconomic struggle.

CONCLUSION

Holistic and liberating mission, fully incarnational and indigenous presence, Spirit-filled and lay leadership, and genuine concern for the poor are the main challenges that face the church in Latin America, and a Wesleyan approach is meaningful, practical, and helpful in formulating missiological responses to the context. The Wesleyan churches in Chile—the one (MCC) responsibly prophetic against political and social injustice but very small in number, the other (MPCC) charismatic and focused on meeting the needs of the people and consequently very large and popular—are important expressions of Wesleyan theology in the Latin

American churches. Together they summarize and exemplify the kind of mission enterprise that must feature the actions of the churches of Wesleyan origins in Latin America. They also provide warning signs of what should be avoided. May God help us get the inspirations and insights the Wesleyan theology of mission can offer, the wisdom to contextualize them, and the courage to implement them in such a way that it becomes life in our practice of mission for the glory of God.

NOTES

1. According to Harvie M. Conn and Manuel Ortiz's book *Urban Ministry: The Kingdom, the City and the People of God* (Downers Grove, Ill.: InterVarsity Press, 2001), the cathedral or "central sanctuary" of the Jotabeche Methodist Pentecostal Church can seat 16,000 people. It has over forty satellite congregations and claims to have more than 350,000 members, which makes it the second largest local church in the world, next to David Young Cho's Full Gospel Church in Seoul, South Korea. "The bridge between the 16,000 and the 350,000," they say, "is the satellite network" (p. 242).

2. Isaías Gutiérrez Vallejos, *Presencia y Testimonio: Enfoque Metodista de un Evangelio Comprometido con la Vida* (Presence and Testimony: Methodist Approach of a Gospel Committed with Life), (Santiago, Chile: CIEMAL, 1989), p. 1.

3. David Martin, *Tongues of Fire: The Explosion of Protestantism in Latin America* (Oxford, Eng. and Cambridge, Mass.: Basil Blackwell, 1990), p. 30.

4. David Stoll (in *Is Latin America Turning Protestant? The Politics of Evangelical Growth*, Los Angeles: Univ. of California Press, 1990) indicates that, "Grateful for the endorsement, the new dictator, General Augusto Pinochet, became a patron of the country's largest

Protestant denomination, the Pentecostal Methodist Church" (p. 112). On the other hand, Stoll disputes Lalive d'Epinay's "assessment of [Chilean] Pentecostalism as a reactionary force," acknowledging that, "many [Pentecostal] believers seem to have voted for the Allende government and its attempt to build socialism" (p. 316).

5. José Míguez Bonino, "Wesley in Latin America: A Theological and Historical Reflection," in *Rethinking Wesley's Theology for Contemporary Methodism*, ed. Randy L. Maddox (Nashville: Kingswood Books, 1998), p. 173.

6. Juan Sepúlveda, "Theological Characteristics of an Indigenous Pentecostalism: The Case of Chile," in *In the Power of the Spirit*, eds. Benjamin F. Gutiérrez and Dennis A. Smith (New York: Presbyterian Church [USA] and AIPRAL/CELEP, 1996), pp. 51–61. Commenting on Jürgen Moltmann's book *The Spirit of Life: A Universal Affirmation* (Minneapolis: Fortress Press, 1992) and the importance of it for Pentecostalism in general, Sepúlveda sees parallels between Moltmann's considerations and the Latin American Pentecostal experiential trajectory. Moltmann speaks of "church theology," which is constructed by and to pastors and priests, in contrast with the

"theology of experience," which is preeminently "lay" theology (Moltmann, p. 17). Sepúlveda concludes that, "Since experience cannot be reduced to concepts, a theology that takes experience as its starting point must be a narrative theology, as is biblical theology, to a large degree" (Sepúlveda, p. 55).

7. Luís Wesley de Souza, "The Assemblies of God in Brazil: Lessons in Indigenization (A Study of the Process of Indigenization of Pentecostalism in Brazil from 1910 to 2000, and Implications for Mainline Protestantism)" (PhD diss., The E. Stanley Jones School of World Mission and Evangelism of Asbury Theological Seminary, Wilmore, Ky., 2003), p. 299.

8. Justo L. González, *Wesley para a América Latina Hoje* (Wesley for Latin America Today), (São Paolo: Editeo, 2003), pp. 16–18. For González, when the Azusa Street revival broke out, "many churches saw themselves obligated to make a decision about it. Most of them rejected what was taking place as a demoniac work . . . [but] many other holiness groups embraced the revival, which later on originated the main Pentecostal churches, [including] the Church of God in Cleveland, Tennessee, and the Assemblies of God" (p. 18).

9. de Souza, "The Assemblies of God in Brazil," p. 15.

10. Howard A. Snyder, *The Community of the King*, revised (second) edition (Downers Grove, Ill.: InterVarsity Press, 2004), p. 76.

11. George G. Hunter III, *To Spread the Power: Church Growth in the Wesleyan Spirit* (Nashville: Abingdon Press, 1987), p. 137.

12. Ibid., p. 169.

13. Richard P. Heitzenrater, *Wesley and the People Called Methodists* (Nashville: Abingdon Press, 1995), p. 182.

14. Ibid.

15. Ibid., p. 91.

16. Howard A. Snyder, *The Radical Wesley and Patterns for Church Renewal* (Pasadena, Calif.: Wipf & Stock Publishers, 1996), p. 155. According to Snyder, "As [John] Wesley's ministry developed and he began commissioning a whole regiment of traveling preachers, two options were open to him to explain biblically what was happening. One would have been a radical affirmation of the doctrine of the priesthood of believers, an assertion that biblically and in God's plan every believer is called to minister and that the various forms of ministry are based on the charismatic work of the Holy Spirit rather on the institutional accreditation of the church. The other option, which Wesley essentially took, was to admit the normal validity of ecclesiastical ordination but to see the Holy Spirit as breaking through this mold and creating an 'extraordinary' pattern of ministry in a fashion outside but somewhat parallel to normal ecclesiastical structures."

17. Ibid., p. 142.

18. Heitzenrater, *Wesley and the People Called Methodists*, pp. 23–24.

19. Snyder, *The Radical Wesley*, p. 15.

20. Howard A. Snyder, *Liberating the Church: The Ecology of Church and Kingdom*, (Pasadena, Calif.: Wipf & Stock Publishers, 1996), pp. 142–43.

21. ———. *The Problem of Wineskins* (Downers Grove, Ill.: InterVarsity Press, 1975), p. 39.

22. Snyder, *The Community of the King*, p. 141.

23. John Wesley had a critical understanding of why some people do not care about the poor: "One great reason why the rich in general have so little sympathy for the poor is because they so seldom visit them. Hence it is that, according to the common observation, one part of the world does not know what the other suffers. Many of them do not know, because they do not care to know: they keep out of the way of

knowing it—and then plead their voluntary ignorance as an excuse for their hardness of heart" (Sermon 98, "On Visiting the Sick," I.3, *The Works of the Rev. John Wesley: Vol. 3*, Jackson Edition, Oxford: Clarendon Press, pp. 387–88).

BIBLIOGRAPHY

Bonino, José Míguez. "Wesley in Latin America: A Theological and Historical Reflection." In *Rethinking Wesley's Theology for Contemporary Methodism*, ed. Randy L. Maddox, pp. 169–82. Nashville: Kingswood Books, 1998.

de Souza, Luís Wesley. "The Assemblies of God in Brazil: Lessons in Indigenization (A Study of the Process of Indigenization of Pentecostalism in Brazil from 1910 to 2000, and Implications for Mainline Protestantism)." PhD diss., The E. Stanley Jones School of World Mission and Evangelism of Asbury Theological Seminary, Wilmore, Ky., 2003.

———. "Classical Pentecostalism: Lessons for Missions." *Caminhando* 12, no. 19 (January–June 2007): pp. 57–68.

González, Justo L. *Wesley para a América Latina Hoje* (Wesley for Latin America Today). São Paolo: Editeo, 2003.

Heitzenrater, Richard P. *Wesley and the People Called Methodists*. Nashville: Abingdon Press, 1995.

Hunter, George G., III. *To Spread the Power: Church Growth in the Wesleyan Spirit*. Nashville: Abingdon Press, 1987.

Martin, David. *Tongues of Fire: The Explosion of Protestantism in Latin America*. Oxford, Eng. and Cambridge, Mass.: Basil Blackwell, 1990.

Moltmann, Jürgen. *The Spirit of Life: A Universal Affirmation*. Minneapolis: Fortress Press, 1992.

Sepúlveda, Juan. "Pentecostal Theology in the Context of the Struggle for Life." In *Faith Born in the Struggle for Life: A Rereading of Protestant Faith in Latin America Today*, ed. Dow Kirkpatrick, pp. 298–318. Grand Rapids: William B. Eerdmans Publishing Company, 1988.

———. "Pentecostalism as Popular Religiosity." *International Review of Mission* 78:309 (January 1989): pp. 80–88.

———. "Theological Characteristics of an Indigenous Pentecostalism: The Case of Chile." In *In the Power of the Spirit*, ed. Benjamin F. Gutiérrez and Dennis A. Smith, pp. 51–61. New York: Presbyterian Church (USA) and AIPRAL/CELEP, 1996.

Snyder, Howard A. *The Problem of Wineskins*. Downers Grove, Ill.: InterVarsity Press, 1975.

———. "The Church as Holy and Charismatic." *Wesleyan Theological Journal* 15, no. 2 (Fall 1980): pp. 7–32.

———. *The Radical Wesley and Patterns for Church Renewal*. Pasadena, Calif.: Wipf & Stock Publishers, 1996.

———. *Liberating the Church: The Ecology of Church and Kingdom*. Pasadena, Calif.: Wipf & Stock Publishers, 1996.

———. *The Community of the King*. Second edition. Downers Grove, Ill.: InterVarsity Press, 2004.

Stoll, David. *Is Latin America Turning Protestant? The Politics of Evangelical Growth*. Los Angeles: Univ. of California Press, 1990.

Wesley, John. *The Works of the Rev. John Wesley*, vol. 3, ed. Thomas Jackson. Oxford: Clarendon Press, 1975–1983, orig. pub. ca. 1846.

9

JOHN WESLEY'S EIGHTEENTH-CENTURY CONTRIBUTIONS TO THE TWENTY-FIRST-CENTURY THEOLOGY OF RELIGIONS

Terry C. Muck

Insights John Wesley articulated in the eighteenth century have important contributions to make to the twenty-first-century missional theology of religions discussion.

That might seem like an odd claim to make for the theological insights of a man who essentially failed in his initial cross-cultural mission experience. Born in Epworth, England, to an Anglican parish priest, Wesley spent two early years in America as a missionary chaplain in the colony of Georgia. They were frustrating years for Wesley and the frustration probably had something to do with his paradigmatic religious experience that occurred upon his return to England.

Yet the case could probably be made that it was this failed mission experience in America that gave him the empathetic understanding of the mission quest necessary to craft a missional theology of religions that has stood the test of time. It has become almost axiomatic that in order to understand a human phenomenon one must experience at least a taste of it for oneself. Outsider (etic) observations and categorizations have their place, but unless complemented by insider (emic) insights, they tend to remain abstract insights rather than life-changing experiences. Wesley learned about mission as an insider in Georgia. Because of this experience he came to understand the difficulties of cross-cultural mission and, eventually, see the way forward.

The lessons he learned in Georgia surely made his subsequent cross-cultural mission experiences (to Ireland, Wales, Scotland, etc.) the successes they were. One can certainly see the influence of Georgia throughout his sermons and letters and his more mature thinking.

What were these missiological contributions so important to us today? Immediately we run into the usual issues of trying to understand the theology of a man who did not pretend to write theology. So, as everyone does, we must mine the sermons for his missiological insights. We will look at three: (1) "The General Spread of the Gospel," a sermon written in Dublin in April 1783; (2) "On Zeal," a sermon first preached in Wales on April 29, 1781; and (3) "Free Grace," a controversial sermon preached and/or written on April 26, 1739.

In trying to apply Wesley's insights to the modern world, we find ourselves faced with the anachronistic problem—Wesley simply didn't have the geographical or demographic knowledge to accurately assess the missional needs of the world. To him the world was divided religiously this way:

Heathens   63%
Muslims   20%
Christians   17%

Obviously, the category called "heathens" is a catchall for anyone not a Christian or Muslim. A modern parsing of the world's religions would be more detailed to include indigenous religions, Chinese religions, Hinduism, Buddhism, and so on. Yet even if we keep Wesley's categories, and even if we accept Wesley's estimates as accurate for his day, we find the religious makeup of the world has changed rather dramatically. To us, if we keep Wesley's categories, the world looks this way:

Heathens   47%
Muslims   20%
Christians   33%

Yet, when we step back and assess Wesley's missional contribution, we find the limitations of theological genre and incomplete statistics mean little when compared with the truth of what Wesley discovered about God and God's work through us in the world. Like all theological truth, its articulation in human, cultural form does and must change. But it is truth all the same.

The most important challenges of the world missional scene today have changed. They are not about challenges that have faced the church in the first two millenniums. Once, resources and capacity were a nagging problem. They are no longer. The mission movement is well funded. Once, access to non-Christian cultures was a problem—access was limited because of remoteness and difficulty of reach (see William Carey). Today, where access is a problem it is because of the intentional rejection of access by governments dominated by other religious forces. Christianity has become unpopular in some places in the world today. And Christianity is seeing the growth and development of sophisticated missional competitors.

And yet even in these changed conditions, Wesley's insights still ring true. Wesley's teachings focused on Christians' relationships to people of the world and different religions; on the importance of respect for all God's creatures; on a hope in a universal reconciliation; on walking the tightrope between being committed to the truth of the Gospel and being compassionate to all in need.

WHY THE GENERAL SPREAD OF THE GOSPEL FALTERS

Wesley based his hope in the general, worldwide spread of the Gospel on passages like Isaiah 11:9, "The earth shall be full of the knowledge of the LORD, as the waters cover the sea" (KJV). According to Albert Outler, he preached on this passage seven times between 1747 and 1755. But it was one of his later sermons on this text that is helpful in our attempts to deal with the modern/postmodern, religiously plural world: "The General Spread of the Gospel."

He begins this missionally auspicious sermon by painting a fairly dismal picture of the current (1783) mission scene. The spread of the Gospel, after a rip-roaring start, has stalled. Both heathens (63%) and Muslims (20%) outnumber Christians (17%) in terms of their percentage of the world population. And even among the Christians, he surmises, there are too many who in terms of faith quality are no better than the heathens and Muslims. I suppose we would today call these nominal Christians.

What has been the reason for this dismal state of affairs? Why has the Christian church plateaued in terms of growth? It seems almost inexplicable, says Wesley: "How astonishing is this, if there is a God in heaven! . . .

How is it possible to reconcile this with either the wisdom or goodness of God?"[1] If God wants the Gospel to spread to the ends of the earth, which Scripture clearly says he does, then why are we no longer making any progress toward that end?

The answer from God's side of things is fairly simple: If God wanted to act irresistibly, he could save the whole world in an instant. But we know that God has chosen not to act that way. When it comes to offering the gift of salvation he does not *do*, he *makes possible*. He stands by each of us, offering the free gift of grace, but has given each of us the moral capacity to choose, and he waits for us to choose. Rather impatiently at times, but he waits all the same.

But answering the why question from the side of God does not solve the problem. There is more to learn. Wesley gives a brief outline of how the Gospel has spread from the time of the apostles until now to show that God's assisting ways have worked at many, many periods of time in the church's history. And since we know God's actions are constant—that is, his assisting grace has always been everywhere present—the periods when the Gospel does not spread (like the period right now) must be a problem on the part of human beings, not God.

So what is the reason for this dismal state of affairs? It must come from the human side of the equation. Yes it does, says Wesley. He calls it the grand stumbling block. It is the lives of Christians themselves. When Christians do not behave like Christians, when they do not exhibit faith, love, and hope, then the heathens and Muslims do not feel compelled to believe. But when Christians do live lives that model the Gospel, Wesley says, God's purposes are accomplished. The Gospel story becomes almost irresistible.

Can there be any more important word for the Christian mission effort today? We believe, with Wesley, that God is still holding up his end of the bargain, that God's grace is as ubiquitous as it always has been—available for all. And we do believe that God wishes all would accept it. But it still falls to us to be like Christians, to live like Christians.

Not that this is all that simple. Geopolitical factors muddy the waters. The Christian church is still identified with nations and the witness of nations is not uniform. As with individuals, the nations often give Christianity a bad name.

Wesley's point endures, however. The problem in areas where the Christian mission has stagnated is not with resources, or techniques, or especially sinful people. The problem is with us. We are the ones who must get our Christian act together and remove the one remaining stumbling block to the dream of the Gospel spreading over all the earth as the waters cover the seas.

Do you believe that the Gospel can spread like this? Are you willing to do what you can to remove any and all stumbling blocks standing in the way of that end?

LOVING ZEALOUSNESS

How exactly does the behavior of Christians create stumbling blocks to the spread of the Gospel? In a sermon preached first in 1781 and many times thereafter, Wesley identifies one of the behavioral culprits: zeal. Christians, he said, misunderstand zeal. And until we are able to improve our zealousness, the spread of the Gospel will continue to stumble.

Wesley is not opposed to zeal per se. The text for the sermon "On Zeal," Galatians 4:18, shows that: "It is good to be zealously affected always in a good thing" (KJV). The text reminds Wesley and us that, "without zeal it is impossible either to make any considerable progress in religion ourselves, or to do any considerable service to our neighbor."[2] No, Wesley was not arguing for a lack of zeal in Christian mission work.

What he was arguing for was a zealousness more consistent with Christ's life and teachings. The kind of zeal he observed in many of his compatriots was inconsistent with the zeal he found in this Bible. And this false zeal was very damaging: "Pride, covetousness, ambition, revenge, have in all parts of the world slain thousands, but zeal its ten thousands."[3]

As a prelude to explaining how one can identify proper zeal, Wesley defines his terms. The original word, he said means "heat." The Greek word used to express it in New Testament texts is *zelos*. When applied to an attribute of the human mind, then, it means a warm emotion or affection. Someone who has zeal has a heated emotion toward something else. For Wesley, zeal referred to an intense commitment. So far, no real difference from the usual understanding of the word.

What, then, makes for Christian zeal? Christian zeal is always affixed to charity or love: "It is not properly religious or Christian zeal if it be not joined with charity. . . . Christian zeal is all love."[4] "True Christian zeal," Wesley said, "is none other than the flame of love."[5] Christian zeal is the same thing as fervent love.

One can begin to see the difficulty of grasping this. The plain and simple meaning of zeal is not difficult to grasp. And we all think we know what love is. But the two don't easily go together in the phrase, "loving zeal." The stakes rise when Wesley goes on to pair zeal with words like "humility," "meekness," and "patience." Zeal without humility, meekness, and patience is dead.

It is true that we sometimes make efforts to rationalize this obvious biblical teaching by talking about having "tough love" for someone. Tough love is an attempt to describe the combination of zeal (toughness) and concern (compassion). But the argument is so easily shifted into the kind of actions we have come to abhor—inquisitional actions, crusading actions, imperialistic actions—that one can see why Wesley was so concerned with describing zeal as a package of affections, a disposition, that can properly be called Christian.

He ends the sermon by recommending activities that call for different quantities of zeal. The most zeal, he says, should be attached to our genuine love for other people. The second most zeal should be attached to our own attempts to develop within ourselves what Wesley calls the holy tempers, that is, the fruits of the spirit—longsuffering, gentleness, meekness, goodness, fidelity, temperance, contentedness, resignation to the will of God. These are proofs and fruits of our living faith.

The third most zeal should be present in works of mercy toward others, the fourth most in works of piety such as prayer, communion, Bible reading, and fasting. And the least amount of zeal should be attached to the building of the church.

Although Wesley does not specifically say it, his list of the gradations of Christian zeal is probably opposite to the ways most of us practice zeal. We are most zealous in activities that have to do with the building of the church and least zealous in activities that have to do with perfecting our own spiritual lives. And that is precisely Wesley's point. If we want to cease being the stumbling blocks that are stagnating the growth of the church, we must reexamine what it is we are most zealous about.

THE OPTIMISM OF GRACE

Wesley's final contribution to the missional theology of religions of today has to do with our attitude toward people who are not Christian.

If calibrating the proper amount of loving zeal has to do with the various tasks of the Christian life, then Wesley's understanding of the optimism of grace has to do with the affections with which we approach people who are not Christian, who are heathen or Muslim (or Hindu or Buddhist, etc.).

In Wesley's day, as in ours, some believed that there were many people in the world who were chosen by God for damnation. Even if this were a small group, a small group of Christians believing such a thing was too much for John Wesley: "[S]ome have answered: The greater part of mankind God hath ordained to death . . . [grace] is not free for them."[6] Wesley countered this by saying that while God did not choose to use his powers to save everyone, God certainly made salvation available for everyone and because of that provision everyone had the chance to be saved.

Wesley objected to predetermined failure on several fronts. One was that it destroyed the Christian's chance of showing meekness and love to all, even non-Christians. If there were two classes of non-Christians, the savable and the unsavable, then it is difficult if not impossible to know which was which and thus to know how to relate to each. If, on the other hand, we approach all with the belief that grace is available to all, then we can approach all with the expectation of mission.

That chance (of showing love and compassion to all) was the prime motivation for mission. By telling the story of Jesus, we increased the chances they would all be saved. But even for those who have not had a chance to hear, God's grace was available everywhere to everyone.

If we don't believe this, however, the motivation for mission becomes nebulous. The most obvious candidates for those chosen to fail are people of other religions who seem to be willfully choosing a false path. And if that is the way we view people of other religions, we tend to see them in a negative light: "It naturally tends to inspire or increase a sharpness or eagerness of temper which is quite contrary to the meekness of Christ," Wesley preached.[7]

Conversely, if we believe all people we meet are children of God, with access to God's grace, indeed, already have God's grace active in their lives, then people of other religions are just a short step away from salvation. Our task is not to judge them negatively, but to help them articulate the presence of God already active in their lives. The best way to do this is to tell the story of Jesus, the quintessential model of God's active grace in a human being's life.

It is possible to interpret the optimism of grace as a subtle theological point, and it is indeed an important one to deliberate and debate. But for Wesley its greatest value was as a tool of evangelism, a way of approaching people with the Gospel story that greatly increased their chances of internalizing the story of Jesus. It is as if Wesley were anticipating modern psychological studies that show that anyone seeking change in other people's lives—whether behavioral or educational or cognitive—has a better chance of success if he or she has positive expectations of the other people's potential rather than negative expectations.

CONCLUSION

These three contributions don't exhaust the contributions John Wesley made to the modern mission movement. Others have noted his tremendous organizational ability—and nothing needs organizing more than a world-encompassing mission movement. And Wesley's insights about personal holiness certainly have enormous importance in assessing the effectiveness of cross-cultural mission workers in a world gone mad with reliance on management skills and communication techniques.

Yet the unique features of today's globalized world demand we pay attention to Wesley's prescience regarding relationships with people of other religious traditions. Hindus, Buddhists, and Muslims remain relatively unattracted to the story of Jesus. Many have heard it, many of those respect it, but few have embraced it. These three populations alone encompass almost half of the world's people.

John Wesley made no secret of the fact that the general spread of the Gospel was not supposed to end until all men and women had heard the story of Jesus and embraced it as their own. He taught that the greatest stumbling block to that spread was the unholy lives of Christians themselves. Until Hindus, Buddhists, and Muslims are attracted to Christian persons, they will not be attracted to the Christian faith. And we can only make ourselves winsome by loving and respecting Hindus, Buddhists, and Muslims for what they are: children of God, to some extent sustained and enlivened by the grace of the one true God of the universe, the God we worship and proclaim to the world.

NOTES

1. John Wesley, Sermon 63, "The General Spread of the Gospel," in *Sermons II*, ed. Albert C. Outler, vol. 2 of *The Bicentennial Edition of the Works of John Wesley* (Nashville: Abingdon Press, 1976–), p. 488. Hereafter cited as *Works*.

2. Wesley, Sermon 92, "On Zeal," in *Sermons III*, vol. 3, *Works*, pp. 308–9.

3. Ibid., p. 309.
4. Ibid., p. 311.
5. Ibid., p. 312.
6. Wesley, Sermon 110, "Free Grace," in *Sermons III*, vol. 3, *Works*, p. 544.
7. Ibid., p. 548.

BIBLIOGRAPHY

Wesley, John. *Sermons*. Ed. Albert C. Outler. Vols. 1–4 of *The Bicentennial Edition of the Works of John Wesley*. Nashville: Abingdon Press, 1976–.

10

WESLEY'S "CATHOLIC SPIRIT" AND GLOBAL CHRISTIANITY

Timothy C. Tennent

INTRODUCTION

John Wesley's reluctance to produce any precise doctrinal formulation for the "people called Methodists,"[1] along with his "catholic spirit" have led a number of scholars and leaders to herald him as an important forerunner in the emergence of the modern ecumenical movement.[2] While Wesley's contribution to the later ecumenical movement cannot be denied, two key developments of the last half of the twentieth century compel a fresh examination of Wesley's understanding of catholicity.

The first development is the dramatic diversity of ways in which the term "ecumenical" is used today, most citing Wesley's famous dictim taken from 2 Kings 10:15: "If thine heart is as my heart, give me thine hand." Therefore, Wesley's understanding of ecumenism as a way of practicing theology is explored in light of the varying ways the word "ecumenical" is being used today.

The second development is the emergence of multiple centers of vibrancy in the world Christian movement due to the rise of the Majority World church.[3] This has stimulated calls for a new understanding of ecumenism, which has been called a "deeper ecumenism" or the "new ecumenism," referring to a return to "ancient consensual scriptural teaching" as experienced in the apostolic and patristic period.[4] Therefore, this essay will also examine how Wesley's "catholic spirit" may illuminate fresh ways for someone to be simultaneously Wesleyan *and* a full participant in the emergence of an increasingly diverse global Christian movement.

MEANING OF THE TERM "ECUMENICAL"

The word "ecumenical" is derived from the Greek word *oikoumenikos*, signifying the entire inhabited world. In early biblical usage the word implies the global scope of the Christian mission. However, over time and with usage, the term has developed three other meanings. First, the term is frequently used to denote the common creedal confessions, such as the Nicene Creed, which unite all branches of Christianity. It is common to hear someone speak, for example, of the "ecumenical" councils referring to the seven church councils that were representative of all three branches of Christianity. Unfortunately, many Christians have not been particularly interested in articulating their theological continuity with the ecumenical councils, even though in practice they may be in broad conformity with them.

Second, the word "ecumenical" is also used to refer to interreligious dialogue between Christian and non-Christian religious groups as well as to the need for greater cooperation among other Christian groups. This is the usage that provokes a negative reaction among some who understand it to be advocating, at best, a gigantic, structural merger of the church around the world, and, at worst, the complete blurring of every distinctive doctrine of Christianity in the face of challenges from other religions. In Latin America, in particular, the word is often associated with Communism or with Protestant churches that have "sold out" to Roman Catholicism.[5] Phrases like "an ecumenical gathering" or "an ecumenical dialogue" can still create a negative reaction among many Christians.

Finally, the term has come full circle to refer to the emergence of global Christianity of which we (despite our various denominations) are all participants. The global church is so large and diverse, it is virtually impossible to comprehend all the many differences. Yet, there are certain great truths—most notably Christ himself who is the Truth—that unite all Christians in every age: those affirmations that have been held *semper ubique ab omnibus*. While, as we shall see, the historic creeds are foundational for Wesley, this kind of ecumenism refers to a deeper unity that cannot be *solely* expressed by a creed or packaged neatly in conceptual theological language. Rather, it refers to a deeper spiritual unity that acknowledges our catholicity because we are all members of the body of Christ and share a common union with Jesus Christ and a burden to bear witness to him in authentic ways throughout the whole world. It has more to do with a shared sense of belonging to Christ and a common commitment to global witness than anything about the specifics of ecclesiastical structures or even precise doctrinal formulations. This usage of the word is implied when we hear statements such as "Lausanne is an ecumenical gathering."[6]

This rather broad semantic range of the word "ecumenical" explains why there has been so much confusion even among Christians about whether the embrace of ecumenism is a sign of ecclesiastical vitality or demise.

In many ways, Wesley's life exemplifies many of the tensions inherent in the word "ecumenism." On the one hand, as noted earlier, Wesley was fascinated by Jehu's greeting to Jehonadab found in 2 Kings 10:15. Jehu said, "Is thine heart right, as my heart is with thy heart? And Jehonadab answered, It is. If it be, give me thine hand" (KJV). Wesley used that text to expound what he called the "catholic spirit."[7] The phrase "warm heart, give me thine hand" has become symbolic of Wesley's commitment to ecumenism. Wesley was able to embrace considerable diversity among Christians who held convictions different from his on various points. Wesley frequently found himself embroiled in various controversies with Roman Catholics, Anglican bishops, and Calvinist thinkers. He held strong theological convictions and firmly upheld all of the historic Christian confessions. Wesley would have been dismayed at the erosion of orthodoxy in mainline churches due to the increasing embrace of secular ideologies and a post-modern epistemology. Wesley was both ecumenical *and* orthodox; he held firm convictions *and* had an irenic spirit and warm heart toward those with whom he disagreed.

How was Wesley able to embrace both of these so ably? The key is to understand how Wesley understood theological inquiry, as well as the ecumenical spirit in which he approached theological controversy. We will now examine Wesley's understandings of ecumenism and how his position might be situated within the varying understandings of ecumenism today.

WESLEY'S UNDERSTANDING OF ECUMENISM

Three key features together form the broad outlines of Wesley's commitment to and understanding of ecumenism. Only by understanding all
three of these aspects of Wesley's thought are we able to have a proper
understanding of how Wesley might be placed within the context of
modern-day ecumenism.

UNITY AND DIVERSITY

First, Wesley makes a firm distinction between the theological unity that
is necessary to our identity as Christians while, at the same time, allowing
for broad diversity in the nonessentials of the faith. Historically, this has
been expressed through the terms *kerygma* and *adiaphora*. The word
kerygma comes from the Greek word meaning "proclamation." It refers to
the core essentials of the Christian faith as expressed, for example, in the
Apostles' Creed and the Nicene Creed. Wesley was firmly committed to
the historic core of Christian proclamation. The word *adiaphora* comes
from the Greek word *adiaforus*, which as used by the Stoics meant "things
indifferent." Thus, the *adiaphora* refers to those differences held by
Christians that "are not sufficiently central to warrant continuing division
or dispute."[8]
     In Wesley's day there was a belief that Christian belief and practice
should conform to the larger national identity. In other words, if someone
lived in England, he or she should follow the faith and practice of the
Church of England (Anglican); if someone was born in Scotland, that
person should follow the faith and practice of the Church of Scotland
(Presbyterian). This meant that Christians in a particular geographic
region were compelled to reach agreement not only on the broad essentials of the Christian faith, for example, the *kerygma*, but also they had to
agree with all the diverse particulars (*adiaphora*) of whatever national
church was in place. However, Wesley forcibly rejected this territorial
understanding of Christian identity. In Wesley's sermon "Catholic Spirit,"
he says:

> I know it is commonly supposed, that the place of our birth fixes the
> Church to which we ought to belong . . . I was once a zealous maintainer

of this; but I find many reasons to abate of this zeal. I fear it is attended with such difficulties as no reasonable man can get over: Not the least of which is, that if this rule had took place, there could have been no Reformation from Popery; seeing it entirely destroys the right of private judgment, on which the whole Reformation stands.[9]

Wesley goes on to argue that Christians should be able to dwell together in harmony even if they disagree about basic convictions such as the forms of church government, the modes of baptism, the administration of the Lord's Supper, and so forth. However, Wesley makes an important distinction between "catholic spirit" and "latitudinarianism." The latter refers to those who wish to engage in endless speculation about the essentials of the Gospel or wish to remain indifferent to holding a particular conviction. In contrast, Wesley argues that "a man of truly catholic spirit" does not have the right to set up his or her own form of religion. Rather, a Christian should be "as fixed as the sun in his [or her] judgment concerning the main branches of Christian doctrine."[10] He calls on his hearers to "go, first, and learn the first elements of the Gospel of Christ, and then shall you learn to be of a truly catholic spirit."[11] Wesley's ecumenism was built on the foundation of a shared theological orthodoxy concerning the historic essentials of the Christian faith.

It is important to remember that "religious diversity" in eighteenth-century Europe meant something quite different than it does today. Religious diversity in the context of most of Wesley's writings is associated with variations within Christian identity. The protagonists in Wesley's sermons and correspondence are the Roman Catholics and the Reformed tradition rather than the adherents of Islam or Buddhism. Thus, the question arises, how might Wesley's "catholic spirit" be applied within the context of today's multireligious firmament?

Wesley would likely have been uncomfortable with the posture of many conservative Christians who embrace the historic Christian confessions but remain reluctant to engage in honest interreligious dialogue that seeks to respond to the objections of Hindus, Buddhists, and Muslims to the Christian faith. Wesley was a staunch defender of orthodoxy, but clearly understood that Christianity is a faith for the world. He knew that the Gospel flourishes when challenged by unbelief, ridicule, and skepticism. Wesley knew that, despite all the risks and vulnerabilities involved, our confidence in the Gospel demands that we do not give space to any kind of cultural, ideological, or religious apartheid whereby we conveniently isolate ourselves from the beliefs and practices of the world we live in. We have been sent out into the world. Wesley knew that we must bear witness to the Gospel in the world we actually live in. Thus, Wesley would have encouraged faithful dialogue with other religions while maintaining a strong commitment to the core essentials of the faith.

Wesley did write about Muslims at various times in his writings. While it is true that Wesley wrote that Muslims were "utter strangers to all true religion" he also conceded that many Muslims bring shame on the church because they lead more holy lives than some nominal Christians.[12] In his sermon "On Faith," Wesley wrote that "their not believing the whole truth, is not owing to want of sincerity, but merely to want of light."[13] Wesley showed a keen interest in engaging those who stood in opposition to the Christian Gospel.

Nevertheless, Wesley would have been deeply disturbed by the modern trend to uncritically embrace the affirmations of other religious traditions in the name of ecumenism or a "catholic spirit." It is not uncommon today for the Christian participants in modern day inter-religious dialogue to fail to defend historic Christian affirmations, i.e., the *kerygma*. These dialogues are often characterized by a lack of vigilance in defending the Gospel, and frequently ground is conceded that lies at the heart of the Christian message. Wesley was thoroughly committed to the absolute truths of the core Christian proclamation. Thus, Wesley's ecumenism should primarily be understood as his willingness to embrace a wide range of Christians in all of their diversity, who share a common experience of being transformed by Christ. He would encourage inter-religious dialogue as a form of listening and learning, but always within the larger context of proclamation that everyone needs to receive the good news of the Gospel of Jesus Christ.

EXPERIENTIAL AND PRACTICAL

It has often been noted that, unlike the earlier sixteenth-century Reformers, Wesley's theology was not set forth in a sustained, systematic fashion. Rather, Wesley's theology is derived from his sermons, short treatises, exegetical notes, journals, and many letters of correspondence. This is because Wesley was rightfully suspicious of a theology that was set forth in isolation from the lived experience of Christians. At the core of Wesley's theological method was his fundamental commitment to the experience of Christian conversion and the need to apply theology to the practical challenges of the Christian life and the social needs of the larger society. Wesley's emphasis on theopraxis and his reluctance to set forth a Methodist "creed" for those in the movement was not because Wesley was indifferent towards theology or the need for doctrinal clarity. Wesley understood that faith in Christ is first and foremost a response to God's saving initiative, as opposed to merely granting mental assent to a certain defined set of dogmatic formulations, however true.

Wesley was a trained theologian and preacher of the Gospel long before his famous heart-warming experience at Aldersgate, which took place on May 24, 1738. Wesley's conversion experience at Aldersgate transformed his preaching and his understanding of the Christian Gospel. Prior to Aldersgate, Wesley saw the Gospel as beginning in the mind of the Christian as he or she learned to affirm the truths of the Christian faith. After Aldersgate, Wesley understood that Christianity begins as a religion of the heart. Wesley's post-Aldersgate theology looks for the initiative of God in the life of the believer—namely conversion. Only then could one respond to God's grace through doctrinal or theological positions. As Wesley scholar Albert Outler has observed, "Christian experience adds nothing to the substance of Christian truth; its distinctive truth is to energize the heart so as to enable the believer to speak and do the truth in love."[14]

This emphasis on conversion created the basis for a new frontier in ecumenism, one that is particularly evident today in the global Pentecostal movement. The emphasis is no longer on whether your brother and sister share your precise view of baptism, or church government, or views regarding predestination. The starting point was to first recognize our common experience as those who have been converted by the work of the Holy Spirit. This is why Wesley added "experience" to the traditional Anglican triad of Scripture, tradition, and reason, forming the famous Wesleyan Quadrilateral.

Wesley's theology became rooted in the shared evangelical experience. Wesley encouraged Christians to embrace the theological distinctives of their tradition, but also to embrace people of genuine Christian experience who differed on matters that did not strike at the heart of historic Christian faith. Wesley said, "The person of a 'catholic spirit' . . . is steadily fixed in his religious principles, in what he believes to be the truth as it is in Jesus; while he firmly adheres to that worship of God which he judges to be most acceptable in his sight; . . . his heart is enlarged toward *all mankind*. . . . This is catholic or universal love. . . . For love alone gives the title to this character: Catholic love is a catholic spirit."[15] The person of "a catholic spirit," while not being indifferent to "opinions," does not base Christian love and concern upon agreement in "opinion." [16]

When we think of the ecumenical movement, we often think of the legacy of the World Council of Churches. However, there are other important examples of Christian ecumenism. For example, one of the most remarkable manifestations of ecumenism today has been through the Lausanne movement, which has brought together more Christians from more diverse backgrounds than any other movement in Christian history. The shared evangelical experience is one of the most basic bonds that allows those who participate in Lausanne to move beyond a more sectarian view of Christianity. Wesley is one of the pioneers in demonstrating the importance of a shared Christian experience in bringing Christians together who may not agree on a number of doctrinal points, but whose lives exhibit the prior work of God's initiative in their lives. For Wesley, theology arises out of a response to God's prior initiative, lest it become a dead letter of endless intellectual speculation untethered from a vibrant, warm heart.

THE WORLD IS MY PARISH

The third and final feature of Wesley's theology as it relates to ecumenism was his early appreciation for the possibility of what we know today as "global Christianity." However, few have given proper recognition that Wesley is one of the leading forerunners of conceptualizing the church in its full global, rather than sectarian, dimensions. In the post-Aldersgate period, Wesley's preaching became so controversial that he was barred from preaching in the pulpits of the Church of England. Since he continued to preach in the open fields, he was charged with "trespassing" on the parishes of other ministers. He replied to this charge in a letter written in March of 1739 with what has become the most famous quote of Wesley, "the world is my parish." In the letter he says, "I look upon all the world as my parish; thus far I mean, that in whatever part of it I am, I judge it meet, right and my bounden duty to declare, unto all that are willing to hear, the glad tidings of salvation."[17]

It is difficult for modern-day Christians to fully comprehend the radical nature of this statement. The territorial conceptions, as noted earlier, were so strong that it was considered heresy to preach the Gospel to those outside your parish. These territorial conceptions were one of the biggest barriers to the emergence of the Protestant missionary movement. In contrast, Wesley was ahead of his time in first conceptualizing the church in its full global dimensions and only secondarily in its particularity as, for example, Methodist Christians. Wesley asked why he should not preach the Gospel in "Europe, Asia, Africa, or America" for, with the apostle Paul, he declared, "woe is unto me if I preach not the Gospel!" (1 Cor. 9:16–19 KJV). Wesley declared that he was prepared "to go to Abyssinia or China, or whithersoever it shall please God by this conviction to call me."[18]

Wesley seemed to understand that the church of Jesus Christ is indestructible, since Christ is the Lord of the church and has promised to build his church. However, the indestructibility of the church is not tied to any particular institutional manifestation of it. With the dramatic rise of Christians from the Majority World church, many of whom do not trace their history to the Reformation, there is a need to discover a deeper ecumenism that can unite all true Christians. Wesley anticipated the future multicultural diversity of the church and the common experience of rebirth from above that unites all Christians of every age.

NOTES

1. The well-known phrase, "people called Methodists" comes from an essay written by John Wesley in October of 1745 entitled "Advice to the People Called Methodists." See John Wesley, *The Works of the Rev. John Wesley*, vol. 8 (Grand Rapids: Zondervan, 1959 reprint of 1872 publication), pp. 351–59. Hereafter cited as *Works*.

2. See, for example, General Secretary Rev. Samuel Kobia's keynote address to the World Council of Churches in 2005, which can be viewed at http://www.oikoumene.org /en/resources/documents/wcc-programmes /ecumenical-movement-in-the-21st-century /foundational-texts/22-10-05-challenges-facing-the-ecumenical-movement-in-the -21st-century.html. See also C. Moeller and G. Philips, *The Theology of Grace and the Ecumenical Movement* (Paterson, N.J.: St. Anthony Guild Press, 1961/1969).

3. I prefer the term Majority World church over all of the alternatives, including the non-Western world, the Global South, the Third World or the Two-Thirds World. For a full discussion of the use of terms for Asia, Africa, and Latin America, see my *Theology in the Context of*

World Christianity (Grand Rapids: Zondervan, 2006), pp. xviii–xx.

4. See, for example, Thomas C. Oden, *The Rebirth of Orthodoxy: Signs of New Life in Christianity* (San Francisco: HarperSanFrancisco, 2003). The doctrinal consensus is often cited as embodied in the Apostles' Creed, the Nicene Creed, and the Athanasian Creed, all of which were affirmed by Wesley.

5. Gamaliel Lugo Morales, "Moving Forward with the Latin American Pentecostal Movement," *International Review of Mission* 87, no. 347 (October 1998): p. 509.

6. Lausanne is shorthand for the Lausanne Congress for World Evangelization, a global organization with a membership of hundreds of different groups, all committed to the evangelization of the world.

7. Wesley, "Catholic Spirit," *Works*, vol. 5, pp. 492–504.

8. John Westerdale Bowker, *The Sacred Neuron* (New York: I. B. Tauris, 2005), p. 120.

9. Wesley, "Catholic Spirit," *Works*, p. 496.

10. Ibid., p. 502.

11. Ibid.

12. Wesley, "On Faith," *Works*, vol. 7, p. 201.

13. Ibid., p. 197.

14. Albert Outler, "The Wesleyan Quadrilateral—in John Wesley," Wesley Center Online, Wesley Center for Applied Theology, http://wesley.nnu.edu/wesleyan_theology/theojrnl/16–20/20–01.htm.

15. Wesley, "Catholic Spirit," *Works*, p. 503.

16. Ibid., pp. 493, 495.

17. John Wesley, *The Works of John Wesley*, vol. 25, *Letters I, 1721–1739*. Ed. Frank Baker (Oxford: Clarendon Press, 1980), p. 616. This quotation is from the 1980 edition because I agree that this famous letter was more likely written to John Clayton on March 28, 1739, rather than James Hervey on March 20, 1739.

18. Ibid., p. 615.

BIBLIOGRAPHY

Jenkins, Philip. *The New Faces of Christianity: Believing the Bible in the Global South*. New York: Oxford University Press, 2008.

Oden, Thomas. *Doctrinal Standards in the Wesleyan Tradition*. Grand Rapids: Francis Asbury Press, 1988.

———. *The Rebirth of Orthodoxy*. New York: HarperSanFrancisco, 2003.

Outler, Albert C., ed. *John Wesley*. New York: Oxford University Press, 1964.

Rack, Henry D. *Reasonable Enthusiast: John Wesley and the Rise of Methodism*. London: Epworth Press, 1989.

Tennent, Timothy C. *Theology in the Context of World Christianity*. Grand Rapids: Zondervan, 2007.

Tuttle, Robert G., Jr. *John Wesley: His Life and Theology*. Grand Rapids: Zondervan, 1980.

Wesley, John. *The Works of the Rev. John Wesley*, reprint of 1872 edition. Grand Rapids: Zondervan, 1959.

Wright, Christopher. *The Mission of God*. Downers Grove, Ill.: IVP Academic, 2006.

11

GOD AT WORK IN THE WORLD

Robert G. Tuttle, Jr.

As John Wesley matured in his theology he emphasized more and more the universal work of the Gospel. Even where God's voice was heard small, God was never without a witness. Wesley believed in the universal work of the Spirit and insisted that Methodists be fully aware of what God was doing in other parts of the world. This had several significant implications.

THE GOSPEL AS WORLD AFFIRMING

Wesley believed that Christianity is, or should be, different in its basic approach to life and creation. There is much in the world of religion that is world denying. It tends to imply dualism—a good God and an evil god. The good God dwells within us, while the evil god (perhaps some Neoplatonic demiurge) creates the universe and the world in which we live. Since (according to some) creation is evil, salvation calls us out of the world (let the world go hang) by contemplating the God within, that we might be absorbed into some kind of cosmic fluff.

Christianity, on the other hand, at its best, is world affirming. Although some forms of Christianity insist that happiness in this world is only an illusion, Wesley believed that the same God whose Spirit dwells within us is the One God who creates and, in spite of the fact that creation has fallen, God wants it back for our enjoyment. Wesley insisted,

Evil did not exist at all in the original nature of things. It was no more the necessary result of matter, than it was the necessary result of spirit. All things then, without exception, were very good. And how would it be otherwise? There was no defect at all in the power of God, any more than in his goodness or wisdom.[1]

Creation is far more important to God than to the ruler of this world (1 John 5:19). In less than six months after beginning to teach at the E. Stanley Jones School of World Mission and Evangelism on the campus of Asbury Theological Seminary, several of my colleagues helped me to see that Christians have conceded far too much to worldwide anti-Christian influences. For example, the evangelistic emphasis on the so-called "10/40 Window" (those European, African, and Asian countries that lie between the tenth and fortieth parallels, north, and stretching from Africa to China) assumed Satan's control of great masses of people with little or no thought to the prevenient work of the Holy Spirit already at work. Although I would be the first to admit that the "10/40" attempt to establish a prayer base upon which to begin evangelistic ministries was noble, I am reminded again and again that God has more invested in creation than we do. God is already at work around the world and *if we can find the tools to communicate the Gospel effectively, then God might well let us in on the privilege of winning planet Earth to Jesus Christ.* Let me illustrate from the works of Wesley.

Soon after his "Aldersgate" experience Wesley preached a sermon entitled "The Almost Christian."[2] In that sermon he spoke about the faith of the "almost Christian" and the faith of the "altogether Christian." There, the faith of the almost Christian implied a "heathen honesty" that paid at least some regard to truth and justice that expressed itself in love and offered assistance one to another. It also implied a "form of godliness" that abstained from excess and avoided all strife and contention. The almost Christian frequently prayed and was sincere toward inward principles of religion extending even to a real design to do the will of God. Unfortunately, according to the earlier Wesley, since the almost Christian lacked the one thing necessary evident in the altogether Christian—the faith that follows repentance and offers the forgiveness of sins—all of this, though noble when enlivened by believing in the Son who brings everlasting life, served only to compound one's condemnation.

Over a quarter of a century later Wesley wrote another sermon entitled "On Faith."[3] In this sermon he contrasted the faith of a "servant"

with the faith of a "child." Here the faith of the servant is directly analogous to the faith of the "almost Christian" referred to in his earlier
sermon. Now, however, the faith of the servant, rather than serving only
to compound one's condemnation, means that one is not far from the
kingdom of God.

It is apparent to me that the "Almost Christian" sermon conceded too
much to the Enemy (the "Accuser"), whereas the later sermon, "On Faith"
acknowledged the influence of the Holy Spirit already at work in the
world. Once John Wesley recognized that evangelism was bearing witness
to a God already at work, ministry became less of a chore and more of an
opportunity. Again, God is never without a witness, *"Nihil est in intellectu
quod non fuit prius in sensu"* (Nothing is in the understanding, which was
not first perceived by some of the senses). His *Works* demonstrate this,
time and again. In his sermon "Walking by Sight and by Faith," he writes
of those in the "unknown regions" of the world:

> God, having "opened the eyes of their understanding," pours divine light
> into their soul; whereby they are enabled to "see Him that is invisible," to
> see God and the things of God. What their "eye had not seen, nor their
> ear heard, neither had it entered into their heart to conceive," God from
> time to time reveals to them by the "unction of the Holy One, which
> teacheth them of all things."[4]

Since God has taken the initiative by the "unction of the Holy One," we
can be bold in our follow-up. We need not be intimidated. Understandably,
Wesley also became more and more sensitive to cross-cultural issues that
would further the Gospel. Let me put this a different way.

THE UNIVERSAL WORK OF THE HOLY SPIRIT

I assume that the Holy Spirit is at work in everyone, the world over. That, linked
with the need to be culturally sensitive in order to cooperate with the
work of the Spirit, is the rationale for this chapter. As strange as this may
sound, if God loves some people more than others, I'm not sure I want to
go to heaven. If God is no respecter of persons, then admittedly the Holy
Spirit must somehow take up the slack, level the playing field. Forgive my
presumption, but since I believe that faith in Jesus Christ alone puts us

right with God, heals the brokenness of our time, and makes us fit to receive the inheritance of God's glory, then *God, by the Holy Spirit, must guarantee that every man, woman, and child has an equal opportunity to respond, if not to the name, at least to the person of Jesus Christ.* How can that be? How can one respond to the person of Jesus Christ without knowing his name?

It occurs to me that knowing someone is far more than knowing his or her name. Early in his ministry Wesley condemned the mystics because they did not specifically call people to faith in Jesus Christ. These mystics were the "rock upon which he nearly made shipwreck." Of all the enemies of revival they were the worst because they stabbed Christianity in the vitals, making a mockery of personal faith in Jesus Christ. Later in his ministry, however, Wesley used the example of several mystical lives to illustrate Christian perfection. Obviously, you cannot have it both ways. So, what happened to change his mind? As he matured in his theology, Wesley began to rely more and more on the fruit of the Spirit as the criterion for faith (Gal. 5:22–23). His conclusion? Even if it looked like a grape vine, if it produced apples, call it an apple tree. So, if the mystical lives manifested fruit that only faith could produce then faith must be present, even without acknowledging it.

Jesus says, "Not everyone who says to me, 'Lord, Lord,' will enter the kingdom of heaven, but only he [or she] who does the will of my Father who is in heaven" (Matt. 7:21 NIV). Obviously I can know someone's person without knowing his or her name. Don Richardson's *Eternity in Their Hearts* describes going to remote parts of the world and among those open to the Holy Spirit already at work within them, speaking the name of Jesus, and getting this response: "So that's his name." Jesus says to his disciples, "Everyone who listens to the Father and learns from him comes to me" (John 6:45 NIV). Furthermore, "The Holy Spirit, whom the Father will send in my name, will teach you all things . . . the Spirit of truth who goes out from the Father, he will testify about me . . . he will convict the world of guilt in regard to sin and righteousness and judgment . . . he will guide you into all truth" (John 14:25; 15:26; 16:8, 13). I am absolutely convinced that in those who remain open to the Spirit, a personal relationship with God will lead inevitably to faith in the person of Jesus Christ, and, if his name is spoken, a recognition of that name will confirm their experience.

I have a ten-rupee note in my wallet with a picture of Gandhi on it. When asked why I would carry such a note I always reply, "If Gandhi is not in heaven he's giving the devil fits and hell is a better place." I can imagine the devil calling Saint Peter about once a week and asking, "Can you take this man off my hands? He clearly does not understand the principle. He's driving us nuts. Listen, I'll trade you for him. Send me one of your so-called hard-nosed evangelicals. I'll take anybody for Gandhi." Now, I'm not sure I have the theology for that but when I get my tongue out of my cheek you will probably get the point.

I shall never forget Gandhi's advice to E. Stanley Jones: emphasize love, talk about Jesus, learn about other religions but never ever adulterate your own religion.[5] I have a Jewish friend who would never trust a Christian who was not trying to convert her. I'm always trying to make her jealous (Rom. 10:19; 11:11, 14). Now, lest you think I've lost my "evangelical mind," let me offer a brief disclaimer.

Note

THE DISCLAIMER

The disclaimer is that none of this should imply universalism. I do not for a moment believe that all religions are the same. Admittedly, most attempts at finding a universal Gospel look for the answers in other religions—what do Buddhism, Hinduism, and Islam already share in common with Christianity? Though I applaud any attempt to learn about other religions as an excellent way of being convinced of the absolute truths of Christianity, for me that is the wrong point of departure. I believe that all religions (including my own) are a "law of sin and death" apart from the power of the Holy Spirit available through faith and trust in Jesus Christ. Let me illustrate.

Some years ago I met a young man in the sauna of a university health center. He was a Muslim from Sri Lanka (actually a minority in a country where most are either Buddhist or Hindu). After a brief time of chatter I decided to ask a straightforward question, "Have you ever considered Christianity?"

He smiled, "No, why should I?"

He seemed genuinely interested so I asked, "What do you do for a living?" He said he was an engineer. For some reason, I then asked, "What do you do when you've got a fifty-ton block of concrete? How do you move it?"

His immediate response, "You've got to have a hoist."

My next comment, "Let me tell you about the hoist," opened the door for some interesting conversation. Over the next few minutes I began in a very introductory way to share with him my own conviction that every religion the world over (including my own) was like a fifty-ton block of concrete without the power of the Holy Spirit available through faith in Jesus Christ. As I left the sauna I lifted my arm like a hoist—"Don't forget the hoist." The next week he noticed me across a crowded room, smiled, and lifted his hand mimicking a hoist. We have had several interesting conversations since.

So, let's be honest. I believe that Christianity picks up where every other religion leaves off. That, however, does not make me right and the rest of the world wrong. Over the years students have asked, "How can you be so narrow-minded as to assume the uniqueness of faith in Jesus Christ?" My response is, "My believing in the uniqueness of faith in Jesus Christ doesn't make me right, but it sure makes me an evangelist."

If God is a triangle and I believe God is a circle, God does not become a circle to accommodate what I believe God to be. God remains a triangle. Truth has never changed to accommodate what I believe truth to be. Nevertheless, I believe that it is faith in Jesus Christ alone that restores fellowship with the living God. If you can convince me that Jesus is not who he said he was and is, I am a dead man. Flesh would not cling to bone any longer. You could gather me up in a basket. That's just how much of me is at stake.

FOLLOWING UP ON GOD'S INITIATIVE, A CULTURAL MANDATE

If God has already taken the initiative in the drama of rescue, even where God's voice is heard small, then an intelligent, winsome witness should bring results. Again, we should not be intimidated. "Those who are with us are more than those who are with them" (2 Kings 6:16 NIV). This does not mean that we abuse another's culture. *Culture should be our friend, not our enemy.* Within every culture there should be clues as to where God is already at work. Look at the stories, myths, symbols, rituals, and especially the music and art of any culture. Those countries where God's voice is heard small are rich with traditions that are packed with transferable concepts that will communicate the Gospel. There are some wonderful biblical precedents.

God in the creation account (Gen. 1–11) does not run roughshod over culture. Biblical scholars tell us that there were contemporary myths that were similar in some respects to the Genesis account of creation. Some see this as a threat to the integrity of the Old Testament. Let me give this a different twist. God wanted to communicate the truth of a divine purpose and (it is suggested) used some of the existing stories from Mesopotamia as transferable concepts to reveal a universal truth. People in the days of Moses knew and supposedly understood these stories. God does not start from scratch. The bits and pieces of reality in the existing myths are cleaned up, sanctified, and woven into a narrative that people could understand. Although the difference between creation as the result of the One God, loving (the Genesis account), and the many gods, warring (the Mesopotamia account), is significant, the overall story is communicated in such a way that people could relate and understand. Again, *the existing culture* (rather than a threat) *is used as a springboard for communicating divine revelation.* Is God smart or what? Another example, however, takes this same concept to still another level.

Within generations of Adam and Eve, God regretted having created our first forebears. It is a bit of an understatement to be reminded that the flood seriously pruned the family tree. Unfortunately, it is a short journey from Noah to Babel. Humankind, still sin prone, once again yielded to inherent desire. God knew that humankind, in community, left to itself, would have perfected its own evil and destroyed itself. There is nothing we cannot do in community. *Unredeemed*, we would have perfected our self-centeredness and devoured ourselves. Perhaps God separated us at Babel to prevent our self-destruction. The confusion of languages served to preserve a remnant that could understand the reality of only *one* God. It has recently occurred to me that Babel, the last paragraph of primeval history (Gen. 11:8–9), mandates the study of different cultures. We need not return to Babel, but we must find ways of communicating across cultural boundaries. In fact, the first paragraph of patriarchal history, the covenant established between God and Abraham (Gen. 11:10*ff*), demonstrates the principle. In effect, the last of primeval history sets the stage for cross-cultural studies.

The story of Abraham is another example where God (and the author[s] of the Pentateuch) used existing culture to communicate the truth. I've had students complain that the covenant with Abraham makes God too bloodthirsty. My response is usually, "God didn't invent the concept of covenant. That was already in place when God chose to be revealed."

How did you establish relationship in Abraham's day? You "cut a covenant." I wrote a book a couple of years ago on the history of evangelism. My publisher wrote to say that it was taking me far too long to get through the relevance of the Old Testament. Besides, I could not assume a historical Abraham. I wrote back. True, it is difficult to prove from the extrabiblical sources the historical Abraham but I can prove the historicity of "cutting a covenant." Clay tablets were discovered beginning in the 1920s and a consensus of sorts emerged that these (Nuzi) tablets document firmly that the custom of cutting a covenant was common practice in the first half of the second millennium B.C.

All this is to say that God's use of covenant was God's way of being culturally sensitive. God related to Abraham in a way that Abraham could understand. The animal was sacrificed and the two parties of the covenant, Abraham and God (God being symbolized by the fire pot), passed between the halves of the divided animal with the promise that if either broke the promise, the same fate would befall them. There were even provisions for covenant renewal. Feast days were established where animal sacrifices—as signs of repentance—underscored the seriousness of sin. Unfortunately, after several generations, these acts of sacrifice degenerated into a form of religion that no longer demonstrated the heart. God wearied, once again, but had promised never again to destroy or confuse creation. In God's infinite mercy a new covenant was established where God provided a complete and perfect sacrifice that would take away the sins of the world, *once and for all*. Nestled in the middle of the longest book in the Bible we find these words:

> "The time is coming," declares the Lord, "when I will make a new covenant with the house of Israel and with the house of Judah. It will not be like the covenant I made with their forefathers when I took them by the hand to lead them out of Egypt, because they broke my covenant, though I was a husband to them," declares the Lord. . . .
>
> "No longer will a man teach his neighbor, or a man his brother, saying, 'Know the LORD,' because they will all know me, from the least of them to the greatest . . . For I will forgive their wickedness and will remember their sins no more." (Jer. 31:31–34 NIV)

First Peter 1:19–20 states that "the precious blood of Christ, a lamb without blemish or defect . . . was chosen *before the creation* of the world" (NIV, emphasis added). The implication here is clear. God took the cultural concept of covenant seriously. From the beginning God knew full well that the very act of creation itself would eventually require the blood of an only Son. It is terribly significant that God was a Redeemer *before* God was a Creator. God loved before God made. Even though the covenant with God was broken time and again, God established a guarantee that our brokenness would no longer rule and that our sins would be remembered no more. That is the story of the work of a triune God.

TO THE FATHER, THROUGH THE SON, BY THE HOLY SPIRIT

The Bible teaches that God has one essence (the *Shema* in Deut. 6:4 reads, "The LORD our God is *one* God") but is manifested in three distinct persons—"Father, Son, and Holy Spirit" (Matt. 28:19). There is no analogy that can adequately explain this. (I am told that heresy is born when little minds try to solve big paradoxes.) For years I used the example of water as liquid, ice, and steam. Water, whether heated or frozen, is still H_2O. This was more helpful for some than for others. So, I continued to search for a way of describing the triune God's anticipating the fall of creation and its ultimate redemption.

Then, late one night, I caught an image. As I was studying the earlier chapters in the book of Genesis, I imagined the three persons of the Trinity discussing the dilemma of creation. Like someone with multiple personalities, I watched and listened as they talked among themselves. That part of God that we call Father was the first to speak: "We want to be known. We will create man and woman 'in our own image' (Gen. 1:26), and we will love them like children." The Son replied, "Will they love us back?" Then, like wind blowing in the trees, I heard the voice of the Spirit, "As we become known, some of them will love us back, because we will be merciful and kind. In spite of their rebellion, our compassion will lead them to repentance and faith."

Then, as they continued to contemplate creation and the fall, their voices dropped. There was a catch. It became painfully apparent that in order to be known fully and to guarantee salvation, one of them would have to "visit and redeem the people" (Luke 1:68). One of them would have to "become flesh and dwell among them" (John 1:14).

Consistent with the nature of covenant, a sacrifice would be required, since "without the shedding of blood there is no forgiveness of sins" (Heb. 9:22). Furthermore, this sacrifice would have to be human and "without blemish" (Heb. 10:1–4). Since all of creation would "sin and fall short of the glory of God" (Rom. 3:23), only the one sent could fulfill such a sacrifice.

Suddenly, I imagined the Son stepping forward to be chosen by the Father as the one who would go (1 Pet. 1:20). He spoke, "Send me. 'I will declare your name to my brothers; in the presence of the congregation I will sing your praises' (Heb. 2:12). I will 'share in their humanity so that by my death I might destroy him who will hold the power of death—that is, the devil—and free those who all their lives have been held in slavery' (Heb. 2:14–15). Make me 'like them in every respect' so that I might be 'a merciful and faithful high priest' in your service, that I 'might make atonement for the sins of the people.' Then, because I too have suffered and been tempted, I will be able 'to help those who are being tempted' (Heb. 2:17–18). They will know that we love them, not because we imagine how they feel when they hurt inside, but because we know how they feel when they hurt inside, because I have been there."

So, even before God created, it was decided. The price of creation would require the death of the Son. Even though that Son would then be raised from the dead in order to demonstrate God's victory over sin and death (no small thing), it was an incredible price to pay.

Does God's initiative to establish a covenant sacrifice that would guarantee victory over sin and death make God bloodthirsty? I think not! Remember, God did not invent the rites of covenant. Covenant relationship is God's attempt to be culturally sensitive to a concept already in place so that love and forgiveness are communicated in a way that could be understood and received. God, as Father, Son, and Holy Spirit, is always taking such initiative, the world over. Let God arise.

NOTES

1. *The Works of the Rev. John Wesley,* 3rd ed., vol. 6, ed. Thomas Jackson (Grand Rapids: Zondervan 1959 reprint of 1872 publication), p. 214.

2. Ibid., vol. 5, pp.17–25.

3. Ibid., vol. 7, pp. 195–202.

4. Ibid., vol. 7, p. 260.

5. E. Stanley Jones told this to the author in Bridgewater, Virginia in 1969.

BIBLIOGRAPHY

Barrett, David and Todd Johnson, eds. *World Christian Trends: A.D. 30–A.D. 2200.* Pasadena, Calif.: William Carey Library, 2001.

Chidester, D. *Christianity: A Global History.* San Francisco: HarperCollins, 2000.

Crossman, Meg. *Perspectives Exposure: Discovering God's Heart for All Nations and Our Part in His Plan.* Seattle, Wash.: YWAM Publishing, 2003.

Hunter, George. *The Celtic Way of Evangelism.* Nashville: Abingdon Press, 2000.

Jenkins, Philip. *The Next Christendom.* Oxford: Oxford University Press, 2002.

Richardson, Don. *Eternity in Their Hearts.* Ventura, Calif.: Regal Books, 1981, 1984.

Stone, Bryan. *Evangelism after Christendom.* Grand Rapids: Brazos Press, 2006.

Tuttle, Robert, Jr. *The Story of Evangelism.* Nashville: Abingdon Press, 2006.

Walls, Andrew. *The Missionary Movement in Christian History: Studies in the Transmission of Faith.* Maryknoll, N.Y.: Orbis Books, 1996.

Wesley, John. *The Works of the Rev. John Wesley.* Ed. Thomas Jackson. Grand Rapids: Zondervan, 1959.

PART THREE
Historical Perspectives

I N THIS SECTION, WE ENCOUNTER A WIDE RANGE OF interesting case studies that illustrate how Wesleyan theology and mission methods were put to use in the establishment of Methodist missions in various parts of the world. The authors of these chapters have written in such a way that we will be able to apply the lessons from history to the practice of mission today.

Dana Robert describes how most early Methodist mission activity was begun by entrepreneurial and innovative individuals who were volunteers and lay people rather than professional clergy sent by the established church. After noting several examples of such pioneers, Robert focuses on how Methodist missions promoted higher education as a mission strategy and then examines the struggles between innovation and consolidation as they relate to the controversy over education in Fuzhou, China, in the 1880s.

Andrew Walls explains that while "the Wesleys saw Methodism as a mission; their successors turned the mission into a church with a mission society." He gives the background to John Wesley's famous phrase, "I look upon all the world as my parish," which helps explain, says Walls, the apparently haphazard early development of Methodist overseas missions. Despite this, Methodist work was already going forward on several continents by the time William Carey wrote his famous "Enquiry" in 1792. Walls analyzes John Wesley's famous sermon "The General Spread of the Gospel," and the supporting hymnody of his brother Charles, to show that for the Wesleys, "the eschatological vision of the conversion of the nations is organically linked with the present calling of Methodists to preach the Gospel in England."

Paul Chilcote shows how the model that the Wesley brothers developed for the Methodist movement was one that drew committed Christians together for discipleship and then sent them out into the world to join in God's mission and to make disciples. Chilcote articulates the elements of this model in the theology and organizational genius of John Wesley, which was reinforced in the hymns of Charles Wesley.

He argues that their purpose was to reclaim mission as the church's reason for being and evangelism as the heart of that mission in the world.

"From its earliest days Methodism linked movement and institution together in inextricable ways," notes Arun Jones in his case study from India. This study draws on sociologist Max Weber's theory to show how movements must transform into institutions in order to survive and how institutions need good leadership to be maintained. Jones portrays the history of the Clara Swain Hospital in Bareilly, as an expression of the Methodist movement in India. In its nearly one hundred forty years of institutional life, the hospital has thrived under good leadership and declined when leadership was not strong. There are many lessons for mission today.

In the next chapter, we stay in India and discover the remarkable and distinguished missionary career of J. Waskom Pickett, spanning a period of forty-six years. Art McPhee provides a riveting picture of this gifted and talented missionary statesman who pioneered missiological theory and was exemplary in the practice of Methodist missions in India. Pickett was a minister, evangelist, and bishop, a champion of hospitals and healing, an author and editor, a practitioner of holistic mission, an advocate for contextualized Christianity in India, and a relief organizer, diplomat, and educator.

The Wesleyan mission moved through the South Pacific from Polynesia in the East to New Guinea in the West. Although European missionaries often led the way, the bulk of the evangelizing and church planting was done by little-known Pacific Islanders. Michael Rynkiewich retraces the history of the spread of Methodist mission outreach in Papua New Guinea and the role that often unknown Polynesian and Melanesian missionaries played in the advancement of the kingdom in the Pacific.

We turn our attention next to West Africa and the story of Thomas Birch Freeman, one of the early British missionaries who played a significant role in establishing Methodism in West Africa. Michael Mozley documents four characteristics of Freeman that enabled him to have such a profound and lasting ministry. Braving a deadly climate that killed his two English-born wives, and courageous in the face of potentially deadly enemies, Freeman persevered in the midst of many difficulties and left a lasting legacy of missionary work.

Finally, we conclude this section of Historical Perspectives with H. T. Maclin's history of the founding of The Mission Society. Maclin provides the historical context out of which the Mission Society for United Methodists emerged in 1984, and we learn that there were three earlier examples of unofficial mission activity being raised up within the American Methodist Church. Understanding the ways in which God has brought The Mission Society into being make us all the more grateful for the ways this mission-sending organization has been used to further the kingdom of God as we celebrate the twenty-fifth anniversary with the publication of this book.

12

INNOVATION AND CONSOLIDATION IN AMERICAN METHODIST MISSION HISTORY

Dana L. Robert

When the Mission Society for United Methodists was founded in 1984, critics condemned it as a violation of the *Book of Discipline* and a retro-evangelistic movement that would perpetuate missionary paternalism. In 2008, however, delegates at the United Methodist General Conference passed a resolution praising The Mission Society for its perseverance, and urging cooperation between the Society and official agencies of the denomination. Similar paths from controversy to acceptance have characterized many of the most important developments in Methodist mission history.

Missionary innovation is usually messy. Methodist mission history has been marked by tensions between grace and order, between individual entrepreneurs and church officials, and between calls to honor the Spirit and references to the *Book of Discipline*. The people whom we honor as missionary pioneers often challenged the system. On the other hand, without organizational support for the experiments of Spirit-led enthusiasts—many of them lay people—there would be little sustained work for us to remember today.

This paper will explore a few of the earlier examples of innovation and consolidation in American Methodist mission history prior to the founding of The Mission Society.[1] These examples show that innovation has typically been characterized by faith in the Holy Spirit, self-sacrificial zeal, and opportunistic pragmatism. In light of the silver jubilee of The Mission Society, it is important to recall the spirit of entrepreneurial voluntarism that has so consistently shaped the history of Methodist missions.

EARLY MISSIONARY VOLUNTARISM

The mystical voice of God catalyzed the founding of the Methodist Missionary Society in 1819. Of mixed African and European descent, John Stewart (1786–1823) was born a free man and Baptist in Virginia. Robbed on his way to Ohio, he tried to drink himself to death. He joined a Methodist camp meeting near Marietta and obtained spiritual relief from his spiritual agony. In a religious experience that reminds one of traditional African summons by the ancestral spirits, he became ill from resisting a call to preach and only recovered after agreeing to obey God.

Stewart heard God calling in the voice of a man and a woman, telling him to preach to the Indians. He set off in a northwesterly direction and sang and preached to the Delawares. Upon reaching the Wyandotts, he sought out Jonathan Pointer, an African-American who had been captured by the Indians and was fluent in Wyandott. With Pointer as interpreter, Stewart began singing and preaching to them in 1816, warning them to "flee the wrath to come." His ministry resulted in the conversion of chiefs, leading women, and others. As was often the case on the frontier, rival missionaries quickly appeared on the scene to steal Stewart's converts. Critics accused him of having no credentials from any organized group of Christians. Stung by the accusation but supported by his native converts, Stewart approached the Ohio Annual Conference and requested ordination.[2]

Today a person who experienced John Stewart's mystical visions probably wouldn't pass through an ordination committee. But in 1819, the Ohio Conference recognized his call from God as part of the divine plan for the expansion of Methodism, and it immediately licensed him. The proof of the pudding, after all, was in the eating. The conference collected money for his work and appointed a regular missionary to follow with a circuit. Back in New York City, the leading Methodists heard of Stewart's success and promptly organized the Methodist Missionary Society to raise money for missions and book publishing. Of the nine ministers who founded the society, six had been circuit rider/missionaries in Canada.

Leading women founded the New York Female Missionary Society, which assisted the missionary outreach through fundraising, an idea that quickly spread to Methodist women in Albany, Boston, and other Methodist centers.[3] In 1825 the women's society sent a circulating library to the Wyandott Indians. The women's society's greatest success came a few years later as a chief support for the new Liberia mission. These two societies, one general and one female auxiliary, were the first significant voluntary organizations American Methodists founded specifically for the mission of the church.

The example of John Stewart demonstrates what became the Methodist pattern during the early nineteenth century—expansion in obedience to the Holy Spirit, backed up by sound organization. Despite requests in 1824 by African-American settlers for a missionary to organize churches, no experienced pastors would volunteer because of Liberia's reputation as the "white man's grave." Finally in 1832 the widower Melville Cox of Hallowell, Maine, volunteered and was accepted because he was already dying of tuberculosis anyway.[4] A heckler at Wesleyan University in Connecticut told Cox that he would die in Liberia. Cox replied, "Then come write my epitaph, 'Let a thousand fall before Africa be given up.'" In the three months before he died, Cox organized the Liberian church according to the *Discipline,* planned a school, bought a building, and held a camp meeting. The first reinforcements after his death lived about a month, with only one unmarried woman missionary who remained. Over the following decades, most missionaries to Liberia died or were invalided home after only brief service.

Despite a permanent haze of malaria and the deaths of nearly all her colleagues, the Liberia missionary who provided continuity for nineteen years was the teacher Ann Wilkins—sustained by her holiness piety and money, prayers, supplies, and correspondence from the New York Female Missionary Society. Wilkins founded the first Methodist girls' school abroad. Her correspondence with her mother also reveals that she was separated or divorced from her husband.[5]

An unlicensed "colored" visionary, a superannuated tubercular, a lay woman of uncertain marital status—these were the risk-taking pioneers of what had become by the early twentieth century the largest American foreign mission force.

JOHN AND HELEN SPRINGER AND THE CONGO MISSION

In 1844 the General Conference of the Methodist Episcopal Church founded a General Missionary Committee that provided national oversight of appropriations and other matters. Founding the committee modified the earliest pattern of voluntary sponsorship for missions through annual conferences. The process of organizational standardization required missions to relate to the entire denomination, and an effective period of Methodist expansion followed the founding of permanent centralized structures. Board of Mission secretaries oversaw Methodist work around the world, thus reducing the power of bishops and conferences over global mission. Historian Russell Richey has argued that when, in 1872, the General Conference transformed all voluntary societies in the church into denominational agencies, the church started down the road of centralized bureaucratization. Methodism went from itself being a mission movement that welcomed the converted "into the family," to being a body that supported missions toward the objects of evangelization.[6]

One result of systematization and consolidation was that the John Stewarts and Ann Wilkins of the late nineteenth century began going outside the denomination to fulfill their missionary callings. The balance shifted away from expansion toward institution building. In the early twentieth century, many of the founders of independent and then Pentecostal missions were originally Methodists—for example, Charles and Lettie Cowman, founders of the Oriental Missionary Society, parent of the third largest Protestant denomination in Korea; Jennie Fuller, earliest leader of the Christian and Missionary Alliance in India; and Willis Hoover, founder of an independent Methodist Pentecostal church that became the largest Protestant denomination in Chile. From the 1870s onward, Methodists who felt called by the Holy Spirit were constantly overflowing the banks of the denomination. On the mission field itself, converts who felt restricted by denominational rigidity sometimes started new churches, for example in 1932 when the evangelist Johane Maranke left Methodism and founded the Vapostori, one of the greatest missionary movements in central Africa.

Within Methodism itself, in a twentieth century of fixed budgets, pioneer innovators struggled to expand the missions. One pair of stubborn innovators were John (1873–1963) and Helen (1868–1946) Springer, founders of Methodism in the Belgian Congo. They met in

Rhodesia where he was head of the Industrial Mission at Old Umtali and she was a linguist and the founder of Methodist girls' education. The Springers married in 1905. Called by the Holy Spirit to fulfill the vision of David Livingstone, Bishop William Taylor, and others to found a chain of mission stations across central Africa, the Springers traveled from Zambia to Angola scouting possible mission locations despite the explicit disapproval of the mission board.

Returning to the United States, the Springers raised such popular support and so much money for a mission in the Congo that the mission board capitulated to public sentiment. The Springers spent an arduous two years planting the mission stations, including founding a Bible training school. Officially approved in 1915, the Congo Mission was headed by John Springer until 1936 when he was elected bishop for Africa. Springer returned after retirement to Mulungwishi where he had personally financed and founded the Congo Bible Institute. Only the nationalist upheavals forced him to leave the Congo at the age of ninety, and he died a few months later.[7]

In John and Helen Springer's struggle to establish the Congo Mission, we see how spiritual conviction and entrepreneurial success— undergirded by grassroots support—permitted individuals to force changes in denominational priorities. The noteworthy successes of Methodist missions have often relied on a healthy if uncomfortable tension between expansion and consolidation, individual entrepreneur- ship and organization, Spirit inspiration and disciplined follow-up. Often individual initiative outran established structures. In many cases, icono- clastic individuals have left the church, as when Willis Hoover became a Pentecostal and took most of the Chilean Methodist church with him in 1909. In other cases, denominational structures managed to retain and then channel the creative energy of pioneers like the Springers.

HIGHER EDUCATION AS MISSIONARY INNOVATION

An important theme in the history of Methodist missions is support for higher education. At first glance, support of educational institutions seems a peculiar emphasis for a movement whose strength was drawn from the anti-intellectual climate of revivalism. Hostility against formal education for clergy continued on a popular level well into the twentieth century. Yet by 1844, American Methodism had established thirteen colleges, making it second only to the Presbyterians with their historical emphasis on a learned ministry. By 1897, the Methodist Episcopal Church alone was sponsoring fifty-four colleges and universities in the United States. By the turn of the century, American Methodists were busy establishing nascent colleges in China, Japan, Korea, Latin America, and India.

Despite the seeming contradiction between goals of expansion and of supporting expensive institutions of higher education,

> a connection between evangelism and education is precisely what fueled Methodist expansion in the late nineteenth and early twentieth centuries. The Methodist message of human cooperation in salvation was popularly understood as a Gospel of self-help in both spiritual and earthly matters. Attaining salvation did not leave Methodist converts passive and complacent about their earthly lot. In fact, the opposite occurred. The acceptance of divine love and mercy by Methodist converts was often accompanied by the urge toward sanctification, which included both moral striving and self-improvement through education.[8]

In the words of church growth expert George Hunter, "redemption and lift," or a bootstraps, self-improvement mentality was crucial to the Methodist appeal. The support for educational institutions exemplified the self-help spirit of American Methodism; by the twentieth century that spirit appealed to people around the world who were seeking to control the forces of modernization in their countries.

Methodism committed itself to liberal arts education for broad segments of its target populations because Methodist identity rested on an optimistic view of human capabilities combined with faith in the democratic potential of educated people. By the 1880s, there was a core group of Methodist missionaries in Asia who had themselves been educated in Methodist colleges. These missionaries understood the importance of education in their own lives, and so they began working toward founding colleges in Asia. The extension of higher education around the world involved heated arguments among missionaries, for many felt that educational institutions distracted from the Gospel ministry.

Another reason for the strong Methodist support of higher education in foreign missions was the active women's movement in the church. Since women typically could not be ordained, unmarried women became missionary-teachers, founding schools for girls in which they hoped to convert them as well as advance women's place in society through education. Methodist women founded the first colleges for women in Asia, including Ewha Womans University of Korea, now the largest woman's university in the world. By 1910, the Woman's Foreign Missionary Society of the Methodist Episcopal Church was supporting the largest number of teachers and more schools and colleges than any other women's missionary organization. The growth of educational, medical, and other social service institutions in late nineteenth and early twentieth century missions was the direct result of Methodist women's passionate advocacy of foreign missions.[9]

The decision of Methodism to support institutions of higher learning was not made without struggle, for there were always those who considered it an expensive luxury. But one major reason behind the founding of schools was that indigenous people came to demand them by the 1880s. Lamin Sanneh has shown how some African chiefs made running schools the price of doing business for Western missions. Once the value of Western education was known, every chief wanted schools in his own territory.[10] What was true for Africa was also true elsewhere.

CONTROVERSY OVER EDUCATION IN FUZHOU, CHINA

Fuzhou, China, where Methodists founded their first college outside the United States, is an interesting case study of the struggle within the church over founding higher educational institutions that offered secular learning. Not only was Fuzhou the site of the first Chinese annual conference and Methodism's first mission college, but the first Methodist girls' boarding school in Asia began there and grew into the first college for women in all of China. In 1881, Chinese pastors in the new Fuzhou Annual Conference petitioned for the mission to found a men's college.

An unbaptized Chinese businessman donated $10,000 for purchasing the property on the condition that the college teach English. Not having time to consult with the mission board in New York, a committee of missionaries accepted the money and formed a Board of Trustees. This decision instantly polarized the mission force, both male and female. At that time, the vast majority of missionaries of all denominations in China opposed the teaching of English, believing it would cause the Chinese to become denationalized and take jobs in the public sector rather than in the church. Some missionaries argued that teaching the Chinese English would "spoil" them and make them "uppity" and refuse to work. The Fuzhou missionaries were split between those who violently opposed higher education for the Chinese and those who felt the highest levels of Western education would meet the felt needs of the converts and would also create a favorable atmosphere for hearing the Gospel.

As the missionaries fought each other over opening the college, they corresponded with the mission board. In one letter, missionary Franklin Ohlinger, the chief supporter of the college, argued against the idea that learning English would make the converts "go bad." The idea of the college was not merely to teach English, but to offer good general education just as in American colleges. Said Ohlinger,

> I trust our first class in Medicine, Theology, Law, will not only have a good knowledge of English and Chinese but also of German and French besides the customary drill in the "ancient languages." We mean to hold out strong inducement for aiming at this standard and our Trustees and Native Conference heartily favor the plan. We do not train men to be cooks and butlers for the foreign merchants, but men who shall be leaders of thought, who shall carry the banner of Christianity and Western Science into every part of these Eighteen Provinces.[11]

The Ohlingers were so strongly in favor of the Anglo-Chinese College that they threatened to appeal for direct support from their grassroots constituency of German-American Methodists.

Although the Anglo-Chinese College opened in 1881, the recriminations between the Chinese pastors and the missionaries who had opposed the college reached all the way to the next General Conference. Fighting over whether to raise the level of instruction in the girls' boarding school broke out in 1883. The Chinese pastors, who controlled the annual conference, responded by refusing to serve communion to several missionaries who opposed the higher-level schools. Two senior women missionaries resigned, and one outraged male missionary took the issue of being disciplined by so-called "natives" to the General Conference.

Methodists in Fuzhou were thus ahead of virtually every other mission in China in the teaching of English and of advanced Western scientific subjects. By the time the Second General Missionary Conference of China met,

Methodists had nearly a decade of experience in the matter.[12] At the conference of 1890, Fuzhou missionary W. H. Lacy argued that teaching the English language was necessary because "the people demand it, and we must meet this demand, or allow the boys to go to Godless schools for their education."[13] Anglo-Chinese College was by 1890 using English for instruction in geometry, conic sections, trigonometry, surveying, astronomy, physics, botany, geology, chemistry, physiology, and premedical studies. It was also teaching the Chinese classics and the Bible. Fuzhou Methodism had found that evangelism was not undercut by the teaching of English, Lacy argued. In the prior two months, eighteen college students had joined the church.[14]

The nasty fighting over higher education in Fuzhou was not repeated elsewhere in Methodism, as far as I know, because the denomination as a whole had decided that opening colleges, including teaching English, was a proper focus of mission policy. From the 1880s through the 1920s, Methodists supported colleges, universities, and medical schools for men and women in all of its established mission fields. Ironically, a denomination that began in revivalism had become one of the greatest sponsors of educational missions in the world. Not only did the church believe in the power of education to change lives and transform society for the better, but converts insisted upon it once they understood how education could help them negotiate the realities of colonialism by giving them Western knowledge. In the case of Latin America, for example in Argentina, Uruguay, and Brazil, one could say that the Methodist Church entered on the backs of the schools. Despite opposition from the Roman Catholic Church, many of the first Methodist missionaries in Latin America were invited by local groups of progressive Latin Americans who sought Western education for their children.[15] The running of educational institutions, with their heavy expenses and staffing needs, was always a partnership between locals and missionaries, both male and female.

CONCLUSION

As the examples in this article show, from a historical perspective, Methodist mission has flourished when there is a healthy balance between expansion and consolidation, between individual initiative and corporate follow-through. Advances are often initiated by individuals willing to challenge the reigning structures of the day. Nothing succeeds like success; eventually the most successful initiatives are accepted by the denominational structures and become part of the normal state of things. While ultimately good organization is necessary for the survival of these innovations, individual initiative and risk-taking have been essential to creative expansion. The founding of the Mission Society for United Methodists a quarter century ago exemplifies the entrepreneurial tradition so essential to the long-term vitality of Methodist missions.

NOTES

1. An earlier, expanded version of this paper was published as "'History's Lessons for Tomorrow's Mission': Reflections on American Methodism in Mission," *Focus* (Winter/Spring 1999): pp. 7–12.

2. *The Missionary Pioneer; or a brief memoir of the life, labours, and death of John Stewart, (man of colour), founder under God, of the mission among the Wyandotts, at Upper Sandusky, Ohio* (New York: Joseph Mitchell printed by J. C. Totten, 1827); N. B. C. Love, *John Stewart, Missionary to the Wyandotts* (New York: Missionary Society of the Methodist Episcopal Church, n.d.).

3. Elizabeth Mason North, *Consecrated Talents: Or, the Life of Mrs. Mary W. Mason* (New York: Carlton & Lanahan, 1870); Susan Warrick, "'She Diligently Followed Every Good Work': Mary Mason and the New York Female Society," *Methodist History* 34, no. 4 (July 1996): pp. 214–29.

4. *Remains of Melville B. Cox, Late Missionary to Liberia, with a Memoir* (Boston: Light and Horton, 1835).

5. Personal communication to author from Susan Eltscher Warrick.

6. Russell E. Richey, "Methodism: Essentially a Missionary Movement, Domestic and Foreign?" unpublished paper presented at ISAE Missionary Impulse in North American History Conference, June 4, 1998, p. 23.

7. The Springer papers were barely rescued from destruction and sent to the United Methodist archives, where they provide a priceless picture of Methodist missions in Africa from the 1890s through the 1950s. On the explorations and founding of the Congo Mission, see John M. Springer, *The Heart of Central Africa; Mineral Wealth and Missionary Opportunity* (Cincinnati: Jennings and Graham; New York: Eaton and Mains, c. 1909); John M. Springer, *Pioneering in the Congo* (New York: printed for the author by the Methodist Book Concern, 1916); John M. Springer, *Christian Conquests in the Congo* (New York: Methodist Book Concern, c. 1927); Dana L. Robert, "Springer, John McKendree and Helen Emily Chapman Rasmussen Springer," in *Historical Dictionary of Methodism*, ed. Charles Yrigoyen, Jr., and Susan E. Warrick (Lanham, Md.: Scarecrow Press, 1996), pp. 201–2; Dana L. Robert, "Springer, Helen Emily (Chapman) Rasmussen," in *Biographical Dictionary of Christian Missions*, ed. Gerald H. Anderson (New York: Macmillan Reference, USA, 1998), pp. 635–36; Dana L. Robert, "Springer, John McKendree," *Biographical Dictionary*, p. 636.

8. Dana L. Robert, "The Methodist Struggle over Higher Education in Fuzhou, China, 1877–1883," *Methodist History* 34, no. 3, (April 1996): pp. 173–74.

9. See Dana L. Robert, *American Women in Mission: A Social History of Their Thought and Practice* (Macon, Ga.: Mercer University Press, 1997), especially chapter 4.

10. Lamin Sanneh, *West African Christianity: The Religious Impact* (Maryknoll, N.Y.: Orbis Books, 1983.)

11. Quoted in Dana L. Robert, "Methodist Struggle," 185. Franklin Ohlinger eventually transferred to the Korean mission, where he ran the Trilingual Press that translated and published tracts, textbooks, and church materials in Chinese, Korean, and English. On literature work in Korea, see Sung-Deuk Oak, "Chinese Protestant Literature and Early Korean Protestantism," in *Christianity in Korea*, ed. Robert E. Buswell, Jr., and Timothy S. Lee (Honolulu: University of Hawaii Press, 2006), p. 75.

12. Jessie Lutz points out that the Episcopalian-sponsored St. John's College admitted students to study English in October of 1881 and subsequently decided to teach subjects in the English language. She sees that as a "major turning point in the history of the China Christian colleges." Jessie Gregory Lutz, *China and the Christian Colleges, 1850–1950* (Ithaca, N.Y.: Cornell University Press, 1971), p. 69. Lutz's book on Christian colleges ignores the Fuzhou Anglo-Chinese College and thus misses the fact that it was founded in 1881 under the assumption that English would be the medium of instruction.

13. *Records of the General Conference of the Protestant Missionaries of China, held at Shanghai, May 7–20, 1890* (Shanghai: American Presbyterian Mission Press, 1980), p. 497.

14. Ibid., p. 498.

15. Many of the earliest Methodist missionaries to Latin America went as teachers under the self-support scheme of William Taylor. William Taylor, *Pauline Methods of Missionary Work* (Philadelphia: National Association for the Promotion of Holiness, 1879); William Taylor, *Ten Years of Self-Supporting Missions in India* (New York: Phillips and Hunt, 1882); Rosa del Carmen Bruno-Jofre, *Methodist Education in Peru: Social Gospel, Politics, and American Ideological Penetration, 1888–1930* (Waterloo, Ontario: Wilfrid Laurier University Press, 1988).

13

WORLD PARISH TO WORLD CHURCH

JOHN AND CHARLES WESLEY ON HOME AND OVERSEAS MISSION

Andrew F. Walls

"I look upon all the world as my parish . . ."

One of the most famous of John Wesley's sayings, uttered quite early in his itinerant career, was "I look upon all the world as my parish." This was not an announcement of a program for world evangelization, but a justification for preaching in other people's parishes, and a declaration of intent to go on doing so. Nonetheless it has a place in the development of a characteristically Methodist doctrine of mission. It signals a breach in the concept of Christendom, to which the parish was integral; and the Christendom concept was foundational to the Western experience of Christianity. It contains a hint of the transition from the church as an essentially Western institution that characterized Wesley's day to the World Church in every continent that characterizes our own.

So there is reason to explore how the idea of a World Parish led to the reality of the World Church, and how the sphere of Methodist activity shifted from English parishes to distant parts of the globe. This paper is confined to the earliest part of the process, the words and actions of John Wesley and the hymnody of his brother Charles. Other studies must consider the transitional figure of the mission, expansionist Thomas Coke,[1] Wesley's troubleshooter in America and the Caribbean, and some significant Methodists of the generation that followed John's death who formed the Wesleyan Methodist Missionary Society and in the process built the Wesleyan Methodist Church.[2] The Wesleys saw Methodism as a mission; their successors turned the mission into a church with a mission society.

WESTERN CHRISTENDOM AND THE IDEA OF PARISH

Europe had become Christian in a process lasting several centuries in which the peoples of the north and west came to accept Christianity as the basis of custom. Christendom, which is only another word for Christianity, became a geographical expression, "the Christian part of the world." The presence of an Islamic world to the east and south as Europe's only near neighbor reinforced the association of Christianity with territory.

This geographically expressed Christianity of Europe was organized in territorial units, of which the basic unit was the parish. The parson (the "person") of the parish notionally had the "cure of souls" of everyone resident within it. All were baptized in infancy, all, notionally, were taught the Christian faith and shared in the Christian worship of the community. The concept implied a single church, a concept unchallenged by the Protestant Reformation, which envisaged the purification of the whole church within each state. And although by Wesley's day some degree of religious plurality was a political reality, the basis of church thinking remained that of the parish minister with the cure of souls for all within his parish. The idea was carried over into parts of the New World, including Georgia, where Wesley's unhappy missionary service took place.

The letter that contains the celebrated phrase about the World Parish is a reply to one from a former Oxford pupil, James Hervey, who now held the cure of souls in the rural parish of Weston Favell, remonstrating with Wesley for his irregular behavior toward the parish system. Favell urged him either to return to college teaching in Oxford or else get a parish of his own.[3] As Wesley says:

> [Y]ou think I ought to sit still; because otherwise I should invade another's office if I . . . intermeddled with souls that did not belong to me. You accordingly ask, "How is it that I assemble Christians, who are

none of my charge, to sing psalms, and pray, and hear the Scriptures expounded . . ."[4]

It is noteworthy that Wesley uses the word "Christians" here where one might have expected simply "people." The point is that those being assembled are baptized members of a community explicitly identifying itself as Christian. As such their spiritual welfare was the responsibility of the clergyman of the parish. Wesley's practices invaded the parish clergyman's sphere both by public preaching (in the church if permitted, out of it if necessary) and by establishing meetings for those "who have the form of godliness and desire the power thereof." This produced a longer-term evangelistic and pastoral instrument, independent of the parish structures.

The concept of Christendom was built on the idea of a community that had a "form of godliness," even if all knew that this was rarely attained in practice. To set up a body consisting of those parishioners "desiring the power of godliness" was to introduce a more radical expression of Christianity than the church structures provided for, now that the Reformation had abolished the monasteries. Wesley's hymnbook was later to speak of "real" Christianity and "inward" over against "formal" religion.[5]

The distinction between "real" or "inward" Christianity and the formal and nominal expressions required or assumed by Christendom is the hallmark of the Pietist and Evangelical movements that transformed Protestant Christianity in the eighteenth and nineteenth centuries. Wesley's expression of it was perhaps the more subversive of the parish structures by *not* establishing a gathered congregation on the Independent or Baptist model. By drawing together societies of "Methodists" committed to radical Christian discipleship inside the parish but independent of its structures and oversight he was setting up an organization for mission not so much *of* the church as *to* the church, outside its lines of authority.[6]

James Hervey, Wesley's correspondent, was himself a radical who asserted the difference between formal and inward religion. A moderate Calvinist doctrinally, he was one of the small group of parish clergy early touched by the Evangelical Revival. He, too, was seeking conversions, but essentially as a mission *of* the church, within, and by means of, the parish system. Charged with the cure of souls within one tiny segment of

Christendom, he saw Wesley's mission project as interfering in the exercise of that responsibility.[7] Both men were aware that there were multitudes of parishes where no one exercised responsibility effectively, and a growing number where no one could. For Hervey, this was irrelevant to the issue: one's duty lay with one's parish. Wesley had a less circumscribed guiding principle:

> If you ask on what principle, then, I acted, it was this: A desire to be a Christian; and a conviction that, whatever I judge conducive thereto, that I am bound to do; wherever I judge I can best answer this end, thither it is my duty to go. On this principle I set out for America, on this I visited the Moravian Church, and on the same am I ready now (God being my helper) to go to Abyssinia or China, or whithersoever it shall please God, by this conviction, to call me.[8]

The letter continues with the scriptural duty to "instruct the ignorant, reform the wicked, confirm the virtuous," duties only possible for one in Wesley's position by entering some other clergyman's parish. And so:

> I look upon all the world as my parish: thus far I mean that in whatever part of it I am, I judge it meet, right and my bounden duty to declare unto all who are willing to hear the glad tidings of salvation.[9]

The argument and the context make it plain that however ready Wesley may have been in principle to go to Abyssinia or to China, he did not expect to go to either; he expected to preach the glad tidings of salvation in English parishes to baptized people in a society that claimed to be Christian. The Evangelical Revival challenged a Christian civil society that was not Christian enough, positing a "real Christianity" over against the formal or nominal. As one of Charles Wesley's hymns puts it, "The Christian world is guilty of damning unbelief." Baptized people need the glad tidings of salvation leading to conversion, just as the Chinese do.

In this view of the preacher's task, there is no place for a special category of "cross-cultural" or even "overseas" mission. Wesley makes a revealing remark after reading Jonathan Edwards's publication of the journal of David Brainerd, missionary of the Scottish Society for Promoting Christian Knowledge to the Native Americans of Massachusetts. Wesley admired Brainerd and made a version of the journal for his Christian Library, but he notes in him the human tendency to overplay the significance of one's own work. Mighty as the movement was where so many of the Indians turned to Christ through Brainerd's preaching, the movement of the Spirit in Northampton under Edwards and in Cambuslang and Kilsyth in Scotland (Wesley modestly goes no further south for his examples) were still more remarkable.[10] But surely, we protest today, Northampton and Cambuslang were communities with a long Christian tradition; Brainerd was preaching to people different in language and culture who hitherto had been outside the Christian faith. This feature does not appear to have struck Wesley; for him revivals of religion are comparable, irrespective of their historical, cultural, or ethnic features.

This helps to explain the apparently haphazard early development of Methodist overseas missions, Wesley's damping down of Coke's enthusiasm for new overseas enterprises, and in particular the long delay in establishing a mission society for Methodists. The 1790s saw the formation of mission societies for most major British Protestant groups; not until 1814 was the Missionary Society for the Leeds District founded, and not until 1818 did the connection-wide Wesleyan Methodist Missionary Society come into being. Yet there were Methodist missions in four continents before 1818. In 1792 William Carey, usually credited with originating missionary societies in Britain, had seen "pleasing accounts" of their success.[11] Nor did Methodism suffer, like the Church of Scotland, where organization of missions was still later, from disputes about the principle of missions. No need was felt for a mission society because missions overseas were not seen as in essence different from other Methodist work. Appointing a missionary was in principle like appointing any other preacher, to be settled by establishing priorities.

" THE FULLNESS OF THE GENTILES' CALL": THE ESCHATOLOGICAL FRAMEWORK

Wesley sets out the theological basis of his approach in Sermon 63, headed "The General Spread of the Gospel."[12] The text is Isaiah 11:9, "The earth shall be full of the knowledge of the LORD as the waters cover the sea" (KJV). The general spread of the Gospel—worldwide mission—is set in the framework of the fulfillment of God's purposes for humanity.

Wesley's eschatology is standard for the period, rooted in the prophecies that speak of the Messiah having the heathen as his inheritance, interpreted in the light of Paul's argument in Romans 9–11 that God's economy involves the call of Israel, its hardening in part, and the admission of the Gentiles to the privileges once unique to Israel. Then, when that process has reached a climax ("the fullness of the Gentiles") comes the recognition by all Israel of its Messiah.

The great themes of this eschatology, intertwining the Old Testament, Romans, and the book of Revelation, are set out by Charles Wesley in the great hymn "Head of Thy Church Whose Spirit Fills":[13]

> *Come Lord, the glorious Spirit cries,*
> *And saints beneath the altar groan;*
> *Come Lord, the Bride on earth replies,*
> *And perfect all our hearts in one.*

The Spirit and the Bride—that is the church—here call for the completion of divine love (all loves excelling), the finishing of God's new creation, the fulfillment of salvation in holiness without which none shall see God. The hymn resumes:

> *Pour out the promised gift on all,*
> *Answer the universal "Come."*
> *The fullness of the Gentiles call,*
> *And take thine ancient people home.*

This is the order of Romans: the fullness of the Gentiles, the completion of the preaching of the Gospel to the nations, followed by the salvation of Israel.

> *To thee let all the nations flow . . .*

[a glance here at Isaiah 2:2ff, where the Gentiles crowd up the temple mount to learn the ways of God, beating their swords into plowshares]

> *Sinners obey the Gospel word*
> *Let all their bleeding Savior know*
> *Filled with the glory of the Lord.*

Oh for thy truth and mercy's sake
The purchase of thy passion claim;
Thine heritage, the nations, take
And cause the world to know thy name.

The climax comes with the second psalm where the King, to whom God has just said, "Thou art my Son," receives the nations as his inheritance—the fullness of the Gentiles.

It is a theme that comes again and again in Charles Wesley's hymns of the kingdom:

Savior whom our hearts adore[14]
To bless our earth again
Now assume thy royal power
And o'er the nations reign.

The subsequent verses enlarge on this call to Christ, "the world's desire and hope," to set up the last great empire in our ruined world, sodden with the blood of murdered millions. By claiming the heathen tribes he begins the endless reign where no one learns war anymore.

But this is not a vision of another world; it is a natural extension of what has already begun as a result of Methodist preaching, as another hymn indicates:

With joy we now approve[15]
The truth of Jesus' love.
God the universal God
He the door hath opened wide.
Faith on heathens hath bestowed,
Washed them in his bleeding side.

The "heathens" that Charles is thinking of do not live in Africa or the Pacific. They are the baptized heathens of London and Kingswood and Bristol, who have been

Purchased and redeemed of old,
Added to the chosen race,
Now received into the fold
Heathens sing their Savior's praise.

It is English heathen who have been incorporated into Israel, a contribution toward the fullness of the Gentiles that will precede the salvation of all Israel. A better-known hymn, "Head of Thy Church Triumphant,"[16] is still clearer:

Thou hast employed thy servants

[that is, the Methodist preachers]

And blessed their weak endeavors
And lo! in thee we myriads see
Of justified believers.

Thanksgiving for this evangelistic success leads into prayer for the completion of the process:

But show thy power and myriads more
Endue with heavenly graces

[that is, bring them not just to forgiveness of sin but to scriptural holiness.]

But fill the earth with glory
And, known by every nation,
God of all grace
Receive the praise of all thy new creation.

Or again, in the hymn "Ye Neighbors and Friends of Jesus Draw Near":[17]

To us and to them

[that is, the blind, lame, dumb, deaf, leprous, and poor]

is published the word
Then let us proclaim our life giving Lord
Who now is reviving his work in our days
And mightily striving to save us by grace.

The mighty work taking place in the writer's days is in the English parishes through Methodist preaching. This leads naturally to prayer for the completion of the process, its extension to all nations:

O Jesus ride on till all are subdued,
Thy mercy make known and sprinkle thy blood
Display thy salvation and teach the new song
To every nation and people and tongue.

In other words, the eschatological vision of the conversion of the nations is organically linked with the present calling of Methodists to preach the Gospel in England. Present ministry, with its divine endorsement shown by repentance, faith, and changed lives, is part of a single continuous process whereby Jesus "rides on" toward the time when all things everywhere are put under his feet.

THE GENERAL SPREAD OF THE GOSPEL

This is spelled out in matter-of-fact prose by John Wesley in the sermon on "The General Spread of the Gospel," already mentioned. It addresses the problem of why five-sixths of the earth was then pagan or Muslim, and why so little of the remaining sixth was truly Christian. The newly discovered peoples of the Pacific, though Wesley could not bring himself to believe that they were actually cannibals, were undoubtedly indiscriminately violent, a standing refutation of contemporary theories of the benevolent effects of natural religion. If Muslims, outnumbering Christians, were without true religion and mercy, their Christian neighbors—Georgian, Circassian, Mengrelian—were proverbial for ignorance and irreligion, and the Christians of Abyssinia little better. Europe might offer more knowledge and more scriptural and rational ways of worship, but two-thirds of it was subject to Roman corruptions of Rome, and the majority of Protestants led far from Christian lives. How can we reconcile this prevailing darkness with the power and love of God?

It is an Arminian problem; high Calvinists may settle it by the mystery of election. Wesley finds in the prophecies the assurance that the darkness will be replaced by the knowledge of God, and, as foretold in that text so beloved by his brother, the Messiah will claim the nations as his inheritance (Ps. 2:8). John, like Charles Wesley, expects this event of the last times to come about by extension from God's present activity in the revival of religion in the Methodist movement. It is possible to conceive how God will work, he argues, by considering how he has already worked, and specifically how he has worked over the last fifty years or so:

> In the same manner as God has converted so many to himself without destroying their liberty, he can undoubtedly convert whole nations, or the whole world.[18]

Wesley urges his hearers to think how from the little circle in Oxford (Oxford, notice, not Aldersgate Street) the leaven has worked throughout England, and then spread to Scotland and Ireland, and a few years later into New York and Pennsylvania and beyond, even to Newfoundland and Nova Scotia. Traditionally, Wesley argues, the pattern has been for large-scale movements of the preaching of justification to last for some weeks or months and then subside, after which progress is by gentle degrees. But the Methodist movement has already lasted for fifty years and it is reasonable to expect its further continuance. The most likely direction for it to spread now would be to Holland and then to the Protestants of France, Germany, and Switzerland, and then to Denmark, Sweden, and Russia. It could then spread to the Catholics in those areas where Catholics and Protestants live on close terms, which would enable true religion to spread to the Catholic countries, Italy, Spain, and Portugal. (Wesley says nothing to indicate that awakening among European Catholics would make them Protestants.) He expects the renewal movement to proceed from the bottom upward, affecting rulers last and the learned last of all.

Such a movement would bring about a return to the model of the church of the Acts of the Apostles, with shared property and the abolition of poverty—but without an Ananias and Sapphira. It would remove the main stumbling block to the conversion of Muslims, which lies in the evil lives of Christians. Muslims will thus turn to the true Messiah and similar considerations will bring in the heathen peoples, beginning with those closest to the European settlements in India.

That leaves only those peoples who do not have regular contacts with Christians. But God will find ways of reaching the Pacific Islanders and the "recesses" of Africa and the Americas. When that happens, it will surely be time for the Jews to return, and all Israel will be saved, and all the promises to the church will have been fulfilled.

Wesley's vision is of the fulfillment of prophecy by contagion: the effect of scriptural holiness that proceeds from the Gospel of forgiveness spreading from community to community. Considerations of culture differences and power relationships are left aside.

The sermon explains why Africa and some other parts of the world moved in and out of consideration for the stationing of Methodist preachers during Wesley's lifetime. On Wesley's principles the stationing of a preacher must relate to the prospects of doing most good at the particular moment.[19] Wesley is sure that the turn of Africa will come, as Providence opens the way; but it never reached the main agenda during his lifetime. Fittingly, the slave trade, the topic of his last letter, was to place Sierra Leone firmly on the agenda soon after his death.[20]

Some parts of Wesley's analysis of the way Methodism might contribute to the general spread of the Gospel have proved sound. Crucial developments have sometimes flowed from Methodists doing Methodist things—praying, preaching, meeting in class or society, singing, talking to neighbors or workmates. Portable Methodist structures, dependent on the gifts and graces of lay men and women and independent of heavy ecclesiastical investment, have sometimes been crucial to new churches.

For the most part, events relating to the general spread of the Gospel have taken a path quite different from Wesley's expectations. He might be amazed (but surely delighted) to find teeming churches and vigorous Christian life in the "recesses" of Africa; he might be puzzled and dismayed at the decline from Christendom in the English parishes where his best years were spent. Perhaps the general spread of the Gospel he foresaw has happened and still in progress, with the missionary movement (now entering a new, non-Western phase) the product of the Evangelical movement he knew. And surely both brothers were right to see that movement stretching into a future in which the Messiah will receive all the nations as his inheritance.

NOTES

1. Meanwhile, see John Vickers, *Thomas Coke, Apostle of Methodism* (London: Epworth Press, 1969).

2. Among recent studies see Andrew Walls, "Wesleyan Missiological Theories: The Case of Richard Watson," in *The Global Impact of the Wesleyan Traditions and their Related Movements*, ed. Charles Yrigoyen (Lanham, Md.: Scarecrow Press, 2002), pp. 27–47; Andrew F. Walls, "Methodists, Missions and Pacific Christianity," in *Weaving the Unfinished Mats: Wesley's Legacy—Conflict, Confusion and Challenge in the South Pacific*, ed. Peter Lineham (North Auckland: Wesley Historical Society of New Zealand, 2007) pp. 9–32.

3. The letter appears in Journal 11, June 1739, *The Journal of the Rev. John Wesley*, vol. 2, ed. Nehemiah Curnock (London: Epworth Press, 1938), pp. 216–18. Hereafter cited as Curnock.

4. Curnock, vol. 2, p. 217.

5. *A Collection of Hymns for the Use of the People called Methodists* by John Wesley first appeared in 1780 and was reissued with successive supplements several times during the nineteenth century. In the preface (dated October 20, 1779) Wesley claims the hymns are "carefully arranged under proper heads, according to the experience of real Christians." These "proper heads" include "Describing Formal Religion" and "Describing Inward Religion."

6. Wesley could cite these lines of authority when it suited his purpose. For instance, when, shortly before the letter recorded, Beau Nash of Bath challenged him for his authority, Wesley's reply is: "By the authority of Jesus Christ, conveyed to me by the (now) Archbishop of Canterbury, when he laid hands on me and said 'Take the authority to preach the Gospel.'" Journal for June 5, 1739, Curnock, vol. 2, p. 212.

7. Hervey (1714–1758), a Holy Club member at Oxford, even formed religious societies similar to the Methodist form, but he kept them under his own eye as parish minister.

8. Curnock, vol. 2, p. 218.

9. Ibid.

10. Under Journal 4, December 1749, Curnock vol. 5, p. 449. See also Andrew F. Walls, "Missions and Historical Memory: Jonathan Edwards and David Brainerd" in *Jonathan Edwards at Home and Abroad*, eds. David W. Kling and Douglas A Sweeney, (Columbia: University of South Carolina Press, 2003), pp. 248–65.

11. William Carey, *An Enquiry into the Obligations of Christians to Use Means for the Conversion of the Heathens . . .* (Leicester, 1792), p. 37 refers to Wesley's ministers "now labouring amongst the Caribbs and Negroes" in the West Indies. Methodism in Antigua had begun through the conversion when visiting England in 1757 of the planter Nathaniel Gilbert and several of his slaves. There were Black Methodists, formerly serving in British regiments in the American Revolutionary War, in Nova Scotia. In 1792 they brought a Methodist society to Sierra Leone. Coke sent a (disastrous) agricultural mission, intended for Futa Jallon, to Sierra Leone in 1796, and a regular missionary was appointed to Sierra Leone by the connection in 1811. The mission party headed by Coke reached Sri Lanka, and Samuel Leigh, Australia, in 1814. Thus there was established Methodist work in every continent before the foundation of the Wesleyan Methodist Missionary Society in 1818.

12. I have used the text in *Sermons on Several Occasions by the Rev. John Wesley*, vol. 2 (London: Wesleyan Conference Office, 1866), pp. 261–71. Hereafter cited as *Sermons*.

13. For convenience I cite the hymns according to their numbers in the 1876 version of *Hymns for the People Called Methodists*, with a new supplement. "Head of Thy Church Whose Spirit Fills" is no. 749. Hereafter cited as *Hymns*.

14. *Hymns*, no. 730.

15. *Hymns*, no. 735, verse 2.

16. *Hymns*, no. 853.

17. *Hymns*, no. 40.

18. *Sermons*, vol. 2, 261.

19. Inevitably Charles Wesley has a hymn, though unpublished, on this economy of preachers. Meditating on how Philip is guided to the Ethiopian eunuch (Acts 8) he says:

Not by voice angelic taught
Yet, Lord, we plainly know

Whether, and to whom we ought
At thy command to go.

From *The Unpublished Poetry of Charles
Wesley,* vol. 2, eds. S T Kimbrough and
Oliver A. Beckerlegge (Nashville:
Kingswood Books, 1990), p. 322.

20. Wesley's last known letter was
written to William Wilberforce in 1791 to
encourage him in the Parliamentary
campaign against the slave trade. See
Letters of the Rev. John Wesley, vol. 8, ed.
John Telford (London: Epworth Press,
1931), p. 265. The next year, 1792, the
Sierra Leone colony was founded, with
many Methodists of African birth or
descent settling there from Nova Scotia.

14

THE MISSION-CHURCH PARADIGM OF THE WESLEYAN REVIVAL

Paul W. Chilcote

John and Charles Wesley's rediscovery of a "mission-church paradigm" in eighteenth-century England fueled the renewal of the church and offers a model of enduring significance for global Christianity today.[1] This paradigm, drawing committed Christian disciples perennially to Jesus and to one another in community (centripetal movement) and spinning them out into the world in mission and service (centrifugal movement), reflected an apostolic vision of the people of God in their view. This essay examines those aspects of Wesleyan theology that provided the foundation for this vision and the hymns of Charles Wesley that inculcated missional praxis.

THEOLOGICAL FOUNDATIONS OF A MISSION-CHURCH PARADIGM

A robust theological foundation undergirded the missional vision that gave birth to a dynamic movement of spiritual renewal under the leadership of the Wesleys. In the mind of these Anglican reformers, mission began with God and not with them.[2] They conceived a "missionary God" because the God they had come to know in Jesus Christ was a God of love who was always reaching out from self to others—an expression of God's love and grace they described as God's prevenient action.[3] The missional practices of the Wesleys and of the Methodist Societies they founded mirrored this understanding of God's nature and character. Moreover, they firmly believed that God was active and at work in the world to save and restore all creation. These primary convictions led the Wesleys to reclaim mission as the church's reason for being and evangelism as the heart of that mission in the world.[4] They developed a holistic vision of mission and evangelism that refused to separate faith and works, personal salvation and social justice, physical and spiritual needs.

The Wesleys anchored this missional vision in the fundamental affirmations of the Christian faith, namely, in the doctrines of creation and redemption, incarnation, and Trinity, all of which point to the "centrifugal nature" of God's activity. They understood God's creation of all things out of nothing, for example, as a sheer act of grace, an extension of God's love motivated by nothing but God's loving character.[5] The incarnation—God taking on human flesh in the person of Jesus of Nazareth—demonstrated the same missional quality. In the fullness of time, God entered human history and reached out to the beloved through Jesus Christ in order to re-create and restore all things in Christ. God's mission—God's evangelistic activity—God's proclamation and embodiment of Good News—in their view, began in creation, continues through redemption, and stretches out toward the consummation. This description of God's missionary character, in fact, even reflects God's triune nature.[6]

The Wesleys built their theology of mission upon the understanding of a Three-One God postured in perpetual, grace-filled, outward movement—Father, Son, and Holy Spirit in perennial interaction with one another and the world in a great dance of love. While mission belongs to God, the Wesleys believed that all people have the privilege of participating in God's mission through their own proclamation and embodiment of the Good News of God's love in Christ. In the same way that God entered human history and took on flesh in the person of Jesus, the Wesleys sought to live incarnationally by investing themselves in the lives of God's children wherever they found them. Charles Wesley used a powerful image to communicate this understanding of mission and God's call to be "Gospel-bearers." He described the Christian as a "transcript of the Trinity." That means essentially that God writes God's self into our very being so that when other people "read" our lives, they perceive God in us:

Cloath'd with Christ, aspire to shine,
Radiance He of Light Divine;
Beam of the Eternal Beam,
He in God, and God in Him!
Strive we Him in Us to see,
Transcript of the Deity.[7]

The theological method of the Wesleys reinforced this foundational vision. Instead of setting aspects of the Christian faith over against each other—for example, forcing a choice between *either* personal salvation or social action—the Wesleys tended to see matters of faith from a *both/and* perspective.[8] Personal salvation, they would argue, must be held together with social action, works of piety with works of mercy, in Christian discipleship. This approach to Christian thought and praxis shaped their understanding of mission and evangelism—and their doctrine of the church, as we shall see momentarily—in profound ways. Several excerpted couplets from a hymn by Charles Wesley illustrate this synthetic method:

Let us join ('tis God commands),
Let us join our hearts and hands

Still forget the things behind,
Follow Christ in heart and mind

Plead we thus for faith alone,
Faith which by our works is shown.[9]

Note the intimate connection of hearts and hands, heart and mind, faith and works. The words of brother John reveal the direct application of this principle to the missional vocation of all Christians:

By experience [the genuine Christian] knows that *social love* (if it mean the love of our neighbour) is absolutely, essentially different from *self-love*, even of the most allowable kind, just as different as the objects at which they point. And yet it is sure that, if they are under due regula-tions, each will give additional force to the other, "till they mix together never to be divided."[10]

Genuine love of self, rooted in God's affirmation—God's prior love—must find expression in love of others. The two must always be held together. One of the most important legacies left by the Wesleys is this effort to hold faith and love, the form and power of godliness, love for God and love of neighbor, together in a growing, dynamic, vital expression of the Christian faith.

This conjunctive method informed the Wesleys' conception of the church and the relation of the Methodist Societies to that larger body, while the cultural and ecclesial context in which they lived helped them to clarify their peculiar vision and mission. Rupert Davies has provided the most incisive analysis of this dynamic tension and identifies, perhaps, the most unique quality of early Methodism:

> A "society" acknowledges the truths proclaimed by the universal church and has no wish to separate from it, but claims to cultivate, by means of sacrament and fellowship, the type of inward holiness, which too great an objectivity can easily neglect and of which the church needs constantly to be reminded. A society does not unchurch the members of either church or sect . . . it calls its own members within the larger church to a special personal commitment which respects the commitment of others.[11]

The Wesleys designed the Methodist Societies, in other words, to function like catalysts of renewal within the life of the larger church. Having rediscovered a mission-church paradigm within the life of their own *ecclesiolae in ecclesia* ("little churches within the church"), their hope was that the leavening action of these small groups of committed missioners would reawaken the Church of England to its primary vocation in the world, namely, the *missio Dei*. The Methodist Societies were like little dynamos spinning inside the church and building momentum in order to reestablish a centrifugal force in the church itself, spinning it out in turn in mission. There can be no doubt that the cell structure of the Methodist organism accounts for the dynamism and growth of the movement and its influence.[12]

It is not too much to claim that three concepts taken together—church, evangelism, and mission—defined early Methodism. A missional ecclesiology emanated directly from the Wesleys' theological vision and method. God forms Gospel-bearers in and through the community of faith, which is itself a manifestation—imperfect though it may be—of the

Gospel in the world. The Wesleys concluded that the central purpose of the church is mission—God's mission. They attempted to replicate the model of the church they discovered in the pages of the New Testament. The church, they believed, is not called to live for itself, but for others. It is called, like Christ, to give itself for the life of the world. It is not so much that the church has a mission or ministries; rather, the church is mission. The church of Wesley's England had exchanged its true vocation (mission) for maintenance, a confusion that often slips into the life of the church in every age. It desperately needed to reclaim its true identity as God's agent of love and shalom in the world. The Wesleys firmly believed that God raised up the Methodists specifically for the task of resuscitating a mission-church.

This vision, as you might well expect, was deeply rooted in Scripture. When John Wesley adapted the Puritan Covenant Renewal Service for use in his own communities, he linked this annual event with one of Jesus' most poignant images for the church, namely, the vine and branches of John 15. In this passage Jesus presents a picture of the church. As we abide in Christ, who is the true vine, we take nourishment from him as the source of all life. We are constantly drawn into the center, to the core, to the source. There is something similar here to the centripetal force in physics, where objects are drawn to the center, something that persistently draws us closer to Christ and closer to one another. But the purpose of the vine is not simply to be drawn in, to revel in our connectedness and fellowship. The vine does not exist for its own benefit, but for the benefit of others through its fruit. What continues to give vitality to the church is the centrifugal force that spins us out into the world with the fruit of the Spirit. As we share this fruit with others, they are enabled to taste and see that God is good. The Wesleys came to believe that a church turned in on itself (that is, only centripetal) will surely die, for it has lost its reason for being. But a church spun out in loving service into the world (that is, also centrifugal) rediscovers itself day by day. "Offering Christ," to use Wesley's own terminology for the work of mission, involves both word and deed, both proclamation and action; it connects the Gospel to the world. Jesus' mission was characterized by healing those who were sick, liberating those who were oppressed, empowering those who stood on the margins of life, and caring for the poor. In all of these actions he incarnated shalom, God's vision of peace, justice, and well-being for all, and his disciples, the Wesleys taught, are called to do nothing less.

In this dynamic conception of a mission-church, the Wesleyan genius was to hold mission and evangelism together without pitting personal salvation against social justice. Mission for the Wesleys meant partnering with God in the realization of shalom in the world. Such a task is necessarily rooted in Christ, for we cannot speak of God's reign apart from Christ, or of Jesus without God's reign. The way in which the Wesleys envisaged this essential connection between evangelism and mission is, perhaps, one of their greatest contributions to the life of the church today.

In her attempt to present an authentic Wesleyan perspective on this relationship, Dana Robert has made recourse to Paul's image of the church as a body.[13] In this paradigm, an organic relationship exists between these two crucial practices of the church; while evangelism is the heart, mission is the body itself. The body moves in different contexts, interacting, engaging, constantly at work. But the heart sends the life-giving blood throughout the whole. Without the heart—without Jesus at the center—there is no vitality, no abundant life. But the body lives to continue the mission of Jesus in the world, namely, to announce and demonstrate the reign of God. The heart and the body, evangelism and mission, Christ and culture, are interdependent and interconnected, and this is the essence of the Wesleyan synthesis—the dynamism of the mission-church paradigm.

In his very last sermon, "On Faith," written in January 1791, John Wesley asked the all-important question about the goal of the Christian life: "How will [the faithful] advance in holiness, in the whole image of God wherein they were created?" He responded with reference to the dual foci of the Christian life and afforded a different language to contemplate the interface of evangelical piety and mission: "In the love of God and man, *gratitude* to their Creator, and *benevolence* to all their fellow-creatures."[14] Benevolence, here, is Wesley's term for mission.[15] But in his sermon "On Family Religion," he demonstrated how the family of God must build this mission upon the foundation of gratitude—the two being distinct but not separate. "And if any man truly love God he cannot but love his brother also," Wesley maintains. "*Gratitude* to our Creator will surely produce *benevolence* to our fellow-creatures. If we love him, we cannot but love one another, as Christ loved us. We feel our souls enlarged in love toward every child of man."[16]

The Wesleys believed that God calls the community of faith to live for others. The primary method of mission in the Wesleyan tradition is for those within the family of God to become God's partners in the redemption of the whole world. As I have written elsewhere:

> The primary question for the Methodist is not, am I saved? The ultimate question is, for what purpose am I saved? For the Wesleys, the answer was clear. My neighbor is the goal of my redemption, just as the life, death and resurrection of Christ are oriented toward the salvation of all humanity.[17]

"Benevolence," for the Wesleys, consisted in all efforts to realize God's shalom in the life of the world. This mission, this good-will toward our fellow-creatures, this ministry of reconciliation, this benevolence manifests itself in particular ways in the Wesleyan tradition, but none more distinctive than outreach to the marginalized and resistance to injustice, both actions expressed through works of mercy that bear witness to God's rule over life.[18] "The first Methodists, who intended to revive the life of the original Christian church," as Tore Meistad attempted to demonstrate, "made a just distribution of economic, educational, and medical resources their top priority. This is evident in John Wesley's sermons as well as in Charles's hymns."[19]

THE MISSION-CHURCH PARADIGM REFLECTED IN CHARLES WESLEY'S HYMNS

Methodism was born in song, and the followers of the Wesleys learned their theology—that is to say, they discovered their missional vocation—by singing it.[20] Mission-church images pervade the hymn corpus of Charles Wesley. Even the most famous of all the hymns, "O for a Thousand Tongues to Sing," is nothing other than a mission manifesto, calling all believers "To spread through all the earth abroad/The honors of thy name."[21] Another favorite hymn reminds all singers of their responsibility before God:

> *A charge to keep I have,*
> *A God to glorify,*
> *A never-dying soul to save,*
> *And fit it for the sky;*

To serve the present age,
My calling to fulfil;
O may it all my powers engage
To do my Master's will.[22]

These words communicate an extremely important principle: God has chosen the faithful for service, not to privilege, and the primary vocation of Jesus' disciples is "to serve the present age" by bearing the Gospel in word and deed to everyone, everywhere. Jesus' disciples are called to use all their gifts, all their powers, to declare the amazing love of God to all.

In one of the great Trinitarian hymns included in John and Charles Wesley's *Hymns on the Lord's Supper*, the singer beseeches God:

Claim me for Thy service, claim
All I have and all I am.

Take my soul and body's powers,
Take my memory, mind, and will,
All my goods, and all my hours,
All I know, and all I feel,
All I think, and speak, and do;
Take my heart—but make it new.[23]

The disciple of Christ asks the Three-One God to claim every aspect of his or her life in an oblation that can only be described as covenantal. In typical Wesleyan fashion, a series of "alls" characterizes the plea. All I have, all I am, all my goods, all my hours, all I know, feel, think, speak, and do. The all-encompassing sacrifice of self—the offer of one's whole being in service to God—rests secure, as Charles makes abundantly clear throughout, on the foundation of a heart transformed by God's prevenient action. One can hear echoes of the baptismal covenant, perhaps, in Charles's use of language. The sacrament of baptism, of course, is that place where discipleship begins, that event in which God claims each person as God's own. It also signals the commitment of the individual and the community to God's mission. Baptism establishes the mission-church and the sacrament of Holy Communion sustains it. The ambiance of many Wesley hymns elicits a profoundly missiological vision of Christian community and engagement with the dominion of God in the *unite Lin service*

world. In hymns like these, Charles Wesley cultivated a profound vision of servant vocation modeled after that of Jesus—a missional conception of Christian discipleship summarized tersely in the simple phrase: "Claim me for Thy service."

Charles Wesley goes to great lengths to specify the character of this Christian service.[24] In the practice of mission, the servant simply offers to others what he or she has freely received from God. "This only thing do I require," sings Christ's co-missioned disciple, "Freely what I receive to give, The servant of thy church to live."[25] Servants, in other words, engage in an evangelistic mission in life—offering God's grace to all in word and deed. The unique feature of Wesley's vision, however, is the way in which he connects the sharing of grace with the restoration of the mind of Christ in the believer. In a composite hymn, opening with a lyrical paraphrase of "Jesus and the woman at the well" (John 4:10–15), Wesley conjoins the "mind" of Philippians 2 with the "action" of James 1, yet another important conjunction in his missional vision:

> *Thy mind throughout my life be shown,*
> *While listening to the wretch's cry,*
> *The widow's and the orphan's groan,*
> *On mercy's wings I swiftly fly*
> *The poor and helpless to relieve,*
> *My life, my all for them to give.*[26]

To have the mind of Christ, in other words, is to care for the poor.

> *Happy soul, whose active love*
> *emulates the Blessed above,*
> *in thy every action seen,*
> *sparkling from the soul within:*

> *Thou to every sufferer nigh,*
> *hearest, not in vain, the cry*
> *of widow in distress,*
> *of the poor, the shelterless:*

> *Raiment thou to all that need,*
> *to the hungry dealest bread,*

to the sick givest relief,
soothest hapless prisoner's grief:

Love, which willest all should live,
Love, which all to all would give,
Love, that over all prevails,
Love, that never, never fails.
Love immense, and unconfined,
Love to all of humankind.[27]

Notice in particular Wesley's language of "active love." A disciple with a living faith is the one whose whole heart has been renewed, who longs to radiate the whole image of God in his or her life *and therefore* hears the cry of the poor and wills, with God, that all should truly live! The Wesleyan vision of mission, thus understood, is a *life*, not just an act, that unites piety and mercy, worship and compassion, prayer and justice. It involves a humble walk with the Lord that is lived out daily in kindness and justice. Healing those who were sick, liberating those who were oppressed, empowering those who stood on the margins of life, and caring for the poor, it must always be remembered, characterized Jesus' mission and models that mission to which all are called in his name.

S T Kimbrough, Jr., articulates the essence of this missional vision succinctly: "to be emptied of everything but love is what it means to serve a God who in Christ was emptied of all but love."[28] Those who are truly servants of Christ in the world, and those communities that redis-cover what it means to be a mission-church, empty themselves, like Jesus, and find their greatest reward in the realization of God's dream of shalom for all. Certainly, the fundamental vision of Christian mission is being sent to continue and participate in that movement of God toward humanity that began with the mission or sending of Christ and the Holy Spirit. The Wesleys and their followers realized that this is a mission of global proportions.

This Wesleyan vision of a "mission-church paradigm" offers much to a church needing to rediscover the central place of evangelism and mission as constitutive practices of the whole people of God. While evangelism includes all of those activities that draw others in, mission reaches out to all, and particularly to those dear to God's heart who are most vulnerable and in need. In imitation of Christ, a mission-church woos others into the loving embrace of God and then helps them to see that their mission in life, in partnership with Christ, is to be the signposts of God's reign in this world. In his hymn "For a Preacher of the Gospel," Charles Wesley reminds us of this transforming call of God upon our lives:

I would the precious time redeem
And longer live for this alone,
To spend and to be spent for them
Who have not yet my Saviour known:
Fully on these my mission prove,
And only breathe to breathe thy love.[29]

NOTES

1. I have discussed the centrality of this "mission-church" theme related to the Wesleyan heritage elsewhere. This essay is based, in large measure, upon these previous publications and addresses, including *Recapturing the Wesleys' Vision: An Introduction to the Faith of John and Charles Wesley* (Downers Grove, Ill.: InterVarsity Press, 2004), esp. chap. 7; *The Wesleyan Tradition: A Paradigm for Renewal* (Nashville: Abingdon Press, 2002); "Evangelistic Practices of the Wesleyan Revival," in *Methodist Evangelism: Wesleyan Mission*, ed. Laceye Warner, *Equipping Global Ministry: Wesleyan Studies Project* (Washington: Wesley Theological Seminary, forthcoming); "Servants of Shalom in the World," *Covenant Discipleship Quarterly* 18, no. 3 (Summer 2003): pp. 1–2; "Emergent and Wesleyan Christians in Conversation," address to the Annual Meeting of the Academy for Evangelism in Theological Education, Ashland Theological Seminary, October 2007; and "'Claim Me for Thy Service': Charles Wesley's Vision of Servant Vocation," address to the Wesley Studies Working Group, Oxford Institute of Methodist Theological Studies, Christ Church, Oxford, August 2007.

2. This vision is consonant with a contemporary missiological consensus summarized in the term *missio Dei*, or the "mission of God." As Darrell Guder has argued, "mission is the result of God's initiative, rooted in God's purposes to restore and heal creation" (Darrell L. Guder, ed., *Missional Church: A Vision for the Sending of the Church in North America* [Grand Rapids: William B. Eerdmans, 1998], p. 4).

3. See the discussion of John Wesley's understanding of prevenient grace in Randy Maddox, *Responsible Grace: John Wesley's Practical Theology* (Nashville: Kingswood Books, 1994), pp. 83–84. Of particular interest is Wesley's sermon "The Promise of Understanding," in which he expounds how "we cannot know till hereafter how God works [graciously] in many cases which are daily before our eyes." See *Sermons IV*, ed. Albert C. Outler, vol. 4 of *The Bicentennial Edition of the Works of John Wesley* (Nashville: Abingdon Press, 1976–), pp. 281–91. Hereafter cited as *Works*, vol. 4.

4. It is important to note that the Wesleys made this discovery without ever using this more contemporary language concerning it. The words "mission" and "evangelism" hardly ever appear in the Wesleyan corpus, but the Wesleyan Revival was at once profoundly missional and evangelistic in nature. David Bebbington has argued that one of the "striking symptoms of discontinuity" between the Evangelical Revival under the Wesleys and the previous two centuries was "a new emphasis on mission." The impetus for this development, in some measure, was the triumph of Wesleyan Arminian theology over entrenched Calvinism by the end of the eighteenth century. See David Bebbington, *Evangelicalism in Modern Britain: A History from the 1730s to the 1980s* (Grand Rapids: Baker Book House, 1989), p. 40.

5. See John Wesley's "Thoughts Upon God's Sovereignty," in *The Works of the Rev. John Wesley, M.A.*, ed. Thomas Jackson, 14 vols. (London: Mason, 1829–31), vol. 10, pp. 361–63.

6. For an interesting discussion of the interface of God's mission and God's triune being, see John Wesley's sermon, "On the Discoveries of Faith," in *Works*, 4, pp. 29–38.

7. John and Charles Wesley, *Hymns and Sacred Poems* (London: William Strahan, 1739), p. 178.

8. I explore this "conjunctive methodology" in *Recapturing the Wesleys' Vision*, where I identify eight primary syntheses, including faith and works, Word and Spirit, personal and social, form and power, heart and head, pulpit and table, Christ and culture, and piety and mercy. Cf. Kenneth J. Collins, *The Theology of John Wesley: Holy Love and the Shape of Grace* (Nashville: Abingdon Press, 2007) where the author employs essentially the same interpretive framework.

9. Franz Hildebrant and Oliver A. Beckerlegge, eds., *The Works of John Wesley, Volume 7, A Collection of Hymns for the Use of the People Called Methodists* (Oxford: Clarendon Press, 1983), p. 698. Hereafter cited as *Works*, vol. 7.

10. Quoted in Chilcote, *Recapturing the Wesleys' Vision*, 47; from John Wesley's *Plain Account of Genuine Christianity*, 6.1.6.

11. Rupert Davies, ed., *The Works of John Wesley, Volume 9: The Methodist Societies, History, Nature, and Design* (Nashville: Abingdon Press, 1989), p. 3.

12. Mike Henderson has identified eight major principles that led to the success of Wesley's system, all of which have missiological import: (1) human nature is perfectible by God's grace; (2) learning comes by doing the will of God; (3) mankind's nature is perfected by participation in groups, not by acting as isolated individuals; (4) the spirit and practice of primitive Christianity can and must be recaptured; (5) human progress will occur if people will participate in "the means of grace"; (6) the Gospel must be presented to the poor; (7) social evil is not to be "resisted," but overcome by good; and (8) the primary function of spiritual/educational leadership is to equip others to lead and minister, not to perform the ministry personally. See *John Wesley's Class Meeting: A Model for Making Disciples* (Nappanee, Ind.: Francis Asbury Press, 1997), pp. 127–60.

13. See Dana L. Robert, *Evangelism as the Heart of Mission*, Mission Evangelism Series, Number 1 (New York: General Board of Global Ministries, The United Methodist Church, 1997).

14. *Works*, vol. 4, p. 196. Emphasis added.

15. See the exceptional study of Tore Meistad, "The Missiology of Charles Wesley: An Introduction," *Proceedings of The Charles Wesley Society* 5 (1998):

pp. 37–60. "Because Wesleyan soteriology begins in the creation and ends in the new creation," he observes, "the transformation of the person becomes a part of the transformation of the entire cosmos (see Col. 1:15–23; see Rom. 8:33–39)" (p. 49). In his examination of "The Messianic Kingdom and the Year of Jubilee," Meistad argues that the concept of "jubilee" shaped the common life of the early Christian community, leading them to share resources and care for the poor. The early Methodists modeled their lives after this pattern.

16. John Wesley, *Sermons III,* ed. Albert C. Outler, vol. 3 of *The Bicentennial Edition of the Works of John Wesley,* (Nashville: Abingdon Press, 1976–), p. 336. Emphasis added. Cf. Wesley's discussion of Paul's conception of "neighbor love" in his exposition of 1 Corinthians 13:1–3, in which he observes: "such a love of our neighbour as can only spring from the love of God. And whence does this love of God flow? Only from that faith which is of the operation of God; which whoever has, has a direct evidence that 'God was in Christ, reconciling the world unto himself'" (*Works,* vol. 3, p. 295).

17. Chilcote, *Recapturing the Wesleys' Vision,* p. 101.

18. For a helpful discussion of "works of mercy" and their intimate connection to mission, see Rebekah Miles, "Works of Mercy as Spiritual Formation: Why Wesley Feared for the Souls of the Rich," in *The Wesleyan Tradition: A Paradigm for Renewal,* ed. Paul W. Chilcote (Nashville: Abingdon Press, 2002), pp. 98–110.

19. Meistad, "The Missiology of Charles Wesley," p. 51.

20. See *Works,* vol. 7, p. 1. Not enough research has been devoted to the topic of how Christian hymnody shapes, or misshapes, mission theology. Certainly, there have been periods in the history of the church in which "mission hymns" have encouraged a triumphalist model of Christian mission. How choral traditions, from "praise songs" to "classic hymns," form the attitudes of believers today with regard to mission remains a major area of concern. It is a part of my argument that the Wesley hymns helped to form a missional vision among the early Methodist people and inculcated healthy practices that balanced evangelism and mission, physical and spiritual concern, warm-hearted faith and compassionate engagement for justice in the world.

21. See the incisive analysis of the entire hymn by Tore Meistad in "The Missiology of Charles Wesley," 52–55. S T Kimbrough, Jr., observes that stanzas often omitted from contemporary hymnals "fuse praise with mission and remind us of the inclusiveness of the Gospel" (S T Kimbrough, Jr., *A Heart to Praise My God: Wesley Hymns for Today* [Nashville: Abingdon Press, 1996], p. 143).

22. *Works,* vol. 7, p. 465.

23. John and Charles Wesley, *Hymns on the Lord's Supper* (Bristol: Farley, 1745), 155: pp. 3–4.

24. The limited space of this essay does not permit elaboration of these particular areas of service. Suffice it to say that texts such as Luke 4:16–19 and Matthew 25:31–46 establish something of a template for mission service in the world. In many of Charles Wesley's lyrical eulogies for Methodist women, these images figure prominently as he celebrates the legacy of their mission in God's world. See in particular *The Journal of the Rev. Charles Wesley, M.A.,* 2 vols., ed. Thomas Jackson (London: John Mason, 1849), vol. 2, pp. 323–98.

25. *Works,* vol. 7, p. 101.

26. Ibid., p. 522.

27. S T Kimbrough, Jr., ed., *Songs for the Poor* (New York: General Board of

Global Ministries, The United Methodist
Church, 1997), Hymn 1.

28. S T Kimbrough, Jr., *"Kenosis* in the
Nativity Hymns of Ephrem the Syrian
and Charles Wesley," in *Orthodox and*

Wesleyan Spirituality, ed. S T Kimbrough,
Jr. (Crestwood, N.Y.: St. Vladimir's
Seminary Press, 2002), p. 283.

29. *Works,* vol. 7, p. 597.

BIBLIOGRAPHY

Chilcote, Paul W. "Evangelistic Practices
of the Wesleyan Revival." In *Methodist
Evangelism: Wesleyan Mission*, ed. by
Laceye Warner. *Equipping Global
Ministry: Wesleyan Studies Project.*
Washington: Wesley Theological
Seminary, (forthcoming).

———. *Recapturing the Wesleys' Vision: An
Introduction to the Faith of John and
Charles Wesley.* Downers Grove, Ill.:
InterVarsity Press, 2004.

———. *The Study of Evangelism: Exploring
a Missional Practice of the Church.* Co-
edited with Laceye Warner. Grand
Rapids: Wm. B. Eerdmans, 2008.

———. *The Wesleyan Tradition: A Paradigm
for Renewal.* Nashville: Abingdon Press,
2002.

Guder, Darrell L., ed. *Missional Church: A
Vision for the Sending of the Church in
North America.* Grand Rapids: William B.
Eerdmans, 1998.

Kennedy, Gerald H. *Heritage and Destiny:
Wesley Commemorative Volume on the
Evangelistic World Mission of Methodism.*
New York: Board of Missions of the
Methodist Church, 1953.

Meistad, Tore. "The Missiology of Charles
Wesley: An Introduction." *Proceedings of
The Charles Wesley Society* 5 (1998):
pp. 37–60.

Padgett, Alan G., ed. *The Mission of the
Church in Methodist Perspective: The World
is My Parish.* Studies in the History of
Missions. Lewiston, N.Y.: Edwin Mellen
Press, 1992.

Robert, Dana L. *Evangelism as the Heart of
Mission.* Mission Evangelism Series,
Number 1. New York: General Board
of Global Ministries, The United
Methodist Church, 1997.

15

MOVEMENT AND INSTITUTION IN METHODIST MISSIONS

The Case of Clara Swain Hospital in Bareilly, India

Arun W. Jones

When you come out of the railway station in the sleepy city of Bareilly, located in the densely populated state of Uttar Pradesh in India, you can ask any *rickshawalla,* or driver of a rickshaw, to take you to the "Mishan Aspitaal," and for 10 rupees (15 or 20 if you are a foreigner) he will take you straight down Station Road to the Civil Lines, and make a left into the capacious compound that houses the Clara Swain Hospital, one of the oldest Methodist institutions in India.[1] Currently an establishment of The Methodist Church in India, the hospital has fallen on hard times, and the most obvious and ominous sign of its dire difficulties is the lack of patients.[2] Most of the wards are empty; on any given day, there are five to six patients for a staff of one hundred and thirty.[3]

The reasons for the abysmal state of this once proud institution—the first hospital for women in Asia—are many and varied. They include previous mismanagement and financial misappropriation; rapid turnover of hospital administrators and doctors; an aging and costly infrastructure; poor quality of health care provided; church officials who have no desire to infuse the church's institutions with life and energy; and a profusion of other clinics and hospitals in Bareilly that give ordinary Indians a great deal of choice in medical care. A few decades ago, Methodist hospitals all over northern India could count on a stream of patients coming for very good, compassionate, and financially reasonable medical treatment. Today this stream has virtually dried up: the reputation of most Methodist mission hospitals, at least in Uttar Pradesh, has been badly tarnished due to poor service and administration, while a host of other medical establishments, most of them run for profit, vie for the patronage of a burgeoning population.[4] Despite the concerted efforts and unflagging good will of a few individuals, the Clara Swain Hospital, like many other Methodist hospitals and schools in India, has become an institution with little life left in its aging structures.

It is easy to jump to the conclusion that the problem with failing religious institutions is that they are institutions rather than religious. In this kind of thinking, the idea of religion is inextricably connected to the idea of movement: Christianity is first and foremost about spirit-filled action, motion, and energy; it is not about committee meetings, business agendas, and administrative reports. Institutions are at best a concession to living in a fallen world—so this thinking goes—and they perpetually threaten to waylay religious people from their real work in life.[5] It is easy to point to the life of Jesus Christ, who was constantly criticizing the religious establishment of his day and who established no religious institution himself, in order to support such a view of religious life. What such thinking forgets is that religious movements can be just as tyrannical and destructive as religious institutions. Indeed we live in a world today where a number of religious movements, eschewing religious institutions, are creating a good deal of havoc with their spirit-filled action, motion, and energy.

MAX WEBER ON MOVEMENTS AND INSTITUTIONS

One of the earliest and most enduring modern theories delineating the relationship between movement and institution was proposed by the German sociologist Max Weber (1864–1920). Weber claimed that there were three basic types of legitimate authority among human beings: legal authority with a bureaucratic administrative staff; traditional authority based on ancient rules and powers handed down through the generations; and charismatic authority found in a person who "is considered extraordinary and treated as endowed with supernatural, superhuman, or at least specifically exceptional powers or qualities."[6] The religious movement founded and led by Jesus of Nazareth would thus rest on the charismatic authority of its leader, as would the religious movements founded by Muhammad and Siddhartha. Invariably in charismatic movements a problem arises, says Weber, when the original charismatic figure's (earthly) life is over, and the community founded on charismatic authority needs to decide upon succession of leadership and upon the way it will make its life in the world.[7] Without such arrangements for succession and for regularized quotidian living, of course, the charismatic movement will simply die out. The community that has heretofore ordered itself according to charismatic authority then needs to find ways to order its life based on legal authority or traditional authority. In so doing, it founds institutions to order its life: something that was not a feature of the community when the charismatic figure was still alive on earth.

However much one agrees or disagrees with Weber's typology, I believe he does alert us to the fact that the inevitable process of going from movement to institution does not entail the necessary downfall or corruption of a religious community. Certainly, there are things that a movement can do that an institution cannot: a movement can be appropriately critical of the status quo; it can breathe new life and energy into a community or society; it can sharply refocus people's attention on the true purpose and meaning of their lives. On the other hand, institutions can do things that movements cannot: an institution can perpetuate the energy and force of a movement for future generations; it can help people decide how to live faithfully when the original charismatic leader is gone; it can expand the original charismatic community to include ordinary people who must live in the everyday world of family, society, business, and politics.

INSTITUTIONALIZATION IN MISSION HISTORY

Good examples of the beginning phases of institutionalization are found in the Book of Acts. In chapter 6, because of problems in the community, seven leaders are elected to take care of some daily chores (although this is not all that they do); it is interesting that once this institution for service—later called the diaconate—is created, Luke tells us in verse 7 that "the number of the disciples increased greatly in Jerusalem." Organization was followed by an expansion of the community. Then in chapter 15, what becomes the institution of a general church council is organized to decide whether Gentiles need to be circumcised in order to gain entry into the movement founded by Jesus of Nazareth. The decision allows the entry of a completely foreign group of people into the community, and the Christian religion (Acts 11:26) is born because Greeks are grafted into the Jewish movement. Again, institutionalization led to the growth of the community, probably in ways never imagined by the Jerusalem Council.[8]

John Wesley was keenly aware of the need for institutions to perpetuate and expand his movement. It has been said that the reason that John Wesley's long-term impact on Christianity was far more profound than the impact of his famous contemporary George Whitefield is that Wesley knew how to organize people. The Methodist movement was not simply a movement of strangely warmed hearts: it was a movement of institutions such as class meetings, annual conferences, and an itinerating group of preachers accountable to a superintendent. We must also not forget John and Charles Wesley's generally strong belief in the necessity of the institutions of the Church of England. For example, John Wesley urged his followers to partake of Holy Communion as often as possible, and this could only be done at the parish church.

As the Methodist movement expanded across the globe, at first most significantly in the United States of America, the spread of the Methodist movement and the spread of Methodist institutions continued to go hand in hand. Itinerancy, episcopacy, annual and general conferences were the bedrock institutions on which American Methodism was founded and flourished, but schools, hospitals, orphanages, and other institutions necessary for society soon followed. Far from being distractions to the purposes of Wesley's movement, institutions such as Methodist schools and hospitals were vital expressions of Methodism. They were the fruit of the movement, providing not only goodly nourishment to its followers and others, but also providing the seeds for future Methodist growth, energy, and expansion. From its earliest days, then, Methodism linked movement and institution together in inextricable ways.

THE FORMATION OF A METHODIST MEDICAL
INSTITUTION IN BAREILLY

The Clara Swain Hospital in Bareilly is a good example of how missionary institutions were an integral part of the missionary movement.[9] Dr. Clara Swain (1834–1910), the first woman missionary doctor, came to work in Bareilly in 1870 due to a newly formed Methodist institution—the Woman's Foreign Missionary Society of the

Methodist Episcopal Church.[10] The idea for this society originated with two Methodist missionary wives: Mrs. Clementina (Rowe) Butler, who with her husband had started the Methodist mission in India and served in North India from 1856 to 1865, and Mrs. Lois (Lee) Parker, who went out with her husband to North India in 1859 and served into the twentieth century.[11] The Butlers had been living in the Boston suburb of Chelsea since 1865, where Clementina went about raising interest among women for foreign missions. In 1869, during a furlough, the Parkers visited the Butlers in the Boston area, and the two women decided to organize a Methodist women's mission society.

The Woman's Foreign Missionary Society of the Methodist Episcopal Church (WFMS) was organized on the stormy day of March 23, 1869, by eight Methodist women in the Tremont Street Church in Boston. The following week twenty-six women gathered, adopted a constitution, and elected officers. The purpose of the society was "to engage and unite the efforts of the women of the Methodist Episcopal Church in sending out and supporting female missionaries, native Christian teachers, and Bible readers in foreign lands."[12] Within two months, the women had also established a newsletter, negotiated with the male officers of the Methodist Board of Missions—many of whom were skeptical of the Society's ambitious aims—appointed Isabella Thoburn and Clara Swain (a teacher and a medical doctor) to India, and adopted a Bible woman in India.[13] A thriving, soon to be large and powerful, mission institution had been born.[14]

When Dr. Clara Swain arrived in Bareilly in 1870, she immediately began to treat women and children. Many of her patients came to her missionary bungalow. Others she visited in their homes in Bareilly. Due to customs regarding social segregation of upper caste Indian women and men, a number of the women that Dr. Swain treated would not otherwise have been able to gain access to a doctor trained in Western medicine, since all European and American doctors serving in India were male. Clara Swain was a member of the pioneering generation of women doctors in the United States of America—women physicians who had to endure ridicule, harassment, and ostracism from their society and the all-male medical establishment until they were able to prove their equality and worth. In India, in fact, Dr. Clara Swain dealt with a society that was far more receptive and appreciative of her professional skills than was American society where her sister physicians were struggling to be given a chance to practice. At the end of her first year in Bareilly, Dr. Clara Swain's records show that she "had treated 70 families, visited in 250 homes of the city, prescribed for 1,225 patients at the mission house."[15]

Even that first year, it seems, she started dreaming of building a woman's hospital and medical school. The dream, however, was not simply an American one; it was an Indian government official who had first given voice to the idea of a woman's hospital in Bareilly.[16] The next year, the Nawab of Rampur, the Muslim ruler of a princely state close to Bareilly, donated 40 acres of his land with a mansion in Bareilly to the Methodist mission so that a hospital could be built.[17] In less than a fortnight, on January 1, 1872, Clara Swain and a missionary colleague, Fannie Sparkes, moved into the mansion and started using it for living and working quarters. That same month they proposed to the Methodist annual conference meeting in Moradabad that a new dispensary be constructed, with an examination room, an operating room, an office, a lecture room for a medical class, and two bathrooms. The conference approved her plans, as it did the next year when she brought in more plans for more buildings.

Within four years of arriving in India, Clara Swain had harnessed the material and moral resources of Indians and Americans to build the first hospital for women in Asia, a medical institution not only for treatment but also for teaching.[18] A hundred years after its founding, the Clara Swain Hospital (renamed in the missionary's honor by 1920)[19] was a 260-bed medical center, often crowded with over 300 patients, with a nursing school, a baby fold, a number of specialty wards, and some of the most up-to-date medical equipment in India. Of course, by 1970 almost all of the personnel of the hospital were Indian, the energetic and visionary super-intendent being Dr. Ernest Sundaram.[20]

CONTEMPORARY PROBLEMS AND POSSIBILITIES

The current decline of Clara Swain Hospital started in the late 1970s, and there is no sign that the institution has reached its nadir. It is certainly within the realm of possibility that the land and hospital will be sold off to some local entrepreneur, to develop as he or she sees fit. Most likely it would cease then to function as a Christian institution, and it may not even continue to function as a medical institution. How can one begin to diagnose the malaise of this once proud and vibrant church establishment?

It is interesting that Max Weber categorizes social groups according to the type of leadership they consider legitimate: legal, traditional, or charismatic. For him, the kind of authority or leadership is the key to understanding human communities and societies. In a completely different vein, when I asked North Indian Methodists about the problems of church institutions (including the institutional church), many of them also pointed to leadership as the critical issue. An examination of leadership, then, may be one of the important keys to understanding the plight of dysfunctional church institutions.

If one compares the Clara Swain Hospital to the few Methodist institutions in Uttar Pradesh that are doing well—for example the Isabella Thoburn College for women and the Nur Manzil Psychiatric Centre, both in Lucknow—one sees immediately what is desperately needed for the medical center: the highest caliber of leadership. This leadership needs to possess vision for the future; a thorough knowledge of planning and practical matters, so that the vision may be implemented; energy to harness resources from a variety of national and international sources; charisma to inspire others to follow her or his vision; wisdom to deal with a rapidly changing social, economic, and cultural context, as well as a highly politicized ecclesiastical context; unshakable integrity to withstand severe ecclesiastical and secular pressures to compromise one's moral standards; and a deep Christian spirituality to hold these qualities together. It is interesting that both movements and institutions often rise and fall because of the same factor: the quality of their leadership. Both movements and institutions need good leadership in ordinary times, and outstanding leadership in critical times, if they are to be signs and participants in the work of the kingdom of God.

One of the important reasons that Christians study history is to provide vision and hope for the future. So lest we despair, we should note that the current crisis in Clara Swain Hospital is not unprecedented. When Drs. Charles and Wilma Perrill arrived in Bareilly in December of 1939 to begin their work at the hospital, the missionary-run institution was also in dire straits.

> The prospect was discouraging. There were the old white pillared out-patient building which Dr. Clara Swain had built in 1873, the long lines of brick buildings containing eighty beds for patients, perhaps thirty of them in actual use. None of the buildings had been whitewashed for several years.

There were the nurses' hostel, the bungalows for the women doctors and the nursing supervisors. The one reserved for them was more like a barn than a bungalow, with its big bare living room and its ceilings 19 feet high. The servants' quarters, teeming with children, goats and chickens, were just behind their garden in the rear. . . . During previous years doctors and nurses had come and gone with disheartening regularity, with overwork, sickness, furloughs, and matrimony constantly depleting the ranks.[21]

Yet Charles and Wilma Perrill, over the next two decades, provided the vital leadership necessary for a powerful renaissance of the Clara Swain Hospital. Their vision, energy, and integrity propelled the hospital into a new era, when some of the finest Indian doctors came to Bareilly to train and work, and the hospital continued to thrive, flourish, and grow under Indian leadership and supervision. For Methodists at least, there is no reason why powerful life-giving movements cannot take place within institutions.

NOTES

1. The Government of India has estimated that there are over 190 million persons in Uttar Pradesh in the year 2008; *cf.* "Census of India" at http://www.censusindia.gov.in.

2. These observations are based on a personal visit in July of 2008, when I toured the hospital and talked with a number of persons in Bareilly and elsewhere who have knowledge of the hospital's current state as well as its history. The research trip to India was funded by a generous sabbatical grant from the Luce Foundation.

3. Statistics are from the Christian Medical Association of India.

4. Some Christian hospitals continue to hold stellar reputations in India, for example the Christian Medical College in Vellore and the Christian Medical College in Ludhiana. In Uttar Pradesh, the Nur Manzil Psychiatric Centre, an institution of the Methodist Church of India, is also an example of a well run and respected

medical facility.

5. See, for example, David J. Bosch, *Transforming Mission* (Maryknoll, N.Y.: Orbis Books, 1991), pp. 50–53; also Darrell L. Guder, ed., *Missional Church* (Grand Rapids: Eerdmans, 1998), p. 252, where a distinction is made between "institutionalized church" and "missional connectedness."

6. Max Weber, *Economy and Society*, ed. Guenther Roth and Claus Wittich (Berkeley: University of California Press, 1978), pp. 212–301; quote from p. 241.

7. Weber discusses this in the section on "The Routinization of Charisma," *Economy and Society*, pp. 246*ff*.

8. One can make the valid case that organization of a movement and institutionalization are two different kinds of activities. I would argue that organizational structures that later become codified into permanent structures (either bureaucratic or traditional, if one uses Weberian terms) are the beginning of

institutions. So although the later diaconate looks different from what Stephen and his cohorts are asked to do, and later ecumenical councils of the church look somewhat different from the Jerusalem Council, the origins of later institutional structures can indeed be found in the necessary organization of the Christian movement.

9. In this I agree with the thesis of Jeffrey Cox, who argues that to understand missionaries in India one must look to the institutions they started and ran. Jeffrey Cox, *Imperial Fault Lines: Christianity and Colonial Power in India, 1818–1940* (Stanford, Calif.: Stanford University Press, 2002).

10. See Dana L. Robert, *American Women in Mission* (Macon, Ga.: Mercer University Press, 1996), pp. 135–37 for a good brief account of the founding of the WFMS. Also see Dorothy Clarke Wilson, *Palace of Healing* (New York: McGraw-Hill Book Company, 1968), pp. 3–12.

11. For the Butlers, see Gerald H. Anderson, ed., *Biographical Dictionary of Christian Missions* (New York: Simon & Schuster Macmillan, 1998), p. 104; for the Parkers, see John N. Hollister, *The Centenary of the Methodist Church in Southern Asia* (Lucknow, India: The Lucknow Publishing House of The Methodist Church in Southern Asia, 1956), pp. xxvii, 243–45.

12. Quoted in Wilson, *Palace of Healing*, p. 8.

13. Robert, *American Women in Mission*, p. 138.

14. The birth and development of the WFMS is a good example of how organized movements become institutions.

15. Wilson, *Palace of Healing*, p. 36.

16. Wilson, *Palace of Healing*, pp. 33–34.

17. Wilson, *Palace of Healing*, pp. 40–43.

18. Wilson, *Palace of Healing*, pp. 44–48.

19. Wilson, *Palace of Healing*, p. 90. It is interesting that Clara Swain herself had proposed that the hospital be named in honor of its first donor, the Nawab of Rampur (Wilson, *Palace of Healing*, p. 43).

20. Wilson, *Palace of Healing*, p. 227*ff*.

21. Wilson, *Palace of Healing*, p. 106.

BIBLIOGRAPHY

Anderson, Gerald H., ed. *Biographical Dictionary of Christian Missions*. New York: Simon & Schuster Macmillan, 1998.

Bosch, David J. *Transforming Mission*. Maryknoll, N.Y.: Orbis Books, 1991.

Cox, Jeffrey. *Imperial Fault Lines: Christianity and Colonial Power in India, 1818–1940*. Stanford, Calif.: Stanford University Press, 2002.

Guder, Darrell L., ed. *Missional Church*. Grand Rapids: Eerdmans, 1998.

Hollister, John N. *The Centenary of the Methodist Church in Southern Asia*. Lucknow, India: The Lucknow Publishing House of the Methodist Church in Southern Asia, 1956.

Robert, Dana L. *American Women in Mission*. Macon, Ga.: Mercer University Press, 1996.

Weber, Max. *Economy and Society*, ed. Guenther Roth and Claus Wittich. Berkeley: University of California Press, 1970.

Wilson, Dorothy Clark. *Palace of Healing*. New York: McGraw-Hill Book Company, 1968.

16

SUM OF THE PARTS

THE LEGACY OF J. WASKOM PICKETT

Arthur G. McPhee

The portraiture of world mission in the Wesleyan spirit is wide-ranging. It takes in colorful stories of evangelists, relief coordinators, healthcare paladins, capacity builders, educators, researchers, theorists, strategists, administrators, diplomats, and old-time heroes. Jarrell Waskom Pickett (1890–1981) was, in various combinations, all of these. More than that, he seemed to pull off each concatenation with aplomb.[1]

Raised in Wilmore, Kentucky, Pickett was from the beginning a wunderkind. At age four, he was reading fluently; at six, he advanced from kindergarten to fourth grade in one day; at seven, he was translating the Greek New Testament; at thirteen, he was in college; at seventeen, he got a masters degree; at nineteen, he was professor of Greek and Latin at Taylor University, the third school at which he had taught. Then, at twenty, he began a remarkable forty-six-year missionary sojourn in India.

Within the bounds of American Holiness sensibilities, omnifarious interests and multifarious pursuits were the rule in Pickett's childhood home. His father, Leander Lycurgus Pickett (1859–1928) was a minister, evangelist, debater, songwriter, author, editor, publisher, financial officer, vice presidential candidate, and, as his gravestone avows, "Patriot." His mother, Ludie Carrington Day Pickett (1867–1953) was a homemaker, college English teacher, musician, hymnist, author, editor, temperance organizer, and speechmaker at the 1928 Democratic National Convention in Houston (she opposed the nomination of Al Smith).

Steeped in the Wesleyan Holiness ethos of his alma mater, Asbury College, Pickett was a lifelong Methodist. When, in 1910, he sailed for India, it was as a missionary of the Board of Foreign Missions of the Methodist Episcopal Church. He would minister there as a Methodist elder, editor, and bishop. When he retired, he would serve for several more years as an international ambassador of the Methodist mission board, as well as a professor at the Methodist's Boston University School of Theology.

MINISTER AND EVANGELIST

As pastor of Lucknow's English church (1910–1914), Pickett's pastoral, administrative, and evangelistic skills, and attention to Anglo-Indians, led to a church flush with new members. Concomitantly, in 1912, he planted a new church. Pitching a *shamiana* (large tent) next to the railway head-quarters at nearby Char Baugh, he began a two-week campaign of open-air preaching. When fifty-eight people, many of them railway workers, became followers of Christ, he followed up with twice-a-month services. So many came that the railway authorities agreed to erect a chapel for sharing with a small Anglican fellowship.

In 1914, Pickett got tuberculosis and went home to die. Isolated on a Florida island, he recovered. In 1916, he married Ruth Robinson, Indian-born daughter of Methodist missionaries in Lucknow. She had just graduated from Northwestern University. The pair sailed for India—to Arrah, Bihar, where there was a small conversion movement of outcaste Chamars. That is where the "Indianization" of Pickett began, where he said he discovered "the real India."

Recognizing his limitations as a Westerner, Pickett learned all he could about village Hindus and Muslims. His relational and organizational apti-tudes led to substantial church growth in the region. Of much help were two Indian colleagues and their wives, Emanuel and Dr. Polly Sukh, and Ishwar and Priavati Dayal; Pickett described them as "the main strength of the church in Shahabad" (the name of the district). Pickett remembered Dayal as "the best all-around village evangelist" he had known during more than four decades in India.

When he began to speak in a village, people from houses all around came close enough to hear him. He talked about favorite gods of Hinduism and always in a way that impressed his hearers and did not offend any of them, despite the fact that he always in a very friendly way introduced a strong Christian thought.[2]

CHAMPION OF HOSPITALS AND HEALING

Pickett's contest with tuberculosis produced an unsated commitment to ministries of healing. This led, *inter alia,* to the establishment and promotion of orphanages, hospitals, community healthcare, and mobile clinics. For example, during the global influenza epidemic of 1918–1919, missionaries would wake to find orphaned infants deposited in desperation on their verandahs. Pickett raised funds for a "babyfold" and personally delivered its first tiny guest. In response, one of those babies would become Pickett's secretary and later receive several graduate degrees and a seminary appointment as a professor of Old Testament.

Throughout his career, Pickett chaired medical association and hospital boards. He recruited doctors and nurses, raised funds for facilities, and secured equipment and supplies, including whole army field hospitals at the end of World War II. His passion for ministries of healing persisted into his retirement, during which he collected more than three million dollars for revitalizing the venerable but senescent hospital and medical college Dr. Edith Mary Brown had established at Ludhiana. According to Dr. Charles Perrill, pioneering surgeon and director of Bareilly's Clara Swain Hospital, "In his day, J. Waskom Pickett advanced Christian medical care in India more than any other individual."[3]

WRITER AND EDITOR

Pickett corresponded prolifically. In one nineteen-day period (a holiday), he wrote 360 letters. His published legacy is equally impressive: an array of articles in church papers and periodicals, scores of editorials from his five-year stint as editor of the *Indian Witness,* chapters in books, entries in dictionaries and encyclopedias, and four impressive volumes relating to the growth of the church. The books were: *Christian Mass Movements in India* (1933), which Donald McGavran would deem "the missiological book of the century," although at the time only a third of the century had come; *Mass Movement Survey Report for Mid-India* (1936), with Donald McGavran and G. H. Singh; *Christ's Way to India's Heart* (1938), a small work but thought by some to be Pickett's best; and *Dynamics of Church Growth* (1963), the initial series in McGavran's annual Church Growth lectureship. He also wrote *The Confirmation of the Gospel* (ca. 1946), but it was never published. It showed how ministries of healing (physical, mental, and spiritual), the transformation of Christians, and the church when at its best corroborate the Gospel.

What led Pickett to think along these lines was the ineffectiveness of his own early preaching. Asbury College had put great emphasis on rhetorical skills. Therefore, when he came to India, it was with, as he put it, "an exaggerated idea of the effectiveness of preaching as an evangelizing force." At first he concluded that he was communicating too much, too rich, too fast, so he simplified his message. However, the plainer he made it, the more firmly his Muslim and Hindu hearers dismissed it. The effect was disillusionment, which slowly led to "the realization . . . that the Gospel that seemed to me so beautiful and appealing was to most of my hearers entirely incredible." Gradually, through reflecting on the benefits of Jesus' routine blending of sermon and sign—often in the form of a cure from some affliction— the necessity of confirming the preaching of the Gospel in actions and Christian character became palpable.

Pickett's writing was always to the point; moreover, there always *was* a point. For example, he was a doughty opponent of social evils. In the influential *Indian Witness*, which he edited from 1925 to 1929, he condemned *sati* (the immolation of widows), caste distinctions, and child marriage as vigorously as John Wesley condemned slavery. When criticized for his forthrightness, he refused to back off.

> There are people . . . who do not like to have social evils in India denounced in a Christian paper edited by a non-Indian. They believe . . . that a Christian from the West should be restrained by the fact that social evils still exist in Western countries. That opinion is utterly repellent to us. We are not in India as Missionaries of Western civilization, nor to preach the morals of Western nations. We recognize no obligation to restrict our preaching in India to such parts of the Christian message as have found full acceptance in some Western land. If we did, we would have nothing to preach.[4]

ADVOCATE FOR WORD AND DEED TOGETHER

Although, as methodological insight, Pickett's notion of Gospel confirmation evolved, in practice he seems to have embraced a holistic approach to mission from the start. His early ministry both in Lucknow and Arrah abounds with examples. His commitment to evangelism, social compassion, and justice were patently of one cloth. Later, in his *Indian Witness* editorials, he spotlighted inhumane working conditions, illiteracy, racism, preventable epidemics, militarism, ethnocentrism, and limited opportunities for women. However, because he regarded the proclamation of the Gospel as equally important, he also pleaded, *inter alia*, for a revival of sapient open-air preaching, using *bhajans* and *gazals* (indigenous songs of praise to God), engaging in purposeful dialogue with those of other faiths, and, above all, reclaiming what he called "Golden Rule Evangelism." By "Golden Rule Evangelism," he meant a commitment to sensitive, nonmanipulative ways of commending Christ—the antipode of proselytism:

> It is a deplorable fact that evangelism has seemed to some people an ugly thing because they have witnessed attempts at it that have not been in harmony with the Golden Rule. It is possible to make truth horrible and charity insulting and evangelism repulsive, but it would be as foolish to turn against evangelism as against truth and charity.[5]

For Pickett, the answer to *bad* evangelism was not *no* evangelism but *good* evangelism—an evangelism that bars pejoratives, refuses to trivialize others' faiths, and abominates ethnic and racial condescension—an evangelism that strives to be as pure an expression as possible of Christ's Golden Rule.

CONTEXTUALIZER

In the pursuit of evangelistic effectiveness and an indigenous church, Pickett urged missionaries and Indian pastors to employ Hindu forms to convey Christian meaning. Thus, in 1925, when Vengal Chakkarai was appealing for funds to build a Christian temple, Pickett's editorial response was positive: "We welcome this proposal as we welcome every action that may draw anyone to Christ and may reveal him more clearly."

However, he cautioned against Hinduising Christians—that is, those who would make Christ into just another Hindu deity.[6]

In his editorials and selection of articles for the *Indian Witness*, Pickett consistently promoted infusing indigenous forms with Christian meaning. With only the proviso that it did not compromise allegiance to Jesus Christ, he lauded creative Christian imagination in the service of naturalizing Christianity. His favorite mantra was, "Love the Lord with all your mind."

Pickett deplored paternalistic attitudes. More than once, he urged getting rid of the "foreign" in missions: "We would like to bury the Board of Foreign Missions and the Women's Foreign Missionary Society," he wrote. "As their successors, and heirs, we would propose a Board of International Missions and the Women's International Missionary Society." He added that the burials should be honorable, with eloquent orations of appreciation, but that the Methodist Church was now American and Indian, and Chinese, German, Swedish, Malaysian, Philippine, Mexican, and Chilean. "The church," he wrote, "is a bond that links countries together and makes for peace and understanding."[7]

Wanting his readers better informed about Indian affairs and culture, Pickett advocated the reading of vernacular newspapers. He had little patience with missionaries who were lackadaisical language learners or were disinclined to read broadly. His own reading ranged from Chinese culture to the poetry of Tilak. As editor of the *Indian Witness*, he published major pieces like Cyril Modak's 17,000-word article on "Hindu Bhakti and Christian Worship," Gertrude V. Tweedie's three-part "Inter-Penetration of Islam and Hinduism in India," and her four-part "The Middle Class Moslem Woman of Lucknow." Inevitably, articles like Modak's brought criticism, but Pickett stood firm. He gave Modak another 2,000 words to respond to critics and personally defended Modak's arguments:

> Mr. Modak has raised issues to which the church must give attention if it is to gain a sympathetic hearing . . . and to help Hindu converts to Christ bring their rich inheritance of spiritual aspiration and discovery into subjection unto Him.[8]

Pickett, however, did not stop with contextualization. Without what he called "the companion of love," efforts to inculturate would be sterile, academic exercises.

RESEARCHER AND THEORIST

In 1928, Pickett wrote an editorial on the need for research in evangelism. More than 80 percent of India's Christians were untouchables, having come into the church via so-called "mass movements." He wanted to see a serious study of these conversion movements. There had been some superficial surveys, but they were more about promoting missions than understanding issues and unearthing insights for evangelization and discipling. For example, although recent Church Missionary Society (CMS) surveys purported to be dispassionate and free from "purple patches of eloquence or emotion," in fact they frequently lapsed into just that, as the following paragraph illustrates:

> Would that we could transport you . . . to the plains of Tinnevelly. There you would see the long lines of laborers, men and women, in the fields—their backs bent, their faces to the soil. It is a parable of their life. As they go to their work, the unimaginably lovely lights of early dawn surround them, but their souls are dark. The singing of birds is heard, but their ears are deaf to the songs of liberty. At evening the flags of sunset stream across the sky and the mountains stand in holy stillness, but not for them![9]

Pickett's plea for research attracted the attention of John R. Mott. In the United States, the Social Survey movement was flourishing. A new kind of survey had come into its own, one that employed combinations of direct observation, interviewing, onsite data gathering through questionnaires and schedules, and data-producing experiments. Mott proposed Pickett lead such a study. Soon thereafter, with the help of the Rockefeller-funded Institute for Social and Religious Research, Pickett directed the first of a series of social surveys of conversion-movement Christians. Based on four thousand interviews that each took an hour to complete, it was the largest social survey ever done outside the U.S. and Great Britain.

Pickett began his research in November of 1930. He published the results, with observations and recommendations, in *Christian Mass Movements in India* (1933). Much of his ideation would find its way into Donald McGavran's Church Growth corpus: (1) the need for research and getting the facts; (2) the importance of giving attention to group—multi-individual—conversions (people movements); (3) the cohesive power of group identity (homogeneity); (4) the mistake of socially dislocating new Christians to mission stations; (5) the foreignness of Western individualism; (6) social lift as a consequence of conversion; (7) the expediency of reallocating resources according to receptivity; (8) critique of the term "mass movement"; (9) the need to avoid foreignness and adopt indigenous forms and symbols in the liturgy and worship of the church; and (10) the focus on the masses as more receptive than the classes.

How many of these concepts were original with Pickett is harder to say—perhaps not many. For example, long before Pickett's day, John Wesley had grasped the principle of allocating resources according to receptivity. Moreover, advocating the use of indigenous forms was certainly no new thing, although, in Pickett's day, he was one of the exceptions in advocating it. Developing missionary strategy from the results of social science investigations was a new thing, however, and Pickett was without question among the pioneers. And certainly, his application to missions thinking of this particular panoply of principles around a core emphasis on group conversions was unique. The sum of the parts in Pickett's panoply was, as McGavran noted in his review of *Christ's Way to India's Heart*, a radically new philosophy of missions, a fresh paradigm.

Besides the data collected, conclusions reached, and ideas garnered, Pickett's study also legitimized enlisting the social sciences. Until then, theology alone mattered. However, with its trove of unearthed data and rich ratiocination, *Christian Mass Movements in India* served as a wake-up call, alerting churches and missions to mistakes of the past—often very destructive ones—and paths to more fruitful evangelization in the future. Hence, the social sciences achieved a new status in evangelistic thinking, planning, and evaluation. Mission personnel and church leaders came to see that research and getting the facts were indispensable for laying bare false assumptions and determining viable trajectories. Until Pickett's work, few saw that potential.

ENTREPRENEUR AND INNOVATOR

Pickett's initiatives and innovations were many and many-colored. Here are two examples, bookends from the beginning and end of his Indian odyssey. In the 1920s, Pickett began sending, to all the Indian newspapers he could find out about, a weekly "clipsheet" of fillers on the dangers of drug and alcohol use. Most of the papers used them! Through the clip-sheet, plus many public addresses and articles, he became a key figure in a national temperance movement that was also supported by Gandhi's noncooperation campaign. In fact, one South Indian politician called Pickett the father of the movement.

More significant missiologically was Pickett's role in founding the United Mission to Nepal (UMN), in which he helped Robert Fleming (an ornithologist) and his wife Bethel Fleming (a medical doctor) secure an invitation from the Nepalese king for a permanent medical mission in that closed land. Although Pickett would serve as its first president, his most important contribution was organizing the mission ecumenically, allowing eight missionary societies working separately along the border of Nepal to come together. That ecumenical spirit was vintage Pickett. "Parties and sects I cast behind," wrote Charles Wesley. Were he alive today, nothing would delight Pickett more than to hear that, fifty years hence, the original eight partners in UMN had grown to thirty-nine, representing eighteen countries, and that wherever the mission had worked, indigenous churches had also emerged.

RELIEF ORGANIZER, DIPLOMAT, AND EDUCATOR

When, in 1947, the British gave India its independence and split off East and West Pakistan, the largest population transfer in history transpired, with millions leaving their homes. With the transfer came communal violence and a great slaughter. Representing India's National Christian Council, Pickett set up refugee camps that, according to the government of India, spared several hundred thousand lives. In fact, no nongovernment person did more to save lives. In the process, Pickett, who sheltered at his own residence more than two hundred Christians of Muslim background, risked his own life repeatedly. When the riots subsided, he organized follow-up relief efforts, from which the Churches' Auxiliary for Social Action (CASA) emerged. It continues strong today.

As Methodism's senior bishop, located in Delhi, Pickett had frequent dealings with Prime Minister Nehru, all the members of his cabinet, and other government officials. When, in the late 1940s, the Constituent Assembly was drawing up India's constitution, both B. R. Ambedkar, "father of the constitution," and H. C. Mookerjee, vice president of the

Constituent Assembly, came more than once to the Pickett home for dinner. Pickett later claimed—and there is some evidence to back him up—that he suggested the language for the constitution's religious liberties clause, which gives the right to "propagate" one's faith.

Pickett also embarked on an unofficial ambassadorial role in which, at various times, he met in India's behalf with U.S. presidents, senators, ambassadors, and fourteen times with a secretary of state. He went to Washington and personally pleaded with President Truman to sell surplus wheat to India to prevent famine. He went again and urged President Eisenhower to change America's policy bias toward Pakistan, then driven by Pakistan's proximity to Communist China.

Bishop James K. Mathews, who served under Pickett in the 1940s, remembered:

> He lent an unusual degree of stability to the church and nation as Indian independence emerged. His friendship with Mahatma Gandhi (with whom he did not always agree and with whom he frequently took issue), with Ambedkar, especially with Jawaharlal Nehru and then his daughter, Indira, and other Indian leaders was of crucial importance and incalculable value to the Christian community.[10]

Pickett left India in 1956, saying he was "leaving home and going to America." He would enjoy a long, active retirement. He continued his multifarious involvements. He lectured at several seminaries; he wrote articles, chapters, and books; he preached on every continent; and he raised millions for medical care training at a hospital in India's Punjab. He was ninety-one when he died in 1981.

NOTES

1. The only comprehensive accounts of Pickett's life are the author's *Road to Delhi: Bishop Pickett Remembered* (2005) and the dissertation that preceded it (McPhee, 2001). In his final years, Pickett worked on a memoir; however, his selective, topical arrangement precluded an orderly narrative. Moreover, his handwritten notes were fragmentary, repetitious, and sometimes included misremembered information. One day, a puff of wind through an open window scattered his pages all over the room. He was never able to reorder them satisfactorily and almost gave up. When the book came out, some of what he had written was missing

(e.g., pages he had written on the start of the United Mission to Nepal), and some of it appeared twice! At least the book—which he called *My Twentieth Century Odyssey*—got published (Pickett, 1980). A third, briefer source, is J. T. Seamands' "J. Waskom Pickett 1890–1981: Social Activist and Evangelist of the Masses" (1994). Other sources include hundreds of letters, many of them in the Methodist archives at Drew University, and his *Indian Witness* articles and editorials.

2. Arthur G. McPhee, *The Road to Delhi: Bishop Pickett Remembered* (Bangalore: SAIACS Press, 2005),

p. 121. Hereafter cited as McPhee, *Road to Delhi*.

3. Interview with the author, 1996.

4. McPhee, *Road to Delhi*, p. 164.

5. Ibid., p. 175.

6. Arthur G. McPhee, "Bishop J. Waskom Pickett's Rethinking on 1930s Missions in India," *International Journal of Frontier Missions* 19, no. 3 (2002): p. 33. Hereafter cited as McPhee, "Pickett's Rethinking."

7. McPhee, *Road to Delhi*, pp. 170–71.

8. McPhee, "Pickett's Rethinking," p. 34.

9. McPhee, *Road to Delhi*, pp. 185–86.

10. Ibid., p. 11.

BIBLIOGRAPHY

McPhee, Arthur G. "Pickett's Fire: The Life, Contribution, Thought, and Legacy of J. Waskom Pickett, Methodist Missionary to India." PhD diss., Asbury Theological Seminary, 2001.

———. "Bishop J. Waskom Pickett's Rethinking on 1930s Missions in India." *International Journal of Frontier Missions* 19, no. 3 (2002): pp. 31–37.

———. *The Road to Delhi: Bishop Pickett Remembered*. Bangalore: SAIACS Press, 2005.

Pickett, J. Waskom. *Christian Mass Movements in India: A Study with Recommendations*. New York: Abingdon Press, 1933.

——— . *Christ's Way to India's Heart*. Lucknow, India: Lucknow Publishing House, 1938.

———. *The Dynamics of Church Growth*. New York: Abingdon Press, 1963.

———. *My Twentieth Century Odyssey*. Bombay, India: Gospel Literature Service, 1980.

Pickett, J. Waskom, D. A. McGavran, and G. H. Singh. *Mass Movement Survey Report for Mid-India: a Study of Nine Areas in mid India from the Standpoint of How Mass Movements Begin, Are Arrested, Revive and Go Forward to the Upbuilding of Great Churches*. N.p: India, 1936.

Seamands, John T. "J. Waskom Pickett 1890–1981: Social Activist and Evangelist of the Masses." In *Mission Legacies: Biographical Studies of Leaders of the Modern Missionary Movement*, ed. Gerald H. Anderson, et. al., pp. 348–54. Maryknoll, N.Y.: Orbis Books, 1994.

17

"IF WE LIVE, WE LIVE, AND IF WE DIE, WE DIE"

POLYNESIAN MISSIONARIES IN PAPUA NEW GUINEA

Michael A. Rynkiewich

INTRODUCTION

The names of E. Stanley Jones, John R. Mott, and J. Waskom Pickett are sure to surface in conversations about mission in the Wesleyan tradition. In contrast, names like Seluaia and Josaia, Sailasa Naucukidi, and Setepano Nabwakulea are rarely heard. And yet, the Wesleyan work in the Pacific Islands would not have been possible without the empowerment of new converts and their deployment to the next group of islands.

How was it that, in this Wesleyan mission field, Euro-Australian missionaries were led to include so many local evangelists, teachers, and pastors in their work? What was the result of recruiting relatively new converts for mission work? Why is it that their stories, for the most part, have not been told in mission histories?[1]

WESLEYAN DISTINCTIVES IN MISSION

First, let us explore some Wesleyan distinctives that help us frame the work in the Pacific. As Tippett points out, it was the Evangelical Revival of the eighteenth century that put Wesleyan Methodist, London Missionary Society, and Church Mission Society volunteers in the Pacific Islands in the first place.[2] Why were Euro-Australian missionaries in the Wesleyan tradition willing to rapidly incorporate new converts into the mission?

First, Wesley's understanding of prevenient, justifying, and sancti-fying grace meant that new converts were already on the journey, that God had imputed righteousness to them, and that, in the context of class meetings and the use of the means of grace, God was in the process of imparting righteousness by transforming their character (that is, they were already moving toward perfection). Thus, Wesley, though he was an Oxford don, used a limited set of criteria for choosing lay preachers: they had to be converted and on their way to sanctification, they had to be able to read (he gave them his compilation called *The Christian Library*), and they had to be ready to itinerate.

Second, Wesley's understanding of the urgency of the revival meant that he could not depend on the clergy, who were, in fact, squeezing him out of parish pulpits, but instead he had to commission and send out lay preachers, appointing them as quickly as societies were formed in new places.

Third, Wesley's understanding of the work of an evangelist meant that he brought the Gospel to the people where they were ("field preaching"[3]), in a language that they could understand ("submitting to be more vile"[4]), and in a social organization in which they could participate (the local societies and class meetings rather than the established churches[5]).

WESLEYAN METHODISTS INTO THE PACIFIC

Wesleyan Methodists began work in the Pacific in Tonga (1822), Samoa (1828), and Fiji (1835). Very early on, South Seas Islanders served as missionaries, as Christians from Tonga led the mission in Samoa and Fiji, even giving their lives there.[6] Often a chief converted, then his people consulted and decided as one. So peace came and the church grew. Bible schools were established in Tonga, Fiji, and Samoa, and from these came pastors, teachers, and evangelists.

ON TO NEW GUINEA

The Reverend George Brown, Methodist missionary teacher in Samoa, convinced the Wesleyan Methodist Church in Australasia (Australia and New Zealand) to support a mission effort in New Guinea where the missionaries would be primarily South Seas Islanders. By the time their ship, the *John Wesley*, arrived in Fiji, a measles epidemic had just killed 40,000 people. Still, Brown challenged the weakened students at the Training Institution for pastors and ministers at Navuloa.[7] He warned them of malaria, violence, and the possibility of being on their own without European missionary help. The next day, 83 out of 83 students volunteered to go. Then the British administrator stepped in to try to talk them out of going. The group chose Aminio Baledrokadroka to respond: "We have fully considered this matter in our hearts; no one has pressed us in any way; we have given ourselves up to do God's work, and our mind today, sir, is to go with Mr. Brown. If we die, we die; if we live, we live."[8]

The ship left Fiji with "Baledrokadroka and his wife, Lavenia Tupou; Ratu Livai Volavola and his wife; Penijimani Caumea and his wife; Mijieli Vakaloloma and his wife, Paseta; Pauliasi Bunoa and his wife, Sieni; and the three single men Elimotama Ravono, Timoci Lase, and Peni Levu."[9] Note the gender difference; we do not have many names of Polynesian missionaries, but when we do it is more likely the names of the men and not their wives.

The ship arrived in New Britain in 1875 carrying also the Samoan missionaries "Setaleti Longova and Misieli Loli and their wives."[10] In the first two years, one teacher (Lase) died, and all the wives, except one Samoan woman, died. In 1876, the *John Wesley* returned with more Fijian missionaries: the Reverend Sailasa Naucukidi, Isoa Wainasikeci, Peni Raiwalui, Josiceni Raguru, Sione Ratunikulu, Anasa Raikabo, and Juliasi Tunaka.[11]

In 1877, Naucukidi, Levu, Livai Naboro, and Timoci Barave were making their way through the interior from one village to another when they were ambushed by warriors led by a "big man" named Talili.[12] All four were killed. Brown pursued an unusual strategy; he joined a party of European and Melanesian men on a "payback"[13] raid, burning houses and destroying gardens and pig herds. Talili sued for peace, was forgiven, and became a compatriot of Brown's. From this unusual beginning, the church grew. Brown also paid a price, as his son and daughter both died on New Britain. But, by 1914, the mission reported 276 lay preachers, 197 pastor-teachers, several schools, a Christian Training Institute and George Brown College, not far from a place now called Talili-gap (Talili-blood).[14]

ON TO PAPUA

In 1889, Sir William Macgregor, Governor of Papua, visited Australia and encouraged the Wesleyan Methodist Church to begin mission work in Papua. In 1890, at the General Conference of the Australasian Wesleyan Methodist Church, delegates decided to send the General Secretary for Overseas Missions, the same Rev. George Brown, to survey eastern Papua. He visited Rossel, Woodlark, Misima, the Trobriands, and the D'Entrecasteaux Islands. Brown considered Dobu to be the best place to begin. Macgregor did not agree. The Dobuans were well known in the region as fierce warriors who carried out cannibal raids and used powerful sorcery.[15] Brown was concerned that, if they settled anywhere else, the Dobuans would raid them anyway. And, he remembered that John Wesley had said, "Go not only to those who need you, but to those who need you most."[16] In fact, the Dobuan language turned out to be a helpful mission language because the Dobuans had travelled over much of Milne Bay both to raid and to trade in the Kula exchange.[17]

Following Wesley's admonition to exhibit a "catholic spirit,"[18] Brown met with William Lawes and James Chalmers of the London Missionary Society (LMS) and Alexander MacLaren of the Anglican mission. They all agreed that the Methodists should work in Milne Bay and the Papuan Islands, while the LMS would work on the south coast and the Anglicans on the northeast coast of Papua. The Australasian Wesleyan Methodist Church wanted to move quickly in order to begin the mission as part of the celebration of the centennial of John Wesley's death.[19] They also invited the relatively new Wesleyan churches of Tonga, Samoa, and Fiji to join them in the mission to the Papuan Islands.

The Australasian Wesleyan Methodist Church assembled a well-prepared group in Sydney, and set sail on the *Lord of the Isles*. They were led by Rev. William E. Bromilow accompanied by Brown, and were met at Dobu by Governor Macgregor. We know the names of the European missionaries, but then the list goes generic: "From Fiji, 15 men, six of them accompanied by their wives; From Samoa, 10 men, all of them accompanied by their wives; From Tonga, 4 men, all of them accompanied by their wives."[20]

We do not know all the names of the Polynesians, but we know some. Three weeks after arrival, just after the mission vessel left, Nehemiah's wife died. The teacher came to Bromilow with these words: "You will not send me back to Fiji because my wife has died? She died for the Papuans as Christ died for us all, and shall I not stay to do the work in which she would have been my helper?"[21] Within a month, another man's wife and child had died.[22]

Bromilow had respect for local customs, becoming a trader in the Kula network and a friend of the local "big man," Guganamore. He took other colonialists to task for their racism, claiming that "the idea that these brown natives are not as other men are dies hard, even among those willing to 'give the beggar a chance.'"[23] Bromilow began to distribute pastor-teachers: two Samoans and their wives on Ware, where, according to the comity agreement, the LMS was leaving a station to the Methodists; two teachers and wives on the island of Panaeati, one couple being the Tongan teacher Josaia and his wife, Seluaia; two Samoan teachers and their wives at Bwagabwaga on Misima;[24] and one Tongan teacher and his wife at Alhoga on Misima. Later a Fijian named Kolinio was placed at Liak on Misima, and he married a local girl and stayed.

The Tongan couple on Panaeati gave more than most to the mission. While home alone with a new baby, Seluaia was attacked by a man named Tonakomkom who was looking to "payback"[25] anyone attached to the colonial administration for an affront he had suffered.[26] In his anger, he came across Seluaia and attacked her with his machete. Josaia arrived in time to hear her last words, messages of comfort for their family and church back home. After serving years in prison, Tonakomkom came home, but stayed away from the church. Josaia sent word that, if he came, the people of the church "would not turn their back on him," implying that they would forgive him rather than shun him. This so surprised Tonakomkom, who expected "payback" rather than forgiveness, that he came to church. After a while, he became a believer.[27]

Setepano Nabwakulea remembered Tonakomkom from the late 1930s as a respectable elder in the church.[28] Nabwakulea, a missionary to the New Guinea Highlands himself, had the opportunity to visit Tonga in 1962 and tell Seluaia's home congregation that "although they had buried her on Panaeati, she was not dead, she had been planted and was growing because the church was growing as a result of the woman they had sent."[29]

A Fijian teacher named Simioni Momiovalu was especially effective. He stood between the people and the colonial administration when there was trouble. He observed local culture and made adaptations "using the

Methodist institution of the lovefeast and supplementing its observance with the prestigious practice of pig-slaughter."[30] The people knew oratory, for it was one of the attributes of a "big man"[31] that he could convince his followers, so Momiovalu was able to adapt "the Methodist practice of individual testimony to local conventions of oratory."[32] Momiovalu served in Papua for twenty-five years.[33]

Another name we know is Joni Kuli. He was a Tongan who served as captain on the missionary ketch and as a teacher on Panaeati. Reverend Watson says of him: "To know Joni Kuli was to love him, brave as a lion, with the gentle heart of a woman and the gaiety of a gladsome schoolboy. With this temperament went a deeply reverent devotion to the Christ who was to him the supreme reality."[34]

It would appear that the South Seas Islands[35] missionaries found it easier to meet Bromilow's goals, which were clearly Wesleyan: "The missionary must not remain an outsider, he must get the point of view of the people he desires to influence."[36] Instead of replacing the culture with European Christianity, Bromilow said that "we aim at saving Dobu not by reconstructions from without but by regeneration from within; we sought not to abolish but to redeem."[37]

In 1895, there was a Fijian teacher named Josephata at Bwagabwaga on Misima. The resident magistrate Alexander Campbell visited the school in 1897 and witnessed a school with seventy-seven pupils who recited and sang for him. In 1898, twenty-two people at Bwagabwaga were baptized and received as full members of the church. The people of Bwagabwaga, in 1998, remembered an early Fijian missionary wife named Laitiba who died and was buried, but without a memorial except that the church is built on that very spot.[38] The people of Eaus remember a Samoan pastor's wife named Ilatiya; so not all the names are lost. By 1914, there were sixty Papuan lay teachers/preachers in the Methodist mission. These reports show that the practice of empowering and commissioning lay teachers and preachers continued; the Europeans empowered the Polynesians, and the Polynesians empowered the Melanesians.

Not all the stories are success stories. In 1912, Percy M. Waterhouse was sent to Rossel Island, but left after a year.[39] In 1914, Walter Enticott was sent to Rossel, along with a Rotuman teacher named Mosese. A Misiman teacher named Onesimo joined them, but after four years all had quit the island, with no church established on Rossel. Not until the

1930s did the mission try again when Earnest A. Clarke went to Rossel accompanied by three Misiman missionaries: Gideon, Watisoni Gadile, and Eluida Campbell.[40] This time a church was established.

By 1929, there were 1,872 baptized members of the Methodist Church in the Louisiade Archipelago. Local tradition names a Fijian missionary named Metuisela Fafita from Viti Levu who worked at Liak and married a woman from Brooker Island. In 1935, another Fijian teacher, Meriesala Fiputa, arrived to work on Panaeati, but he died in 1939. Though the Misiman missionaries continued to work on Rossel, the mission did not have enough personnel to put an Australian missionary either on Rossel or Sudest.

THROUGH THE WAR

During World War II, the people found themselves in the midst of battle-fields. The New Guinea Islands were occupied by Japanese forces, and the Papuan Islands suffered through the Battle of the Coral Sea and the rise of a cargo cult movement.[41]

In the Papuan Islands, Isikeli and Mele Hau'ofa, Tongan missionaries who had arrived in 1932, were reassigned to Loaga Mission Station on Misima in 1937. The story of how they held the church together and resisted the Buliga cargo cult movement has been told elsewhere.[42]

A week after the attack on Pearl Harbor and other British and French installations around the Pacific, Resident Magistrate R. A. Woodward at Samarai sent a radio message that all the Australian women and children, except missionaries and nurses who wished to remain, were to be evacuated.[43] By early 1942, the Japanese military had taken the New Guinea Islands and the north coast of New Guinea itself, as well as Bougainville and the Solomon Islands. Attention was focused on Milne Bay and the Papuan Islands, the funnel through which the Japanese military would have to move to get into a position to attack northern Australia. Another radio message was received, though the source is still in dispute,[44] and Resident Magistrate Champion responded by ordering all Australians to immediately evacuate. Early on a Sunday morning, three boats made for Samarai, leaving the Tongan missionary couple behind. Here is how Hau'ofa remembered the day:

. . . it was a dreary day in the lives of my wife and I. I remember when we came back home the place [Loaga Mission Station] was very quiet and lonely. My wife clung to me and said, "All the white people and their wives and children have left the island and left us behind to . . . ?" I looked at her and said, "God called us here for this very hour."[45]

Indeed, Hau'ofa spent the next years negotiating between three white miners who had stayed on the island and were out of control, the local pastors who wondered what to do, Buliga (whose influence grew steadily), nine hundred mine laborers from elsewhere in Papua, and the ANGAU administration that eventually arrived to rule without the experience to do so justly. Hau'ofa writes:

I felt it my duty to go and stop the fighting. . . . I went out and made to pass through the midst of the sign-on boys, holding the lantern and calling out, "Friend, Friend. Stop a while and listen to me." I spoke to them in haste for the other side was marching quickly in our direction, and were not very far distant. One of the boys said, "Speak to the other side. We hear you and accept the reconciliation. But if they will not hear you, please let us fight to the end." I went to the other side and spoke to them, but they were worse than the first. However, they stopped and listened to me. Praise the Lord they both accepted the reconciliation in His Name's sake![46]

In the midst of all these troubles, and the feeling of abandonment by the missionaries, the local teachers and pastors were afraid and confused. It may have seemed that the church could not go on without the Euro-Australians and the cloth, rice, boat, and church hierarchy that they brought.[47] In order to speak to these fears and questions, Hau'ofa decided to go ahead with a Quarterly Meeting. Hau'ofa told the teachers not to expect any salary or support from the mission. He offered to release anyone who wanted to leave, but encouraged them to put up with the hardships and not be like the hirelings who fled when the wolves came. "I again reminded the teachers that the welfare of the people depended on them alone now."[48] After the meeting, Hau'ofa reported that no one left his post.

After an outbreak of cargo cult violence, ANGAU arrived in force. In the end, ten men were sentenced; Buliga hung himself in jail the night before, eight were hanged in public, and another man was under a doctor's care[49] and the doctor refused to release him.[50] All the people were forced to watch the hangings,[51] including, by his own testimony, the fifteen-year-old son of Buliga's sister.[52] Going the second mile, Isikeli and Mele Hau'ofa took in some of the orphaned children of the men who were hanged and raised them at Loaga Mission Station.[53]

During the war, it was clearly South Seas Islands missionaries like Isikeli and Mele Hau'ofa, Jonathan Meleke Fonua on Bwaidoga, Filemoni Faitele at Bunamu, and David Mone on Salamo, who not only held church and society together when abandoned to their fate in the middle of a war between other people, but even saw church growth under the circumstances.

After the war, though the mission recovered, there were never enough Australian and New Zealand missionaries for the work. Thus, when the New Guinea Islands Synod and the Papuan Islands Synod, in the same year, decided that it was time to send missionaries into the Highlands of Papua and New Guinea, the local people also took up the mission. Following the Wesleyan practice, Papuans and New Guineans from the islands and coast went as missionaries into the Highlands. Their story is yet to be fully told.[54]

HISTORY AND MISSION

Doug Munro and Andrew Thornley, in a review of studies of Pacific Islander pastors and missionaries, lament the dearth of published materials.[55] This, in spite of the fact that "the introduction of Christianity throughout most of the Pacific was not accomplished by European missionaries alone but by a veritable army of islander teachers and pastors, themselves often recently converted."[56] That army certainly included more than fifteen hundred South Seas Islands missionaries from islands in Polynesia to other Polynesian and Melanesian islands.[57]

Wesleyan theology encouraged both European missionaries and new converts to discover what the Holy Spirit had already been doing and then come alongside God's ongoing work. Wesleyan practice meant that even new converts were thought to be Spirit-gifted and ready to be trained and commissioned as missionaries themselves, and thus the work went farther and faster than European missionaries alone could have accomplished. Wesleyan anthropology assumed that every new culture and language, indeed, every new generation deserves a fresh hearing of the Gospel in metaphors and meanings that they can understand. Thus it was that the Word became flesh in the Pacific.

NOTES

1. A notable exception is Alan R. Tippett's *The Deep Sea Canoe: The Story of Third World Missionaries in the South Pacific* (Pasadena, Calif.: William Carey Library, 1977), which includes the names and stories of a number of Tongan, Samoan, and Fijian missionaries. There is a helpful list of Polynesian missionaries to the New Guinea Islands in Neville Threfall, *One Hundred Years in the Islands: The Methodist/United Church in the New Guinea Islands Region, 1875–1975* (Rabaul, Papua New Guinea: The United Church [New Guinea Islands Region], 1975), pp. 249–65; a few names and stories appear in William Bromilow, *Twenty Years among Primitive Papuans* (London: Epworth Press, 1929).

2. Tippett, *The Deep Sea Canoe*, p. 3.

3. A. Skevington Wood, *The Burning Heart, John Wesley: Evangelist* (Lexington, Ky: Emeth Press, [1967] 2007), p. 107.

4. Wood, *The Burning*, pp. 101, 108.

5. Ibid., pp. 157–65, 222–23.

6. Ibid., p. 25.

7. Ibid., p. 28.

8. Ibid., p. 29. Tippett notes that another missionary was asked if he was afraid to die and responded: "No, we died before we went!" (*The Deep Sea Canoe*, p. 38).

9. Ibid., p. 29.

10. Ibid., p. 29. In this article I am intentionally placing these names in print, some for the first time, and some recovered from dated publications.

11. Ibid., p. 42.

12. A "big man" is a Melanesian leader. There are few leaders in Melanesia who could properly be called "chiefs," just as there are few groups in Melanesia who could properly be called "tribes." Thus, concepts developed elsewhere to describe the dynamics of group formation and leadership tend to fail miserably in Melanesia.

13. Payback refers to the practice of retribution that dominated Melanesian political life in ages past. See Garry W. Trompf, *Payback: The Logic of Retribution in Melanesian Religions* (Cambridge: Cambridge University Press, 1994).

14. I have visited this site and the testimony of the martyrs still lives there.

15. See Reo Fortune, *Sorcerers of Dobu* (London: George Routledge, 1932).

16. Ronald G. Williams, *The United Church in Papua, New Guinea, and the Solomon Islands: The Story of the Development of an Indigenous Church on the Occasion of the Centenary of the L.M.S. in Papua, 1872–1972* (Rabaul, Papua New Guinea: Trinity Press, 1972), p. 181.

17. See Bronislaw Malinowski, *Argonauts of the Western Pacific: An Account of Native Enterprise and Adventure in the Archipelagoes of Melanesian New Guinea* (New York: E. P. Dutton and Company, [1922] 1961); see also Edmund Leach and Jerry Leach, eds., *The Kula: New Perspectives on Massim Exchange* (Cambridge: Cambridge University Press, 1983).

18. Note that a "catholic spirit" is not a "latitudinarian spirit." See Wood, *The Burning*.

19. John Wesley died in 1791, so the centennial celebration of his death would be 1891.

20. Diane Langmore, *Missionary Lives: Papua, 1874–1914* (Honolulu: University of Hawaii Press, 1989), pp. 289–91.

21. Bromilow, *Twenty Years*, p. 68.

22. The dangers still exist. One of my own children suffered through three malaria attacks while on Misima and later in the Highlands.

23. John Garrett, *To Live Among the Stars: Christian Origins in Oceania* (Suva, Fiji: Institute of Pacific Studies, 1982), p. 235.

24. Bwagabwaga, Alhoga, and Liak are all villages on Misima Island.

25. "Payback" (pidgin English "peybek" or "bekim bek") refers to an understanding of the world where every action calls for a reaction. Gifts are paid back with other gifts, killings are paid back with other killings. See Trompf, *Payback*.

26. It is not clear whether his wife was raped by a policeman or ran off with a policeman.

27. Bromilow, *Twenty Years*, pp. 166–69.

28. Interview with Setepano Nabwakulea on Misima in 1998.

29. Ibid.

30. Garrett, *Live Among the Stars*, p. 234.

31. See Doug Oliver, *A Solomon Island Society: Kinship and Leadership among the Siuai [Siwai] of Bougainville* (Cambridge, Mass.: Harvard University Press, 1955); Marshall Sahlins, "Rich Man, Poor Man, Big-Man, Chief: Political Types in Melanesia and Polynesia," *Comparative Studies in Society and History* 5, no. 3, (1963): pp. 285–303; Michael A. Rynkiewich, "Big-Man Politics: Strong Leadership in a Weak State," in *Politics in Papua New Guinea: Continuities, Changes and*

Challenges, ed. Michael A. Rynkiewich and Roland Seib (Goroka, Papua New Guinea: The Melanesian Institute, 2000) Point 24.

32. Garrett, *Live Among the Stars*, p. 234.

33. Bromilow, *Twenty Years*, p. 235.

34. Ibid., pp. 160–62.

35. The missionaries from the Cook Islands, Samoa, Tonga, and Fiji were called South Seas Islands missionaries at the time. More frequently today people from these islands are called Polynesians.

36. Williams, *The United Church in PNG*, p. 190.

37. Ibid., pp. 191–92.

38. Interview with Hemphrey on Misima in 1998.

39. Langmore, *Missionary Lives*, p. 293.

40. Kathleen Henderson (née Benson), "The History, Development and Status of the Protestant Christian Church in Rossel Island, Papua New Guinea," (typewritten manuscript on Misima, 1997), p. 5.

41. See classic treatments of cargo cults as religious movements of the oppressed (Vittorio Lanternari, *The Religions of the Oppressed: A Study of Modern Messianic Cults* [New York: Mentor Books, 1963]; as nascent political responses to colonialism (Peter Worsley, *The Trumpet Shall Sound: A Study of "Cargo" Cults in Melanesia* [New York: Shocken Books, 1968]); and cargo cults as the logical development of a Melanesian worldview (Peter Lawrence, *Road Belong Cargo* [Manchester: Manchester University Press, 1964]).

42. See Michael Hess, "Misima–1942: An Anti-Colonial Religious Movement," *Bikmaus* 3, no. 1 (1982); Martha Macintyre, "Christianity, Cargo Cultism, and the Concept of the Spirit in Misiman Cosmology," *Christianity in Oceania: Ethnographic Perspectives*, ASAO Monograph No. 12, ed. John Barker (New York: University Press of America, 1990), pp. 81–100; Ross Mackay, "The War Years: Methodists in Papua

1942–1945," *The Journal of Pacific History* 27, no. 1 (1992): pp. 29–; Maria Lepowsky, "Soldiers and Spirits: The Impact of World War II on a Coral Sea Island," in *The Pacific Theater: Island Representations of World War II*, ed. Geoffrey M. White and Lamont Lindstrom (Honolulu: The University of Hawaii Press, 1989), pp. 210–11; Michael A. Rynkiewich, "Person in Mission," *Missiology* 31, no. 2 (2003): pp. 155–68.

43. Mackay, "The War Years," p. 30.

44. Maria Lepowsky, "Soldiers and Spirits," pp. 210–11; see also Mackay, "The War Years," p. 30; and Michael Hess, "Misima—1942."

45. Hau'ofa, "Notes," p. 1.

46. Ibid., p. 2.

47. Ibid., p. 2.

48. Ibid., p. 4.

49. Interview with Dr. Jethro, on Misima, 1998.

50. Hank Nelson, *Black, White and Gold: Goldmining in Papua New Guinea, 1878–1930* (Canberra: The Australian National University Press, 1976), p. 46; see also Hess, "Misima—1942," p. 53.

51. Lepowsky, "Soldiers and Spirits," p. 215.

52. Interview with Romanigu, on Misima, 1998.

53. Ibid.

54. Williams, *The United Church in PNG*, outlines the story and gives the names of many Papuan and New Guinean missionaries. I was able to interview Setepano Nabwakulea, Vilo Kemp, and Late Kwadegu on Misima and get a statement from Libai Tiengwa on Rossell Island. The first Methodist missionaries into the Mendi area included the Rev. Gordon Young and Kamiliel Ladi from the New Guinea Islands region and the Rev. Ernest Clarke, Libai Tiengwa, Stephen Moyalaka, and Thomas Tomar from the Papuan Islands Region. Following them were Daniel Amen and Sydney To Iara from the New Guinea Islands and Timoti Newai, Setepano Nabwakulea and wife, Kiloi, from the Papuan Islands region. Then came Inosi Kwabiana (Goodenough Is.), Alphius Alekera and John Pirah (Solomon Islands District), David Mone (Tonga, NGI district), Epineri Kopman, Peniel To Tabu, Daniel Keskes, Kenas To Vugal, and Enosi Kwabiaona (all NGI); Libai Tiengwa (Rossel), Kemp Kabalua and Vilo (Misima), and Saulo Wenoku (Goodenough). Vilo Kemp served as a nurse, and reports on the strong division between women's and men's lives that affected how women missionaries could do their work. In 1960, Ephraim Jonathan and his wife, Elsie, (PI) were sent to Tari as teachers. In 1963, Lali Bulilau (Misima) with his wife, Ailin, were sent to Tari. In 1965, Lote Kwadegu and his wife, Jean, were also sent to Tari. Lote reports that he lost his congregation when they were routed in a tribal war. Lote walked the whole area, talking with both sides and helping them move toward reconciliation. A Solomon Islands minister, Matthew Beaso, also served in the Highlands.

55. Doug Munro and Andrew Thornley, "Pacific Islander Pastors and Missionaries: Some Historiographical and Analytical Issues," *Pacific Studies* 23, nos. 3/4 (2000): pp. 1–31.

56. Ibid., pp. 17–18.

57. Ibid., pp. 2–3.

BIBLIOGRAPHY

Bromilow, William. *Twenty Years Among Primitive Papuans*. London: Epworth Press, 1929.

Crocombe, Ron, and Majorie Crocombe, eds. *Polynesian Missions to Melanesia: From Samoa, Cook Islands, and Tonga to Papua New Guinea and New Caledonia*. Suva, Fiji: Institute of Pacific Studies, University of the South Pacific, 1982.

Fortune, Reo. *Sorcerers of Dobu*. London: George Routledge, 1932.

Garrett, John. *To Live Among the Stars: Christian Origins in Oceania*. Geneva: World Council of Churches; Suva, Fiji: Institute of Pacific Studies, 1982.

Hau'ofa, Isikeli. [no date] *Notes Made by Isikeli Hau'ofa—1942 to 1945,* a type-written manuscript archived in the local government offices in Bwagaoia, Misima, Milne Bay Province, Papua New Guinea. The notes were appar-ently written in 1946 as part of a set of records of wartime events, as there are similar typewritten or handwritten "statements" by the local clerk, Kenneth Kaiw (1946); another local official, Ebenezer Konau (1946); as well as a statement by the missionary Ernest Clarke (1946) addressed to "Resident Magistrate Hall."

Henderson (née Benson), Kathleen. "The History, Development and Status of the Protestant Christian Church in Rossel Island, Papua New Guinea." Typewritten manuscript lodged on Misima, 1997.

Hess, Michael. "Misima—1942: An Anti-Colonial Religious Movement." *Bikmaus* 3, no. 1 (1982): pp. 48–56.

Langmore, Diane. *Missionary Lives: Papua, 1874–1914*. Honolulu: University of Hawaii Press, 1989.

Lanternari, Vittorio. *Religions of the Oppressed: A Study of Modern Messianic Cults*. New York: Mentor Books, 1963.

Latekefu, Sione. "The Impact of South Sea Islander Missionaries on Melanesia." In *Mission, Church, and Sect in Oceania*, ed. James A. Boutilier, Daniel T. Hughes, and Sharon W. Tiffany, pp. 91–108. Ann Arbor: University of Michigan Press, 1978.

———. "Oral History and Pacific Islands Missionaries: The Case of the Methodist Mission in Papua New Guinea and the Solomon Islands." In *Oral Tradition in Melanesia*, ed. Donald Denoon and Roderic Lacey, pp. 175–87. Port Moresby: University of Papua New Guinea and Institute of Papua New Guinea Studies, 1981.

Lawrence, Peter. *Road Belong Cargo*. Manchester, Eng.: Manchester University Press, 1964.

Leach, Edmund, and Jerry Leach, eds. *The Kula: New Perspectives on Massim Exchange*. Cambridge: Cambridge University Press, 1983.

Lepowsky, Maria. "Soldiers and Spirits: The Impact of World War II on a Coral Sea Island." In *The Pacific Theater: Island Representations of World War II*, ed. Geoffrey M. White and Lamont Lindstrom, pp. 210–11. Honolulu: University of Hawaii Press, 1989.

Macintyre, Martha. "Christianity, Cargo Cultism, and the Concept of the Spirit in Misiman Cosmology." In *Christianity in Oceania: Ethnographic Perspectives*, ASAO Monograph No. 12, ed. John Barker, 81–100. New York: University Press of America, 1990.

Mackay, Ross. "The War Years: Methodists in Papua 1942–1945." *The*

Journal of Pacific History 27, no. 1 (1992): pp. 29–43.

Malinowski, Bronislaw K. *Argonauts of the Western Pacific: An Account of Native Enterprise and Adventure in the Archipelagoes of Melanesian New Guinea*. New York: E. P. Dutton and Company, 1992/1961.

Munro, Doug, and Andrew Thornley, eds. *The Covenant Makers: Islander Missionaries in the Pacific*. Suva, Fiji: Pacific Theological College and Institute of Pacific Studies, University of the South Pacific, 1996.

———. "Pacific Islander Pastors and Missionaries: Some Historiographical and Analytical Issues." *Pacific Studies* 23, no. 3/4 (2000): pp. 1–31.

Nelson, Hank. *Black, White and Gold: Goldmining in Papua New Guinea, 1878–1930*. Canberrra: The Australian National University Press, 1976.

Oliver, Douglas. *A Solomon Island Society: Kinship and Leadership among the Siuai [Siwai] of Bougainville*. Cambridge, Mass.: Harvard University Press, 1955.

Rynkiewich, Michael A. "Big-Man Politics: Strong Leadership in a Weak State." In *Politics in Papua New Guinea: Continuities, Changes and Challenges, Point 24*, ed. Michael A. Rynkiewich and Roland Seib, pp. 17–43. Goroka, Papua New Guinea: The Melanesian Institute, 2000.

———. "Person in Mission." *Missiology* 31, no. 2 (2003): pp. 155–68.

Sahlins, Marshall. "Rich Man, Poor Man, Big-Man, Chief: Political Types in Melanesia and Polynesia." *Comparative Studies in Society and History* 5, no. 3 (1963): pp. 285–303.

Threfall, Neville. *One Hundred Years in the Islands: The Methodist/United Church in the New Guinea Islands Region, 1875–1975*. Rabaul, Papua New Guinea: The United Church, 1975.

Tippett, Alan R. *The Deep Sea Canoe: The Story of Third World Missionaries in the South Pacific*. Pasadena, Calif.: William Carey Library, 1977.

Trompf, Garry W. *Payback: The Logic of Retribution in Melanesian Religions*. Cambridge: Cambridge University Press, 1994.

Williams, Ronald G. *The United Church in Papua, New Guinea, and the Solomon Islands: The Story of the Development of an Indigenous Church on the Occasion of the Centenary of the L.M.S. in Papua, 1872–1972*. Rabaul, Papua New Guinea: Trinity Press, 1972.

Wood, A. Skevington. *The Burning Heart, John Welsey: Evangelist*. Lexington, Ky.: Emeth Press, 1967/2007.

Worsley, Peter. *The Trumpet Shall Sound: A Study of "Cargo" Cults in Melanesia*. New York: Shocken Books, 1968.

18

THOMAS BIRCH FREEMAN

THE MOST FAMOUS WESLEYAN MISSIONARY OF WEST AFRICA YOU HAVE NEVER HEARD OF

Michael Mozley

INTRODUCTION

In the Methodist mission tradition, there was prolific expansion in the nineteenth and twentieth centuries. Most of the ones who carried the Gospel message were obscure, itinerant, local preachers who sensed the call to "go and make disciples of all nations."[1] Some of the most famous missionaries of that era were William Carey, Robert Moffatt, C. T. Studd, and David Livingstone. They have been seared in the memory of mainline Protestant Christianity. They were the heroes and the headliners of world missions.

Although Methodist mission outreach was prolific throughout the world, many of the names of those who went and died in the name of Christ are lost in obscurity. The few who survived were by no means famous. There were hundreds of missionaries who gave their lives in missionary service throughout the world. Men and women responded to the call, went out, served and many times died within a few weeks, months, or a few years after arriving at their destinations. Sierra Leone was the first West African area that the Wesleyan Methodist Missionary Society decided to invest in and it gained the reputation of being called "The White Man's Grave." Yet the Gospel was still conveyed throughout the world by these champions of the faith who risked their lives in the most extreme conditions.

In 1849 William Taylor began his ministry in California and was probably the most famous Methodist missionary in the nineteenth century in

American Methodism,[2] yet if most Methodists were questioned today, very few would know of his life and ministry. Thomas Birch Freeman, similarly, is largely unknown in American Methodism and only faintly remembered in England. Yet his life and ministry helped shape the Methodist movement and established the Methodist Church that stretched from the borders of modern-day Cote d'Ivoire to Nigeria. His adventurous spirit, which propelled him, at the age of twenty-eight, to leave England for circumstances that would lead to almost certain death on the Gold Coast of West Africa was unheralded. His ability to initiate change in the status-quo mentality of nineteenth-century missionary methods was transformative and innovative. His humility in the midst of difficulty was a lasting legacy among his colleagues and the Ghanaian people. Lastly, his ability to learn and grow with the natives that he worked among, as well as the expatriate community, made him famous in the environs in which he lived and worked.

HISTORY OF THOMAS BIRCH FREEMAN FROM 1809–1838

Thomas Birch (Freeman was added later in his life) was born in Twyford, England. His mother, Amy, had been previously married to John Thomas Birch and they had four sons: William, Thomas, Henry, and Joseph.[3] Assuming Mr. Birch died or moved away, Amy remarried an African named Thomas who was a yeoman and a gardener on the estate where Amy worked. They had a son Thomas who would become Thomas Birch Freeman. It was recorded in the St. Mary's Parish records in Twyford that he was born on December 6, 1809, but Freeman himself records in his own journal that his birthday was November 29:

> Nov. 29, 1841: "I was rather poorly. The heat was very intense during the middle of the day, with a strong harmattan. My age this day numbered thirty-two years; but how small a portion of my life have I spent in the service of God!"[4]

The Africans, not knowing that Freeman's father was black, always regarded him as a white man. And such he felt himself to be. England was his native land; he was English by education, training, and culture. Nothing about him suggested African parentage. In his early manhood his complexion was so light that he was invariably taken for a European.

John Milum, in his book, *Thomas Birch Freeman: Missionary to Ashanti, Dahomey and Egba,* and F. Deaville Walker, in *Thomas Birch Freeman: The Son of an African,* both mention that Freeman's father died when young Thomas was six.[5] Freeman, in his youth, used to gather with the local village boys and climb on top of the cobbler's home where the local Methodist meeting was being held and tie a string to a brick and drop it down the chimney to cause a disturbance.[6] One Sunday evening young Thomas came earlier than his village friends and eavesdropped on the service as he listened intently through the cobbler's door. It was reported that through that divine eavesdropping Freeman was converted to Christ.[7] Very little else is mentioned of Freeman's education or his upbringing from that point on. The next mention of him, he is called Thomas Birch Freeman in Ipswich, England. He was the head gardener and botanist for Sir Robert and Lady Harland at Orwell Park. During this time he was also active as a local preacher for the Methodists and was visiting the sick and poor during his free time.

An issue arose with the Harlands and Thomas Birch Freeman had to choose between being the head gardener or serving as a local preacher with the Methodists. He chose the Methodists! Soon after his release from Orwell Park, Freeman saw a notice in the *Methodist Times* of a missionary calling for assistance in the Gold Coast. Mr. George Wrigley had sent word that two of his colleagues, Rev. and Mrs. Peter Harrop, and his own wife had passed away and he was calling for reinforcements. When Freeman heard this news, this is how he responded in his journal:

> Woe is me if I preach not the Gospel and woe unto me if I am not prepared to forsake home, and friends, and all that I hold dear to me, to preach the Gospel to the heathen . . . If I hesitate to go to a sickly clime at the command of the Lord of Hosts, because in so doing I may risk the shortening of my days in this life, cannot He who bids me go strike me here, while surrounded with all the advantages of this sea girt isle? The noble pagan, who when about to embark on an expedition of danger, answered to the remonstrances of friends, "It is necessary for me to go; but it may not be necessary for me to live."[8]

Freeman set out for London to be approved as a missionary and to be ordained as a Methodist minister. He was approved as a missionary in July 1837, was ordained on October 10, and married on October 12 to

Miss Elizabeth Boot, a servant lady at Orwell Park. They set sail for the Gold Coast on November 5, 1837. Freeman wrote in his journal in November 1837:

> Blessed be God, I find my mind composed and prepared for leaving my Native Land. I trust I am going forth with a single eye to the promoting of the glory of God in the welfare of my fellow creatures. O that I may ever feel an increasing anxiety to be useful in my day and generation. Come O my God and warm my heart with heavenly charity. Send me forth I beseech Thee in Thine own strength and make me and my beloved partner a blessing to the poor benighted and opprest Africans.

> *My life, my blood, I here present,*
> *If for Thy truth they may be spent.*[9]

> Help me, O Lord, to live in the enjoyment of vital Religion, that I may know how to feed Thy sheep in the wilderness, through Christ Jesus my Lord.[10]

Mr. and Mrs. Freeman were anticipating to see Mr. Wrigley upon arrival in Cape Coast but that was not to be. Wrigley had died in November just as they were setting off from London. They arrived alone. Five missionaries had fallen before the Freemans had even set foot on the Gold Coast.[11]

FOUR MAJOR CHARACTERISTICS
THAT MADE FREEMAN FAMOUS

Adventurous Spirit

Sierra Leone was already nicknamed "The White Man's Grave," and the reality that five missionaries had already fallen could have discouraged and struck fear into the hearts of Thomas and Elizabeth. They reached the beaches of Cape Coast on January 3, 1838, only to be greeted with the bad news that Wrigley had died three months past. After being welcomed at the castle, they went to visit the mission house where all five missionaries had resided. Freeman wrote, "Blessed be God, we are resigned to do His Will, and should He speedily call us away also, we hope to die in His embraces. Not that we expect to be suddenly removed; not that we have any fear. We hope long to be useful in this part of the world."[12] Both Mr. and Mrs. Freeman picked up where the other missionaries had left off. Freeman saw that Wrigley had begun to build a church in Cape Coast and though not a builder, used his common sense skills and assisted the natives to continue in the building process.

Within six weeks after arriving, both Thomas and Elizabeth fell ill from the heat and "seasoning fever," which was most likely malaria. While Thomas was recovering in one bedroom he had not realized that his wife had fallen deathly ill and passed away within one day of her sickness.[13] Freeman wrote in his journal just after the passing of his wife, "I stand in the deadly breach with humble confidence that God will long spare my life."[14] Though he grieved over the loss of his wife, Freeman continued to carry out the ministry of planting churches, raising up native leaders, and looking for new territory to claim for Christ.

His most famous expedition was his virgin journey to Kumasi in the Asante Region. The purpose of this journey was to meet and share the Good News with the Asantehene, Kwaku Dua, the king of the Asante people. In the nineteenth century, Kumasi was known as the "City of Blood" because of its many human sacrifices, mostly in relation to the death of royal family members. Foreigners, especially the British, feared the Asante because in November of 1823, Governor Charles McCarthy took a group of twenty-five hundred men, mostly Africans, to attack the Asantes over a dispute with the British government. During the battle McCarthy was separated from his men and was surrounded. He knew his death was imminent and ended his own life and then was beheaded by the Asante warriors.[15]

Freeman desired to share the Gospel with these feared warriors and started on his way to Kumasi on January 31, 1839.[16] Though it took him two months, he was the first European Christian to meet with and share the truths of the Gospel to the Asantehene and these feared warlike people. Freeman's adventurous spirit led him to many towns and villages throughout modern Ghana, Togo, Benin, and Nigeria.

After returning from England from his furlough in 1841, Freeman was asked to go and assist the believers in Egba to set up a Methodist post there. Yoruba Christians who were stationed in Sierra Leone had made their way back up the Niger Delta to the town of Abeokuta and were looking for someone to assist them in starting a church. Freeman took his Ghanaian assistant William De Graft in hopes that he would be stationed along the coast in Badagry and work with the believers on the coast and inland at Abeokuta.[17]

On his return journey Freeman also stopped in Dahomey to negotiate with Ghezo, the chief of that area. Ghezo had fierce, female Amazon warriors and was renowned for his slave trading. He was similar to the Asantehene in that he sacrificed many slaves for various purposes. His entire village was surrounded by the skulls of victims that had been killed in battle or in sacrifice.[18] After meeting with Freeman, he requested that a missionary also be stationed in his area on the coast at Whydah.

While in this coastal area of Dahomey, Freeman met with one of the most notorious slave traders in that era, Don Antonio Da Souza. Freeman was a man of diplomacy even in the midst of dangerous situations. Da Souza clearly realized that Freeman stood against him in the slave trade, yet he befriended him.[19] Freeman befriended him yet clearly stood his ground on the evils of slavery and continued to press forward to establish Christian outposts in these most difficult areas.

Whether with Kwaku Dua, the Asantehene of the Gold Coast; Shodeke, the king of Abeokuta and the Egbas; King Ghezo of Dahomey; or slave traders like Da Souza, Freeman was fearless in approaching these men and sharing the Gospel with them. He was a man of adventure and a man of mission. His goal was to present Christ in areas where Christ was not known. If the evils of slavery still persisted, Freeman pressed in, not as a political spokesman for his homeland of England but as an ambassador for the King of Kings.

Initiating Change

Whether from changing the housing accommodations where his colleagues had recently died, spending time with traders on the coast, or implementing an alternative to the slave trade, Thomas Birch Freeman was known as a man who initiated change. He was never seen as cocky or arrogant; he was known and remembered for his humility. Even in his humility, he used wisdom and common sense to create change that saved lives and built relationships.

The first mission house that had been acquired by the Wrigleys had poor ventilation and was very hot and uncomfortable. Freeman observed where most of the traders had lived in Cape Coast and saw that they were thriving rather than succumbing to the brutal elements along the coast. His first courageous act was to find another house that was suitable for him and his wife. It took less than a month for him to find a healthier residence. On January 25, Freeman recalls, "A day of much anxiety. Finding the old mission house very hot and unwholesome I hired our present dwelling for 36 pounds per annum and immediately commenced moving into it trusting that the change is in the order of Divine Providence."[20] It was his sheer determination and observation skills that literally saved his life as he utilized the wisdom of the traders who had found accommodations that were more elevated and airy so that the ocean breeze would help to ventilate the houses.[21] Freeman also was not opposed to drinking the local homemade wine called "palm wine," which was fermented and more healthy than the local water, which carried bacteria.

Freeman also befriended the merchants who were living along the coasts. Some of the former missionaries had isolated themselves from them because they weren't Christian. Freeman rather built relationships with them because he needed their wisdom and resources and he realized they needed God. Birtwhistle states, "His tact with Europeans and Africans alike was part of the same practical gift. He always stood on good terms with the people he lived with: unfailing courtesy and an obvious love for them were the secret."[22]

Freeman was a botanist and a gardener by profession but a minister of the Gospel by calling. As he journeyed back to England on his first furlough, he and William De Graft stopped over in Sierra Leone to visit the work that was going on there. He noticed the plantations that were in existence to compensate for the slave trade. Though he doesn't mention the genesis of the idea in his journal, he implemented the plan on his return to Cape Coast in 1840. His first venture failed miserably but he persisted and began a farm in Accra in the mid 1850s and was producing grapes, pineapples, and various other fruits and vegetables for export. His initiative was to try and stimulate the natives to create an economic alternative to slavery. T. F. Buxton, in his book *African Slave Trade and Its Remedy,* makes this insightful comment:

> It appears, then, that these three cases, Sierra Leone, Gambia, and the Gold Coast, as far as they go, illustrate and strengthen my views. When the errors which have been committed in their management shall be rectified, when education and Christian instruction shall prevail, and when an effective impulse shall have been given to commerce and agriculture, we, seeing what has already been done,

may reasonably hope that a salutary change will be effected in this unhappy continent.[23]

Freeman was an initiator on all three points. From the moment he arrived he invested in the education of the natives to train them in ministry and Christian education. He encouraged commerce between the Fantes and the Asantes, thereby trying to breakdown the tribal stigma, and he believed that agriculture would be an alternative to compensate for the slave trade.

Humility in Difficulty

Two major events happened during Freeman's long stint on the Gold Coast that caused him deep hurt. He was wrongly accused by a fellow missionary during his time of service and, second, he decided to step down from the mission in 1857 for a period of sixteen years.

When Freeman returned from his first furlough in England he brought with him five new missionaries. One of the missionaries who returned with him was John Watson, and he was stationed at Dixcove. After two-and-a-half years of service, Watson returned to England. While Freeman was on his second furlough in England in 1844, Watson wrote an anonymous letter in the *Times* newspaper where he slandered Freeman and accused him of supporting concubinage and raising a sum of five thousand pounds. He accused Freeman of raising funds "from the credulous English, and he now intends to pocket a like sum, under the plea of teaching the benighted Africans."[24] The Wesleyan Missionary Society found Watson's accusations as "untrue and altogether calumnious."[25] A merchant, Mr. J. H. Akhurst, also defended Freeman in the *Times* on October 31, 1844, by stating:

> Having been many years a resident on the Gold Coast, and having had the best opportunities of observing the conduct of Rev. Thomas B. Freeman during the whole period of his superintendence of the Wesleyan mission in that part of Africa, I consider that I owe it to the cause of truth and justice to bear testimony to the excellence of his character, and the unwearied diligence and fidelity with which he has endeavoured to discharge the important duties which have devolved upon him, and to express my deep conviction that the serious allegations preferred against him by "Omega" in *The Times* of Friday last have no foundation in truth. I do not believe him to

be capable of such a dereliction of principle as he is charged with by your correspondent. The improvement in the character and condition of the natives of the Gold Coast, which Mr. Freeman, with his fellow labourers, has been instrumental in promoting, has secured for him the esteem of all who are interested in the advancement of Christian instruction and civilization; and from the judicious manner in which, from my own personal observation made upon the spot, he commenced operations at Badagry and Whydah, I entertain the persuasion that similar benefits will result from his labours in those important places, and am confident that his return to the shores of Africa will be welcomed by all classes of society there.

Freeman replied to "Omega" in the the *Times* and was vindicated on all counts. He did not lash out or return slanderous accusations on his accuser; he simply and humbly defended his actions and character. In a time when Freeman was truly one of the most popular and famous missionaries in England, accusations and slander came but were proved faulty and fruitless. Akhurst's description well defends Freeman's character.

As the strain of multiple missionaries arriving on the Gold Coast increased and the expansion of the work grew larger and larger, Freeman found himself bogged down with the details of administrative oversight and missionary care. These were not his strengths. He was a visionary pioneer, a man of action. He believed his constant movement and traveling was partly the reason he remained as healthy as he did. The burdens grew larger and larger, debts were mounting, and Freeman continued to borrow money from the merchants and the home office in London. He exceeded his budget for the sake of the expansion of the work.

In 1856, the Wesleyan Methodist Missionary Society (WMMS) sent two missionaries, Daniel West and William West, to give some oversight to the work on the Gold Coast.[26] William was being sent out as the financial secretary to the mission and Daniel was to look into and report back to the committee on the state of the work. After the tour was over, Daniel had visited most of the coastal stations and even ventured to Lagos and Abeokuta. On his return journey to report back to the WMMS, Daniel died. All that could be given were his written reports. Walker describes the situation:

Feeling that he [Freeman] had lost confidence of the committee, he asked to be relieved of his office as chairman and general superintendent of the mission, as he had already been relieved of financial control. For the good of the work he felt that it would be best to have a new leader, and he offered freely to step aside. There is not a trace of anger or resentment in his letter. He wrote:

> In standing aside I should not deprive the mission of any services I may be able to render, and I would most willingly act as a local preacher under Mr. William West or any brother who may fulfil the duties of General Superintendent. I would aid the work by every means in my power."27

This was a major blow to the mission in the Gold Coast but Freeman knew that the financial situation was greater than he could handle and so he graciously stepped down. Providentially, the governor of the Gold Coast at that time knew the great gifts of Freeman and hired him as the commandant of Accra in order to be a liaison between the British government and the natives inhabiting the greater Accra region.

Relational Excellence

From the time of Freeman's humble beginnings as a garden boy, when he first bent his ear to that keyhole to listen to the cobbler's message that captured his heart for Christ, Freeman had always shown the ability to relate and respect every human being with whom he came in contact. When he was first confronted by Sir Robert and Lady Harland about the choice of choosing gardening or Methodism, with tact and respect he chose the latter. He continued his friendship with Lady Harland long after his departure, even bringing her botanical samples from Africa for her garden. When he landed at Cape Coast the person he was most endeared to was Governor Maclean, whom he considered a colleague and friend for his entire ministry. Freeman was equally endeared to his native co-workers, Joseph Smith and William De Graft. Freeman realized early on in his mission work that the greater part of the expansion of the ministry would be done by natives and not by missionaries—a keen insight at an early stage of his missionary development. Freeman's greatest asset as a missionary was his ability to relate to people from all walks of life.

One of the best training aids to assist him in that was that he had to travel by foot or by carriers in a basket throughout the country. Every village was an opportunity for him to meet the chief, greet the local leaders, and explain what his mission was. He learned to emulate the customs of the people that he had come to work with. Walker explains this insight Freeman had learned:

> Freeman soon gained an almost magic influence over African chiefs. His sound judgement, his tactful manner of approach, and his never-failing courtesy almost invariably triumphed, and he soon became known as "the great white prophet." Quickly learning the customs of the country, he adopted such as would serve his purpose. Thus, when going to visit a chief, he would send on before him (as a chief would do) a messenger with an official "stick" to announce his approach. Attention to such little courtesies and points of African etiquette greatly pleased the chiefs and opened the way for his great message. "He knows our customs," they said, as they prepared to receive him.[28]

Indeed, Freeman was gifted at communicating with merchants, governors, local chiefs, and village people. But his most extraordinary gift was coupled with the courage to meet some of the most feared and notorious leaders of West Africa. His first visit to meet the Asantehene, Kwaku Dua, was renowned. His venturing over to Abeokuta to meet Shodeke was pioneering, and his desire to meet King Ghezo of Dahomey was sheer fearlessness. Freeman was remarkable at disarming the fears and prejudices that many chiefs held against Europeans.

The most famous engagement between Thomas Birch Freeman and the Asantehene happened in early January 1842. He had returned from his first furlough in England with two of the Asantehene's nephews and delivered them to Kumasi. This was one of the greatest gestures of faith and reconciliation between the British government and the Asante King. The boys were sent to Cape Coast in 1835 as a sign of peace with the British government and later to England for education.

Upon their return, it meant that all was well between the Asantes and the British. The king invited the two newly returned princes; Mr. Brooking, the newly arrived missionary from England; Freeman's interpreter; and Freeman. During the meal the king rose up and greeted them and several cultural expressions were translated for their understanding. Then the king danced. He had never danced in front of his wives before and he explained to Freeman that it was in honor of the queen of England and in gratitude for showing kind gestures to his nephews and to himself. But the most significant gesture was when the Asantehene went over to Freeman and shook his hand. In that day and in that culture, the Asantehene *never* did that to any foreigner. The women in the court sang a song in reflection and honor of what he had done:

> *The Englishman lives in Sebu Seki.*
> *Today he has come to visit the King.*
> *The King has danced before him*
> *In the presence of his wives,*
> *And done what he has never done to*
> *An European before. He has walked*
> *Up, and shaken hands with him.*[29]

It seems a minor incident that one man would shake another's in a gesture of greeting or gratitude, but in the culture of the Asante, this was an unheard of act. It could be compared to the queen of England coming off her throne and stepping down to greet the common people whom she ruled.

Whether Sir Robert and Lady Harland, the president of the Methodist Church, Governor Maclean of the Gold Coast, Joseph Smith, William De Graft, Thomas Fowell Buxton, King Ghezo, or slave trader Da Souza, Freeman treated them all with dignity and respect. He never compromised his beliefs or values in the presence of any of them. He was a man of honor, humility, courage, and relational brilliance. Though he had his shortcomings in the accounting of finances, he persevered and finished his ministry well on the Gold Coast. He buried two English-born wives in Cape Coast, and then in 1848 he married Rebecca Morgan, who was also called Naa Gyamfi. Later in life she was called Nee Nsaadu. She delivered four beautiful children: Thomas Birch Freeman, Jr.; Vincent Freeman; Lucy Freeman; and Evangelina Freeman. Freeman reentered the ministry officially in 1873 and served fifteen more years. He was the keynote speaker for the Golden Jubilee in 1885.

His spirit of sacrifice, innovation, and grace in the midst of many dangers and conflicts reveals character that is rarely found in most missionaries today. Freeman was famous because he was adventurous, creative, humble, and above all, a lover of all people. He was called Kwaku, The Great White Prophet, but finally in his later years he was endearingly called Father Freeman.

NOTES

1. Matthew 28:19 NIV.

2. David Bundy, "William Taylor 1821–1902: Entrepreneurial Maverick for the Indigenous Church," in *Mission Legacies: Biographical Studies of Leaders of the Modern Missionary Movement*, ed. Gerald Anderson, et al., (Maryknoll, N.Y.: Orbis Books, 1994), pp. 461–68.

3. A search of baptisms and burials under the alphabetical name of Birch reveals all dates of birth and death of the children. The first Thomas was not baptized but was buried on August 11, 1793. The following link to St. Mary's Anglican Church in Twyford, England, contains parish records dating back to 1626: http://www.stmarytwyford.fsnet.co.uk/

4. Thomas Birch Freeman, *Journal of Various Visits to the Kingdoms of Ashanti, Aku, and Dahomi* (London: Frank Cass and Co., 1968), p. 111.

5. John Milum, *Thomas Birch Freeman: Missionary Pioneer to Ashanti, Dahomey and Egba* (New York: Fleming H. Revell Company, 1893), and F. Deaville Walker, *Thomas Birch Freeman: The Son of an African* (Edinburgh: Turnbull and Spears, 1929).

6. Walker, *Son of an African*, p. 13.

7. Ibid., p. 13: "One Sunday evening Thomas reached the cottage before his companions, and to pass the time away he stole softly to the door and did a little eavesdropping. As he stood there in the darkness, his ear pressed against the spacious keyhole, he heard words that arrested his attention and sank deeply into his heart. The young tormentor in the current phrase of the period, 'became serious'—very serious—and his companions found him poor company that night."

8. Walker, *Son of an African*, pp. 20–21.

9. Allen Birtwhistle, *Thomas Birch Freeman: West African Pioneer* (London: The Cargate Press, 1950), pp. 5 and xv.

10. Birtwhistle, *West African Pioneer*, p. 5.

11. Joseph Dunwell was the first missionary sent out by the Wesleyan Methodist Missionary Society. He arrived on January 1, 1835, and died on June 24. He was buried in Cape Coast. The Wrigleys arrived on September 15, 1836, and the Harrops arrived in January 1837.

12. Birtwhistle, *West African Pioneer*, p. 7.

13. Walker, *Son of an African*, pp. 39–40.

14. Ibid., p. 41.

15. Wesleyan Methodist Missionary Society Archives, Special Collection Box 6, School of Oriental and African Studies, University of London. The only documentation that I found where T. B. Freeman's father's name is on record is the marriage license that was made when T. B. Freeman married Lucinda Cowan in 1840. It states that Freeman's father's name was Thomas Freeman and his profession was a yeoman.

16. Freeman, *Journal*, p. 13.

17. Birtwhistle, *West African Pioneer*, pp. 75–81.

18. Ibid., p. 85.

19. Walker, *Son of an African*, p. 164: "But there was one slave-merchant different from the rest—Don Antonio Da Souza . . . A few days after landing, Freeman found it advisable to call on Da Souza, and to his surprise found him exceedingly polite and kind, and prepared to help by any means in his power. Even when Da Souza understood that his guest was a Christian missionary and a determined enemy of the slave trade, it made no difference. Throughout Freeman's long stay in Whydah, as well as on subsequent occasions, Da Souza treated him with unfailing kindness and courtesy."

20. School of Oriental and African Studies Methodist Missionary Series/Special Series/Biographical/West Africa/Freeman/FBN Box 4, pp. 47–48.

21. Walker, S*on of an African,* p. 44.

22. Birtwhistle, *West African Pioneer*, p. 9.

23. Thomas Fowell Buxton, *African Slave Trade and Its Remedy* (London: Dawsons of Pall Mall, 1968), p. 399.

24. Pitts Library, Candler School of Theology/Special Collection: Wesley, 1844–Hust; "Malicious Slanders upon Wesleyan Missionaries Exposed and Refuted, in Three Letters to The Editor of the Cork Examiner, with an appendix containing the vindication of The Rev. T. B. Freeman." By Robert Huston, Wesleyan Irish Missionary, Youghal, printed by J. W. Lindsay, 1844.

25. The *Times*, November 7, 1844, "To the Editor." http://archive.timesonline.co.uk/tol/archive/

26. Birtwhistle, *West African Pioneer,* p. 99.

27. Walker, *Son of an African,* p. 204.

28. Ibid., p. 48.

29. Freeman, *Journal,* p. 149.

19

HISTORICAL PERSPECTIVES OF THE MISSION SOCIETY

H. T. Maclin

In the second half of the twentieth century John Wesley's combination of salvation through Jesus Christ followed by good works, especially those relating to the poor and oppressed, became separated in parts of The United Methodist Church (UMC). This was particularly true in the General Board of Global Ministries (GBGM). Concerned laity and pastors, attempting to return emphasis to a balance, began efforts to resurrect Wesley's duality. But seldom if ever have changes and reform come from those in the inner circles of the church. The struggles for the needed reform and the new organization that resulted, the Mission Society for United Methodists (now incorporated as The Mission Society), show God's work in the lives and hearts of many believers. Its founding, while unofficial, was not as unusual as one might think. From our own church we have three earlier examples.

The Methodist Episcopal Church in America, organized in 1794, had viewed its primary mission to be the ever-expanding immigrant and Native American populations, and it established churches in many areas. By 1820, however, the Methodist Missionary Society (MMS) was founded in spite of open opposition to "foreign" mission, which insisted that the churches had more opportunities for urgently needed service in their local communities than were being met.[1] By 1824 enough money had been received to support one missionary and the Society petitioned the Council of Bishops to send someone. Since no action was taken, the petition was again sent to the Council at the General Conference of 1828, which then chose the newly formed nation of Liberia (founded in 1822 by freed slaves) as its first mission outside the U.S. Four years later in 1832, eight years after the money was received, Rev. Melville B. Cox was appointed to go there. Already ill with consumption, he was nevertheless chosen. Family and friends pleaded with him not to go, but he was persuaded he was following God's purpose for his life.[2] Though he lived only four more months after reaching Liberia in March 1833, God empowered him to begin a movement in the Wesleyan tradition that has, through periods of challenge, difficulty, and triumph, continued to this day.

Another movement within American Methodism began in 1869, the Women's Foreign Missionary Society (WFMS), which was organized by just seven women inspired by the wife of a missionary to India. They had tried in vain to persuade the MMS to send women doctors for Hindu and Muslim women who would not see male physicians. When their appeals failed, they unilaterally formed the WFMS as a voluntary society to found hospitals and schools. Their first missionaries, Clara Swain, M.D., and Isabella Thoburn, arrived in India in January 1870. They and their supporters were heavily criticized by the bishops, who accused them of interference, causing disunity in the church, being incompatible with Methodist connectionalism, and diverting funds from the General Society.[3] Not until the General Conference of 1884 were the women's efforts finally recognized as valid ministry and given official status. The WFMS eventually became the UMW (United Methodist Women), whose undesignated giving today supports the Women's Division of the GBGM.

A third movement was the work of evangelist William Taylor. His missionary vision, based on the principle of "self-sufficiency" without MMS support or direction, founded work in India, South America, Liberia, and Angola. After he was elected as a missionary bishop and later retired, his work that survived was taken over by MMS.

By the early 1920s the Methodist churches had over 2,700 foreign-service missionaries, more than any other denomination in North America (counting those from three predecessors of today's United Methodist Church: The Methodist Episcopal Church, the Methodist Episcopal Church South, and the Methodist Protestant Church).[4] Missionary numbers decreased during the late 1920s, the 1930s, and the early 1940s because of the Great Depression and World War II. Communism's success in China in the 1950s led to the closing of what had been the largest foreign field with over 300 Methodist missionaries working in various provinces.

At the end of World War II, however, in spite of the apparent setback in China, a new surge of missionaries arrived in Africa, Latin America, Southeast Asia, and India. My wife and I with two young daughters were among these, having been appointed to the Belgian Congo in 1952 by the then Board of Missions of The Methodist Church. Profound and unexpected changes were in store for all of us: in our society in the U.S., in mission boards, missionaries, and especially in Africa, in political independence that came much faster than anyone had foreseen. The one unchanged and unchangeable factor was—as it is still—". . . the necessity for a confrontation with Christ." As Trueblood pointed out,

> The greatest danger in modern mission is not the one which existed previously, that of evangelism without service, but rather that of service without evangelism . . . Because the service which is not grounded in a message will soon cease to be even a service . . . if it stands alone it will soon cease to stand at all.[5]

Many observers of mission policies of what was then the Board of Global Ministries (BOGM) of The United Methodist Church, myself among them, saw that evangelism had become an embarrassment to Board leadership. Evangelism was associated in the minds of many with colonialism and imperialism. Independence and self-determination, an inevitable, positive development in national churches, seemed to make the decision to no longer directly support the church overseas desirable and politically possible.

During our years in Kenya other "signs of the time" became apparent, among them an article titled "A Look to the Future," written by the General Secretary of the BOGM, Dr. Tracey K. Jones. I read with some amazement that he saw ". . . the test of discipleship to Christ in terms of adult decisions dealing with complex and ambiguous issues" and that "the arena of missionary activity will be the public sector—to liberate men from hunger, war, fear and human degradation; to confront political and social power groups that take advantage of the weak; and to cooperate with governments in the private sector in serving mankind."[6]

I was soon to discover that his prediction would become a basis for Board policy.

The change in strategy to support social and political programs rather than people, formerly called "missionaries" but now referred to as "persons in mission," soon became apparent. Such persons were rarely related to church development. Allocation of funds changed, with as much spent on New York staff as for persons in world mission. Liberation theology emphasized action in the political and social realms rather than in the heart. Attempts to change the trend—by pastors, laity, conferences, and some bishops—were unsuccessful. Ten years of dialogue begun in 1974 by Good News, an evangelical renewal effort within the UMC, with the BOGM was fruitless.

Finally, in 1983, many laity having already left The United Methodist Church, several events converged to bring about the formation of the Mission Society for United Methodists. Dr. L. D. Thomas, pastor of First United Methodist Church in Tulsa, Oklahoma, and Dr. Ira Gallaway, pastor of First United Methodist Church in Peoria, Illinois, covenanted to organize pastors of large churches, whose positions were reasonably secure, to bring about change outside the denominational structure if necessary.

That same summer Good News' Evangelical Missions Council sponsored a national mission conference where Bishop Ole Borgen of Norway gave a startling address, "One Mission, One Missional Purpose: The United Methodist Church in Mission Today."

[The church's] uncertainty and lack of clarity of purpose is confounded by what appears to be a conscious redefinition of . . . traditional concepts, usually without mentioning that a redefinition has taken place . . . [for example] *evangelism* has been corrupted to mean receiving members into the church whether they have committed themselves to Christ or not . . . *Conversion* now indicates any turning around or change of attitude. . . . *Salvation* no longer indicates the new relationship with God, but just as much any kind of "salvation" within the socio-political realms. . . . We have almost imperceptibly moved to a position which . . . will end up . . . where man himself is the acting and redeeming agent.[7]

The next event in 1983 to lay the foundation for The Mission Society came in early October. Dr. Gerald H. Anderson, long regarded as one of Methodism's foremost church historians and missiologists, had no contact with the Evangelical Missions Council of Good News or with Thomas or Gallaway. He had spent, however, nearly a decade of private protest and consultations with colleagues both within the Board and the wider church before deciding to go public in Dallas, Texas. At a meeting of ministers, he chose as his topic "Why We Need a Second Mission Agency."[8]

The defining moment came later that same month when the Board elected a new Deputy General Secretary for what was then the World Division, a key position, responsible for the support of missionaries and projects overseas. Many had hoped for a change in the Board's focus and leadership. But when Ms. Peggy Billings, whose writings showed her to be a strong advocate of liberation theology, was elected, clearly an even more radical stance had been set in place.

Many interested United Methodists previously unrelated began to discuss strategies for organizing a new association. News of Dr. Anderson's address in Dallas came as the Evangelical Missions Council of Good News was already finalizing plans for a second mission agency since the previous ten years of dialogues with the GBGM had accomplished nothing. Drs. Thomas and Gallaway invited a select group to meet at the St. Louis airport on November 28 and asked Dr. Anderson to share his perspectives. Thirty-four pastors and professors of mission responded and, after much prayer and discussion, determined to organize the Mission Society for United Methodists as a voluntary, supplemental agency within the framework of The United Methodist Church. Dr. Anderson summed up the concerns of the group with words similar to those of his Dallas address:

> [It is] difficult to discern that those who are now responsible [in the World Division] really believe that it makes any difference whether or not one believes in Jesus as Savior and Lord.[9]

The thirty-four pastors and professors of mission present at this historic meeting pledged $130,000 for start-up expenses. Now a person was needed to be the executive director.

Ira Gallaway, secretary of the steering committee, came to see me in Atlanta looking for leads to possible candidates. Our long friendship went back to the early 1950s in Dallas at the Perkins School of Theology. From there I was ordained and my wife and I were commissioned as missionaries to Africa, where we served in both the Congo and Kenya.

When we returned to the States I was invited in 1974 to be on the Board's executive staff based in Atlanta as its Field Representative for

Mission Development in the Southeastern Jurisdiction (region) and served in this position for almost another ten years. During this thirty-year period in missions I traveled throughout Africa, Europe, the Middle East, and Asia, gaining some understanding of the church in many areas of the world.

When Gallaway asked me for possible names of potential candidates, I glanced at Alice and replied, "How about me?" Gallaway was astounded. Having already served for nearly three decades with what was earlier called the Board of Missions of the Methodist Church, by now renamed the General Board of Global Ministries (GBGM) of the UMC, he was quite sure I would retire from there, but I had already decided that I could not remain on the GBGM staff.

"What," he asked, "will be their reaction?"

"That's easy," I replied. "They won't like it at all!"[10]

We talked until well after midnight and committed ourselves to join hands with those who stepped forward and pledged their support. The Mission Society for United Methodists was incorporated on January 6, 1984. Expressions of alarm from official sources were very similar to the opposition faced by the 1869 announcement of a small group of seven women who organized the Women's Foreign Missionary Society within the Methodist Episcopal Church.

"A Letter to Autonomous Churches" was sent out to Methodist church leaders around the world in late January 1984 by the head of the GBGM's World Division, Peggy Billings, to tell them:

> I regret to share the news that some clergy here are unhappy with the GBGM and have organized a group called, "the Mission Society for United Methodists." They say they will send missionaries to other places . . . and have hired H. T. Maclin, former staff member of this board, to be their staff . . . This organization could be disruptive of the administrative order of the church and it could also be disruptive of the internal good order of the life of our colleague churches. We will do all in our power to minimize any difficulty, and we would appreciate any information you have to share.[11]

The names of all the directors of the new Mission Society were included in the letter.

Ms. Billing's letter reached around the world with the intent of undermining our efforts. But the news was picked up by the press, both religious and secular, and within a very short time our curbside home mailbox began to fill up with letters, 97 percent of them congratulatory, including inquiries from four overseas Methodist bishops/presidents wanting more information about how they could establish a relationship with us.

In mid-March, Dr. Gerald Anderson, one of the founding members of the Society's Board of Directors, was invited to address the World Division of the GBGM. He came straight to the point in his opening statement:

> We are engaged today in nothing less than a struggle for the soul and survival of The United Methodist Church. It is essentially a struggle about the Gospel of Jesus Christ, the nature of the Gospel, what it means to be a Christian, and what the mission of the church is in the world.[12]

In April 1984 the quadrennial General Conference of the UMC met in Baltimore, where I was asked to provide an account of our actions before the Legislative Committee on Global Ministries. After much debate, the conference passed a petition calling on the

> directors and staff persons of the General Board of Global Ministries [to] confer with directors and staff persons of The Mission Society with the purpose being . . . to strengthen and enhance the witness to our Savior, Jesus Christ, through the mission of the UMC throughout the world.[13]

The Council of Bishops was also requested to

> . . . mediate the differences in mission philosophy and practice that prevail in our church today . . . The resolution provides an arena in which [The Mission Society] can be heard.[14]

Three of eventually eighteen or more dialogue sessions were held during the General Conference. Some of the bishops felt there was really only one question to consider: What did they (the bishops and the GBGM) have to do to get The Mission Society to "go out of business"? Our response was that it was too late for such a question to be raised, for during more than a dozen previous years, twenty-two dialogues had taken place to try to achieve understanding without serious change. We were there to make another attempt and called upon the World Division to affirm its *primary* mandate as stated in the *Discipline* of the UMC, a mandate we ourselves gladly affirmed and asked them to do no less.

> The World Division exists to confess Jesus Christ as divine Lord and Savior to all people in every place, testifying to His redemptive and liberating power in every sphere of human existence and activity and calling all people to Christian obedience and discipleship.[15]

In the meantime The Mission Society would be open to further dialogue but found it difficult to believe the outcome would be any different from that at the end of the earlier effort of the Evangelical Missions Council of Good News led by Dr. Virgil Maybray. He had joined our staff shortly after the General Conference of 1984 to take over our growing files of applicants for missionary service.

The loss of our first board chairman came in September of the same year when Dr. L. D. Thomas died suddenly of a heart attack. At our next board meeting, Dr. Ira Gallaway was elected to succeed him as chairman.

Twenty congregations (0.05 percent of UM churches) served by the founding Board of Directors made a promise in faith of providing $130,000 in start-up funds for 1984. More than $239,000 was received and enabled us to move ahead faster than anticipated. Our first group of ten missionaries was commissioned and sent in May 1985 to Africa, Latin America, and the South Pacific. From then to the present more than eight thousand more donor partnerships have been affirmed, providing a budget in 2008 of approximately $11,000,000.

Since 1985 nearly four hundred men and women have been trained and confirmed to serve Christ in thirty-two nations. As a voluntary agency, the Society receives no apportioned funds through denominational channels but depends on the direct support of individuals, foundations, and local congregations who, with us, affirm the Lordship of our Savior, Jesus Christ. A staff of twenty-seven dedicated individuals work out of our home office in the Atlanta area to make it possible for more than 210 missionaries to be in ministry around the world, nearly 75 percent of them serving from three to sixteen years or more, especially to areas where the Gospel has been least heard. There they introduce individuals to Christ, disciple new believers, plant churches, work with national leaders to help them reach their own nations for Christ, and further community development and relief efforts where needed.

Action by the quadrennial General Conference of 1984 regarding The Mission Society was quite different from the 2008 session when petition 81140, calendar item 1366, came before the Legislative Committee on Global Ministries. The Committee approved it and sent it to the floor for plenary action where it was adopted by 508 votes for and 323 against. The petition resolved that

> The United Methodist Church acknowledge and commend the positive contribution to the work and mission through The Mission Society and that furthermore the General Board of Global Ministries develop new conversations and liaisons with The Mission Society for new and ongoing partnerships in areas of mutual concern . . . that we encourage bishops, Cabinets and annual conferences to acknowledge and support, where appropriate, those individuals and projects associated with The Mission Society.[16]

These words encourage us for future relationships.

The Mission Society celebrates its twenty-fifth anniversary in 2009. Those who have in faith served and helped the Society during this quarter century are too numerous to name individually, but we thank God for each one of them and trust their numbers will increase as we move ahead in this new century.[17]

The Development Timeline, 1985–2008[18] can be seen on the following page.

Development Timeline, 1985–2008

YEAR ENTERED 1985–2008	NEW MISSIONARIES COMMISSIONED*	COUNTRIES, AREAS ENTERED+	SELECTED NEW MINISTRIES PROGRAMS/PROJECTS
1985–1989	81	New Mexico Ghana Mexico South Pacific Paraguay The Philippines Costa Rica Columbia	Foreign students in U.S.; Navajo-Shiprock; Evangelical Seminary of Costa Rica; More than 30 cooperative agreements with other evangelical agencies.
1990–1994	103	Tanzania Guinea Haiti China Kazakstan France Russia (as part of Co-Mission Project) Japan Bolivia	*Get Ready* (U.S. Youth), Ankase Hospital, Ghana; Hispanic Church, Wash., DC, with Fairfax, VA District of UMC; Mobile Medical Clinic to Kazakhstan and Small Business Training Center.
1995–1999	92	Peru Ukraine India	Bible Institute, Paraguay; Living Vine Church, Kazakhstan; CoMissions first missionary; International Leadership Institute launched; Training for 70 district supts. and 7 bishops in India; World Parish Ministries; joins Co-Mission II for church planting in Russia.
2000–2004	102	Hungary Kenya Nicaragua	Community Health Evangelism, Ghana; Church Ministry Dept. launched (U.S. churches); sends staff to Wesley Foundations in U.S. colleges/universities; Mission Mobilization Conferences in Ghana (2003).
2005–2008	112	Brazil Israel Cuba Togo Zambia Venezuela Honduras Ecuador	Church Ministry (formerly World Parish); Mission Mobilization in Ghana, Kenya, Costa Rica, Brazil, and Mexico.

*Includes missionaries seconded to partnership agencies   +Some countries omitted for the safety of missionaries

NOTES

1. Wade C. Barclay, *Missionary Motivation and Expansion,* vol. 1, *Early American Methodism 1769–1844,* History of Methodist Missions (New York: Board of Missions and Church Extension of the Methodist Church, 1949), p. 209. Opposition to the new Society was so great that eleven of the original thirty-two members of the General Board of Managers resigned amidst excuses that the whole church itself is missionary and they opposed "foreign" mission because the church was too poor to support anything outside the local church.

2. Roger S. Guptill, *Though Thousands Fall: The Story of Melville B. Cox* (New York: The Methodist Book Concern, 1932), p. 209. Six years after the death of Cox in Monrovia, his brother, Rev. Gershom F. Cox, published *Remains of Melville B. Cox, Late Missionary to Liberia*, in 1840 for the Methodist Episcopal Church. Many letters to and from M. Cox are included in this book.

3. Wade C. Barclay, *The Methodist Episcopal Church, 1845–1939: Widening Horizons 1845–1895*, vol. 3, *History of Methodist Missions* (New York: The Board of Missions of The Methodist Church, 1957), p. 141.

4. H. T. Maclin, *The Faith that Compels Us* (Atlanta: The Mission Society for United Methodists, 1997), p. 16.

5. Elton D. Trueblood, *The Validity of the Christian Mission* (New York: Harper & Row, 1972), p. 26.

6. Tracey K. Jones, "A Look to the Future," *World Outlook* (April 1969): p. 34.

7. Ole E. Borgen, "One Mission, One Missional Purpose: The United Methodist Church in Mission Today" (unpublished paper), July 11, 1983.

8. Gerald H. Anderson, "Why We Need a Second Mission Agency," *Good News*, (March–April 1984): pp. 55–62.

9. Gerald H. Anderson, unpublished minutes (Rodeway Inn, St. Louis airport, November 1983). Asked to share his perspectives on the state of missions in The United Methodist Church, Dr. Anderson gave a summary of the address he had given to local church pastors in Dallas, Texas.

10. H. T. Maclin, unpublished comments to Dr. Ira Gallaway (Atlanta, December 1983). After expressing an interest in becoming associated with the yet-to-be-formed mission agency, we talked and prayed together well into the night, committing ourselves to organizing it and asking that God would bless our efforts to expand the message of salvation available to all who are willing to trust in Jesus as Lord.

11. Peggy Billings, unpublished letter to autonomous Methodist churches around the world (January 1984).

12. Gerald H. Anderson, unpublished address to World Division, GBGM (March 1984).

13. Proceedings, Legislative Committee reports and other records of the 1984 General Conference (*Daily Christian Advocate*, Roger. L. Burgess, ed., Nashville, 1984).

14. Proceedings, Legislative Committee reports and other records of the 1984 General Conference (*Daily Christian Advocate*, Richard J. Peck, ed., Nashville, 1984).

15. *The Book of Discipline of The United Methodist Church* (Nashville: United Methodist Publishing House, 1984), para. 1302.

16. Legislative Committee on Global Ministries petition 81140, calendar item 1366.

17. Current information about The Mission Society is updated regularly on its Web site, http://www.themissionsociety.org.

Here you can learn about the scope and nature of this ministry around the world, its missionaries, staff (short- and long-term), applications, and other information including downloadable podcasts and Global Outreach programs for the local church.

18. Development Timeline, The Mission Society, 1985–2008. Currently 211 missionaries serve in thirty-two countries supported by over eight thousand donor partnerships. The Society is a member of the Evangelical Council for Financial Accountability (which monitors its finances) and the Evangelical Fellowship of Mission Agencies. For full information visit The Mission Society's Web site at http://www.themissionsociety.org.

PART FOUR

Cultural Perspectives

MISSION ALWAYS OCCURS WITHIN A CULTURAL context and understanding that context is most important for effective mission and evangelism to take place. This section, therefore, focuses on cultural perspectives that inform our mission.

We begin with A. H. Mathias Zahniser's discussion of dealing with a difficult cultural and theological issue in interacting with Muslims, namely, the problem of the death of Jesus. Zahniser receives insight from Wesley's understanding and practice of repentance, prayer, fasting, almsgiving, and intercessory prayer that enable us to build a bridge toward Muslims' understanding of the death of Jesus.

Ajith Fernando presents a case study from Sri Lanka where the ethics of shame and honor are dominant rather than ethics based on sin and guilt. It is therefore a challenge to develop strong accountability groups for discipleship in such a cultural context. He finds that Wesley's structures for spiritual formation are effective in helping new converts, from cultures where shame and honor are important values, to adopt a Christian value system which results in holiness of heart and life.

Contextualization is an important approach to connect the Gospel to the culture in which people live. Dean Gilliland draws on his missionary experience in Nigeria with African students to discuss how biblical truth relates to the major concerns in their society. Then Gilliland explores the question of whether or not John Wesley was a contextual theologian, connecting Christian living to eighteenth-century British society.

People in oral cultures learn best through proverbs, rituals, and stories. Jay Moon explores ways in which Wesley's understanding of prevenient grace is found in the proverbs, rituals, and stories of people which can be used as stepping stones to connect people with the Gospel and to understand better what it means to be a follower of Jesus in their culture. His exploration takes us to Ghana, Nigeria, and a Native American sweat lodge.

In the Islamic world today, many Muslims are becoming followers of Isa al Masih (Jesus the Messiah) while remaining within their religious and cultural context. Wilbur Stone explores this phenomenon and notes that traditional evangelistic approaches to Muslims have failed miserably for the past fourteen hundred years. He suggests we need a change in our attitude, a change in our approach, and a change in our actions to approach Muslims effectively with the saving knowledge of Jesus.

The last chapter in this section turns our attention to three case studies from Asia. Hwa Yung illustrates that when mission activity is tied to wealth and promotes affluence instead of focusing on sacrifice, suffering, and the way of the cross, the growth and vitality of the church suffers. In contrast, where followers of Jesus have endured suffering, deprivation, and economic hardship, the church has often flourished.

20

WESLEYAN SYNERGISM AND THE DIALOGUE WITH MUSLIMS

A. H. Mathias Zahniser

In 2003, Sheikh Fawzial-Zafzaf, president of al-Azhar University's Permanent Committee for Dialogue with the Monotheistic Religions, addressed a largely Christian audience at Ridley Hall, an Anglican Theological College in Cambridge, England. The Sheikh described for his audience some of the common ground Muslims and Christians share, arguing that the "core messages" of Christianity and Islam agree in essence.

But what about the core Christian message of the cross? I said to myself as I listened. In my interactions with Muslims, I have found them almost consistently denying that Jesus was crucified. Does the Qur'an not contain this denial, "they killed him not, nor crucified him" (The Women [4]:157)?

In their dialogue with Islam, some Christians have interpreted the qur'anic denial verse mentioned above so as to deny its denial. Early on, the Nestorian Patriarch Timothy I of Baghdad (d. 823) pointed out to the Muslim Caliph al-Mahdi (reigned 775–785) that the Qur'an denies only the claim of the Jews to have crucified Jesus.[1] Some early Qur'an authorities as well as some more recent ones also have departed from the usual Muslim denial of the cross to stand for its historicity.[2]

A MUSLIM AFFIRMATION OF THE DEATH OF JESUS

Mahmoud M. Ayoub, a devout Muslim and an appreciative student of Christianity and Christian-Muslim relations, is one of these modern

Muslim interpreters. He believes in the Qur'an as the exact words of God and shows that the Qur'an does not deny Jesus' death. He offers his own conclusion about the crucifixion: "Only the human body of Jesus suffered and died"; his soul did not suffer and die, but went to be with God. Ayoub believes this "provides a good starting point for Muslim-Christian understanding."[3] In another context, Ayoub has this also to say about the last days of Jesus' life: "Throughout the trial and subsequent crucifixion Jesus showed himself as an absolute Muslim, that is to say, as one who absolutely submitted his life and his will to the will of God [*muslim* means 'one who submits' in Arabic]."[4]

But does not Ayoub set aside the cross of Jesus as a sacrifice for sin? True, he does not reach a Christian doctrine of redemption—he is after all a Muslim—but he is self-consciously building a bridge in the Christian direction. I am convinced that Wesleyan theology offers an important platform for building a bridge toward Muslims. I refer particularly to the fact that Professor Ayoub sees the crucifixion as evidence of Jesus' absolute submission to God's will. An important passage for Jesus' teaching about his death and resurrection relates to Ayoub's conviction.

JESUS' TEACHING ABOUT HIS CROSS AND RESURRECTION

Jesus clearly placed his crucifixion and resurrection at the heart of his way of being the Messiah. The central section of the Gospel of Mark (8:22–10:45) is structured around three explicit predictions Jesus made of his suffering, death, and resurrection. Each prediction is followed by a misunderstanding on the part of the disciples, and a teaching. The first teaching is that the life of the followers of Jesus is also to be a sacrificial "taking up" of one's own cross (8:34–38). Does this not suggest a submission to God's will on the part of the disciple—and is not Jesus' own death a prime example of such submission? Second, Jesus taught, "Whoever wants to be first must be last of all and servant of all" (9:35). Is not submission the role of a servant? Jesus' third lesson was similar: "[W]hoever wishes to become great among you must be your servant, and whoever wishes to be first among you must be slave of all" (10:43–44).

Mark's servant-shock narrative climaxes in the next verse: "For the Son of Man came not to be served but to serve, and to give his life a ransom for many" (10:45). This ransom image from the emancipation of slaves shows that the death and resurrection of Jesus is a redemptive event. But the verse also epitomizes the lessons Jesus attached to his predictions, showing that redemption involves a transformed life—of submission.

AYOUB'S FOUR MODELS OF REDEMPTION

In addition to affirming the death of Jesus on a cross as an act of "absolute submission" to the will of God, Mahmoud Ayoub extends his bridge of understanding by examining models of Christian redemption and models of Muslim redemption. One model, dominant in Western Christianity, focuses on the cross as sacrifice, Jesus' death taking the place of the Jerusalem Temple's sacrificial system, offering believers forgiveness. Another model, dominant in Eastern Christianity, focuses on redemption as victory, in which through suffering, dying, and rising Jesus gains the victory over sin, death, and the demonic.

In yet another model, Muslim believers deal with their own sins through repentance, fasting, prayer, and giving to the needy. In the fourth model, Muslims are redeemed through intercession. Intercession may be offered by the Prophet Muhammad and other great Muslim figures of piety such as the Prophet's martyred grandson, Husayn ibn Ali. Intercession can also be offered by ordinary believers praying for each other.[5]

Laying aside our first tendency as Christians to label both Muslim types of redemption "salvation by works," let's see how Wesley's theology can help us start a bridge from our side of the valley toward the Muslim side.

HUMAN WORKS AND RESPONSIBLE GRACE IN
JOHN WESLEY'S THEOLOGY

Wesleyan theologian Randy L. Maddox characterizes grace in the theology of John Wesley as "responsible grace." God's grace represents God's self-chosen responsibility to provide for humankind the power and the possibility of redemption. But God's responsibility does not relieve human beings of their responsibility to respond appropriately to God's will and to "work out" their "own salvation" (Phil. 2:13),[6] a type of "synergism."

Synergism derives from the Greek word *synergéo*, "work together with."[7] A form of this verb occurs in the book of James relating directly to redemption: "Was not our ancestor Abraham justified by works when he offered his son Isaac on the altar? You see that faith *worked with (synergei)* his works, and by the works faith was brought to completion."[8] This passage may be one cause of Martin Luther's lack of enthusiasm for the book of James, although he did not remove it from the canon. Nevertheless, the controversy over synergism during Reformation times was a Lutheran issue.

Synergism represents an alternative to the Augustinian view of Martin Luther (*The Bondage of the Will*, 1525) and other Lutherans, such as the early Philipp Melanchthon (*Loci communes*, 1521),[9] who held that the natural human person could conform to civil law, but was as unresponsive as a statue to the law of God or to the call of the Gospel. Therefore, humans "had to be justified by God's free grace before they could repent and believe." This view of redemption, known as monergism, represented the "genuine" (*Gnesio-*) Lutheran position.[10]

Later on, Philipp Melanchthon, followed by others, departed from his early monergism, concluding that it resulted in irresponsible discipleship. In the two later editions of his doctrinal treatise *Loci communes*, Melanchthon wrote that three causes were "conjoined" in redemption: "The Word, the Holy Spirit, and the [human] Will not wholly inactive, but resisting its own weakness . . . God draws, but draws him who is willing . . . and the will is not a statue. . . ."[11]

A reading from the preface to Martin Luther's commentary on the book of Romans provided the context in 1738 for Wesley's deeply influential heart-warming experience of God's grace. That experience drew him even closer to the Reformers' position of salvation by faith alone. But over time he came to believe that salvation by faith is compatible with and requires good works as well. People only lack the power of will to accept the Gospel invitation if they reject the grace of God that awakens their capacity for faith and obedience—a grace God grants to everyone (John 1:9). This understanding of grace was a product also of Wesley's reading of both Eastern and Western theologians.[12]

It is well known that Wesley was a student of the Eastern fathers. He was influenced by Gregory of Nyssa (d. 395), Ephrem Syrus (d. 373), and especially the Syriac ascetic piety found in the *Homilies* of Macarius (d. 391). Randy Maddox finds this to be the source of Wesley's early attraction to holiness and his lifelong teaching about the therapeutic or healing dimension of redemption.[13] Wesley's resultant theology integrates the two Christian models of redemption that Mahmoud Ayoub cites: the juristic focus in the West with its emphasis on pardon and the cross as an atoning sacrifice; and the Eastern focus on power over the disease of sin, the threat of the demonic, and the fear of death. Wesley's theology also addresses Ayoub's two Muslim types of redemption: good works and intercessory prayer.

REPENTANCE, PRAYER, FASTING, ALMSGIVING, AND INTERCESSORY PRAYER IN WESLEY

To return to the book of James, works of piety and prayer cannot be separated from faith as co-workers in the process of redemption. Wesley's integrative theology is at work here as well. He comments on James 2:22 where Abraham's willingness to sacrifice his son is in focus: "[F]aith has one energy and operation; works, another: and the energy and operation of faith are before works, and together with them. Works do not give life to faith, but faith begets works, and then is perfected by them."[14]

Wesley believed that human engagement in such forms of submission and service as repentance, prayer, fasting, and almsgiving are essential in the process of redemption. In his 1748 sermon "The Great Privilege of Those Who Are Born of God,"[15] Wesley describes the role of works as a response to grace in redemption: "[T]hose in whom God's Spirit is [graciously] acting must, by a spiritual re-action, return to God the grace which they receive, for God does not continue to act upon a soul unless the soul re-acts upon God by praise, prayer, and good works."[16] In another sermon, Wesley insists: "[W]hoever improves the grace he has already received . . . will surely retain it. . . . Whereas whoever does not improve this talent, cannot possibly retain it."[17] Does this not sound like the "taking up" of one's cross that Jesus requires?

If individuals wish to experience the grace of God, they must "cease to do evil, learn to do good" (Isa. 1:16–17). While turning from evil and turning to the good do not, as mentioned above, merit one's redemption, they do meet a condition for the working out of redemption in that without human response, grace will be withdrawn.[18]

I say "withdrawn" because, according to Wesley, the grace to respond to God's work in human experience is given to all people, enabling their awakening to their need of God and a good life. Such grace, termed by

Wesley "preventing" grace, is now called prevenient grace. God gives this grace that precedes repentance, faith, and nurture to all, including those born where no Gospel witness is present.[19] Acts 10:4 is part of an interaction between Cornelius, a Roman officer, and an angel God sent to him. "What is it Lord?" the centurion asks. The angel replies, "Your prayers and your alms have ascended as a memorial before God." John Wesley comments: "Dare any man say these [prayers and alms] were splendid sins; or that they were an abomination before God?"[20] "Splendid sins" was a phrase used by monergists for good works offered by the unregenerate. As good works they were "splendid," but because offered in self-justification they amounted to sins and "an abomination before God." Wesley is here insisting that human beings cooperating with God's grace who are not believers in Christ have access to God's favor.[21]

Ways of responding to grace effective for the ongoing success of redemption include, among other things, prayer, fasting, meeting together for worship and mutual support, attention to the Scriptures, and meeting the needs of others. Wesley wrote, "One of the principal rules of religion is, to lose no occasion of serving God. And, since he is invisible to our eyes, we are to serve him in our neighbor."[22] Again these works are forms of submission, are they not?

Fasting is one of those works important in redemption, according to Wesley, whose works include 150 instances of the gerund "fasting." The word frequently occurs in a list of indispensable means of grace. In his seventh discourse on the Sermon on the Mount, Wesley applies Scripture, tradition, creation, reason, and experience to fasting and concludes:

> And with fasting let us always join fervent prayer, pouring out our whole souls before God, confessing our sins [and] humbling ourselves under his mighty hand. . . . [And] add alms thereto [and] works of mercy, after our power, both to the bodies and souls of men.[23]

Finally, intercessory prayer, Ayoub's second Muslim model of redemption, amounts to a redemptive event in Wesley also: "God does nothing but in answer to prayer; and even they who have been converted to God without praying for it themselves . . . were not without the prayers of others."[24]

In redemption, Wesley brings the Eastern emphasis on power over sin, death, and the demonic, which leads to holiness, together with the Western emphasis on the cross of Christ as a sacrifice for sin, which yields pardon. He also insists that divine grace works together with the human efforts of repentance, fasting, prayer, intercession, study of Scripture, worship, and almsgiving in Christian redemption. In other words, in Wesley the four types of redemption mentioned by Ayoub come together. The faith and works of all humanity are the result of the prevenient grace of God, and their "prayers and alms ascend as memorials before God." Following Wesley, we can widen our understanding of the process of redemption to include human works of submission, all empowered by the grace of God. Surely here we have begun a bridge of responsible grace in the direction of Islam.[25]

IMPLICATIONS OF WESLEYAN SYNERGY FOR THE DIALOGUE WITH MUSLIMS

A Wesleyan synergistic view of redemption has at least four implications important for Christian dialogue with Muslims: (1) it fleshes out the Eastern and Western Christian models of redemption to include the models already recognized in Islam; (2) it emphasizes the prevenient and pervasive engagement of responsible grace throughout the process of redemption, motivating and enabling such submissive acts as repentance, prayer, fasting, and intercession; (3) its stress on the *necessity* of good works and the value of intercession in redemption will lead Christians to appreciate and to take seriously human engagement in the Islamic process of redemption; and (4) it will hopefully lead to an awareness of the deep engagement of God in redemption revealed in the death and resurrection of Jesus.[26]

NOTES

1. Neal Robinson, *Christ in Islam and Christianity* (Albany, N.Y.: SUNY, 1991), pp. 107–8.

2. See Todd Lawson, *The Crucifixion and the Qur'an* (Oxford: Oneworld, 2009).

3. Mahmoud M. Ayoub, *A Muslim View of Christianity*, ed. Irfan A. Omar (Maryknoll, N.Y.: Orbis Books, 2007), p. 167.

4. *Newsletter of Christian-Muslim Concerns* 43 (July 1990): 3, published by Interfaith Relations of the National Council of Churches of Christ in the U.S.A.

5. Ayoub, *A Muslim View*, pp. 91–94.

6. Randy L. Maddox, *Responsible Grace: John Wesley's Practical Theology* (Nashville: Kingswood Books, 1994), p. 19, but see also pp. 55, 147–48.

7. James P. Louw and Eugene A. Nida, eds., *Greek-English Lexicon of the New Testament Based on Semantic Domains*, 2 vols.

(New York: United Bible Societies, 1988), vol. 2, p. 235.

8. I have altered the New Revised Standard Version translation of James 2:21–22 for a more literal rendering of the passage.

9. See Heinz Schiebel, "Melanchthon, Philipp," in *The Oxford Encyclopedia of the Reformation*, ed. Hans J. Hillerbrand, 4 vols. (New York/Oxford: Oxford University Press, 1996), vol. 3, p. 42.

10. Luther D. Peterson, "Synergist Controversy," *The Oxford Encyclopedia of the Reformation*, vol. 4, p. 133.

11. Quoted by C. George Fry, "Synergism," *Evangelical Dictionary of Theology*, ed. Walter A. Elwell (Grand Rapids: Baker, 1984), p. 1063.

12. Maddox's discussion of the synergism issue in Methodism concludes with this statement: "If synergism is understood as simply the preservation of a role for grace-empowered human co-operation in salvation, then it too reflects a concern of Wesley's understanding of Prevenient Grace" (*Responsible Grace*, p. 91).

13. Ibid., pp. 84–86, 147–52.

14. John Wesley, *Explanatory Notes upon the New Testament*, 2 vols. (Peabody, Mass.: Hendrickson, [1754] 1986), *apud* James 2:22. The Qur'an treats the event referred to in James 2 and narrated in Genesis 22, also *combining faith and works*: "Peace be upon Abraham; we reward in this way those who do well; he is indeed among our servants the believers" (The Ranks [37]: pp. 109–11).

15. John Wesley, Sermon 19, "The Great Privilege of Those Who are Born of God," §II.1 and §III.3, *Works*, 1:435, p. 442. Cited in Maddox, *Responsible Grace*, p. 87 n. 154. Most citations of *The Works of John Wesley* refer to The Bicentennial Edition, ed. Frank Baker, 26 vols. (Nashville: Abingdon, 1980–2003). Hereafter cited as *Works*. Some references

cited as *Works* (Jackson) refer to *The Works of the Rev. John Wesley*, ed. Thomas Jackson, 14 vols. (London: Wesleyan Conference Office, 1872).

16. John Wesley, Sermon 19, §II.1, *Works*, 1: p. 435. Cited in Maddox, *Responsible Grace*, pp. 86–87.

17. Ibid., p. 87, n. 154, Sermon 90, "An Israelite Indeed," §I.5, *Works*, 3: p. 284.

18. See "Minutes of Several Conversations between the Rev. Mr. Wesley and Others," Q. 77 in *Works* (Jackson), vol. 8, p. 337. For an excellent treatment of Wesley's view of grace see James Stuart, *The John Wesley Code* (Wellington, New Zealand: Philip Garside, 2008), chap. 8.

19. In his essay "The Doctrine of Original Sin," Wesley went so far as to say that God will not condemn "one child of man" because of Adam's sin (§6, *Works* [Jackson], vol. 9, p. 332).

20. Wesley, *Explanatory Notes*, *apud* Acts 10:4.

21. This is discussed in "Minutes of Several Conversations," Q. 77 in *Works* (Jackson), vol. 8, p. 337, where Wesley says that among the unevangelized, an individual will be accepted of God who "according to the light he hath, 'feareth God and worketh righteousness.'"

22. John Wesley, *A Plain Account of Christian Perfection*, §25, Q. 38, 8 in *Works* (Jackson), vol. 11, p. 440.

23. Wesley, Sermon 27, "Upon our Lord's Sermon on the Mount," §IV.6, 7, *Works*, 1: p. 610.

24. Wesley, *Plain Account*, §25, Q. 38, p. 5, *Works* (Jackson), vol. 11, p. 437.

25. For Muslims, humans are born with the capacities Wesley attributes to the work of responsible grace. See A. H. Mathias Zahniser, *The Mission and Death of Jesus in Islam and Christianity* (Maryknoll, N.Y.: Orbis Books, 2008), pp. 232–33.

26. Ibid., pp. 246–55.

21

WESLEY'S SMALL GROUPS AS KEYS TO NURTURING GODLINESS AMONG CONVERTS FROM ECONOMICALLY POORER BACKGROUNDS

A CASE STUDY FROM SRI LANKA

Ajith Fernando

The rapid growth of the church in the non-Western world has happened primarily through people seeing God meet their needs through the display of his power. The church is facing many challenges as it seeks to nurture the new believers into mature, Christlike Christians. Some of those who profess a dramatic conversion to Christ continue with their old habits such as telling lies, acting dishonestly, taking revenge, and abusing their wives. Though holiness has been preached, the fact that its outworking is often not evidenced suggests that some key elements of the Christian message have not entered into the worldview of the new believers.

It is well known that John Wesley viewed the primary calling of the Methodist movement as being to spread scriptural holiness in the land. This certainly happened in Britain and North America so much so that Methodism was given the name "the holiness movement." Can this become a reality in cultures that do not have any background knowledge of a holy God informed by the teachings of the Bible? Wesley liked to call the Methodists "Bible Christians." This is what evangelical Christians are called today in Sri Lanka. But the behavior of many of our Christians often contradicts the teaching of the Bible.

SHAME AND HONOR IN OUR CULTURES

I believe a major reason for the slowness of our new believers to demonstrate in their lives major aspects of the biblical teaching on daily living is the cultural background where right and wrong are evaluated based on whether a given action produces shame or honor rather than whether it makes one guilty before a holy God. The guilt orientation gives a more *personal* awareness of sin, which acts as an incentive to holiness. Shame and honor are more *community-oriented* values.[1]

Sometimes when a father does something wrong, everyone in the family knows it. They may talk about the problem but they do not attribute wrong to the father as he must not be shamed and his honor must be preserved. A girl who is sexually abused by an uncle or stepfather tells her mother about it. The mother tells her not to talk about that again as it would bring dishonor to the family. She may even scold her daughter saying that for this to happen the girl must have first provoked him through her behavior. We had a president in Sri Lanka who is reputed to have kept files detailing all the corrupt practices of his ministers. He did not bring these up until they fell out of line and appeared to be disloyal to him. Sin was brought up not because it was morally wrong but because it was politically expedient to bring it up at a certain time. In this culture when someone's sin is brought up by another it is viewed as an act of disloyalty or of political maneuvering rather than something coming out of a commitment to the sinning person, to God, or to morality.

The above examples show that the strong community orientation in our cultures can serve as a disincentive to the accountability that fosters holiness. Yet, in the Bible, holiness is very much of a community value. Over the years I have come to the conviction that we must labor to transfer the community solidarity that is strong in shame cultures so that it applies to personal holiness also. Earlier it was considered a shame to own up to having sinned. What if by pressing biblical principles we develop an attitude of shame over *not* owning up to our sin? What if people once used to ignoring personal sins now view these sins as bringing shame?

In my thirty-two years as leader of Youth for Christ (YFC) in Sri Lanka and twenty-eight years on the leadership team of a Methodist church in the outskirts of Colombo, I have worked primarily with the urban poor from other faiths. We have attempted to follow John Wesley's system of nurture through small groups. There have been groups focusing on applying the Scripture to day-to-day life (which Wesley called Class meetings) and on those focusing on accountability (which Wesley called Bands).[2] The ministry of YFC currently has about 275 small groups. This was harder to do with consistency in the church. However, I can confidently say that all those who made it to some level of maturity were part of this small group system. I am convinced that the nurture structures advocated by Wesley are effective in helping new converts from cultures where shame and honor are important values to adopt the Christian value system, which results in holiness of heart and life.

NEW CRITERIA FOR SHAME AND HONOR

Practicing community in this way helps develop new criteria for identifying shame and honor. Wesley placed a strong emphasis on "rules" for the various groups within Methodism. These practices were considered normative for Methodists especially when they met for their regular meetings like leaders' meetings and local preachers' meetings. Therefore, he included questions about the personal lives of the members of the society, especially its leaders. The format for the meetings included questions about the beliefs and practices of the people. While these questions are still asked, at least in some Methodist churches in Sri Lanka, not many regard them with much seriousness.

In my study of the journals of John Wesley one of the most striking differences I saw between the church then and now was how little we discipline our members today. Wesley would "examine" the societies during his visits. That is, he would ask the leaders about the conduct of each member and decide what should be done about that member. The membership of many members was revoked as a result. Today disciplining is often associated with shame and honor. When a person is disciplined motives are attributed to the action taken: "The minister is against him because he criticized his wife."

Disciplining is part of the culture of a biblical community and the result is that there is a fear of sinning in that community. This is what happened after Ananias and Sapphira died (Acts 5:5, 11). Paul told Timothy, "As for [elders] who persist in sin [after carefully establishing that the sin was actually committed], rebuke them in the presence of all, so that the rest may stand in fear" (1 Tim. 5:20 ESV). I must confess that this is one directive that we have found very difficult to follow. Because of following it there was a holy fear of sinning in the early church that is missing in today's church. Through his practice of questioning and examining, Wesley initiated new criteria for shame and honor. He brought personal life into the public eye and affirmed that people could not profess to be Methodists if their personal lives did not give evidence of pursuing scriptural holiness.

This is an essentially biblical methodology where shame and honor is used in the promoting of holiness. Paul, for example, said that sexual sin "must not even be named among you, as is proper among saints" (Eph. 5:3 ESV); that filthiness, foolish talk, and crude joking was "out of place" (Eph. 5:4); and that "it is shameful even to speak of the things that they do in secret" (Eph. 5:12 ESV). When rebuking the Corinthians for unholy behavior, he said, "I say this to your shame" (1 Cor. 15:34 ESV; see also 2 Thess. 3:14). Even in biblical times honor and shame were used to foster holiness, just like Wesley did by bringing members' personal lives into public scrutiny through his probing questions to be asked at meetings.

COMMUNITY SOLIDARITY

The community solidarity in Christ fostered by Wesley's small groups served as an incentive to adopting Christian values. Wesley's bands have been described as belonging to the affective mode.[3] His "Rules of the Bands" begins with the words: "The design of our meeting is to obey the command of God, 'Confess your faults to one another, and pray for one another that ye may be healed' (James 5:16)."[4] Wesley recommends questions to ask about the personal life. This was what we today call a personal accountability group. So the band was a homogenous group consisting of the same kind of people—young men, or young women, or adult men, or adult women.

For three decades, I have been preaching about the need for Christian leaders to have this kind of accountability relationships and I have even written a book on this.[5] The constant response I get from leaders is that they cannot trust people enough to talk to them about their weaknesses and sins. Many describe how they have tried to do this and got hurt through the betrayal of trust. I am convinced that we need to create a new culture where people will trust each other so as to be willing to be vulnerable before them.

For such a culture we need a fresh understanding of grace. Grace tells us that we are all sinners but that God has done all that is necessary for our sins to be forgiven and forgotten. If we have such a strong sense of grace we would not be afraid to bring up our sins before trusted people. Those who hear of such sins would not go gossiping about them because they know that their own identity is only because of grace that was showered upon them despite their sinfulness. For a forgiven sinner to gossip about the sins of others would be the height of hypocrisy. This grace perspective pervades the New Testament, which is unafraid to highlight the sins and weaknesses of the key leaders of the early church.[6]

In early Methodism, attendance at Class meetings was compulsory. No "tickets" for the Sunday society meetings were given for those who missed more than three meetings in a quarter.[7] These Methodists were serious about their community life. And the small groups helped them to get serious about it. Wesley's "Specialised Bands" placed further incentives to pursue together a common task such as overcoming alcoholism. This has been described as operating in the rehabilitative mode.[8] Today we call this group therapy. A group of peers is formed so that they can help each other to overcome a problem they commonly share.

APPLICATION-ORIENTED BIBLE STUDIES

A major achievement of Wesley's famous class meeting was that it helped people to apply the Word. Michael Henderson describes this as operating in the behavioral mode.[9] Many new believers among the poor are semi-literate in that they are unable to grasp and internalize what the Bible teaches by reading it. It is very humbling at the end of a Bible study to notice how little of what the Bible teaches has gone into the mind. Many of these people revered the teaching in the books of their previous religion but no one expected them to adhere to all that was taught. Though many Sri Lankans daily recite that they will not lie, lying is very much a part of their daily lives. It would be something new to have teaching that is intended to influence their personal behavior.

Application-oriented Bible discussions help such individuals to internalize the teachings of the Bible. Here the teaching in the Bible is brought right down to their personal behavior at home and at work. They discuss how they are going to respond to specific situations they are facing. Then the truth of the Word can go into the lives of people who may not be used to learning from intellectual discussions about biblical concepts.

Many of today's small groups do not really grapple with the text of Scripture and with how to apply it to daily life. Usually today's meetings have times of praise (called "worship"), testimony, praying for the needs of people, and a short "devotional." We are missing a good opportunity to foster holy living among Christians.

SOLIDARITY HELPS DEVELOP SELF-ESTEEM

Poverty, combined with a class system that looks at the poor as inferior, can severely damage a person's self-esteem. What they sense is a far cry from the significance and identity that comes with being a child of God. Like many other Christian values, this is not something that people automatically grasp after conversion. Not having much to be proud about, they often do not have enough self-esteem to keep them from doing shameful things. Self-esteem, as we shall see, is a great incentive to holiness. Lacking it, they may betray those who have sacrificially helped them by stealing from or lying to them. Often those who have been betrayed by the poor get disillusioned about helping them.

The key to overcoming this problem is practicing what the Bible says about a new community where earthly distinctions have been broken (Gal. 3:28; Eph. 2:11–22). There is great power when a poor person, who is despised in society, enjoys fellowship in a small group together with rich and socially esteemed persons. They realize that they are treated as equals with the rich and that they are even helping the rich spiritually by what they share and do. When they sense that they are treated as equals in Christ self-esteem begins to grow. That, in turn, gives them new standards for behavior. It becomes below their dignity as princes and princesses in God's kingdom to steal and lie and betray their brothers and sisters in Christ. We must not expect to be successful in raising up a generation of saints from among the poor if we do not attack the terrible class distinctions that are still prevalent in the church.

It is beyond the scope of this article to deal with the great wealth that comes to economically rich people by such close fellowship with the poor. Let me only say that, by confining their growth experience to highly specialized homogenous groups, Christians will miss a lot of the enrichment that is available to them. Wesley's class meetings were heterogeneous groups based on geographical location. Rich and poor, young and old, men and women met to apply the Scriptures together and they enriched each other out of their own unique experiences.

ATTACKING SOCIAL EVILS

Another by-product of having rich and poor Christians meet together in the early Methodist class meetings was that influential people heard first-hand of the sufferings of poor laborers. This caused them to develop a social conscience, which led to actions to rid society of social evils. It promoted societal holiness.[10] While a student in a Buddhist University in Sri Lanka, I looked into an encyclopedia of economics in the university library to see whether it had anything to say about John Wesley. I will never forget my joy as I read that the Wesleyan revival may have helped prevent a repetition of the bloody French Revolution in the United Kingdom. This was because necessary social changes resulted as a by-product of this revival.

MAINTAINING THE ETHOS

Fellowship of the kind advocated by Wesley is not easy to maintain over a long period of time. As movements get bigger, the members naturally tend to lose some of the discipline required for such accountability. This challenge is intensified by the fact that, given the radical individualism that pervades contemporary life, this kind of community accountability is somewhat out of step with life in contemporary church and society. The Methodist system of changing ministers every few years can result in an occasional minister not being as enthusiastic about Wesleyan-style accountability. This adds to the challenge. But if the lay leaders doggedly persevere in meeting for such fellowship it can survive the challenge until a minister who is more open to it arrives.

In YFC we have not yet had the problem of leaders who are out of step with this aspect of our ethos. I have been the leader of the movement for thirty-two years of its forty-three-year existence. So the ethos was generally accepted, at least in theory. The challenge has been to maintain the principles of accountability and fellowship as the movement has grown in size. We have tried to meet this challenge in several ways.

- Like Wesley I have tried to write frequently about our ethos to the body of Youth for Christ through letters, memos, and articles.

- I travel regularly to our centers primarily to teach the staff. Unlike Wesley, I let those who supervise these centers "examine" (see above) the centers. During my visits to the centers I have tried, like Wesley, to focus on teaching the staff and volunteers and on visiting the homes of the leaders. I have also tried to spend long hours chatting to them about the things of God. Therefore, whenever possible, I have tried to spend most of my time in their homes. One of my big challenges has been to prevent the leaders from keeping me busy with public programs, which reduces the possibility of my spending time in fellowship with the leaders.

- We have attempted to have deep fellowship among the twelve or so national leaders through two- to four-day-long leadership team meetings held three times a year and majoring on spiritual fellowship and strategy rather than on business. My hope has been that the priority given to fellowship by the leaders would result in that emphasis trickling down to the rest of the movement. Maintaining this "unity of the Spirit in the bond of peace" (Eph. 4:3) among the leaders has been the hardest and most absorbing challenge I have faced in all my years of ministry.

- I have consistently shared publicly about the blessing I have received from my "band" of five friends who have known each other well for thirty to forty years (reduced from six after the death of one). I have hoped that my sharing may challenge some to seek such spiritual accountability with others.

NOTES

1. For a description of shame-honor cultures see Joseph Plevnik, "Honor/Shame," in *Biblical Social Values and their Meanings*, ed. John J. Pilch and Bruce J. Malina (Peabody, Mass.: Hendrickson Publishers, 1993), pp. 95–104; Bruce J. Malina, *The New Testament World: Insights from Cultural Anthropology* (Louisville, Ky.: Westminster John Knox Press, 2001), pp. 27–57; Timothy C. Tennent, *Theology in the Context of World Christianity* (Grand Rapids: Zondervan, 2007), pp. 77–101; Duane Elmer, *Cross-Cultural Connections* (Downers Grove, Ill.: InterVarsity Press, 2002), pp. 171–81; and Hannes Wiher, *Shame and Guilt: A Key to Cross-Cultural Ministry* (Bonn, Ger.: Verlag für Kultür und Wissenschaft, 2003).

2. For a description of these groups see D. Michael Henderson, *John Wesley's Class Meeting: A Model for Making Disciples* (Nappanee, Ind.: Evangel Publishing House, 1997).

3. Hendersen, *Class Meeting*, p. 112.

4. Ibid., p. 117.

5. Ajith Fernando, *Reclaiming Friendship: Relating to Each other in a Frenzied World* (Scottdale, Pa.: Herald Press, 1993).

6. See Ajith Fernando, *Jesus Driven Ministry* (Wheaton, Ill.: Crossway Books, 2002), pp. 134–52.

7. Henderson, *Class Meeting*, p. 108.

8. Ibid., p. 125.

9. Ibid., p. 93.

10. Allan Coppedge made this point in a seminar on the theology of John Wesley during the 1989 Minister's Conference of Asbury Theological Seminary.

BIBLIOGRAPHY

Elmer, Duane. *Cross-Cultural Connections*. Downers Grove, Ill.: InterVarsity Press, 2002.

Fernando, Ajith. *Jesus Driven Ministry*. Wheaton, Ill.: Crossway Books, 2002.

———. *Reclaiming Friendship: Relating to Each other in a Frenzied World*. Scottdale, Pa.: Herald Press, 1993.

Henderson, D. Michael. *John Wesley's Class Meeting: A Model for Making Disciples*. Nappanee, Ind.: Evangel Publishing House, 1997.

Malina, Bruce J. *The New Testament World: Insights from Cultural Anthropology*. Louisville, Ky.: Westminster John Knox Press, 2001.

Plevnik Joseph. "Honor/Shame." In *Biblical Social Values and their Meanings*, ed. John J. Pilch and Bruce J. Malina. Peabody, Mass.: Hendrickson Publishers, 1993.

Tennent, Timothy C. *Theology in the Context of World Christianity*. Grand Rapids: Zondervan, 2007.

Wiher, Hannes. *Shame and Guilt: A Key to Cross-Cultural Ministry*. Bonn, Ger.: Verlag für Kultür und Wissenschaft, 2003.

JOHN WESLEY AS
A CONTEXTUAL THEOLOGIAN

Dean S. Gilliland

MY BEGINNING IN CONTEXTUALIZATION

You will see that this essay aims to answer the question, "If John Wesley were here today would he have a favorable opinion of contextual theology and would he, perhaps, contribute to it?"

Even though it is some forty years since the widespread discussion on contextual theology began, what it is and attempts to do is still not clear to many. I want to relate briefly how I became involved in this different way of thinking about theology. It began during our missionary years in Nigeria (1955–1976). In 1974 the memorable gathering of the Lausanne Committee for World Evangelization (LCWE) produced the *Lausanne Covenant*. At that time I was principal of the Theological College of Northern Nigeria, a center for pastors' training, with students coming from seven denominations. I posted the *Lausanne Covenant* on the campus bulletin board and immediately it attracted attention. The college, including faculty, met to discuss the entire document and how it would relate to the seminary curriculum. It turned out that two paragraphs were more important for us than others. These were headed "Christian Social Responsibility" and "Evangelism and Culture." For years these topics had created difficulties among conservatives, including missionaries. I had been teaching theology much as I had learned it in my own seminary, yet I knew I was not really in touch with African issues.

In the days following, while attempting to find a biblical basis for contextualization, I came to understand the incarnation in a different way. I began to see it as an astonishing model for constructing theology in diverse cultures. The prologue to John's Gospel, especially John 1:14, communicated a new vision for me: *"The Word became flesh and dwelt among us."*

At the time, I had already been living and teaching in Africa for twelve years. I saw in a new way that God, personally, came into the world to be "at home" with each and every people, living with them in their own place. I could now see that by the incarnation, God gave us an astonishing demonstration of divine contextualization. Why don't we teach theology by first dealing with the real world where people live, just as God, personally and intimately, came among his own? This, then, will give the data that we can take to the Bible, while also referring to historical theology where appropriate. In short, this would mean that when people of Christian faith are asked the right questions, the Scriptures and the Holy Spirit can be trusted to guide the body of Christ into truth (John 16:13).

I decided, therefore, to start down a new path in our theology course. Granted, it would be an experiment, but I was convinced that two factors had made classical theology inappropriate for these mature African students. One is that the "systematic" approach to theology is based on a way of thinking (philosophical logic) that is foreign to Africa, and, second, an authentic theology for Africa cannot simply be a "warmed over" Western product. Rather, while integrating biblical revelation and insights from systematics, theology for these African pastors must begin with the thought forms and felt needs of their own society.[1]

The first assignment was to set the agenda, so to speak, by encouraging the class to agree on which categories of African culture/worldview were of most importance. In other words, we were going to theologize from the areas of deepest meaning for African life. This is where the critical questions will arise. Whether these issues fit the order of or correspond to "official" theology would not be the criteria. After several days of truly good participation it was agreed that we should cover six major areas of truth in the African world. These were: (1) community and family, (2) nature, (3) God and gods, (4) rituals, (5) the Spirit and spirits, and (6) ancestors.

I knew, at once, that these concerns were not abstractions but concrete issues of the heart. I soon found that the Bible does speak forcibly to these important matters and, along with the class, I had an awakening to the importance of the Old Testament as never before.[2]

1. By beginning with *community and family* we covered the fundamental issues of our relationship to God and the human family, the relationship of unbelievers to the community of faith and all that this means for those inside and outside of the body of Christ. We dealt with the way other Christians become a "second" family and how the church provides a broadening of true fellowship. Christians are not alienated from earthly families, rather, the community now rises above narrow ethnocentrism and connects the regional faith-family with believers everywhere.

2. The section on *nature* as a source of truth and a factor of power reminded me of how cautious I was taught to be about what we often called "natural revelation." Because of this, the African awareness of everything about nature as a messenger giving testimony to God was enlightening (and humbling) for me. Creation truly became the beginning place for knowing the biblical God, with awe, mystery, reliability, immanence, and power. For the African, nature does not lead away from God but to God. Jesus' authority over nature in miracles and healing was profound in this context.

3. One of the longer sections was on the subject of *God and gods*. The High God in African religion(s) is usually not an approachable or present reality. Generally, it is a god who went far away after creating the world. In a class of twenty, there were thirteen different names for God. It was liberating to the students to discuss how their ethnic High God differs from or is similar to the God of the Bible. The many "tribal gods," so closely related to African culture and worldview, did present major problems. All discussion was brought to the Bible, requiring an encounter with the first commandment such as I and the students had never before experienced.

4. An African view of the world requires that long-practiced *rituals* be performed in the correct way and by the right persons. When prescribed rites are carried out, it is believed that the continuity of individual and community life is assured. Major life events, such as, birth, puberty, marriage, death, planting, harvesting, etc., are ritually provided for. Often, the forms of these rituals can be misunderstood by outsiders. By discussing rituals we became highly aware of the ritualistic nature of biblical life. The class carefully analyzed cultural rituals as to which are fitting, objectionable, or can be changed for Christian life and worship.

5. Practically all that came up, regardless of the topic, seemed to connect to *Spirit and spirits* in one way or another. Pneumatology, as I had

studied it, focused almost exclusively on a rational approach to the Holy Spirit and did not touch the needs of everyday life. To the African, the world is literally charged with spirits (clean and unclean), nature spirits, spirits of the dead, both good and bad. Uninhibited discussion about the reality of the spirit-world was spontaneous and included everyone. With this, the Bible truly came alive as we studied it through a lens of discerning the spirits.

6. It is no exaggeration to say that when Africans die, especially the elders, they become *ancestors* that are not truly dead. The phrase "living-dead" describes the powerful influence that the dead continue to have after they have physically departed. The class had a debate that lasted an entire day to deal with the question of "ancestor worship." The consensus was that all rituals to commemorate the dead are "rituals of respect," not worship. We did take note of the great honor given to the "fathers" in the Old Testament.[3] Even the genealogy of Jesus as recorded in Matthew proved how important it was to the Jews to honor his ancestral line.

JOHN WESLEY AND CONTEXTUALIZATION

Thinking through theology in this innovative way[4] proved to open up the heads and hearts of African Christians, allowing even the untrained to participate in the drama of real life with Holy Scripture. After having taught classes in contextualization at Fuller Theological Seminary for twenty-five years with students from all over the world, I have had unforgettable, often surprising, experiences in finding new ways to communicate Christian truth in a variety of religious traditions.

WESLEY'S TIME AND OUR TIME

It has been 218 years since John Wesley's death. The changes in these two hundred-plus years would make Wesley a stranger in our world today. Wesley's now famous statement, "I look upon the world as my parish," was actually written in an almost off-handed way in a letter defending his right to preach in areas of England that some said were out of his territory.[5] This phrase carries implications for our time that Wesley could never have imagined. We could wonder what his reaction would be to the role of the United States in the world today, remembering, as we must, that he held the colonists in contempt and saw the entire American enterprise as a traitorous experiment.[6] Common terms that are precious to us today, such as *conversion, evangelism, revival*, and even *mission*, were virtually unknown in the theological language of the eighteenth century. Preaching with these new expressions created serious problems for Wesley as he worked to keep his loyalty to the Church of England. Anglican antagonism toward the "Methodist connexion" was always painful.[7]

What would the conversation be if two great evangelical elders, John Wesley and Billy Graham, could spend a day talking together, sharing about how God was at work in their time, through their ministries? Even though their worlds are radically different, God gathered people in great numbers to hear the Gospel in fitting, contextual ways. What would Wesley say to the fact that today the majority Christian church has moved out of the West to the nations of the Southern Hemisphere? He said even more than he knew with his words, "In whatever part (of the world) I am, I judge it my right and my bounden duty to declare unto all that are willing to hear, the glad tidings of salvation."[8] This open, uncompromising love for people, whoever and wherever they are, was a theme of Wesley's life, repeated in his sermons, letters, and in daily relationships.

Were Wesley with us today he would be in touch with everything contemporary and would communicate the Gospel in a way that the most needy would desire it, understand it, and accept it. In principle, this is contextualization. His obituary, published in *The Gentleman's Magazine* (March 1791) carried the following testimony: "(Through Wesley) morals and religion was introduced into the lowest classes of mankind, the ignorant were instructed, the wretched relieved, and the abandoned reclaimed."[9]

THE WESLEYAN QUADRILATERAL

Contextualization is a response to the human condition. It takes seriously the existing situations of people and how to do something about them. Forty-five years ago the idea of a Quadrilateral as a way to think through Wesleyan theology was introduced by Albert Outler.[10] The point of this Quadrilateral idea was that Wesley's thinking about the Christian faith moves interactively around four dimensions: *Scripture, tradition, reason,* and *experience*. Literature that emerged from the discussion is abundant, taking up arguments both for and against.[11] It became clear that I must ask if this Quadrilateral idea accurately reflects John Wesley's theology and, if so, is it helpful in understanding what his attitude toward contextualization would be were he with us today?

First, two cautionary words need to be made. One is that Wesley himself had nothing to do with framing the Quadrilateral. As we have said, it was Outler's analysis of Wesley's thinking when helping to find mutuality between the Methodist and the Evangelical United Brethren churches during merger discussions. No one will dispute Outler's right or good intentions in constructing the Quadrilateral because his scholarly work on John Wesley is unquestioned.

As a second point, the Quadrilateral has been a subject of controversy for both liberals and conservatives.[12] The main problem is that the four dimensions must not be taken as equal sources for truth. This would be a gross distortion of Wesley. He had no tolerance for anyone or anything that would diminish his high view of Scripture. Those who want to quote Wesley as their authority for liberal social issues tend to pass laterally through tradition, reason, and experience for ground to stand on, with only superficial regard for Scripture. This would offend Wesley. The only way to picture the Quadrilateral is to envision a three-sided pyramid that stands on Scripture as the base upon which the others rest.[13]

Still, with this being said, there is no reason to throw out the baby with the bathwater. Wesley was, without question, responsive to the social issues of his day. By recognizing this, contextualization is a hinge, as it were, connecting our present with his time. The poor, the enslaved, the sick, and the nonliterate were Wesley's mission. Wesley's influence on Wilberforce is fixed in history. His letters to Wilberforce, for example, witnessed openly that slavery was, "an execrable villainy which is the scandal of England and of human nature."[14] He recognized that in England's courts, "a black man's word is never accepted against the testimony of a white man."[15] Such convictions came to Wesley by looking at the real situations of ordinary people and bringing these human realities to the Scriptures in an incarnational way. Wesley recognized reason (and tradition) as God's gift to be used reasonably and thankfully. Taking not one iota away from Scripture he wrote, "I would as soon put out my eyes to secure my faith as lay aside my reason."[16]

PREVENIENT GRACE

In contextualization it is the Spirit of God that draws the body of Christ to think about values and conduct in light of the Word, which is a gift of the teaching Spirit.

The emphasis on prevenient grace is so Wesleyan that it must be reckoned with before the rest of John Wesley's evangelical theology can be understood. This special grace explains why the unredeemed mind can even incline toward or desire God. This grace exists prior to and without any connection to human activity. "Prevenient" is not a word we use today, which limits our ability to grasp Wesley's meaning. Tom Oden defines it as, "the capacity to respond to grace (so that) the person then may . . . become an active, willing participant in receiving the conditions for justification."[17] In his book *The Silver Chair*, C. S. Lewis puts beautiful words in the mouth of Aslan, the lion, "You would not have called to me unless I had been calling you."[18] This is fully in the spirit of what is meant by prevenient grace.

But what does this have to do with contextualization? It would be incongruent with Wesley's view of prevenient grace to say that the grace that calls a person to salvation has no continuing function. The prevenient grace of God is not some kind of vacuous or temporary activity. Just as the Spirit of God constrains a person to incline toward God, so the same Spirit is, "shed abroad in the heart of the believer."[19] Wesley would affirm that the same Spirit that brings the human person to salvation is also the Spirit who guides into all truth (John 16:13). As at justification, the convert, "feels in his heart the mighty working of the Spirit of God. (so) . . . God is continually breathing in, as it were, upon his soul and his soul is breathing unto God."[20]

Therefore, contextualizatiion is first and always the work of the Holy Spirit. The prevenient Spirit of grace is the saving Spirit and the saving Spirit is also the teaching Spirit. Contextualization is the dynamic reflection carried out by believers in any given situation or time. Wesley's greatest conviction was that the Word be truly and clearly understood among the people in this or that particular place. Wesley took a lifelong, uncompromising stand against the Calvinists (even his friend George Whitfield) by standing firm that, "*whosoever will* let him drink of the water of life freely."[21] The same prevenient Spirit that called these simple believers to conversion now also helps them to discern and appropriate biblical truths in the context of their own world.

WESLEY RESISTED DOGMA

The problem with systematic theology is that it is taught as a finished exercise to be transmitted fait accompli among all believers and churches, regardless of local situations or cultural differences. In 1990, while in Papua New Guinea, I taught a course in contextualiztion for missionaries of several denominations. Each student in the class was required to produce a theological project dealing with issues related to the people where they worked. One student said he would like to write a contextualized *Westminster Confession*—one that would be more appropriate to his churches in Irian Jaya. When he spoke to his mission head about contextualizing the *Confession* for his tribal people, the administrator told him that such an exercise would be inappropriate. The reason, he said, was that all twenty-eight chapters of the ancient Reformed document were as relevant in Irian Jaya today as they were in Geneva in the seventeenth century!

Rather than working on every jot and tittle of dogma, John Wesley was, himself, in a lifelong quest for personal holiness. No single word describes his own struggle in faith better than "seeking assurance." In contrast, pursuing absolute belief and defending unrelenting dogma was not Wesley's approach to theology. Knowing the witness of salvation and promoting holiness of life was the implicit purpose of his every activity. While he was knowledgeable about and fully engaged in theological discussion, he was not a speculative or systematic theologian. For Wesley, theology was the "handmaid of piety."[22] Translated into modern speech, "theology must bring wholeness in Christ." In his own words Wesley wrote:

> I design plain truth for plain people . . . I labour to avoid all words which are not easy to be understood, all which are not used in common life and in particular those kinds of technical terms that so frequently occur in bodies of divinity, those words of speaking which men of reading are intimately familiar but which to common people are an unknown tongue.[23]

Wesley's greatest arguments were with the Calvinists who challenged his Arminian convictions, especially in the area of "election." Predestination was an abhorrent idea to Wesley and contrary to his message of "whosoever will." For him, predestination opened the way to "antinomianism" (living without law), which he felt promoted unconcern about holiness.

Why are we making a point of Wesley's negativity to hard dogma? It is because for him, making truth practical in life and finding clarity of faith in one's daily routine superseded being absolute in theology. This openness to searching for ways to "make sense" for ordinary people and his emphasis on "experience" is required for any theology in context. Lists of what to *believe* is not Wesleyan religion. Rather, the experience and assurance of saving faith, even though it may not be fully explained, is Wesleyan. "His theology must be appreciated as a living and growing body of thought and way of thinking."[24]

WESLEY WAS CLOSE TO THE PEOPLE

We raise a very important dimension in contextualization when speaking about the interaction between formal (official) theology and unofficial theology. In saying this, we take seriously the way ordinary folk think about biblical truth as well as truth derived from their everyday lives. Contextualization is a dialogue carried out by the joining together of what is sometimes called the "big tradition" and the "little tradition." Contrary to what might first be imagined, the "little tradition" is made up of the few who know formal "head" theology while the "big tradition" lies with the body of ordinary Christians who bring insights of the "heart" to the conversation (informal theology).

By conviction, Wesley was a missioner to the masses. In his speech, his writing, and his style of life he was, indeed, close to the less educated. Let us look at three dimensions of his life that show how clearly he listened to and was informed by those whom he often referred to as the "poor and plain people."

HEALING AND FOLK MEDICINE

In his book *The Life of John Wesley* (2003), Roy Hattersley has given us a valuable look at who Wesley was as a person. In working through his convictions and in his courage to declare new ideas, Wesley was always motivated by practical and helpful services to the lower classes. The spirit of contextualiztion is an openness to new ideas and readiness to commu-nicate in the most practical ways. Hattersley says,

John Wesley insisted that he rarely acted hastily. But he felt a constant temptation to snatch at new ideas. Spiritual revelations were rare but intellectual revelation was frequent and he always accepted new truth with a zealous determination.[25]

Not only was Wesley open to manifestations of the Holy Spirit in physical healing that frequently occurred during his field preaching, he was, himself, a bold practitioner of home remedies. His widely publicized medicines caused disbelief and ridicule from the elite, even though the concoctions that he recommended were not much different from some of the popular treatments practiced by our own ancestors.

Even some of his own "preachers" were skeptical about the miraculous healing that occurred. However, one of these preachers, named George Bell, claimed he had the gift for healing. Bell made the case of one, Mary Spead, who came to him with an advanced stage of breast cancer. Bell prayed for her and she witnessed that, "the previously ravaged breast returned to its youthful shape" and there was no more pain. This aroused contention on the part of the "preachers" but not from Wesley. His response was, simply, "Here are the plain facts: (1) She was ill, (2) she is well, and (3) she became so in a moment. Which of these with any modesty can be denied?"[26] His own folk remedies, for almost every pain or sickness, were well known and published far and wide through his booklet *Primitive Physick: An essay on easy and natural methods of curing most diseases* (1747). These cures were actually offered as one of the services at the Foundry which had become the official headquarters of the Methodist Connection.[27] Space does not allow descriptions of his medications for common illnesses, which included many types of treatments with electricity. Always practical, he rated his treatments as "tested," "tried," and even "infallible." Finally, he said, "Do not forget the old unfashionable medicine—prayer," and "have faith in God who killeth and maketh alive."[28]

The point for contextualization is to help us see that in both divine healing and medicine, John Wesley had an appreciation for what neither professional churchmen nor medical doctors would accept. Still, in the face of opposition from these upper-class professionals, all his life Wesley was committed to down-to-earth ways of meeting the "folk" on their own level, making no apology for innovations that brought endless criticism.[29]

LOYAL RESISTANCE TO THE CHURCH OF ENGLAND

Contextualization is not a rootless exercise. It is not something that springs up spontaneously as new forms or with no connection to historic thought and practice. Wesley never doubted his attachment to the Church of England. Loyalty to the church was bred in him through family and training. However, it was always a struggle to keep this loyalty intact and persevere in his call to minister to the common people who were beyond reach of the churches of his day, particularly the Anglican Church.

The long history of Christianity, the theology of the church, and the role of the church itself is taken very seriously in contextualization. Two of the earliest models for contextualization were labeled as "adaptation" and "accommodation," meaning that formal or Western academic theology was always the norm. Then, as these set forms were taken into new, uninitiated situations, the teaching was adjusted to "conform" or "fit" the variables of each place. Wesley's lifetime problem was how to renew the Anglican Church that he loved while communicating with the masses who were untouched by the churches. As time passed, "Methodism" began to look like a distinct religion with an independent theology, leaving Wesley and his followers open to attack. Hattersley writes that the hardest thing for John's brother, Charles, to bear was that John had become so "contextual" that he feared the Methodists were causing schism in the Church of England.

> (Charles) was dubious about his brother's ability to walk the theological tight-rope between orthodoxy and heterodoxy and must have realized that John's ability to satisfy the (Methodist) societies without prejudice to the Church was also immensely hampered by his (John's) life style.[30]

John knew intuitively that the Anglican Church was out of touch with the poor and the lower classes. He was deeply attached to the Church of England but he was even more attached to his own societies, which caused him to write, "I love the rites and ceremonies of the Church. But I also see, well pleased, that our Lord can work without them."[31]

Indeed, the success of field preaching and the building of local meeting houses was a break-through in communication and relationships. Antagonism was high but John's commitment to the people was firm. He saw his unorthodoxy as something sanctioned by the highest authority.

"God commands me to do good work among all men, to instruct the ignorant, reform the wicked and confirm the virtuous."[32] Necessity and God's
will combined helped him ignore the scorn from the Anglican Church.

On one hand, contextualization requires the use of historical theology
and church tradition and, on the other, it demands understanding human
need and finding the terminology that best addresses each situation. It is
a tribute to Wesley that Heitzenrater can say,

> Wesley sensed the spirit of the English people perhaps as well as any
> person in his day. He was to remain an Anglican clergyman to his
> dying breath and at the same time, was able to harness the energies of
> revival into a new form that was to become a major force in Protestant
> Christianity.[33]

WESLEY'S "SONS OF THE GOSPEL"

One of the most controversial issues that arose out of the Wesleyan
emphasis on "experience" and "witness of the Spirit" was spontaneous
preaching by the unordained and untrained whom John liked to call his
"sons of the Gospel." Lay preaching would later become a characteristic
of the Methodists, but at first it was a burden for Wesley to bear. There
were already several movements similar to the Methodists that irritated
the leadership of the Anglican Church. Each was aimed at some sort of
reform that the organizers felt should take place within the Anglican
Church. A problem raised by these groups and by the Methodists was that
these lay preachers were zealous and highly motivated but not recognized
as legitimate clergy. The bind for John Wesley was this: to refuse these
"preachers" the right to speak openly about their experience in Christ
would "grieve the Spirit" but to encourage them would cause greater rift
in relations with the Church.

Unlettered and unordained as they were, John Wesley moved from
restraint to acceptance and finally to actually recruiting lay preachers.
This openness to their right to speak and teach shows how contextual
Methodism was becoming. Nothing meant more to Wesley than sharing
the Good News of saving faith regardless of who the messenger was, as
long as they were living what they preached. In light of his loyalty to the
church, this was not an easy road for Wesley but in the end, the "sons of

the Gospel" were given more and more responsibility. He even got to the point that he argued publicly with the hierarchy of the Church of England that the nonordained could serve communion and could receive ordination outside of the church structure.

What is important to contextualiztion is the fact that lay preachers would bring insights to the Bible based on their own stories. Wesley was much like the apostle Paul, who encouraged even relatively new converts to speak publicly about their spiritual experiences and in their own way. Like Paul, also, the greater emphasis was on right behavior rather than on exact knowledge of the doctrine. "John Wesley accepted the inevitability of minor doctrinal differences so long as the preacher believed in salvation by faith with good works as redemption's consequence."[34]

In addition, much could be said about the use of hymns in Methodist worship. This was another departure from the Anglican tradition. Hymn-singing was a violation in the Anglican Church because devotions should be based on texts, not "human inventions."[35] While his brother, Charles, did not like certain of John's innovations (causing considerable tension between them) Charles did agree heartily that congregational singing was a change that Methodists loved. Charles's many hymns were a gift to the emerging Methodist movement and are witness to the support he brought to this contextual dimension of worship.

In the end, John Wesley's openness to lay preachers left no question about the contribution of his "sons of the Gospel." Finally, he wrote to the Anglican hierarchy:

> Will you condemn a preacher because he has not university learning or has not a university education? What then? He saves those sinners from their sins whom the men of learning and education cannot save.[36]

IN CONCLUSION

While this essay has been an enriching exercise for me, it now seems almost arrogant to conclude how John Wesley would react to contextualization if he were with us today. This we know: he had no other motivation but to bring men and women into salvation by faith and lead them in the process toward holiness. Neither formal theology nor a static church system could stand in his way. Since Wesley was so in touch with ordinary people, so committed to clarity in presenting the Gospel, and so able to make irresistible his appeal to accept divine grace, I do feel that he would embrace contextualization.

However, in saying this, there is a great caution that he would raise. No human basis of truth, no habits or customs of any culture can ever become the final word. All of life must ultimately surrender to the Truth which, as Wesley said, "[God] hath written down in a Book. Oh, give me that book. At any price give me the book of God. . . . Here," he said, "is knowledge enough for me. . . . Let me be *homo unius libri* [a man of one book]."[37]

John Wesley would probably say, "Yes, let us work at contextualization but remember that regardless of how good or well-intentioned our efforts may be, they will stand approved only as they come under the judgment of the Word and the Spirit."

NOTES

1. In 1978, I began teaching at the School of World Mission (Fuller Theological Seminary), knowing very little about theory in contextualization. The following year, my colleague and friend, Charles Kraft, published his classic volume *Christianity in Culture* (Maryknoll, N.Y.: Orbis Books, 1979). The aim of that book and my own efforts coincided. Kraft wrote, "Here we are not working in abstractions or western ethnocentric thinking. Rather, thought forms, habits of culture and manifest human needs are identified and brought to the Bible for discussion and appropriate action" (*Christianity in Culture*, p. 12).

2. Theologians who had been trained to do theology in only one way felt quite defensive, even threatened, in these early days of contextualization. Again, Kraft was firm in his convictions about developing new pathways for an ethno-biblical approach to theology. "[The] communication of the Gospel cannot be simply to learn the culture of the people . . . in

order to better force on them . . . understandings developed by other people, in other times to answer other questions" (Ibid).

3. Great respect for the dead in the Old Testament connects in dynamic ways with the African world. For example, consider the commands regarding Joseph's bones (Exod. 13:19) and the elaborate, extensive celebration of Jacob's death in Canaan, granted without question to Joseph by Pharaoh (Gen. 50).

4. We developed together a methodology of four steps: (1) Observe and identify problems, cultural themes, values, and needs of the context; (2) Describe fully these problems, themes, values, needs; (3) Once described, seek for meanings/truths that underlie the problems, themes, values, needs; and (4) Bring the insights of this work to the Bible (and theology) to find appropriate (contextual) answers for relevant proposals and action.

5. The comment appears in a letter from John Wesley to his friend, John

Hervey. Quoted in Richard Heitzenrater, *The Elusive Mr. Wesley* 2nd ed. (Nashville: Abingdon Press, 2003), p. 108; also Roy Hattersley, *The Life of John Wesley: A Brand from the Burning* (New York: Doubleday, 2003), p. 151.

6. As time passed, Wesley relented from his early resentment of the American colonists. A benevolent monarchy was his ideal for government: "Democracy to John Wesley was the work of the Devil." Hattersley, *The Life of John Wesley*, p. 409.

7. Hattersley, *The Life of John Wesley*, pp. 266–68. By 1755 the issue of separation from the Church of England became critical yet Wesley's decision was that separation would damage the "societies" and turn member against member, p. 267.

8. Heitzenrater, *The Elusive Mr. Wesley*, p. 108.

9. Ibid., p. 338.

10. Albert C. Outler, "The Wesleyan Quadrilateral in John Wesley," *Wesleyan Theological Journal* 20 (1985): pp. 7–18.

11. Donald A. D. Thorsen, *The Wesleyan Quadrilateral: Scripture, Tradition, Reason and Experience as a Model of Evangelical Theology* (Grand Rapids: Zondervan, 1990) and Ted Campbell, *Wesley and the Quadrilateral: Renewing the Conversation* (Nashville: Abingdon, 1997), p. 9.

12. The problems led Outler to witness publically that he regretted coining the term "Quadrilateral" since it had become so widely misunderstood. Thorsen, *The Wesleyan Quadrilateral*, p. 23.

13. Ibid., p. 71.

14. Hattersley, *The Life of John Wesley*, p. 395.

15. Ibid.

16. "A Dialogue Between an Antinomian and His Friend" in *The Works of John Wesley*, vol. 10, ed. Thomas Jackson (London: Epworth Press, 1872), p. 7.

17. Thomas Oden, *John Wesley's Scriptural Christianity* (Grand Rapids: Zondervan, 1994), p. 243.

18. C. S. Lewis, *The Chronicles of Narnia: The Silver Chair* (New York: Harper-Collins, 1953), p. 23.

19. Romans 5:5.

20. Colin W. Williams, *John Wesley's Theology Today* (Nashville: Abingdon, 1960), p. 102.

21. Revelation 22:17.

22. Heitzenrater, *The Elusive Mr. Wesley*, p. 140.

23. Ibid., p. 142.

24. Ibid., p. 393.

25. Hattersley, *The Life of John Wesley*, p. 211.

26. Heitzenrater, *The Elusive Mr. Wesley*, p. 291.

27. The Old Foundry where cannons had been manufactured was purchased in 1739 for 150 pounds. It had suffered an explosion but Wesley set to rebuilding it from what he called, "an uncouth heap of ruins." The Foundry became the center for a variety of ministries, including a clinic, for the growing Methodist Society. *John Wesley*, ed. Albert C. Outler, (New York: Oxford University Press, 1964), p. 420.

28. Heitzenrater, *The Elusive Mr. Wesley*, p. 134.

29. Hattersley, *The Life of John Wesley*, p. 230.

30. Ibid., p. 151.

31. Ibid.

32. Ibid.

33. Heitzenrater, *The Elusive Mr. Wesley*, p. 22.

34. Hattersley, *The Life of John Wesley*, p. 247.

35. Ibid., p. 115.

36. Ibid., p. 248

37. Heitzenrater, *The Elusive Mr. Wesley*, p. 143.

BIBLIOGRAPHY

Cosby, Michael R. "Using the Wesleyan Quadrilateral to Teach Biblical Studies in Christian Liberal Arts," *Teaching Theology and Religion* 4, no. 2 (2001): pp. 71–80.

Hattersley, Roy. *The Life of John Wesley: A Brand from the Burning.* New York: Doubleday, 2003.

Heitzenrater, Richard P. *The Elusive Mr. Wesley.* 2nd ed. Nashville: Abingdon, 2003.

Kraft, Charles. H. *Christanity in Culture.* Maryknoll, N.Y.: Orbis Books, 1979.

Oden, Thomas C. *John Wesley's Scriptural Christianity: A Plain Exposition of His Teaching on Christian Doctrine.* Grand Rapids: Zondervan, 1994.

Outler, Albert C., ed. *John Wesley.* New York: Oxford University Press, 1964.

Pudney, John. *John Wesley and His World.* New York: Scribner and Sons, 1978.

Stone, Ronald H. *John Wesley's Life and Ethics.* Nashville: Abingdon, 2001.

Thorsen, Donald. *The Wesleyan Quadrilateral: Scripture, Tradition, Reason, Experience as a Model for Evangelical Theology.* Grand Rapids: Zondervan, 1990.

Tuttle, Robert, Jr. *Mysticism: The Wesleyan Tradition.* Grand Rapids: Francis Asbury Press (Zondervan), 1989.

Waller, Ralph. *John Wesley: A Personal Portrait.* London: SPCK Publishing, 2003.

Williams, Colin W. *John Wesley's Theology Today.* Nashville: Abingdon, 1960.

2 3

INDIGENOUS PROVERBS, RITUALS, AND STORIES

Evidence of God's Prevenient Grace in Oral Cultures

W. Jay Moon

INTRODUCTION

A story is told of a young man, sitting by the river bank, discouraged since he could not swim across the river. An elderly man walked up, rolled up his pants, and then walked across the surface of the water. The young man was in disbelief until another elderly man arrived, rolled up his pants, and also walked across the surface of the water. Eventually, a third elderly man arrived and did the same thing! Finally, the young man decided to try for himself. He rolled up his pants and tried to walk across the surface of the water—only to sink and be carried away by the swift current. The three elderly men looked back and replied, "If only he had asked us—we could have told him where the stones were placed to cross over the river safely!"

When approaching oral cultures, God has placed stepping stones to move people from the river bank of unbelief or young faith to mature faith. While these stones may not be readily apparent to literate learners at first glance, careful observation reveals that missionaries catch up on a conversation that God has already started. Wesley understood that we do not bring God to a culture; rather, God brings us there. In Wesleyan terms, this is called "prevenient grace."

The purpose of this chapter is to apply Wesley's concept of prevenient grace to oral cultures. After briefly explaining the concepts of prevenient grace and orality, I will explore three areas where God often is revealed in oral cultures. The purpose is to help missionaries find the stepping stones that God has placed in oral cultures. Overlooking these stones often leads to frustration or failure. These stones provide a good starting point for Christian mission since this furthers the work that God has already started with the indigenous people.

WESLEY'S CONCEPT OF PREVENIENT GRACE

Prevenient grace is the undeserved love of God that precedes human actions. It is rooted in the fact that God has created this world and has called it good (Gen. 1). Humankind has been shaped and created in God's image; therefore, God's image exists in every culture. Prevenient grace is

> . . . the divine love that surrounds all humanity and precedes any and all of our conscious impulses. This grace prompts our first wish to please God, our first glimmer of understanding concerning God's will, and our "first slight transient conviction" of having sinned against God. God's grace also awakens in us an earnest longing for deliverance from sin and death and moves us toward repentance and faith.[1]

Prevenient grace assures us that God precedes the missionary in every culture, amidst the stain of sin that also exists in every culture. This balances a creation theology with a redemption theology, and it provides a helpful starting point for missionaries approaching new cultures.

ORAL CULTURES

When approaching a new culture, the host peoples' learning preferences can be characterized along a continuum between the poles of oral vs. literate. People in oral cultures learn best and have their lives most transformed when they receive communication in oral forms.[2] In primary oral cultures, this means that the people cannot read or write. They do not follow literate thinking patterns; rather, they appreciate and follow oral patterns of thought. In secondary oral cultures (like many postmodern contexts), the people can read and write but they still prefer oral communication forms instead of literate communication forms.

Oral does not mean simplifying or "dumbing down" the message. Quite to the contrary, oral communicators have developed elaborate forms of thought that are very creative, ornate, and highly organized. The problem is that this organization is "of a sort unfamiliar to and often uncongenial to the literate mind."[3] Literate learners use methods of analysis such as lists, three-point sermons, note-taking, outlines, word studies, apologetics, and complex chains of abstract logical arguments. Oral communicators, on the other hand, have developed creative means to make the message memorable. Since oral learners cannot refer to notes or outlines, oral communicators rely upon mnemonic patterns in proverbs, rituals, stories, songs, dance, drama, etc., to create messages that can be recalled later. For the remainder of this chapter, I will focus on three of these oral communication forms —proverbs, rituals, and songs— in order to demonstrate how they can be useful in cooperating with God's prevenient grace in oral cultures.

PROVERBS

Many oral cultures rely upon proverbs to make the message memorable and understandable. Proverbs are like large, time-tested stepping stones placed in a river to take you from the river bank of what you know to the other bank of what you do not know. Good oral communicators wisely place these stepping stones. One Nigerian explained to me, "If one does not speak in proverbs, he will not carry people with him for long."[4]

Indigenous proverbs have been described as the wisdom of many with the wit of one. Indigenous proverbs capture many of the core values of a culture using terms and metaphors that the people recognize as "their own."[5] When using proverbs in a sermon in Ghana, a man commented, "Now I know that this message is from God and not just from the white man since our own proverbs confirm it."

When looking for the prevenient grace of God in the Builsa culture, I noticed how people relied upon proverbs to create lively, engaging, entertaining, and powerful communication. Many of these proverbs also contain the time-tested wisdom of elders that people have come to rely upon. Who is the author of wisdom—is it not God? Did not God use the form of proverbs to also communicate with the Jews in the Old Testament? The existence of proverbs in an oral culture can provide evidence of the image of God in culture. This can be a good starting point to help oral people understand God as revealed in Jesus.

After being away for awhile, one day I returned to Ghana to visit a Muslim friend who was an oral learner.[6] Knowing my interest in proverbs, with a smile he shared with me, "I knew that you would return to see me. We have a proverb in Hausa that says, 'What the heart loves, there the legs will go.'" He shared how he knew that I would return to see him. Since my heart was there, my legs would find a way to follow.

As I pondered further the meaning of this proverb, I responded, "Do you think God's heart is close to us?" A discussion ensued whereby he considered how God's heart is with us since he created humans; therefore, God must find a way for his feet to follow.

Eventually, I explained, "God's heart pulled so strongly that his feet had to come to earth and live among us. That is why Jesus came. Jesus was the feet of God!"

He seriously pondered the meaning and implications of what was discussed. As a Muslim, he agreed that Jesus was a good person but he did not understand why Jesus was necessary. Why would God want to come to earth anyway? He understood God as the creator and ultimate judge but he had not considered before how God's heart may be drawn to live among the people God created. It was a new thought to him but it made perfect sense using the logic and time-tested wisdom of the Hausa proverb.

He was beginning to see God in terms and concepts that he could understand. This explanation of Jesus connected with aspects of his own worldview. It described the meaning of Jesus in terms and metaphors that were uniquely Hausa and also fully Christian. Previously, Christianity was presented to him in ways that were foreign, using literate points, analysis, comparisons, etc. By using Hausa metaphors and concepts contained in his own proverbs, Jesus' coming to earth started to make sense and was congruent with some of the deeply held core values of my friend's culture.

"There is a God whose heart pulls so strong that his feet must come to be with us," he concluded. "That is good news. I would like to know more about this."

Could this proverb then be a stepping stone, placed by God, to help my Muslim friend understand and appreciate the Gospel? This is an example of God's prevenient grace among an oral people that becomes an excellent beginning point to help people understand the Gospel, using oral patterns that can be appreciated and understood.

RITUALS

Rituals are also used in oral cultures to help people understand and experience God. Rituals help people to experience the ultimate God meeting their intimate needs.[7] Instead of merely a logical assertion alone, oral people want to have their hearts touched as well as their minds. In oral cultures, people want to experience the mystery of God. Particularly during times of crisis or transition, they need to be reminded that the ultimate God cares about their intimate needs. Rituals are used to maintain continuity amidst the transitions of life.[8]

Symbols, the building blocks of rituals, are used to help people feel, touch, taste, see, or smell God's presence. The five senses are involved to motivate and move people. Symbols have been simply defined as "something present that stands for something absent"[9] or something seen that points to something not seen. When a Native American walked into a room and smelled the burning sage, she exclaimed, "That is the smell of forgiveness."[10] While she could not see this concept of forgiveness, the distinct smell of the burning sage, along with the sight of the rising smoke, was a symbol of something she could not see. The symbol of the sage touched her heart as well as her mind.

When symbols are combined in a ritual, the presence of the Ultimate God is invited to become intimate with people. In the Bible, God used existing cultural rituals to communicate deep new meaning with people, whether it was a covenant ceremony with Abraham that involved walking in the midst of slaughtered animals (Gen. 15), or circumcision (Gen. 17), or baptism (Matt. 3). In oral cultures, some existing rituals may be another example of the prevenient grace of God, preparing people to understand and experience the presence of God.

The Native American ritual of the "sweat lodge"[11] is a ritual of purification[12] involving several symbols that can be used to connect the ultimate God with the intimate concerns of people. Before entering the sweat lodge, we each prayed to Jesus with the burning sage representing cleansing and forgiveness. On hands and knees, we crawled into the dome-like structure that was composed of willow branches covered with tarps. Once inside, water was poured over hot rocks to create steam, and then the entrance to the sweat lodge was closed. It was pitch dark. Between four rounds of additional hot rocks being added to the center, worship songs were offered, prayers from the heart were given by each person, and words of wisdom and Scripture were given to address our deep concerns. Amidst this hot, dark, intimate, and moist environment, I cried out to Jesus—Jesus' presence became very intimate and intense. This ritual of Native Americans was such a profound spiritual experience that I knew I had to do this again.

This time, I brought seminary students. After preparing themselves with prayer and confession, the students entered the sweat lodge together. One student later remarked, "I have never felt closer to Jesus than during the sweat lodge." In further discussions, we learned how students were deeply touched by this purification ritual. The symbols of the sage, rocks, water, steam, fire, etc., all helped us to feel the Ultimate God become intimate in our lives. The day after the sweat lodge, some students remarked, "I now feel stronger in my faith—God met me in the sweat lodge."

Could the sweat lodge ritual be an example of God's prevenient grace in oral Native American cultures? Could this be evidence of God preparing Native Americans to receive and experience the Gospel in ways that are congruent with their own culture? The sweat lodge may be a good starting point for ministry to Native Americans in ways that continue the conversation God started long ago.

STORIES

In addition to rituals and proverbs, God has been conversing with people throughout the ages by stories. It seems that everyone likes a good story. In literate contexts, stories are used to illustrate a point being made. In oral cultures, however, the story itself is the point. Oral learners like to keep the story intact as one complete whole. Instead of dissecting a story and analyzing points to be made, oral learners will listen and remember the whole story. Throughout the storytelling and long beyond, oral learners will draw guidance from the story, similar to the way you would draw food from a buffet line—you take what is needed for that moment.

In oral cultures, stories tend to be very concrete and relational instead of abstract. At times, the stories are very earthy or exaggerated in order to make them memorable. Animals may be used to talk about people that exhibit certain characteristics. In this indirect way, the storyteller tells tales involving owls, spiders, rabbits, wolves, monkeys, and so forth, while really talking about people they know who are wise, crafty, greedy, etc. Instead of relying solely upon a strict chronological recounting, oral performers often start at the place of the most action or intensity. This is done to grab or "hook" the listener. The storyteller knows that the audience needs to be hooked in the beginning in order to convince the listeners to listen to the rest of the story.[13] Good oral performers often use sounds and gestures to create a pleasing and memorable experience. Participation from the audience is often engendered. This may be in the form of a refrain that is sung at key points, questions asked, or simple role-playing. All of these techniques are used to aid people in remembering the story. Since oral learners cannot refer to written materials later to recall the story, the oral performer must embed some of the above mnemonic aids in the storytelling in order to set deep memory hooks. In this way, oral learners can remember the story later when needed.

God transforms our lives by stories as well. The largest percentage of the Bible is written in narrative format. Jesus' prolific use of stories (Mark 4:34) among oral people exhibits the value he placed on the Gospel as a storytelling tradition.[14] Could it be that God also reveals prevenient grace by some of the local stories within the various cultures of the world? If so, could this be a useful entry point for the Gospel to these people?

The Builsa people of Northern Ghana remember the stories when the slave raiders came into their villages to take their people away.[15] The last slave raid was estimated in the year 1896, and these battles are an important part of the identity of the Builsa. One story explains how the raiders were approaching on horseback and a sheanut tree, *Acham*, warned the Builsa ahead of time. This helped them to prepare well and defeat the enemy. The Builsa also climbed up on the rocks in order to find protection from the raiders. The raiders' horses could not maintain good footing on the rocks; therefore, the rocks helped to rescue the Builsa again.

Several Builsa church leaders reflected upon this story and asked the question, "Is there any evidence of God's presence during this time?" They were looking for stepping stones in the river during that period of history. In discussion with the Builsa church leaders, they considered, "Who created the sheanut tree? Only God could make this tree talk. Who created the mountains that we could run to for safety?" Are these not evidence of God's prevenient grace during the darkest days of their history? Builsa church leader, Atemboa,[16] noted how God provided the rock in the desert during the Israelites' time of need so that Moses could strike this rock and find water (Exod. 17:1–7, Num. 20:1–13). First Corinthians 10:3–5 explains that this rock was Christ, even though the Israelites were not aware of this at the time. Could it be that the rocks that rescued the Builsa are also evidence of the presence of Christ during their darkest time in history? In Scripture, God often reminded the Jews of times when God used creation to rescue and protect them, whether it was a river to flood the Egyptians, a donkey to talk with Balaam, hail to beat back the invaders, and so forth. Could the above Builsa story also be a good starting point to explain God's prevenient grace?

Atemboa concluded:[17]

If not for God's timely intervention, the slave raiders could have forced the Builsa to become Muslims. In many other areas, Babatu[18] forced people to become Muslims or be killed. As it stands today, very few Builsa are Muslim but many are now open to receive the good news of Jesus Christ. I see this as Jesus' intervention in Builsa history.

Since the Builsa church leaders saw evidence of God's prevenient grace in their past stories, this may be a good starting place for ministry there.

CONCLUSION

When approaching oral cultures, Wesley's concept of prevenient grace directs the missionary to look for evidence of God's presence long before they arrived. In oral cultures, good places to start this search are in the local proverbs, rituals, and stories of the people. In order to continue what God has already started among the local people, these aspects of oral cultures are good entry places for ministry to the local people. If we look long enough, God's fingerprints will be evident such that coming to Christ will be congruent with some aspects of their own culture. This can create an indigenous understanding and appreciation of the Gospel in local cultures, utilizing the very stepping stones that God has placed in culture to lead them toward mature faith.

NOTES

1. Harriet Jill Olson, ed. *The Book of Discipline of The United Methodist Church.* (Nashville: The United Methodist Publishing House, 2004), p. 46.

2. Grant Lovejoy, ed., "Making Disciples of Oral Learners: Lausanne Occasional Paper 54" in *2004 Lausanne Forum Occasional Papers*, ed. D. Claydon, et al., http://www.lausanne.org/documents/2004forum/LOP54_IG25.pdf (Lausanne Committee for World Evangelization, 2004).

3. Walter J. Ong, *Orality and Literacy* (London: Routledge, 1982), p. i.

4. W. Jay Moon, "Sweet Talk in Africa: Using Proverbs in Ministry," *Evangelical Missions Quarterly* 40, no. 2 (2004): p. 163.

5. Stan Nussbaum, ed., *The Wisdom of African Proverbs CD-ROM, version 1.03.* (Colorado Springs, Colo.: Global Mapping International, 1996–1998).

6. For a more full description of this encounter in narrative form, see W. Jay. Moon, "Using Proverbs to Contextualize Christianity in the Builsa Culture of Ghana, West Africa" (PhD diss., Asbury Theological Seminary, 2005). This was published in the American Society of Missiology Scholarly Monograph Series in 2009.

7. A. H. Mathias Zahniser, *Symbol and Ceremony: Making Disciples Across Cultures, Innovations in Mission* (Monrovia, Calif.: MARC, 1997), pp. 32–41.

8. Onno Van der Hart, *Rituals in Psychotherapy: Transition and Continuity* (New York: Irvington Publishers, 1983).

9. Wendy Leeds-Hurwitz, "Semiotics and Communication: Signs, Codes, Cultures," in *Communication Textbook Series,* ed. J. Bryant (Hillsdale, N.J.: Lawrence Erlbaum Associates, 1993), p. 6.

10. This occurred at the North American Institute for Indigenous Theological Studies conference held at the Sioux Falls Seminary on November 29 to December 1, 2007, during the closing ceremony, which included the burning of sage, drumming, and a farewell dance involving all of the seminar participants.

11. I was first exposed to this powerful ritual by Randy Woodley, president of Eagles' Wings Ministry, during a class at Asbury Theological Seminary. It was such an intense spiritual experience of Christ that I eagerly participated in other "sweat lodge" ceremonies later. Richard Twiss, president of Wiconi International Ministries, and I take seminary students once a year to the Rosebud reservation in South Dakota in order to experience and discuss contextualization. Among other events, the students participate in the Lakota-Sioux "sweat lodge" called the *Inipi* ceremony.

12. For a good treatment of the Inipi and other Lakota Sioux rituals, see Joseph Epes Brown, ed., *The Sacred Pipe: Black Elk's Account of the Seven Rites of the Oglala Sioux*, vol. 36, *The Civilization of the American Indians Series*, ed. J. E. Brown, (Norman: University of Oklahoma Press, 1953, 1989).

13. John Walsh, *The Art of Storytelling: Easy Steps to Presenting an Unforgettable Story* (Chicago: Moody, 2003).

14. Thomas E. Boomershine, *Story Journey: An Invitation to the Gospel as Storytelling* (Nashville: Abingdon Press, 1988).

15. The Builsa people are roughly 100,000 in number and they live mainly in the Upper East Region of Ghana. In 1998, leaders from the Bible Church of Africa and SIM Ghana discussed the history of the slave trade in Northern Ghana. Many stories were collected and shared at this event. In addition, I met with the paramount chief of the Builsa,

Azantilow Asandow, and his elders to discuss these events. He explained to me that he was born in 1901 (only five years after the final slave raid), and his father participated in the final battle against these Zambara slave raiders from the North. His father passed these stories onto him. The story above was attested to by both Azantilow Asandow and George Atemboa. These stories are embedded in the Builsa identity. Each year, a Fiok festival is held to remember this story, while dancers from all over the Builsa villages come to Sandema to act out the war dance and commemorate this event.

16. George Atemboa, "The Impact of the Slave Trade on the Builsa," in *The Slave Trade and Reconciliation: A Northern Ghanaian Perspective*, ed. A. Howell (Accra, Ghana: Assemblies of God Literature Centre, 1998), p. 29.

17. Ibid.

18. The slave raiders were Muslims from the Zambarama people group in the region of Niger. The names of these leaders are still remembered by the Builsa—Babatu and Samori are the most famous. Babatu was reportedly on a jihad into and surrounding the territories of the Builsa people.

24

ISLAMIC STUDIES— THE INSIDER'S APPROACH

Wilbur Stone

In surveying past and present attempts to communicate the message of Christ among Muslim people groups, it would appear that something has gone terribly wrong for there have been few successful attempts to establish an indigenous movement or church among Islamic peoples. As the saying goes, "If we keep doing what we've been doing, we'll keep getting what we've been getting," and that isn't much! A viable solution will only come when we are able to admit to ourselves that there has been a problem in the past and that there is a problem with our present efforts.

Perhaps the following question based on a biblical passage can provide us direction as to how to proceed. Are we willing to become all things to all people that by all means we might win some?[1] Careful consideration of past and present approaches suggests that changes are needed in at least three areas: (1) changes in attitude, (2) changes in approach, and (3) changes in action. Such changes have the potential to enhance the effectiveness of cross-cultural communications among people groups adhering to the Islamic faith.

Based on the premise that all religious faiths, including Islam, are authentic, though not necessarily true, these faiths represent an authentic intention and attempt by some group of people to relate to the divine or a trans-human reality that provides the meaning for their religious activities and their very meaning of existence itself.[2] I contend, *"All roads do not lead to God, but God can be found walking on all of those roads."*

Those involved in efforts to communicate Christ among Muslims should examine or perhaps reexamine their personal attitudes toward both Islam and toward Muslim peoples.

Although I am not arguing that one need accept Islam as a viable way to obtain salvation, the fact that others do view Islam as the correct and only way for them to relate to God[3] should cause the cross-cultural worker to respect these persons' religious efforts as representing their sincere attempts to encounter and gain the approval of God through following the various practices related to Islam. Muslims typically have a great appreciation for the ultimacy and transcendence of the sovereign God. Their stated concern for cleanliness and purity in every aspect of their lives, and their commitment to and emphasis upon the importance of prayer, reveals a deep desire to honor and please God. My point is simply that in relating to sincere Muslims we might gain insights into our own faith and even be challenged spiritually at times.

My arguments are based on another premise, namely that the attitude we take toward another people and their religious faith will greatly impact, enhance, or impede our efforts to build meaningful personal relationships with them through which we might then share Christ. If we view their religious faith and religious practices as mere superstition, or worse as demonic or satanic, then we typically approach the followers of such faiths in a condescending, confrontational, even combative way.

On the other hand, if we embrace their religious efforts as being an authentic attempt to encounter the divine, we can then work to build upon points of contact within Islam to demonstrate how Christ is the ultimate fulfilment of their religious quest. Perhaps like the apostle Peter, we need to learn that God is aware of and respects every person who is genuinely seeking to relate to him.[4] Do we really respect Muslims' religious pursuits? Such attitudes and approaches tend to reduce the potential for conflict, and enhance one's efforts at building personal relationships, thus facilitating attempts to share the Gospel message.

Such an approach also is based on yet another premise, namely that the Holy Spirit is actively working among Muslim peoples. This is being clearly demonstrated in the reports of dreams and visions among them around the world.[5] Christ is clearly working among Islamic peoples in a loving, seeking, and nonjudgmental way. Perhaps we can and should learn from these encounters, and seek to share our faith in more vulnerable and less confrontational ways. Other great evangelists such as John

Wesley, the founder of the Methodist movement, emphasized the importance of recognizing the fact that God is always and everywhere at work in the lives of all peoples to bring them to repentance and saving faith. This activity is sometimes referred to as "prevenient grace."[6]

Elenctic approaches, approaches that recognize and place emphasis on the essential role the Holy Spirit plays in an evangelistic witness, genuinely show value for the other person's faith and points of view. Such approaches pave the way for dialogue, for building bridges, and for greater understanding and mutual respect. This type of approach thereby creates liminal opportunities, or moments of openness or vulnerability, through which the Holy Spirit is able to pursue his work of conviction or of convincing others of the truth of the Gospel.[7] We do not take God to any people group, we only enable them to discover the God who has been ever present in their midst![8]

One Christian Islamic scholar argues that "Christian-Muslim relations have been characterized by fear, unfair criticism, inappropriate comparisons, arrogance, ridicule and violence."[9] A Christian evangelist working among Muslims and an advocate of new and creative approaches to evangelism among Muslim peoples argues that instead of perpetuating our traditional views that "Muslims are hardhearted, inherently unresponsive or resistant people to the Gospel," it might be more appropriate for the Christian church to confess its own sins, failures, and ethnocentric attitudes and actions towards the Muslim world.[10]

In addition to acknowledging our past failures, perhaps we also need to confront our fear of syncretism. While acknowledging that any attempt at contextualization must deal with the real danger of syncretism, perhaps we need rather to accept that such risks are acceptable as we seek to develop more effective approaches to communicating the Gospel among Muslim peoples. In fact, my definition of contextualization is "positive syncretism"! Of course, attempts at contextualization are best developed by those coming to faith within the Islamic community rather than by outsiders to the Islamic community and faith. Paul Hiebert's work related to the topic of critical contextualization is helpful in addressing this need.[11]

Changes in attitude must necessarily be accompanied by changes in approach. One Christian writer once stated, "The most important word in the English language is relationship."[12] Perhaps that should provide us a clue as to how to facilitate more effective Christian witness among Muslims. In fact, numerous Muslim "converts" and Christian workers among Muslims argue that there is a need for more relational approaches to sharing a Gospel witness versus the more confrontational approaches advocated by missionaries in the past.[13]

Incarnational approaches as modeled by our Lord Jesus reveal and emphasize the crucial importance of building personal relationships and friendships through which one can share Jesus with Muslims. It is said that St. Francis of Assisi once told his followers, "Wherever you go, preach the Gospel; if necessary, use words." Of a truth our lives often do speak louder than our words. Relational or friendship approaches to evangelism would appear to be far more effective than the typical Western confrontational models advocated and utilized in the past.

Muslims, like many other peoples, truly value their friendships. Perhaps in our desire to share the Gospel, we fail to realize the significance of taking time to build genuine friendships with our Muslim acquaintances. One Christian group which I had the privilege of working with has the following motto: "Be a friend, Make a friend, Lead your friend to Christ." And, surprise, surprise, it really does work!

In advocating more relational approaches to sharing Christ among Muslims, the need for another change in approach is revealed. Muslims find their identity within their community. In fact, Islam, perhaps more than any other religious movement, is built around the centrality of the community. This reveals the need to replace the extractionist types of approaches of the past with approaches that allow an individual, or even larger groups, to remain members of their families and the wider Muslim community.

The methods of the past have typically brought the "converts" into conflict with their immediate family and the wider community, even jeopardizing their lives and the lives of their family members. Often such "converts" had only one choice and that was to flee to the West or to some safe haven. And, perhaps even worse from a missiological standpoint, that person's potential influence for sharing Christ within his or her own community was virtually destroyed. In other words, by demanding that they come out from the Muslim community, we in effect eliminate any possibility of that person going back into that same community as a witness for Christ.

More effective approaches would allow a Muslim follower of "Isa al Masih"[14] to remain within his or her family and community while seeking to provide that person the necessary support and encouragement needed to be "salt and light" within his or her own world. Perhaps the formation of small groups (cells) of believers who could meet in their homes for Bible study, prayer, and worship might serve as one alternative approach to demanding that such persons identify themselves openly with a Christian church.

Some advocate approaches that allow persons to continue to call themselves Muslims, even including repetition of the Islamic creed, while identifying themselves as follower of *Isa*. Still others suggest that the "Jesus Mosque" might be an appropriate response. It is my conviction that we must allow the Muslim followers of Jesus to determine the best way of maintaining relationships with their existing community and the best way to form appropriate contextualized communities of believers within the larger Muslim community.

Must a Muslim become a member of a "Christian church" in order to be a true follower of Jesus Christ? Must the Muslim "convert" be baptized and publicly declare his faith before the entire Muslim community? Can a Muslim believer remain a secret believer? Is it necessary that a Muslim follower of Jesus be called a Christian? Questions such as these must be dealt with in an appropriate manner.

This paper has thus far violated yet another area that calls for change. There is a need to rethink the use of certain vocabulary typically associated with the Christian missionary movement, namely such terms or expressions as: "Christian," "church," "convert," "conversion," "ex-Muslim," "former Muslim," "becoming a Christian," "baptism," "evangelism," "missions," and so forth. Such terms or expressions carry negative or offensive (pejorative) meanings to the Muslim community.[15] "If we are to witness a turning to Christ within Islam, this kind of conversion language must not be used in our interaction with Muslims nor in our mission reports and prayer letters."[16]

More acceptable terminology might be the use of the term "believers" for the Muslims who have made a commitment to follow Jesus as their Lord and Savior. As with the approach to forming an appropriate community of believers, we perhaps must leave the selection of a name for themselves as well as the selection of appropriate vocabulary, and other forms and symbols they will use to express their faith, to these followers themselves. We must trust and allow the Holy Spirit to lead these followers of Jesus in determining the solutions to such issues.[17] We perhaps must answer the same question dealt with in the Jerusalem Council in Acts 15. Must a person become a "Jew" before he or she can become truly "surrendered" to Christ as Savior and Lord? Conversely, must a Muslim become identified as a "Christian" in order to be a true follower of *Isa*?

Changes in attitude and in approach must also necessarily be followed by changes in action. The foregoing model places great emphasis upon the personal lifestyle of the would-be evangelists, and demands the employment of incarnational approaches and identification, as complete as is possible, with the peoples to whom one is seeking to share a viable witness. We must be willing to eat with, to dress like, to live like, and even to pray like and fast with the people to whom we wish to share a witness. When asked how far one should go in identifying with another people, one of my former teachers, Dr. Darrell Whiteman, stated that, "We should go just as far as our consciences will allow us to go."

One area fraught with controversy is whether one should use the Qur'an in seeking to share a "Gospel" witness among Muslims. Again, the issue of attitude is at the heart of the problem. What attitude should the Christian witness take toward the Qur'an, the holy scriptures of Islam? Is the Qur'an a work of Satan, or just the work of a man (Muhammad) who was either misled or deceived? Does it contain points of contact that can be employed to present Jesus as Savior and Lord of the Muslim too?

One Christian author, Don Richardson, argues that there are no "redemptive analogies" in Islam.[18] While it may be simply an argument over semantics, I strongly feel that there are many points of contact or bridges within Islam and in the Qur'an that one can utilize to effectively communicate the message of Christ to Muslims. Did not the apostle Paul quote from Greek secular poets and philosophers in his attempt to communicate the Gospel message to those in Athens?[19]

In light of the honor and respect the average Muslim feels toward the Qur'an, it is perhaps foolish to think that we can completely ignore the Muslim scriptures in witnessing to them. Indeed, some Muslim "converts" and Christian workers feel that the Qur'an provides the most natural bridge to sharing the Gospel among Muslims.[20] In fact, the Qur'an, especially in the Arabic edition, seems to speak very positively of Jesus Christ, of the Old Testament Scriptures, of the Gospels, of Jews and Christians. And, perhaps more important, there are many points of contact related to Jesus in the Qur'an. While one must admit that there are major differences between the

Bible and the Qur'an in relation to Jesus, there would appear to be enough commonalities to at least begin a dialogue with a willing Muslim.

However, this approach demands that the evangelist be as familiar with the Qur'an as the average Muslim. In actual fact, many would-be evangelists have never even read the Qur'an, let alone made a serious effort to study and memorize portions of it. If we feel that Muslims need to read and understand the Bible, then perhaps we too need to show our respect for them by spending an adequate amount of time studying their scriptures as well. And, although it would require an extraordinary effort and commitment on the part of the evangelist, the best possible method would seem to be to master the Arabic language so as to be able to interact and dialogue with Muslims in the only truly accepted version of their holy scriptures.

Finally, we must recognize that our efforts will be fruitless apart from the work of the Holy Spirit. Our best efforts will bear little fruit unless they are bathed with much prayer, and the anointing of the Holy Spirit. Sharing a witness for Christ among Muslims is surely among the most difficult challenges facing the Christian community today. We must acknowledge that the employment of our best strategies, and the expenditure of vast amounts of resources, will accomplish precious little unless we acknowledge our total dependence upon the Lord. If we do it without prayer and the unique work of the Holy Spirit, then God has no part in it. There must be recognition of the centrality and importance of intercessory prayer to the successful communication of the Gospel among Muslim peoples.

We must seek to partner with the Holy Spirit who is already at work among the Muslim peoples. Perhaps as stated by a Christian missionary in a previous period of time, we need to recognize that when we enter in among another people to share a Gospel witness, we should take off our shoes for we are standing on holy ground—we are standing where God, the Holy Spirit, is perhaps most present and most at work.[21]

The foregoing comments and suggestions are meant to be just that. I do not pretend to have the answers to the many difficult issues raised in this paper. Nor do I pretend to be an expert on Islamic studies. I do however trust the Holy Spirit to empower us to meet the challenges that face us in successfully communicating the Gospel to Muslim peoples.

Be reminded that all we do or attempt in sharing Christ among Muslims must be unique to a particular context. Muslims are not all the same—in other words Muslims in one area may be quite different from Muslims in another area. "Insider's approaches" are obviously working in certain Islamic circles, and may be especially appropriate with high-identity Muslims. However, many Muslims do not know Islam very well. Many are not even familiar with the Qur'an. For many, their faith is more of a cultural tradition than a heart-felt religion. We must adjust our approaches to our particular context and people group based on their knowledge of and commitment to Islam, their knowledge of and use of the Qur'an, their unique needs and beliefs, and the sincerity of their pursuit of God. Of a truth, we need a variety of approaches to reach the Muslim world! In the words of a Muslim background believer, "Don't proclaim Christ as a religion, but rather proclaim him in terms of a relationship! Before one can preach the Gospel, one must wear the Gospel!"[22]

NOTES

1. 1 Corinthians 9:22.

2. Harold W. Turner, *From Temple to Meeting House: The Phenomenology and Theology of Places of Worship* (New York: Mouton, 1979), p. 348.

3. Muslims use the term *Allah* for God. While not all scholars or theologians will agree, this author views the term *Allah* as synonymous with any of the normally accepted terms used by Christians for God.

4. Acts 10:34–35.

5. Rick Love, *Muslims, Magic and the Kingdom of God* (Pasedena, Calif.: William Carey Library, 2000), pp. 155–57, 160–163; Richard Tucker, "A Move of God in a Muslim Land," in *From the Straight Path to the Narrow Way*, ed. David H. Greenlee (Secunderabad, India: OM Books, 2005), p. 260.

6. Matthias H. Zahniser, "Close Encounters of the Vulnerable Kind: Christian Dialogical Proclamation Among Muslims," *Asbury Theological Journal* 49, no. 1 (Spring 1994): p. 75.

7. John H. Bavinck, *An Introduction to the Science of Missions* (Philadelphia: The Presbyterian and Reformed Publishing Company, 1960), pp. 221–33.

8. Matthias H. Zahniser, "The Trinity: Paradigm for Mission in the Spirit," *Missiology* 17, no. 1 (January 1989): p. 75.

9. Zahniser, "Close Encounters," p. 74.

10. D. O. (pseudonym). From an unpublished article entitled "A Jesus Movement within Islam," p. 13.

11. Paul G. Hiebert, *Anthropological Insights for Missionaries* (Grand Rapids: Baker Book House, 1985), pp. 186–92.

12. W. Oscar Thompson, Jr., *Concentric Circles of Concern* (Nashville: Broadman Press, 1981), p. 13.

13. Fouad Elias Accad, *Building Bridges: Christianity and Islam* (Colorado Springs, Colo.: Navpress, 1997), pp. 30–33; Zahniser, "Close Encounters," p. 72.

14. *Isa al Masih* is the Arabic term for "Christ the Messiah," which is used in the Qur'an and other Islamic writings.

15. D.O., pp. 14–17.

16. Ibid., pp. 14–15.

17. Ibid., pp. 16–17.

18. Don Richardson, *Secrets of the Koran* (Ventura, Calif.: Regal Books, 2003) pp. 17–20.

19. Acts 17:16–33.

20. Accad, *Building Bridges,* pp. 12–24.

21. John V. Taylor, *The Go Between God: The Holy Spirit and the Christian Mission* (London: SCM Press, 1972), pp. 3–7, 179–197; Zahniser, "The Trinity," pp. 74–75.

22. In a personal conversation with Syed Kamran at a seminar in Taipei, Taiwan, in 2001.

BIBLIOGRAPHY

Accad, Fouad Elias. *Building Bridges: Christianity and Islam.* Colorado Springs, Colo.: Navpress, 1997.

Bavinck, Johan H. *An Introduction to the Science of Missions.* Philadelphia: The Presbyterian and Reformed Publishing Company, 1960.

Hiebert, Paul G. *Anthropological Insights for Missionaries.* Grand Rapids: Baker Book House, 1985.

Love, Rick. *Muslims, Magic and the Kingdom of God.* Pasedena, Calif.: William Carey Library, 2000.

Richardson, Don. *Secrets of the Koran.* Ventura, Calif: Regal Books, 2003.

Stone, Wilbur P. "Prophet or Priest? The Paradox of Ministry." Unpublished Sermon, The Southern Baptist Theological Seminary, Louisville, Ky.: 1996.

Taylor, John V. *The Go Between God: The Holy Spirit and the Christian Mission.* London: SCM Press, 1972.

Thompson, W. Oscar, Jr., *Concentric Circles of Concern.* Nashville: Broadman Press, 1981.

Tucker, Richard. "A Move of God in a Muslim Land." In *From the Straight Path to the Narrow Way,* ed. David H. Greenlee, pp. 255–65. Secunderabad, India: OM Books, 2005.

Turner, Harold W. *From Temple to Meeting House: The Phenomenology and Theology of Places of Worship.* New York: Mouton, 1979.

Zahniser, Matthias H. "The Trinity: Paradigm for Mission in the Spirit." *Missiology* 17, no. 1 (January 1989): pp. 69–82.

———. "Close Encounters of the Vulnerable Kind: Christian Dialogical Proclamation Among Muslims." *Asbury Theological Journal* 49, no. 1 (Spring 1994): pp. 71–78.

25

THE CROSS AND MISSION

Hwa Yung

INTRODUCTION

For Christians who take the New Testament seriously, it is a truism to say that the cross is central to mission. I use the cross here as a symbol of the spirit of sacrifice, suffering, simplicity, and servanthood that is entailed in the call of the Gospel. Our Lord, in his words uttered shortly before his death, clearly draws attention to the centrality of the cross: "I tell you the truth, unless a kernel of wheat falls to the ground and dies, it remains only a single seed. But if it dies, it produces many seeds" (John 12:24 NIV). But how much is this really so in actual mission thinking and practice?

Writing from the context of East Asia, a region that has seen spectacular economic growth in the last few decades and where the wealth of some churches is beginning to match that of their counterparts in Europe and North America, it is sometimes difficult for this theme to be taken seriously. Why the need for all this emphasis on sacrifice, suffering, and the cross? Such talk surely belongs to the past. God has now blessed us materially beyond our wildest dreams. Just look at the megachurches springing up in places like Seoul, Singapore, or even Jakarta, and the Mercedes and BMW cars parked outside churches in Hong Kong or Kuala Lumpur! With hundreds of millions of dollars or, perhaps, even billions poured into Asian missions today, the churches have become increasingly confident about themselves. Many see this as an unalloyed blessing!

Yet, within the Wesleyan tradition, that was not how John Wesley himself saw the matter. God's blessing of riches also has its down side. Wesley in the revival had seen how many poor people, after conversion, had their lives transformed. The resultant personal discipline, hard work, and thrift led to what sociologists call "social lift," with many converts becoming more wealthy and middle class. But this unfortunately gave rise to pride, self-indulgence, love of money, and a subsequent loss of interest in spiritual things, which in turn threatened the whole revival! Two years before his death, Wesley asked in one of his sermons, "Does it seem . . . that true scriptural Christianity, has a tendency in process of time to undermine and destroy itself?"[1] It was out of this concern to prevent riches from destroying the faith of his converts that he coined his famous formula: Gain all you can, save all you can . . . give all you can! "Otherwise," he continues, "I can have no more hope of your salvation than that of Judas Iscariot." [2]

Wesley's struggle with the destructive power of money in spiritual life clearly illustrates the relation between the cross and mission in a negative manner. When sacrifice and simplicity are set aside, spiritual vitality and the cause of mission inevitably suffer. Similarly his pattern for itinerant ministry illustrates the same theme positively. E. Dale Dunlap has noted that itinerancy, which began under Wesley in England, underwent its greatest development under Francis Asbury in America. He writes: "The cost of the system in human effort and sacrifice was fantastic. The preachers were constantly on the go, exposed to all kinds of weather, especially vulnerable to epidemics and disease, for which . . . they received less than $100 cash per year. Most of the men were young when they died."[3] Indeed, Dunlap notes that Frederick Norwood commented that the early Methodist itinerancy came as close as Protestantism could to Catholic monastic orders with its absolute vows! Yet the results were plain. American Methodism quickly overtook British Methodism numerically before the end of the eighteenth century, and outgrew every other church in America in the nineteenth century.

THREE CASE STUDIES

Numerous other examples can be drawn from history to illustrate this theme, both positively and negatively. I will use three case studies from twentieth century Asia for this purpose. The first comes from South Korea and Taiwan.

Case Study One

One of the puzzles in church growth in modern Asia is that of the relative growth of the churches in South Korea and Taiwan. As far as I know, this has never been examined. Careful study shows that both countries shared a rather similar history. Both cultures are rooted in Confucianism. Both were colonized by Japan at the end of the nineteenth century or early twentieth century, with Christians experiencing varying degrees of persecution subsequently. The populations in both countries went through experiences of war with the Communist armies after World War II. Many Chinese fled mainland China for Taiwan, and many Koreans fled from the north of the country to the south. Both countries benefited from very substantial aid and missionary efforts after World War II. Yet the church in South Korea took off and continues to thrive with some 30 percent of the nation Christianized. By contrast, the church in Taiwan has only grown slowly in the same period. How do we explain this? I suggest the answer may be found when we examine how Christians in the respective countries lived in relation to the cross.

In the case of South Korea, various factors contributed to the rapid growth of the church in the post–World War II era. But what is also undeniable is that the church had during the years leading up to the end of the Japanese colonial era taken a heroic stand on nationalism and religious freedom. In 1919, when a countrywide. revolt against Japanese rule occurred, fifteen out of the thirty-one signatories of the declaration of independence were Christians—even though the percentage of Christians in Korea at that time was small! Many Christians were at the forefront of the refusal to participate in the emperor worship enforced at Japanese Shinto shrines in Korea. Many were imprisoned and killed for their stand on these matters. When Korea was liberated in 1945, more than three thousand Christians were released from prison![4] The church went through yet more suffering when Christians were singled out by the Communists for elimination during the Korean War, leading to about half of all Protestant pastors being killed or disappearing. Having lived faithfully for two generations under the shadow of the cross, the church that emerged in the aftermath of the Korean War in 1953 had a public moral standing second to none! On this solid foundation, the rapid growth of the church in the next three decades was built.

The story of the church in Taiwan up till the end of World War II is similar in many ways to that of Korea, with the pressures from the Japanese being perhaps less intense. After the war, the island was handed over to China under the Kuomintang government. But resentment to the mainlanders as occupiers led to a revolt in 1947 in which thousands of Taiwanese died. When Chiang Kai-Shek was defeated in China, he moved his government over to Taiwan in 1949. But it is unlikely that this in itself would have hindered church growth there, to the extent described in the latest edition of *Operation World* as "the only major Han Chinese population in the world where the spiritual breakthrough has yet to come."[5] After all, a substantial portion of the population after 1949 was composed of mainlanders.

Furthermore, Chiang Kai-Shek, the leader of Taiwan until his death in 1975, was supposed to be a Christian and warmly disposed toward missionary efforts. How can this slow growth of the church in Taiwan be explained? The answer, I believe, is partly found in the fact that Chiang Kai-Shek's Christianity was, in truth, barely nominal.[6] Any supposed deep-seated Christian commitment was for all intents and purposes a sham, a myth promulgated by paid Washington lobbyists for various reasons—as well as almost certainly by Chiang himself. The reality was that he and his wife's family, together with many of the senior military and government leaders, were deeply mired into the systemic corruption of the Kuomintang government, which was one of the key reasons for the Communist victory in 1949. Some years after President Truman stepped down from government, and on the basis of hard evidence, he said this of Chiang and his wife's family, the Soongs: "They're all thieves, every damn one of them . . . They stole seven hundred and fifty million dollars out of the $3.8 billion that we sent to Chiang. They stole it, and it's invested in real estate down in Sao Paulo and some right here in New York . . . And that's the money that was used and is still being used for the so-called China Lobby."[7]

At the time of the Communist victory in 1949, many senior Kuomintang officials left China with bundles of U.S. dollars and gold bars, almost all looted from the people, or stolen from government funds and American aid. Yet, I personally know a man, a general in the Kuomintang army, who left China penniless in 1949, having refused to be sucked into the corruption of the Kuomintang government. There were almost certainly others, but probably not a large number. This man had taken such a stand because of his strong Confucian convictions. For within Confucianism, there has always been a very strong tradition in China historically of the *qing-guan*, the incorruptible servant of the state, who would rather lose everything, including his privileged positions, than to soil his hands through ill-gotten gain. Of course, this man also had an utter disdain for Chiang and many of his cronies in the Kuomintang leadership because of their shameless self-seeking and corruption! The clear implication therefore is that, in the eyes of the people of Taiwan, the Gospel could not have been held in high regard and therefore not worthy of a positive response.

On this point, the contrast with the Korean church could not have been more complete! Without denying that other factors have also been at play, I suggest that this is a crucial key to explaining the puzzle of why the church in South Korea took off, whereas that in Taiwan stagnated during the last fifty years.

Case Study Two

This brings us to the second case study. Whereas the church in South Korea experienced what has been described as "wild-fire" church growth from the 1950s onward, what many do not know is that since the early 1990s, church growth in Korea has stagnated. Recent discussions with Korean church leaders indicate that this is still an ongoing problem. What lies behind this stagnation after decades of spectacular growth?

Studies by two scholars have pointed in similar directions. Bong Rin Ro, in a paper analyzing the growth and decline of the Korean church, suggested that the factors that had led to the earlier growth have since been overtaken by other problems that have brought about a loss of vitality. These include rampant schismatic church divisions and the perception that, despite contributions to nationalism and reforms in the past, the church has failed to take Christian social responsibility seriously in more recent years. Further, the emergence of megachurches has often resulted in insufficient pastoral oversight and weaknesses in the discipling process. Finally, there are problems associated with growing affluence and modernization, such as materialism, hectic lifestyles, influence of secularism and other modern ideologies, including theological liberalism.[8]

Similarly, Young-gi Hong, in a study on nominalism in Korean Protestantism, states that government statistics shows that Christian numbers levelled off at around 26 percent of the whole population by 1995.[9] Hong also quotes a Gallup poll carried out in 1998 which showed that Protestant Christianity compared unfavourably with Buddhism and Roman Catholicism in the eyes of the Korea people. Of the three religious groupings, Protestantism has the highest defection rate (46.1% compared with 29.4% and 39.9% for Buddhism and Catholicism, respectively). Among people not belonging to any religious group but who are willing to consider joining one later, Protestantism holds the least attraction (21.4% compared to 41.8% and 36.7%, respectively, preferring Buddhism and Catholicism). Hong also found that some of the key reasons why people have been deserting Protestant churches included distrust of the church arising from the improper conduct of pastors, shortage of time for church because of hectic lifestyles, and disappointment with fellow church members. Further, many nominal Protestants who have not left the faith but have ceased to attend church indicated that they were affected by "shortage of time, the bad conduct of church leaders and members and a negative image of the church."[10] Among other things, Hong also notes that much more effort needs to be given to the discipling process in individual lives.

What Ro and Hong have shown is that economic success, growing affluence, materialism, secular pressures, and other pressures of modern life are clearly taking a toll on Protestant Christianity. But Hong's study also shows that the public image of Protestantism is poor compared to Buddhism and Catholicism, clearly implying that Protestantism has demonstrable weaknesses peculiar to itself. Problems such as distrust of the leadership, improper conduct of members, inadequate pastoral oversight associated with large churches, and weakness in the discipling process all combine to suggest that the present stagnation of the church in South Korea is in many ways caused by its own earlier success.

As we have already noted, this was a problem that Wesley had already noted much earlier in another form. It appears that Korean Christianity failed to take seriously Wesley's question that we quoted earlier: "Does it seem . . . that true scriptural Christianity, has a tendency in process of time to undermine and destroy itself?" In the midst of its success, the vision of the cross and what it stands for appear to have begun fading in the church, with disastrous consequences as a result!

Case Study Three

For the third illustration of the thesis of this paper, we return once more to the Chinese church in the twentieth century. The Protestant church in China in the first half of the twentieth century was weak and struggling. Despite more than a hundred years of Western missions, it numbered around a million members when the Communists took control in 1949. Vast numbers of missionaries had worked in China, many sacrificially. Huge sums of money had been poured into evangelistic work as well as social, medical, and educational outreach. Almost all the best universities and hospitals in the country came out of missionary efforts. Still the church grew slowly! Why?

John Sung, the outstanding Chinese evangelist and revivalist of the first half of the century, saw clearly that it was the Western control of the church on the one hand and the Chinese dependence on foreign funds on the other that were the key causes of the church's stagnation. Repeatedly he urged the church to stop relying on missionary funds. Instead it should look "to the Lord of all things and realize that the time has come for the church to be self-propagating, self-governing and self-supporting—truly independent!"[11] This vision found its out-working in the ministry of many, including especially Wang Mingdao, Sung's contemporary and Beijing pastor of later fame.[12]

Asked shortly before his death about the future of the Chinese church, John Sung revealed that God had showed him that a great revival was coming. But the Western missionaries would all have to leave first, together with their money.[13] Sung died in 1944 and the Communists came to power in 1949. All the missionaries had to leave and all church properties were confiscated. For the next thirty years, many thought that the Chinese church had died through intense persecution. Then in the late 1970s, the rumbling of a tremendous revival in China began filtering out through the Bamboo Curtain. As they say, the rest is history—and we have yet to see its full unfolding!

Again by way of contrast, it is interesting to compare what happened to the church in some other parts of Asia where Western missions also poured in similarly vast amounts of human, financial, social, medical, and educational resources. In South Asia, for example, anecdotal evidence indicates that the mainline churches are hardly growing, despite having inherited so much materially from Western missions. Instead, church leaders often have large chunks of their time taken up in administering property and dealing with legal disputes over them!

SUMMING-UP

The three cases studies examined can be replicated by many others drawn from the growth of the church since its very beginnings. As we think and pray together about mission in the twenty-first century, we are still faced with a choice between the same two basic approaches to Christian mission. One approach places self-giving, sacrifice, simplicity, and humble service, symbolized by the cross, at its heart; the other pushes it to the periphery. The ever-present temptation is to ignore the lessons of two thousand years of mission history!

NOTES

1. John Wesley, Sermon 122, "Causes of the Inefficacy of Christianity," in *Sermons IV,* ed. Albert C. Outler, vol. 4 of *The Bicentennial Edition of the Works of John Wesley,* (Nashville: Abingdon Press, 1976–), p. 95.

2. Ibid., p. 96.

3. E. Dale Dunlap, "The United Methodist System of Itinerant Ministry," in *Rethinking Methodist History: A Bicentennial Historical Consultation*, ed. Russell E. Richey and Kenneth E. Rowe (Nashville: Kingswood, 1985), p. 21.

4. Bong Rin Ro, "The Church in Korea," in *Church in Asia Today: Challenges and Opportunities*, ed. Saphir Athyal (Singapore: Asia Lausanne Committee on World Evangelization, 1996), pp. 54–71.

5. Patrick Johnstone and Jason Mandryk, *Operation World* (Carlisle, Eng.: Paternoster, 2001), p. 187.

6. For a good account of the man, see Jonathan Fenby, *Generalissimo: Chiang Kai-Shek and the China He Lost* (London: Free Press, 2003). Whether there was a real conversion in Chiang Kai-Shek's life after the 1949 debacle is not known by the author, and certainly is not the issue here.

7. Cited in Sterling Seagrave, *The Soong Dynasty* (New York: Harper & Row, 1985), p. 437. More details are found in the book, and also in Fenby, *Generalissimo: Chiang Kai-Shek and the China He Lost.*

8. Bong Rin Ro, "The Korean Church: Growing or Declining?" *Evangelical Review of Theology*, 19, no. 4 (October 1995): pp. 336–52.

9. Young-gi Hong, "Nominalism in Korean Protestantism," *Transformation*, 16, no. 4 (1999): p. 136.

10. Ibid., p. 138*ff.*

11. Cited in Leslie T. Lyall, *A Biography of John Sung* (Singapore: Armour, 2004), p. 99; originally published as *Flame for God: John Sung and Revival in the Far East* (Sevenoaks, Eng.: OMF, 1961).

12. See Thomas A. Harvey, *Acquainted with Grief: Wang Mingdao's Stand for the Persecuted Church in China* (Grand Rapids: Brazos Press, 2002), especially pp. 27–46.

13. William E. Schubert, *I Remember John Sung* (Singapore: Far Eastern Bible College Press, 1976), pp. 65*ff.* But see also John Sung, *The Journal Once Lost: Extracts from the Diary of John Sung*, compiled by Levi Sung (Singapore: Genesis Books, 2008), pp. 271, 476.

BIBLIOGRAPHY

Dunlap, E. Dale. "The United Methodist System of Itinerant Ministry." In *Rethinking Methodist History: A Bicentennial Historical Consultation*, ed. Russell E. Richey and Kenneth E. Rowe, pp. 18–28. Nashville: Kingswood, 1985.

Engel, James F., and William A. Dyrness. *Changing the Mind of Missions—Where Have We Gone Wrong?* Downers Grove, Ill.: InterVarsity Press, 2000.

Harvey, Thomas A. *Acquainted with Grief: Wang Mingdao's Stand for the Persecuted Church in China*. Grand Rapids: Brazos Press, 2002.

Hong, Young-gi. "Nominalism in Korean Protestantism." *Transformation,* 16, no. 4 (1999): pp. 135–41.

Lyall, Leslie T. *A Biography of John Sung.* Singapore: Armour, 2004, p. 99; originally published as *Flame for God: John Sung and Revival in the Far East.* Sevenoaks, Eng.: OMF, 1961.

Ro, Bong Rin. "The Korean Church: Growing or Declining?" *Evangelical Review of Theology*, 19, no. 4 (October 1995): pp. 336–52.

Schubert, William E. *I Remember John Sung*. Singapore: Far Eastern Bible College Press, 1976.

Stott, John R. W. *The Cross of Christ.* (Leicester: InterVarsity Press, 1986.

Sung, John. *The Journal Once Lost: Extracts from the Diary of John Sung,* compiled by Levi Sung. Singapore: Genesis Books, 2008.

PART FIVE
Strategic Perspectives

A MISSION MOVEMENT, LIKE THE EIGHTEENTH-century Wesleyan revival in Britain and mission today, must be grounded biblically and developed theologically. It will generate a historical record from which to learn how to become and remain culturally relevant. But unless there is a clear strategy in place, that takes into consideration the biblical, theological, historical, and cultural perspectives, it will eventually flounder. Hence, we conclude this book on *World Mission in the Wesleyan Spirit* with strategic perspectives.

George Hunter's essay on "Mission Strategy in the Wesleyan Spirit" argues that John Wesley was a strategic genius and anticipated many of the developments that would emerge two hundred years later in church growth lore and the academic field of organizational development. Hunter warns that it is easy for a dynamic movement to lose its way when the means for fulfilling the objectives of a movement become more important than the ends, and participants in the movement become caught in the "activity trap"—keeping busy but going nowhere that advances the kingdom of God.

At first blush, missiologists and missionaries in the Wesleyan tradition may not consider environmental issues a legitimate part of their agenda for mission. Norman Thomas, however, reminds us in the next chapter that a dimension of our biblical and Wesleyan heritage embraces the understanding that all of God's creation is groaning to be renewed and healed. After giving a brief but dismal "state of the earth" summary, Thomas suggests some appropriate missional responses and challenges us to enlarge our mission to embrace the healing of the earth along with humanity.

Lindy Backues draws on his eighteen years of holistic mission and community development work in Indonesia to create a model of how we can relate to the very people we want to serve in mission. He looks at the incarnation of Jesus and derives six characteristics that we can use to guide and evaluate our participation in mission and community development activities.

Global strategies for world mission were anticipated at the great World Missionary Conference in Edinburgh in June 1910, and shaped much of mission activity in the following century. As we prepare to celebrate and critique that significant event one hundred years later, Daryl Balia discusses how Wesley's notion that the world was his parish seems initially constrained to nominal Christians in Great Britain. Another Methodist, John R. Mott, who was the architect of the 1910 Edinburgh conference had a different emphasis. Now, as preparation is underway for Edinburgh 2010, we see that the face of world Christianity has changed dramatically with substantial growth in the global South and retraction in the North, so that mission is from everywhere to everywhere.

Next, we look at leadership training as an important element in mission strategy. Brazilian Norival Trindade examines briefly three growing Christian movements and their need for leadership training. He then suggests a model of leadership training for mission that is open to new and diverse ideas, relies on Scripture, is created in the context of community, is culturally relevant, and is experiential and transformative for those who are trained.

Finally, we conclude this section and this book with a chapter that is inspired by William Carey's 1792 pamphlet, "An Enquiry into the Obligations of Christians to Use Means for the Conversion of the Heathens." Darrell Whiteman, drawing on research data from the *Mission Handbook 2007–2009*, explores the multiple means used in evangelical mission activity today to fulfill the Great Commission and model the Great Commandment. He notes seven trends and several ecclesiological and missiological issues of evangelical mission organizations, and concludes with The Mission Society as a case study of an agency that is holistic and kingdom-centered in its ministry.

26

MISSION STRATEGY IN THE
WESLEYAN SPIRIT

George G. Hunter III

Strategic thinking is the "red-headed stepchild" in the minds of most church and mission leaders. Strategy's role in the mission family is marginal compared to theology, history, perpetuating "our tradition," keeping supporters happy, advancing clergy careers, and many other ecclesiastical concerns that claim *priority* attention. Insufficient attention to strategy, however, is usually a major contributor to the stagnation or decline that many churches, missions, and denominations are now experiencing.

George Odiorne, the twentieth-century management guru, used to describe the life history of virtually all organizations (including churches) by tracing the following scenario over time: organizations typically begin with a clear mission. They understand their "main business," and they focus on several objectives that they must achieve if their mission is to succeed. To achieve the objectives of their mission, they organize and deploy their people in a range of activities that will move the organization toward fulfilling the objectives; the activities are clearly understood to be the *means* for achieving the mission.

Let enough time elapse (years or decades), however, and the people long involved in the activities have usually forgotten what their activity was supposed to achieve; what was once a means has become an end in itself. Odiorne declared that the organization is now caught in "the activity trap," and it needs the "renewal" that comes from, and not without, the recovery of a worthy strategy. This may involve essentially returning to its earlier mission; but if the world has changed, then the old mission is less relevant. The mission may need refining, or redefining.[1]

So, for instance, a church worships at 11:00 AM every Sunday and its board meets on the second Tuesday of each month because that is their tradition; the church schedules the Spring Revival (or the Vacation Bible school, or the rummage sale) because they scheduled it last year, and the year before, and so on. So, a mission (say) that once established schools and hospitals in a land where there were none, now struggles to maintain those institutions in a new era when the government provides schools and hospitals. Or a mission that once established leprosy ministries when lepers were seen everywhere, still labors to perpetuate the leprosy mission in a setting where leprosy is all but defeated—while malaria and AIDS are now epidemic. Welcome to "the activity trap."

The term "strategy" derives from the Greek term *strategos*—which referred to "the art of the general" in deploying forces and resources to achieve military objectives, but the term has long informed what other kinds of organizations achieve with intentionality. The Jesuits, for instance, did not become history's greatest educational mission without serious strategic thinking and planning.[2]

Scholars of the field[3] are agreed that effective strategy development, for any type of organization, involves several components: (1) defining the *objectives* or goals that the organization intends to achieve, and by when; (2) gathering the kind of *intelligence* about the historical, social, and cultural context in which the organization will make its contribution; (3) making the crucial strategic *decisions* that will steer the organization's direction;[4] (4) developing the *policies* that facilitate (rather than frustrate) the mission's achievement; and (5) developing the *programs* that will take the organization, step by step, toward its objectives. The organization's *strategy*, then, refers to the pattern that integrates the intelligence, objectives, decisions, policies, and programs for the organization's mission.

Christianity's history has not been devoid of strategic geniuses. Names like Paul, Patrick, Boniface, Ignatius of Loyola, Matteo Ricci, William Carey, William Taylor, Rufus Anderson, and Henry Venn come to mind. More recently, Roland Allen, Donald McGavran, and Ralph Winter catalyzed strategic thinking in many missions, and Vatican II and the Lausanne Movement for World Evangelization have advanced the strategic perspective in the church's service. McGavran's church growth movement raised mission strategy to more prominence within mission's academy.

Historically, Methodism once modeled the strategic perspective. John Wesley, the movement's founder, was a movement leader and a strategic genius. Early Methodism was driven by a contagious strategic vision. The movement was characterized by the kind of objectives, intelligence, decisions, policies, and programmatic ministry initiatives that we now know are essential to a Christian movement's success.

For example, eighteenth-century Methodism was "purpose driven." Wesley and the movement's other leaders often reminded each other of the movement's objectives. For instance, in 1744—six years into the movement—Charles Wesley rehearsed their strategic vision poetically:

When first sent forth to minister the word,
Say, did we preach ourselves, or Christ the Lord?
Was it our aim disciples to collect,
To raise a party, or to found a sect?
No; but to spread the power of Jesu's name,
Repair the walls of our Jerusalem
Revive the piety of ancient days,
And fill the earth with our Redeemer's praise.[5]

In the movement's "annual conference" of the pastors, John Wesley typically reminded the leaders of the movement's priority objectives— which were so un-negotiable that anyone who did not own them was "not one of us." With the *objectives* as a given, Wesley was then usually content for the gathered pastors to work out the decisions, policies, and strategies that reasonably followed.

Wesley was disciplined in gathering the *intelligence* that would inform Methodism's expansion. He traveled England extensively for decades. He observed more than one hundred communities, and trends in those communities, every year. He recorded his observations, nightly, in his journal. He studied the available demographic data. He engaged in extensive correspondence with many local leaders, and interviewed many local leaders, converts, seekers, and backsliders, and thereby gained their perceptions of the state of their churches, communities, and the culture. He observed and reflected upon the trends in early Methodism's churches (then called "societies") and the life of their small groups (then called "class meetings"), including the available statistical data. (He took statistical data so seriously that he scolded pastors who inflated their annual reports!) The following lengthy reflection from Wesley's *Journal* demonstrates how he studied field data, numbers, and trends to make sense of what was happening and to inform more effective local mission:

> How is it, that almost in every place, even where there is no lasting fruit, there is so great an impression made at first upon a considerable number of people? The fact is this: Everywhere the work of God rises higher and higher, till it comes to a point. Here it seems for a short time to be at a stay; and then it gradually sinks again.
>
> All this may easily be accounted for. At first, curiosity brings many hearers; at the same time, God draws many by his preventing grace to hear his word, and comforts them in hearing. One then tells another. By this means, on the one hand, curiosity spreads and increases; and, on the other, the drawings of God's Spirit touches more hearts, and many of them more powerfully than before. He now offers grace to all that hear, most of whom are in some measure affected, and, more or less moved with approbation of what they hear, have a desire to please God, with good-will to his messenger. And these principles, variously combined and increasing, raise the general work to its highest point. But it cannot stand here, in the nature of things. Curiosity must soon decline. Again, the drawings of God are not followed, and thereby the Holy Spirit is grieved: He strives with this and that man no more, and so His drawings end. Thus, the causes of the general impression declining, most of the hearers will be less and less affected. Add to this, that, in process of time, "it must be that offenses will come." Some of the hearers, if not Teachers also, will act contrary to their profession. Either their follies or faults will be told from one to another, and lose nothing in the telling. Men, once curious to hear, will hear no more; men, once drawn, having stifled their good desires, will disapprove what they approved of before, and feel dislike instead of good-will to the Preachers. Others who were more or less convinced, will be afraid or ashamed to acknowledge that conviction; and all these will catch at ill stories, true or false, in order to justify their change. When, by that means, all who do not savingly believe have quenched the Spirit of God, the little flock that remains go on from faith to faith; the rest sleep and take their rest; and thus the number of hearers in every place may be expected, first to increase, and then to decrease.[6]

Wesley and his people understood Methodism's identity as an Apostolic ("sent out") Order within the Church of England. Methodism's main business was to reach and make new Christians of the new urban populations that the established parish churches could not (or would not) reach, and to develop these socially marginalized people into the kind of disciples, and local movements, that could serve and reach many others. Early Methodism developed some distinctive policy perspectives; "itinerant" Methodist preachers, for instance, were deployed to advance Methodism's mission (*not* to advance their careers). Wesley developed strategic initiatives that shocked more conventional church leaders. He typically engaged the pre-Christian people of a community through the "vile" practice of open-air field preaching; he opened the Lord's Supper to seekers, and declared it to be "a converting ordinance."

Wesley anticipated the six themes that substantially account for effective local Christianity, everywhere, today.[7] (1) Early Methodism was *culturally relevant*. The movement adapted to indigenous cultural forms and expressions—as reflected in its language, architecture, and music. (2) Early Methodism was *emotionally relevant*. Wesley joined Jonathan Edwards in offering "a religion of the heart" that liberated people from destructive emotional lives into the new emotional world of the kingdom of God. (3) Early Methodism reached and developed local Christians through *small groups*; this was a movement of small groups—class meetings, bands, penitent bands, and others. (4) Early Methodism was essentially a *lay movement*; in assigning most of the ministry that matters to laity, Methodists believed they had recovered a core principle of the "primitive Church," which was later obscured by the third century mistake that reassigned virtually all ministry to priests. (5) Early Methodism pioneered (what we call today) *outreach ministries*. They knew that you do not reach most people through evangelism alone; you get in ministry with them (in homes, hospitals, neighborhoods, and even prisons), and then you get in conversation with them, and you include God in the conversation, and you involve them (often before they have believed or experienced anything) in the life of a class meeting and a local Methodist society. (People typically "belong" *before* they "believe!") (6) Wesley declared "the world is my parish," and he deployed Francis Asbury, Thomas Coke, and many others in the kind of *world mission* that reached and served peoples in lands far beyond Great Britain.

Wesley's strategic mind anticipated several of the strategic principles that were later crystallized in church growth lore. Consider the following four principles.[8]

1. Wesley prioritized *evangelism* within the movement's ministry and mission. He taught his preachers and other leaders that their main business was to "save souls," by which he meant not merely going to heaven but "a restoration of the soul to its primitive health" which enables people to *live* "in righteousness and true holiness, justice, mercy and truth."[9] Wesley believed that everything else the movement wanted to do for people and the nation depended upon the movement's expanding base of committed people: "We all aim at one point, (as we did from the hour when we first engaged in the work), not at profit, any more than at ease, or pleasure, or the praise of men; but to spread true religion through London, Dublin, Edinburgh, and, as we are able, through the three kingdoms."[10]

2. Wesley taught his leaders to reach out to *receptive* people and populations—while they are receptive. He believed that, due to the Holy Spirit's "prevenient grace" working in people and populations, there are always fields that are "white for the harvest"—for a season. In contrast to the usual assumption in Christian mission, Wesley observed that (what McGavran was to call) "the masses" are usually more receptive than "the classes." Furthermore, Wesley perceived (theologically) why this is the case: He reasoned, "Religion must not go from the greatest to the least, or the power would appear to be of men."[11] Wesley's published (Question and Answer) conversations with other Methodist leaders give us his most cogent expressions of the principle:

Q. Where should we endeavor to preach the most?
A. 1. Where there is the greatest number of quiet and willing hearers.
    2. Where there is the most fruit. . . .

Q. Ought we not diligently observe [where] God . . . pour[s] out his Spirit more abundantly?
A. We ought; and at that time to send more laborers than usual into that part of the harvest.[12]

While counseling outreach to receptive populations, Wesley would not abandon resistant populations; it was important to also "plant seeds." So Wesley even preached to mobs, and Methodism found other ways to engage hostile, resistant, and indifferent populations. Wesley observed that many communities shifted from resistance to readiness over time; people are "softened by degrees." Nevertheless, he often counseled his leaders, "Go to those who want you, and go most to those who want you most."

3. Donald McGavran observed that the faith spreads most naturally and contagiously across the kinship and friendship networks of Christians, especially new Christians. Social networks provide "the bridges of God." Wesley glimpsed this principle and wrote about it occasionally, as in the reflection quoted above: "One then tells another. By this means, on the one hand, curiosity spreads and increases." Wesley did not, however, understand this principle as deeply or teach it as explicitly as he did the receptivity principle. Nevertheless, the published testimonies of eighteenth-century Methodist converts reveal that relational bridges were typically involved in helping people to discover The Way.

Wesley, however, emphasized more prominently than the later church growth movement the role of *conversation* in engaging pre-Christian people. His *Journal* reflects hundreds of conversations with seekers and new Christians in his travels. One-to-one conversation that involved listening as well as talking was the method to "get within" people, and to adapt to "their several conditions and tempers." While public proclamation is indispensable in getting the Word out, the "labor of private instruction" is even more reproductive. "For, after all our preaching, many of our people are almost as ignorant as if they had never heard the Gospel. . . . I have found by experience, that one of these has learned more from one hour's close discourse, than from ten years' public preaching."[13]

4. While the church growth movement has emphasized new church planting and in the 1970s kept that cause alive until denominations rediscovered it, church growth people have not consistently perceived the broader and deeper strategic principle as clearly as John Wesley did. Wesley saw that a whole range of *structural* additions, not merely new Methodist "societies," were a prerequisite for the movement's further expansion. He anticipated (what I have called, from botany) the principle of "proliferation." Some plants do not grow primarily by remaining the same but growing bigger. Like bamboo, banyan trees, and (especially) aspen trees, they grow by proliferating trunks, limbs, and branches that were not earlier visible. In time, they extend their roots and (what appears to be) another young tree emerges from the soil; that second tree proliferates new trunks, limbs, and branches and extends the root system further, and so on.

For instance, Wesley was obsessional about starting new "classes"—Methodism's small groups in which people ministered to each other and helped each other to live as Christians, and in which they received "awakened" seekers and helped them experience grace. (The faith was "taught" and "caught.") One goal of field preaching was to start new classes for awakened people. He coached his leaders to start new classes everywhere, and *not* to preach where they could not enroll seekers in groups—lest they leave spiritually vulnerable people to the wiles of "the Murderer." Methodism's overall strategy called for reaching and building people through a society-wide network of classes, as well as other groups to serve distinct purposes—such as the bands—and for planting a Methodist church (then called a "society," and composed of multiple classes and other groups), as well as a range of lay-led outreach ministries, in every community in the nation. In time, the movement in many communities would call for multiple churches. Moreover, every structural addition required the proliferation of leaders—for the groups, ministries, and societies, and the proliferation of itinerant preachers.

Such strategic thinking once enabled the momentum that energized Methodism's growth in John Wesley's lifetime and for two or three generations beyond his death in 1791. In time, however, two problems afflicted Methodism that hound most Christian traditions, sooner or later.

In some nations, a generation of leaders simply perpetuated the strategy of the previous generation (or the previous century), but in such a changed context that the strategy no longer fit. So, for instance, when the populations were once scattered across the landscape, Methodism planted a church in every hamlet. In many nations, covering the territory is still Methodism's strategy; it still looks impressive on a map, but most people now live in the cities—where Methodism has astonishingly fewer churches per capita than across the hinterland.

In other nations, a generation of leaders emerged who assumed that they knew better than the founding genius. They quietly hijacked the movement and turned it into an institution, and in time the people lost their theological and strategic vision; they no longer recalled what their tradition once did, or why. By now "the activity trap" is entrenched, and the members mistake the beehive of activities for normal Christianity; Wesley once forecast the possibility that Methodism would one day retain "the form of religion, but without the power."

NOTES

1. See George S. Odiorne, *Management and the Activity Trap* (New York: Harper & Row, 1974).
2. See Chris Lowney, *Heroic Leadership: Best Practices from a 450-Year-Old Company that Changed the World* (Chicago: Loyola Press, 2003).
3. Henry Mintzberg, Joseph Lampel, James Brian Quinn, and Sumatra Ghoshal, eds., *The Strategy Process: Concept, Contexts, Cases*, 4th ed., (Upper Saddle River, N.J.: Prentice Hall, 2003). With articles from many contributors from the management and leadership academy, this is a widely used comprehensive source.
4. Donald McGavran's *Momentous Decisions in Missions Today* (Grand Rapids: Baker Book House, 1984) is still an excellent discussion of the issues around which strategic thinking in mission turns.
5. Franz Hildebrandt, *Christianity According to the Wesleys* (London: The Epworth Press, 1956), 46.
6. John Wesley, *The Works of John Wesley*, 3rd ed., vol. 13, ed. Thomas Jackson (Grand Rapids: Baker Book House, 1978 reprint of 1872 ed.), pp. 338–39.
7. I elaborate upon these themes in *The Apostolic Congregation: Church Growth Reconceived for a New Generation* (Nashville: Abingdon Press, 2009).
8. In this section I am often drawing from my book *To Spread the Power: Church Growth in the Wesleyan Spirit* (Nashville: Abingdon Press, 1987), in which the following insights (and others) are more fully developed.
9. Wesley, *Works*, vol. 8, p. 247.
10. Ibid., pp. 380–81.
11. *The Journal of John Wesley*, May 21, 1764.
12. Thomas Jackson, ed., *The Works of John Wesley*, 3rd ed. (Grand Rapids: Baker Book House, 1872, reprinted 1978) Vol. 13, pp. 300–301
13. Wesley, "Minutes of Several Conversations Between the Rev. Mr. Wesley and Others," *Works*, vol. 8, pp. 300–303.

BIBLIOGRAPHY

Hunter, George G. III. *To Spread the Power: Church Growth in the Wesleyan Spirit*. Nashville: Abingdon Press, 1987.
———. *The Celtic Way of Evangelism*. Nashville: Abingdon Press, 2000.
———. *Radical Outreach: The Recovery of Apostolic Ministry and Evangelism*. Nashville: Abingdon Press, 2003.
———. *The Apostolic Congregation: Church Growth Reconceived for a New Generation*. Nashville: Abingdon Press, 2009.
Lowney. Chris. *Heroic Leadership: Best Practices from a 450-Year-Old Company that Changed the World*. Chicago: Loyola Press, 2003.
McGavran, Donald A. *Momentous Decisions in Missions Today*. Grand Rapids: Baker Book House, 1984.
———. *Understanding Church Growth*, 3rd ed. Grand Rapids: Eerdmans, 1990.
Mintzberg, Henry, Joseph Lampel, James Brian Quinn, and Sumatra Ghoshal, eds. *The Strategy Process: Concept, Contexts, Cases*, 4th ed. Upper Saddle River, N.J.: Prentice Hall, 2003.
Odiorne, George S. *Management and the Activity Trap*. New York: Harper & Row, 1974.
Wesley, John. *The Works of John Wesley*, ed. Thomas Jackson. Grand Rapids: Baker Book House, 1872, reprinted 1978.
Winter, Ralph W., and Steven C. Hawthorne. *Perspectives on the World Christian Movement*, 3rd ed. Pasadena, Calif.: William Carey Library, 1999.

27

HEALING THE EARTH

A WESLEYAN IMPERATIVE

Norman E. Thomas

"Mission and the Groaning of Creation" was the theme in October 2008 of the world's most widely circulated mission studies journal. In the editor's introduction, Jonathan J. Bonk made the bold judgment that addressing environmental issues "is perhaps the most pressing missiological agenda of the twenty-first century."[1]

The contemporary neglect of ecotheology and ecojustice in mission studies is not confined to those of Wesleyan heritage. Peruse *Evangelical Dictionary of World Missions,* published in 2000, and you will find not a single article related to environmental issues.[2]

This paper is based on the premise that environmental awareness and care for the earth is critically important for effective mission in this century. After outlining six areas in which our fragile planet is at risk, I will make a case that these concerns are not some left-wing, tree-hugger, New Age fad, but in fact are essential to a Wesleyan understanding and practice of Christian faith. I will argue that followers of John Wesley who embrace their heritage will have a creative contribution to make. Next, I will explore an approach to ecojustice based on Scripture and the Earth Charter. Finally, I will suggest implications for The Mission Society seeking to be creative in mission in this its silver jubilee year.

A FRAGILE PLANET AT RISK

Six times mass extinctions have occurred since life began on earth. The first five had natural causes such as the asteroid that eliminated the dinosaurs 65 million years ago. The sixth is occurring in this century and humans are the primary cause. Give a comprehensive physical examination to our fragile planet and the report is grim. Life systems are in peril or near collapse.

Global warming: Jim Hansen, a top climate specialist at NASA, claims we have just ten years to reduce greenhouse gases before global warming reaches a tipping point—a point at which climate change acquires a momentum that makes it irreversible. The current annual rise in the atmospheric CO_2 level is four times what it was in the 1950s, largely because of increased emissions from burning fossil fuels. The more that CO_2 accumulates in the atmosphere, the more temperatures rise. Scientists fear that some feedback mechanisms will begin to kick in to further accelerate the warming process. As highly reflective Arctic Ocean sea ice melts it is replaced by darker open water that absorbs more heat from the sun. Melting permafrost threatens to release billions of tons of carbon, some as methane—a potent greenhouse gas with a global warming effect per ton twenty-five times that of carbon dioxide.[3]

Water scarcity: Africa's Lake Chad, once a landmark for astronauts when circling the earth, is now difficult to locate. Surrounded by nations with burgeoning populations (Cameroon, Chad, Niger, and Nigeria), the lake has shrunk 96 percent in forty years. Due to declining rainfall and soaring demand for irrigation, Lake Chad may soon disappear entirely. Equally alarming is the global depletion of certain underground aquifers. Under Beijing deep wells now have to reach one thousand meters (more than half a mile) to tap fresh water. Water tables are now falling in those countries that contain more than half the world's peoples, including the three biggest grain producers (China, India, and the United States). Even though we use fresh water at double the rate of aquifer replenishment, half of humanity lacks proper sanitation facilities. In Mexico, to pick just one developing world example, 50 percent of water is unsafe to drink.[4]

Shrinking forests: I shall never forget my visit to Haiti in 1978. High on a hill above the crowded capital Port-au-Prince, I saw the denuded hillsides, and below me a river running yellow with silt; for Haiti, once a tropical paradise, was now 96 percent deforested. First the trees go, then the soil. Will the Amazon, the world's largest carbon sink, suffer a similar fate? Author Lester R. Brown fears that as more land is cleared by logging, and for grazing and family, the rainforest weakens and may be approaching a tipping point beyond which it cannot be saved.[5]

Soil depletion: "The thin layer of topsoil that covers the planet's surface is the foundation of civilization," Brown declares. Typically six inches or so deep, it is eroding faster than it is being formed in perhaps a third of the world's cropland. It is the degradation of cropland in Mexico that is the "push" factor prompting some 700,000 Mexicans each year to leave the land in search of work in nearby cities or in the United States. Globally, the explosive demands of growing numbers of humans and live-stock are converting land into desert. Saharan dust storms—once rare—are now commonplace. They both drain the African continent of its fertility and deposit dust in Caribbean waters that clouds the water and damages coral reefs.[6]

Collapsing fish populations: In 1975, I read the Club of Rome's Second Report containing vivid graphs on the overfishing and subsequent collapse of major fish populations.[7] More than thirty years later, we live at a time when 75 percent of species are being fished at or beyond their sustainable capacity. James Martin, a futurist, believes that 90 percent of the edible fish in the oceans have been caught. Consider the plight of 200,000 West Africans recently dependent on fishing for their livelihood. While the explosion of their own numbers of *pirogues* contributed to over-fishing, the bigger threat came from a vast flotilla of industrial trawlers from the European Union, China, and Russia that thoroughly scoured northwest Africa's ocean floor resulting in the collapse of major fish popu-lations. As a consequence 31,000 desperate Africans in more than nine hundred boats sought to migrate to Europe, with 6,000 estimated to have died or disappeared in the effort.[8]

Endangered species: As an extended letter to a Southern Baptist minister, famed Harvard University biologist E. O. Wilson writes: "If current deterioration of the environment by human activity continues unabated, half of Earth's surviving species, plants, and animals will be extinguished or critically endangered by the end of the century. One quarter, it's been estimated, could leave us in the next 50 years due to climate change alone."[9]

Today we must hear anew such biblical texts as Romans 8:22 that "the whole creation has been groaning in labor pains until now" as it awaits its redemption. We also will find distinctive emphases in our Wesleyan theology that can undergird our missional response.

OUR WESLEYAN HERITAGE

From childhood, as son and grandson of Methodist pastors, I have sung with conviction the hymn Charles Wesley wrote in 1747: "Love divine all loves excelling, joy of heaven to earth come down. . . . Finish then thy new creation. . . . Let us see thy great salvation perfectly restored in Thee." Theodore Runyan argues that the thought of the Wesleys is grounded in a theology of the "great salvation" that is cosmic in its grasp of the "new creation" that transforms both personal and social dimensions of human existence.[10]

Admittedly John Wesley's central concern was theocentric and human-centered. Wesley believed that every person is loved by God, enlivened by God, and enlightened by God. Emphasis on the primacy of grace, the inability of humans on their own to do any good, and our full responsibility to respond to God's gift and call are the foci of Wesley's theology. John Cobb argues that Wesley "did not set human beings entirely apart from the remainder of creation. God's presence is not limited to humanity." He cites as a clear and most emphatic passage Wesley's third sermon, "Upon our Lord's Sermon on the Mount":

> God is in all things, and . . . we are to see the Creator in the glass of every creature . . . we should use and look upon nothing as separate from God, which indeed is a kind of practical Atheism; but with a true magnificence of thought, survey heaven and earth and all that is therein as contained by God in the hollow of His hand, who by his intimate presence holds them all in being, who pervades and actuates the whole created frame, and is in a true sense the Soul of the universe.[11]

Rather than this being an isolated usage, Cobb finds the immanence of God in all human beings to be "a major and emphatic theme of Wesley." By implication that immanence extends to the whole of creation, for God "is the only agent in the material world; all matter being essentially dull and inactive, and moving only as it is moved by the finger of God. And He is the spring of action in every creature, visible and invisible, which could neither act nor exist, without the continual influx and agency of His almighty power."[12] In his 1783 sermon "The General Spread of the Gospel," Wesley elaborated on the new creation: "[God] is already renewing the face of the earth: And we have strong reason to hope that the work he hath begun, he will carry on . . . until he has fulfilled all his promises . . . and re-established universal holiness and happiness, and caused all the inhabitants of the earth to sing together."[13]

Although Cobb finds in Wesley's thought the dualism of Newtonian physics (God as cause of any motion of inanimate matter, but acting through living things, causing humans to be God's agents), he finds Wesley's principle that God is active in all movement to be applicable to contemporary physics. Now we perceive that what once appeared to be inanimate is in fact composed of energy in motion. Wesley's principle of "the interactive character of the relation between God and creature," so brilliantly developed by Wesley in relation to grace and responsibility of humans, can for Cobb "illumine the whole of the God-World relation." Affirming this theology, Wesleyans have an important contribution to make in the ecumenical discourse on "the integrity of creation."[14]

COMPONENTS OF WESLEYAN ECOJUSTICE

A creative Wesleyan approach to environmental justice will grow out of an interaction between our best current experience and reason, on the one hand, and the Bible on the other.[15] As a minimum it would include the following convictions:

The Earth is the Lord's, not ours: The phrase "the earth is the Lord's" (Ps. 24:1) was first used by Moses as part of a struggle for the liberation of God's chosen people. It was a warning to the arrogant, oppressive, and possessive Pharaoh of Egypt (Exod. 9:29). We bring this truth to the table of public debate in which our self-interest and national pride can dictate policy concerning the use and exploitation of limited resources.

Care for the least: Who are of the family of God? For centuries Christians have interpreted Jesus' words, "just as you did it to one of the least of these who are members of my family" (Matt. 25:40) as a command to care for the poor persons. With ecological sensitivity we now ask: Do these words also imply caring for the least of God's creation—the birds and the lilies and the grass (Matt. 6:26–30)? The cofounders of the Forum on Religion and Ecology expressed this conviction well as they wrote: "This is not about stewardship of the Earth, but about embracing our embeddedness in nature in radical, fresh, and enlivening ways."16

Living as the new creation: When we sing our prayer to God—"finish then thy new creation"—we ask God to enable us to live in perfect love. As Wesleyans we strive to go on to perfection—not as a state to be achieved but as a daily process of growth in grace. To love God means to love all God's creatures, not just humans. It includes discerning what God is doing in the world and giving ourselves to working with God in making all things new.17 It involves living in heightened intimacy with all created beings—in communion with them.18

For decades environmental issues were considered the concern only of the technocrats—the scientists, lawyers, and policy makers. Now the ethical dimensions of the crisis are becoming obvious. What is our moral responsibility to the generations that follow us? How can we ensure equitable development for Chinese, Indian, African, and other peoples as well as ourselves that does not destroy the environment? Can persons of faith help solve environmental challenges? Yes!

I commend for your reading and reflection two seminal documents. The first document is the Earth Charter, a document of enormous potential that emerged out of the United Nations Conference on Environment and Development (also known as the Earth Summit) held in Rio de Janeiro, Brazil, in 1992. Thousands of groups and individuals helped to shape the Earth Charter, giving principles for guiding sustainable development. These are grouped in an integrated vision for a viable future based on respect and care for the community of life. The interdependent principles are three: (1) ecological integrity, (2) social and economic justice, and (3) democracy, nonviolence and peace. The Preamble highlights the crisis:

> We stand at a critical moment in Earth's history, a time when humanity must choose its future. As the world becomes increasingly interdependent and fragile, the future at once holds great peril and great promise.
>
> The choice is ours: form a global partnership to care for Earth and one another or risk the destruction of ourselves and the diversity of life.19

The charter concludes with three laser beams of wisdom concerning the way forward. First, it requires "a change of mind and heart" with "a new sense of global interdependence and universal responsibility." Next, it calls for a recognition that "life often involves tensions between important values" that can mean difficult choices. Finally, it invites all to hold ours to be "a time remembered for the awakening of a new reverence for life, the firm resolve to achieve sustainability, the quickening of the struggle for justice and peace, and the joyful celebration of life."[20]

The second document I commend to you is an urgent call for action published in 2007 by scientists and evangelicals. At a meeting convened by the National Association of Evangelicals and the Center for Health and the Global Environment of Harvard Medical School, thirty scientists and theologians searched for common ground in protection of the creation. Their signed statement, entitled "An Urgent Call to Action: Scientists and Evangelicals United to Protect Creation," proclaimed the following:

1. We believe that the protection of life on Earth is a profound moral imperative. It addresses without discrimination the interests of all humanity as well as the value of the non-human world. It requires a new moral awakening to a compelling demand, clearly articulated in Scripture and supported by science, that we must steward the natural world in order to preserve for ourselves and future generations a beautiful, rich, and healthful environment. For many of us, this is a religious obligation, rooted in our sense of gratitude for Creation and reverence for its Creator.

2. One fundamental motivation that we share is concern for the poorest of the poor, well over a billion people, who have little chance to improve their lives in devastated and often war-ravaged environments. At the same time, the natural environments in which they live, and where so much of Earth's biodiversity barely hangs on, cannot survive the press of destitute people without other resources and with nowhere else to go. . . .

3. We pledge to work together at every level to lead our nation toward a responsible care for creation, and we call with one voice to our scientific and evangelical colleagues, and to all others, to join us in these efforts.[21]

ECOJUSTICE—OUR WESLEYAN MISSION IMPERATIVE

While it is possible to treat the separate elements of the environmental crisis in purely practical ways, it is John Cobb's insight that "many environmentalists, even those not generally interested in religious ideas, have come to the conclusion that it is most fundamentally a religious crisis."[22]

Wesleyans sing with fervor Charles Wesley's hymn, "A Charge to Keep I Have" (1762):

To serve the present age, my calling to fulfill,
O may it all my powers engage to do my Master's Will!
Arm me with watchful care as in thy sight to live,
and now thy servant, Lord, prepare a strict account to give.

It is strategic that our mission (evangelism and discipleship) be connected to the whole of creation that is groaning to be renewed. The Mission Society was formed "to join in God's mission for the redemption of humanity."[23] In this jubilee year it has an opportunity to creatively enlarge that mission to embrace the healing of the earth.

NOTES

1. Jonathan J. Bonk, "Mission and the Groaning of Creation," *International Bulletin of Missionary Research* 32, no. 4 (October 2008): p. 170.

2. A. Scott Moreau, ed., *Evangelical Dictionary of World Missions* (Grand Rapids: Baker, 2000).

3. Lester R. Brown, *Plan B 3.0: Mobilizing to Save Civilization* (New York: W. W. Norton, 2008), pp. 50, 65–66.

4. Ibid., pp. 68, 72; Larry Rasmussen, "Green Discipleship," *Reflections* 94, no. 1 (Spring 2007): p. 68.

5. Brown, pp. 89–90.

6. Ibid., pp. 90–97.

7. Mihajlo Mesarovic and Eduard Pestel, *Mankind at the Turning Point: The Second Report to the Club of Rome* (New York: E. P. Dutton, 1975).

8. Brown, *Plan B 3.0*, pp. 97–101; James Martin, "The Great Challenges of the Twenty-First Century," *The Futurist* 41, no. 1 (January–February 2007): p. 21; Sharon LaFraniere, "Europe Takes Africa's Fish, and Migrants Follow," *The New York Times*, January 14, 2008, A1 and A10.

9. E. O. Wilson, *The Creation: An Appeal to Save Life on Earth* (New York: Norton, 2007); see also Brown, *Plan B 3.0*, pp. 101–5.

10. Theodore Runyan, *The New Creation: John Wesley's Theology Today* (Nashville: Abingdon, 1998).

11. John Wesley, *The Bicentennial Edition of the Works of John Wesley*, Par. I.11, vol. 1 (Nashville: Abingdon Press, 1976–) pp. 516–17; hereafter cited as Wesley's *Works*.

12. Wesley's *Works*, "Upon Our Lord's Sermon on the Mount, VI," Par. III.7, vol. 1, p. 581; John B. Cobb, Jr., *Grace and Responsibility: A Wesleyan Theology for Today* (Nashville: Abingdon, 1995), pp. 50–51.

13. Wesley's *Works*, vol. 2, p. 499.

14. Ibid., pp. 52–55. See Larry L. Rasmussen, *Earth Community, Earth Ethics* (Maryknoll, N.Y.: Orbis Books, 1996), pp. 98–110, for a concise summary of ecumenical thought on the integrity of creation. Ted Runyan adds that Wesley himself was an amazingly ecumenical product, drawing for his theology from five distinct traditions: Puritanism, Anglicanism, Lutheranism by way of Moravian Pietism, Roman Catholicism, and Eastern Orthodoxy by way of the Eastern Fathers. His unique contribution is to be found in the way he drew from the sources, critiqued them, and combined them ("The New Creation," *Wesleyan Theological Journal* 31 (Fall 1996): p. 5.

15. For components from other Christian traditions see Allan Effa, "The Greening of Mission," *International Bulletin of Missionary Research* 32, no. 4 (October 2008): pp. 171–76.

16. Mary Evelyn Tucker and John Grim, "Daring to Dream: Religion and the Future of the Earth," *Reflections* 94, no. 1 (Spring 2007): p. 6.

17. Cobb, *Grace and Responsibility*, p. 113.

18. See Thomas Berry, *The Dream of the Earth* (San Francisco: Sierra Club, 1988), and Jay B. McDaniel, *With Roots and Wings: Christianity in a Age of Ecology and Dialogue* (Maryknoll, N.Y.: Orbis Books, 1995) for development of this theme.

19. The full text of the Earth Charter, and of *Toward a Sustainable World: The Earth Charter in Action,* the story of the actions that have transformed the Earth Charter into a global movement, can be read at http://www.earthcharterinaction.org.

20. Ibid.

21. "An Urgent Call to Action: Scientists and Evangelicals United to Protect Creation" can be read at http://www.pbs.org/now/shows/343/letter.pdf.

22. Cobb, *Grace and Responsibility*, p. 20. See also Max Oelschlaeger, *Caring for Creation: An Ecumenical Approach to the Environmental Crisis* (New Haven: Yale University Press, 1994), pp. 1–18.

23. http://www.themissionsociety.org/go/whyweserve.

BIBLIOGRAPHY

Berry, R. J., ed. *The Care of Creation: Focusing Concern and Action*. Leicester, Eng.: InterVarsity Press, 2000.

Brown, Lester R. *Plan B 3.0: Mobilizing to Save Civilization*. New York: W. W. Norton, 2008.

Cobb, John B., Jr. *Grace and Responsibility: A Wesleyan Theology for Today*. Nashville: Abingdon, 1995.

Effa, Allan. "The Greening of Mission." *International Bulletin of Missionary Research* 32, no. 4 (October 2008): pp. 171–76.

Hessel, Dieter T., and Rosemary Radford Ruether, eds. *Christianity and Ecology: Seeking the Well-being of Earth and Humans*. Cambridge, Mass.: Harvard University Press, 2000.

Jenkins, Willis. "Missiology in Environmental Context: Tasks for an Ecology of Mission." *International Bulletin of Missionary Research* 32, no. 4 (October 2008): pp. 176–84.

McDaniel, Jay B. *With Roots and Wings: Christianity in an Age of Ecology and Dialogue*. Maryknoll, N.Y.: Orbis Books, 1995.

Rasmussen, Larry L. *Earth Community, Earth Ethics*. Maryknoll, N.Y.: Orbis Books, 1996.

Runyan, Theodore. *The New Creation: John Wesley's Theology Today*. Nashville: Abingdon, 1998.

Wesley, John. *The Works of John Wesley*, begun as The Oxford Edition of the Works of John Wesley (Oxford: Clarendon Press, 1975–1983); continued as *The Bicentennial Edition of the Works of John Wesley* (Nashville: Abingdon Press, 1984–); also as an electronic resource, edited by Richard P. Heitzenrater (Nashville: Abingdon Press, 2005).

28

THE INCARNATION AS MOTIF
FOR DEVELOPMENT PRACTICE

Lindy Backues

INTRODUCTION

The Word became flesh and blood,
and moved into the neighborhood.
—John 1:14 (*The Message*)

Evening was approaching and I was sitting at the station in Jakarta, Indonesia, waiting for the last train headed to the city of Bandung where I lived. The day had been a long and sweaty one and I was looking forward to getting home. I spied a woman making her way past those on the benches waiting for the train. Due to her rather daring attire and due to the fact she was striking up conversation exclusively with males, it was obvious that eventually I would receive a proposition.

At that moment, a notion popped into my head, as if uttered by a voice deep inside me: What would Jesus do in such a situation? It suddenly became clear to me that this was precisely the sort of person he often paid special attention to. Would he not see her as a human *just as he, himself, was human*? The thought precluded my brushing her off this time as a taboo to be avoided.

When she reached me, she began to treat me as a potential "John." It was not long before I learned her name and other facts about her and, as I did, Anis (her name) took that to mean I was interested in her services.

As a consequence, she came on even more strongly. But, even so, I still pressed on asking about her life. After a while, she found herself telling me in broad strokes what had brought her to this point.

She had an eight-year-old daughter that she left with her mother. Even though her mother knew what she did every night for a living, she insisted with pride that her daughter did not know. When I asked her how long she could keep the secret from her daughter, her eyes welled with tears, but she quickly shook off her sadness. This would not be a problem, she answered, since her boyfriend—a man from Holland— would be back soon enough to take her away from this life. She told me that she had not heard from him for about eight months but she believed she would be hearing from him soon.

I hated that I knew how this story would end—I wished things were different for her. It seemed she could see in my eyes that I was at that moment very present to and for her and, yet, the conversation was not in the least tinged as sexual. On the contrary, I was having a conversation with a sister, with one for whom I wanted a better way of life.

Just then, the train came. I was disappointed to leave her and ready to be gone from her at the same time. I reasoned that I had done my duty—I had treated her as a person. She had been humanized.

But, to my surprise, she claimed that she, too, was heading to Bandung on the train and she asked to sit next to me so that we could continue our conversation. I paused—we were now heading to my hometown! What about my reputation? But, the voice spoke to me again, what would Jesus do? So, I agreed—and we rode the train together, side by side.

In the end, we had a meaningful conversation for the duration of the trip. When we finally went our separate ways, she shook my hand gently, wishing me well with sincere respect and kindness. Even though I lived in that city for several years to come, I never saw her again. But she made a lasting impression upon me.

Such an interaction was the fruit of a notion that has since grown with intensity and clarity over the years. In what ways is Jesus the model for our work with the marginalized and disenfranchised?

I will attempt to develop a model of missional involvement based upon the incarnation: an outline of its central features which offers a suite of defining characteristics in an "incarnational approach to participation." This guide will be focused upon the incarnational notion of being "with." As Ruth Page puts it, [a hierarchical] . . . relationship among humans has become suspect. It is widely perceived among Christians of very different theological stand-points that vertical relationships of command and obedience make possible oppression, dehumanization or at least perpetual immaturity. . . . "With" is a word which has vast theological potential. . . .[1]

The potential of "with" holds not just for Christians, nor is it simply theological in import, but sociological and political as well. This is the core idea that has led me to explore this issue.

THE SIX MARKS OF THE INCARNATIONAL MOTIF

1. Narrative Enactment—Providing Chronological Commonality and Strangeness

Is not this the carpenter's son? Is not his mother called Mary? And are not his brothers James and Joseph and Simon and Judas? And are not all his sisters with us? Where then did this man get all this? (Matt. 13:55–56)

Jesus' neighbors were astounded at his teaching in the synagogue (Mark 6:2). They had watched him grow into an adult and they knew the names of his family members. The people in the synagogue were confronted with a *commonality* that they knew all too well. By living amongst them Jesus incarnated into their history, developing his own narrative not only with, not only within, but also against their firmly estab-lished narrative.

Thus, from one angle the notion of *Narrative Enactment* coalesces well with humanity's quest for embodied meaning. We all have a story line similar to that of persons the world over. It is equally true, however, that our story becomes an alternative to established ways of living and firm modes of doing things. To live next to others at times is to live prophetically; to challenge settled ways and to question rooted assumptions.

Living narratively in a particular community is absolutely crucial if we truly wish to initiate anything close to missional participation. And in doing so, we must bear the risk that the possibilities our presence opens up might seem strange—even threateningly so.

2. Residential Nearness—Providing Proximity and Distance

> And the Word became flesh and lived among us, and we have seen his glory,
> the glory as of a father's only son, full of grace and truth. (John 1:14)

The notion of *nearness* is included in the theological motif of incarnation. Often termed the *scandal of particularity*,[2] the Word became flesh in a specific place, amongst specific persons, and thereafter he did not travel far over the entire course of his life. He made his home amongst local persons and he became a *stakeholder*.

Such a posture supplies proximity as well as distance. The proximity comes when a single environment is shared by at least two individuals in a manner that allows recognition and familiarity. It is also true that, as one draws near to another, what previously looked similar often looks more foreign as well. Minute features end up compared and unfamiliarity accentuated.

The concept of incarnation requires such nearness. It is commonplace to speak of causes coming in two forms: necessary as well as sufficient. Residential nearness is necessary to community formation and participation. By itself, it certainly cannot assure adequate levels of participation since the term means more than mere propinquity. However, what can be assured is that no significant level of participation is remotely possible without it. We simply cannot hope for authentic incarnational participation unless we move into the neighborhood and become stakeholders within it.

3. Physical Encountering—Providing Tangibility and Vulnerability

> We declare to you what was from the beginning, what we have heard,
> what we have seen with our eyes, what we have looked at and touched
> with our hands, concerning the word of life. . . . (1 John 1:1)

The apostle Thomas refused to believe in the resurrection appearance of Jesus. It is interesting that at Jesus' next appearance amongst them, instead of upbraiding Thomas, Jesus offered to him an opportunity to do just what Thomas said he needed: "Then he said to Thomas, 'Put your finger here and see my hands. Reach out your hand and put it in my side. Do not doubt but believe'" (John 20:27). The offer of touch was to answer doubt.[3]

Such an offer also seems paradigmatic in Jesus' quest to bring healing—note the many persons restored to health by way of physical contact. Presumably, if there were a divine presence extant in the person of Jesus, he could have easily healed by way of fiat—through a word spoken. So, why the repeated instances of touch? Perhaps healing without touch somehow falls short of human authenticity. There was tactility to the incarnation that often seemed the impetus for wholeness and comfort.

But, there is a dual edge to this sword. Local cultural norms dictate acceptable boundaries of touch in given places—especially in tradition-based societies as gender comes into play. But, such restrictions simply underscore, once again, that our involvement must be narratively enacted and residentially near. Sustained engagement in a given community is what will instruct us concerning limits, helping us to interface with local persons. Nonetheless, the fact remains that we must be bodily involved in the work at hand. All of this is included in our physical involvement in local conditions.

An additional facet needs to be explored. At a deeper level what seems most characteristic here is our potential to be wounded through vulnerability. Babies are a joy to hold but being present to an enemy exposes our weakness. The instinct is to shield ourselves where we feel most exposed. That is not Jesus. In situations like these, he rendered himself vulnerable.[4] Such a paradoxical strength—resilience couched in vulnerability—must be a discernible part of our efforts of empowerment in communities of privation.

4. Social Embedment—Providing Accountability and Reconciliation

> The angel said to [Mary], "The Holy Spirit will come upon you, and the power of the Most High will overshadow you; therefore the child to be born will be holy; he will be called Son of God. And now, your relative Elizabeth in her old age has also conceived a son; and this is the sixth month for her who was said to be barren. . . . (Luke 1:35–36)

We are told that one woman was a young teenager; the other was advanced in years. Both found themselves supernaturally with child. What is often overlooked is that the children of these two were actually blood cousins, born of women with kinship ties.

So we see that the text places Jesus as one deeply embedded and genuinely enmeshed in webs of local relationships—accountable and responsible to his community. Such an image stands squarely positioned in the normal stream of the biblical tradition.

> Puzzling as it may be to postmodern individualists, [the regaining of community] is the nature of the language of the biblical documents. The corporate sense of human personhood, the sense that sociocentric personalities live in interconnected balance, is present linguistically as well as sociologically. The frequency of plural forms that address the group, not the individual; the rarity of descriptions of solitary experience; and the absence of a sense of self as a discrete, autonomous entity all focus reconciliation on the person-in-community.[5]

Consequently, it should come as no surprise that Jesus is presented in terms directly contrasting the lone, mytho-poetic, cinematic cowboy.

There is another dimension to be underscored here: incarnational participation curbs flight as we are faced with the need to reconcile. A key distinctive of our lifestyle is a radicalization of choice.[6] Consequently it seems, the modern person's capacity to work through problems in community has atrophied. Flight into choice has dulled the modern person's ability to work through issues in community, leaving the person with very little of what could be called "relational endurance."

The image of the incarnation staunches the tendency to flee.[7] From this perspective, individuals need each other in order to be human. Identity here is largely defined by the community into which one is enmeshed. Consequently, there is greater motivation to cooperate with others since choosing another community is simply not an option.

An incarnational development practitioner must embed in a local community, becoming accountable to the residents living there. Furthermore, she may be called upon to bring about reconciliation between parties in the local community long at odds with each other. Such an undertaking will take great patience—sometimes even implicating the practitioner, in which case she may need to reconcile with others in the community as well.

5. Flexible Availability—Providing Access and Preference

> Then little children were being brought to him in order that he might lay his hands on them and pray. The disciples spoke sternly to those who

brought them; but Jesus said, "Let the little children come to me, and do not stop them; for it is to such as these that the kingdom of heaven belongs." (Matt. 19:13)

Little children are a supremely inefficient lot. Once watches are synchronized, schedules consulted, and promises made, a child often gums up the works. Hunger reasserts itself, diapers need changing, and good planning comes to naught.

But, are we not here brought face-to-face with some of the apparatus of the modern world—watches, calendars, appointments? Are these not some of our modernist icons showing us where it is that we place our priorities? Are they not also often the tools of our trade in the development industry?

Being flexibly available, Jesus extended an invitation to children to *participate* in the "kingdom of heaven." Perhaps this indicates something about our priorities as we look for guidance from the incarnational motif. Flexibility on the part of Jesus does not seem a rare quality. As one traces his wanderings throughout Galilee, one is struck by the number of times his schedule seems spontaneously altered. For instance, after drawing quite a crowd by restoring the Gerasene demoniac in Mark 5:1–20, Jesus crosses the Sea of Galilee and encounters Jairus, a leader in the synagogue, who requests him to come heal his daughter (Mark 5:21b–24).

Just then ". . . there was a woman who had been suffering from hemorrhages for twelve years . . . [who] came up behind him in the crowd and touched his cloak . . ." (Mark 5:25, 27). She, too, wished to be healed—and was, by virtue of this contact.[8] Jesus is then once more approached by people from Jairus's household—"while he was still speaking . . ." (Mark 5:35). Jairus's daughter had died. Jesus carries on to her home and gives her back to her parents.

The shift in agendas is palpable but not unusual. In communities of tradition, the most crucial events often defy scheduling: death, birth, floods, fire, and so forth. Development practitioners need to stay open and be flexible; there is no other way to be involved in daily affairs of villages.

But flexibility is not unchecked aimlessness. Jesus' adaptability points to his priorities.[9] When the Syrophoenician woman begged him to deliver her daughter of evil spirits (Matt. 15:21–28; Mark 7:24–30), Jesus answers her by saying that "the children [of Israel must] be fed first, for it is not fair to take the children's food and throw it to the dogs" (Mark 7:27). Yet, in the end, he does what she requests. What can we tell about his priorities by way of this event? Mark's Gospel places the story in the flow of a discussion concerning cleanness and uncleanness (cf. Mark 7:1–23)—this woman's "uncleanness," in the end, was more acceptable to Jesus than the "cleanness" of religious leaders. Jesus turns prevailing purity classifications on their head, giving evidence of what has been called Jesus' "preferential option for the poor"—his focus on the needs of the dispossessed.

By urging us to live amongst the poor, encountering actual privation face-to-face, the incarnational motif pushes such preferences to the fore. To be flexible is to be available—especially for those most in need of assistance.

6. Verifiable Emptiness—Providing Authenticity and Challenge

> The hour has come for the Son of Man to be glorified. Very truly, I tell you, unless a grain of wheat falls into the earth and dies, it remains just a single grain; but if it dies, it bears much fruit. (John 12:23–24)

While today's society at-large emphasizes upward mobility, the incarnational motif counters with downward mobility as the mark of its success and discernible servitude as its outgrowth.

This is most evident in the life of Jesus in the Gospel of Mark. W. H. Vanstone, in his book *The Stature of Waiting*,[10] says that, after being handed over to the chief priests by Judas Iscariot, Jesus willingly ". . . exchanged action for passion, the role of a subject for that of object."[11] Vanstone notes that, before he is handed over to the authorities, Jesus is on the scene making things happen, the subject of sentences centered on action.

All of this radically changes following the appearance of Judas in the garden (Mark 14:43*ff*). With this, Jesus becomes the *acted upon,* not the actor.

> . . . From this point to the moment of Jesus' death on the Cross, a period which occupies . . . one hundred lines of narrative, Jesus is the grammatical subject of just nine verbs. . . . He is no longer there as the active and initiating subject of what is done: He is there as the recipient, the object, of what is done.[12]

It seems possible that the temptation before Jesus might be an enticement to carry on being the *subject* of events, not their passive *object*. With this, Jesus takes on obedient surrender for the sake of others, a stance Vanstone calls "the posture of waiting."[13]

As those involved in a vocation concerned with the less powerful, development practitioners must embrace this trajectory by being inspired by the divesting image of the incarnation and its example of verifiable emptiness. As we are faced with periods of necessary subjection to the logic of forbearance and renunciation, we take on this incarnational "posture of waiting" so as not to impatiently assert professional privilege to rights. Such a posture is nothing other than love. Authentic participation cannot exist without it.

We now have before us a barometer for evaluating participatory schemes. Whatever endeavours we choose to take up stand little chance of issuing forth in true participation unless they are done in a manner that is

- narratively enacted;
- residentially near;
- socially embedded;
- physically encountered;
- flexibly available; and
- verifiably emptied.

Those involvements that take these six marks seriously will find themselves deeply involved in local communities giving rise to results more in keeping with the notion of *participation* in the first place.

BEING "WITH" AS A WESLEYAN IMPULSE

This volume is looking at models of world mission in the Wesleyan spirit. That being the case, it is now fair to ask if the model put forth here aligns with such a spirit. While space permits only general exploration, I believe that a brief glance at the topic validates incarnational approaches as ones in harmony with the style John Wesley himself endorsed.

First, it is interesting to note how many of the persons who ended up attracted to Mr. Wesley's ministry were comprised of the poor themselves. As Richard Heitzenrater reminds us,

The "poor of Society," to use Wesley's common phrase, were not outsiders who were the occasional object of his external outreach—they were, by and large, the people who made up a relatively large proportion of his societies and for whom he and the Methodists had specific pastoral responsibility.[14]

But, we should go on to ask whether the approach Wesley advocated for assisting these poor is alligned with the incarnational approach put forward here. Wesley maintained an emphasis on what the Christian becomes, not simply what the Christian does. And, as Heitzenrater points out, the way Wesley saw a believer becoming what he or she should become is by being conformed to the image of Christ.

> True religion, for the Oxford Methodists, was not basically a collection of actions that were determined by obedience to various sets of rules. It was conformity to a model: Thomas à Kempis' *De imitatione Christi*, one of the first books in a crucial series of readings for Wesley in the mid-1720s, became the cornerstone of his ethical approach and established the perspective for much of his later thinking on the Christian life.[15]

Thus, we can confidently say that models of world mission along the lines of the pattern recommended here correspond not only to the image we have of Christ but also to that recommended by John Wesley for the people called Methodist.

A RETURN TO THE TRAIN

We may now return to my encounter with Anis on the train that day in Bandung. How does that encounter fare in the light of our model?

In terms of physical encounter, flexible availability and verifiable emptiness, my ride on the train seems a worthy example of incarnational involvement. Physical encounter calls for tangible and vulnerable involvement, flexible availability bids unguarded access and a preference toward the poor, and verifiable emptiness invites authenticity of involvement and a challenge of direction—wherein the one seeking participation is brought face-to-face with undeniable contexts of privation that test the participant's trajectory. Through our discussion, both Anis and I were indeed rendered vulnerable by way of a spontaneous conversation flexibly brought about through chance encounter at that Jakarta train station. And, these many years later, I am still challenged by my experience with her. As I look at the event from that angle, it now makes more sense why I seemed providentially nudged to change my focus, my mind, and my schedule as Anis struck up a conversation with me.

However, when examined in light of the three remaining features of the incarnational model, my experience does not stand up to scrutiny quite as well.

First off, our meeting was a chance encounter and, as such, I never again ran into Anis, in spite of the fact Bandung was my home for many years after that exchange. I did not thereafter reside in her narrative, over time, alongside her—consequently, I was decidedly non-incarnate in her history and my narrative did *not* develop alongside hers.

One of the reasons for this, of course, is the fact that I lived nowhere near her—in fact, I never found out precisely where she in fact did live. A few years later, I moved to another city, losing all track of Anis except for the memory she left with me. I did not participate in Anis's life with any manner of proximity. And, by virtue of physical and narrative distance, which only increased as time went by, I certainly was not socially embedded in her world—which obviated any sort of true communal accountability or reconciliation between us or, through me, between Anis and God. In a word, there simply was not enough time, space, nor social interweaving for any of that to happen.

So, when gauged against the more complete pattern of Jesus' incarnational model, it was not enough for me to be flexible, vulnerable, and concretely present to Anis. True missional development practice on my part would have stipulated that I be more narratively involved in her world over time, residing near her, socially embedding myself in her world. Without that, my efforts would always fall short of the depth of incarnational involvement that Jesus modeled.

CONCLUSION

As stated above, the six marks of the incarnation offer us an important template for evaluating development practice and missional participation. Such a word-picture makes accessible an adjudicating guide in order to appraise our own involvement in communities of privation and tradition; as was said above, with this we now possess a suite of defining characteristics which, together, give insight into what is entailed in an "incarnational approach to participation." Other approaches to development practice and missiological participation can now be evaluated utilizing this model—and, in the process, the incarnational model itself can continue to be weighed in terms of its usefulness, its practicality, and its appropriateness.

NOTES

1. Ruth Page, *The Incarnation of Freedom and Love* (London: SCM Press, 1991), pp. 53–54, emphasis in the original.

2. On the *scandal of particularity*, note the following from Lesslie Newbigin, *The Open Secret: An Introduction to the Theology of Mission*, Revised Edition (Grand Rapids: William B. Eerdmans, 1995), p. 67:

> The scandal of particularity is . . . the problem of relating God's universality to his particular deeds and words. God is over all and in all; not a sparrow falls to the ground without his will. Yet the Bible talks of God acting and God speaking in particular times and places. How are these related? With what propriety can we speak of particular acts of God if God is universal Lord of all? How can we relate this universality to this particularity?
>
> The attentive reader of the Bible will note how constantly these two themes are interwoven without any apparent sense of incompatibility. In Romans 10:12–13 Paul makes a statement of sweeping universality: "There is no distinction between Jew and Greek; the same Lord is Lord of all and bestows his riches upon all who call upon him. For, 'everyone who calls on the name of the Lord will be saved.'" But this leads him straight into the assertion of the need for the missionary to go and preach (Rom. 10:14–15). In John 4:24, the text that has often been used to deny the need for "form or sign or ritual word" in religion, "God is Spirit, and they that worship him must worship him in spirit and truth," follows immediately on the blunt statement that describes the Samaritan worship as ignorant and asserts that "salvation is from the Jews" (4:22). Universality and particularity do not contradict one another but require one another: How can this be so?

3. The point made here stands irrespective of whether Thomas actually did take up the offer to validate Jesus' presence by means of touch or not, since that being underscored is the offer of tactility on the part of Jesus.

4. Such does not preclude astute discernment and the need to assess opportunities in terms of desired impact and strategic implementation. In other

words, a concern for vulnerability and susceptibility does not mean that we blindly entrust ourselves to any and all—such an approach could threaten to undo that which we are attempting to accomplish. Even when faced with increasingly positive response on the part of followers in Jerusalem, ". . . Jesus on his part would not entrust himself to them, because he knew all people and needed no one to testify about anyone; for he himself knew what was in everyone" (John 2:24–25). In short, while there is a biblical concern for gentleness and strength in weakness, there is also a balancing admonition toward shrewdness (See also Luke 16:1–8).

5. David Augsburger, *Helping People Forgive* (Louisville, Ky.: Westminster John Knox Press, 1996), pp. 148–49.

6. Peter Berger puts the matter well: "In most of the world today, traditional frameworks of meaning are under severe stress and are in the process of changing their fundamental character. In other words, the matter is complicated by the global fact of *modernization*. There are many facets to this process, but a crucial facet may be expressed as follows: *Modernization is a shift from givenness to choice on the level of meaning.* Tradition is undermined to exactly the degree in which what previously was taken for granted as a 'fact of life' becomes something for which an individual may or may not opt. Consequently, in any situation undergoing modernization, it is often unclear which of the two versions of the 'right to meaning' should pertain—the right to choose freely or the right to be left alone in the old givenness. This unclarity is not just in the mind of the outside observer; it marks the minds of those who are in the modernizing situation. It has often been remarked that individuals in the throes of modernization

are torn, divided within themselves. A decisive aspect of this division is the ambivalence between givenness and choice. It is not difficult to see that anomie is a powerful threat under such conditions" (*Pyramids of Sacrifice: Political Ethics and Social Change* [New York: Penguin Books, 1974], pp. 196–97, emphasis in the original).

The thesis of another of Berger's books, *The Heretical Imperative: Contemporary Possibilities of Religious Affirmation* (London: Collins, 1979)—a sociological examination of Westernized, modern concepts of religion—is almost entirely focused upon this choice as the one and only "imperative" still functioning in Western society.

7. Though it must be said, it does not guarantee reconciliation. Like residential nearness to community formation, social embedment is a necessary cause for reconciliation, but it is not sufficient in and of itself. Persons can remain unreconciled in spite of it; but they can scarcely become reconciled without it.

8. Note the emphasis on touch once again—further buttressing the point made above concerning tactility, healing, and incarnation.

9. Note that Jesus' delay caused by this woman resulted in the "death" of the daughter of one of the leaders of the synagogue—surely, this was not the way to curry favor from those in command.

10. W. H. Vanstone, *The Stature of Waiting* (London: Darton, Longman and Todd, 1982).

11. Ibid., p. 32.

12. Ibid., p. 20. Later in the book Vanstone also makes a similar point in reference to the Gospel of John.

13. One is reminded of educational theorist Paulo Freire who states that the poor of the earth are customarily treated as objects by outsiders, who

inevitably place themselves as subjects to all activities in the context (see his *Education for Critical Consciousness* [New York: Harper & Row, 1973]). He goes on to say that the only way in which this *subject–object* coupling can be deconstructed, becoming a subject–subject partnering model, is by way of what he calls a *conscientization*, a new awareness on the part of both parties of the similarity one has with the other. This sort of new awareness requires new pictures and new possibilities placed before those

participating—with each thereby embracing new conceptions of the other. What we have in the picture of Jesus, here, is just such a new possibility.

14. Richard P. Heitzenrater, "The *Imitatio Christi* and the Great Commandment: Virtue and Obligation in Wesley's Ministry with the Poor" in *The Portion of the Poor: Good News to the Poor in the Wesleyan Tradition*, ed. M. Douglas Meeks (Nashville: Kingswood Books, 1995), p. 52.

15. Ibid., p. 59.

BIBLIOGRAPHY

Augsburger, David. *Helping People Forgive*. Louisville, Ky.: Westminster John Knox Press, 1996.

Berger, Peter L. *Pyramids of Sacrifice: Political Ethics and Social Change*. New York: Penguin Books, 1974.

———. *The Heretical Imperative Contemporary Possibilities of Religious Affirmation*. London: Collins, 1979.

Freire, Paulo. *Education for Critical Consciousness*. New York: Harper & Row, 1973.

Heitzenrater, Richard P. "The *Imitatio Christi* and the Great Commandment: Virtue and Obligation in Wesley's

Ministry with the Poor." In *The Portion of the Poor: Good News to the Poor in the Wesleyan Tradition*, ed. M. Douglas Meeks, pp. 49–63. Nashville: Kingswood Books, 1995.

Newbigin, Lesslie. *The Open Secret: An Introduction to the Theology of Mission*. Revised Edition. Grand Rapids: William B. Eerdmans Publishing Company, 1995.

Page, Ruth. *The Incarnation of Freedom and Love*. London: SCM Press, 1991.

Vanstone, W. H. *The Stature of Waiting*. London: Darton, Longman and Todd, 1982.

29

EDINBURGH 2010

Implications for Wesleyan Witness

Daryl Balia

WORLD MISSIONARY CONFERENCE (1910)

The foundations of the modern ecumenical movement are held by many to have been laid by the landmark 1910 World Missionary Conference in Edinburgh. The renowned Archbishop of Canterbury, William Temple, himself a student delegate at the conference, would later observe that it was "the greatest event in the life of the Church for a generation." This was not a far-fetched insight if we concur with similar views that "Edinburgh 1910" was unique for the impetus it gave to Christian mission in many different ways and that it served to inaugurate a new era of international and interchurch cooperation at a level never before known. Writing much later, the mission historian, Brian Stanley, points out that the conference was not in fact a gathering of all associations of Christianity and suffers from "the distortions of hindsight."[1] It was not geographically representative nor were churches delegated to attend to the same extent that mission agencies were, let alone "younger churches" of the time.

Edinburgh 1910 was a prototype, nonetheless, in that it stood out as the first "world" gathering of missionaries and the scope of its work embraced missionary efforts (albeit Protestant) from more parts of the world than had been possible before. Its purview was intentionally global and those who gathered came from some of the remotest parts of the mission landscape. Wesleyans were as well represented then, as they have been at most subsequent world mission conferences organized by the World Council of Churches (WCC). It might be interesting at this juncture to inquire if the people called Methodists have in some way been prepared to anticipate a view of world mission from their venerable founder, John Wesley, and explore the extent to which such a view (if it exists) might be corroborated with our understanding of mission in the twenty-first century.

THE WORLD IS MY PARISH

The Wesleyan spirit, as far as world missions go, is premised, of course, on that famous journal entry of 1739 which John Wesley made and we shall attempt to understand in the context of its time:

> I look upon all the world as my parish; thus far I mean, that, in whatever part of it I am, I judge it meet, right, and my bounded duty to declare unto all that are willing to hear, the glad tidings of salvation. This is the work which I know God has called me to; and sure I am that his blessing attends it.[2]

Wesley, initially at least, seems to have succumbed to the temptation of seeing the parish as his world for if mission meant going to mostly nominal Christians who happened to be located abroad, he was content to rather spread "scriptural holiness" at home. Yet, such was Wesley's impact on the "home missions" front that he is sometimes credited for having prevented sedition in England during his time. Wesley's hope for the riches of God's grace to be shared by all was not fully realized as the early Methodists sought to be a church within the church, giving emphasis to elements of the Christian faith they felt were being neglected. It is therefore no accident, says Henry Rack, that Methodist missions were acquired the way the British acquired their colonies, "in a fit of absence of mind, coming to terms with them in an official way afterwards."[3] There was clearly no strategic formulation or policy at work except the drive to recognize new circuits that were evolving abroad.

While Thomas Coke was agitating for missions abroad, Wesley remained somewhat negative. This might have arisen in part from his own early missionary encounter with native Indians in Georgia. The tide might have changed in 1778 when the Methodist conference debated the matter of a mission to Africa, but it was only in 1786 when the Methodist conference for the first time sanctioned the sending of William Warrender for "heathen" missions, that is, to minister to black persons in the West Indies. This was before William Carey had formed the Baptist Missionary Society, though the first Wesleyan society for foreign missions was only formed in 1813 after Wesley's death. Then too, it was not the usual voluntary society but one meant to operate as a department of the emerging church structure.

If the nineteenth century was the "great century" for world missions, it is hardly surprising to encounter resistance in earlier times to the notion of "reaching the unreached" among mainstream Protestants. Some believed that the Great Commission had been directed to the apostles only while others, under Calvinist influences, dared not attempt to do God's work for God. Having come through two centuries of struggle for the survival of its heart and soul, Protestantism might be forgiven for having misplaced its missionary zeal for conversions in the eighteenth century.

Not in the case of John Wesley, though, who saw the world as his parish and shared a deep desire for the conversion of all people to Christ, including the other "stranger in our midst." This "other" in Wesley's England was the black slave, the object of commercial transactions, human abuse, and the "sum of all villanies." Slave owners and slave traders found justification for upholding their capitalistic impulses in slave dealing with the belief that blacks were barbaric and uncivilized. This justification of oppression on the grounds of race was made on ideological grounds, therefore, as it served their interests to propagate such a view, which seems to have also been held by the likes of George Whitefield and John Newton. Both were never opposed to slavery as they were to its darker side.

Contrary to Whitefield, Wesley held that the hot climate of Georgia was no excuse for slave holding as for him it was a case of, "Better no trade, than trade procured by villany."[4] Wesley's understanding of natural law, human liberty, and inherent equality would not allow him to sit comfortably in the midst of such eighteenth-century cultural superiority. Europeans were in no respect superior to other peoples or races. For Wesley then, the Negro slave was no more the object of evangelical zeal for conversion than the English nominal Christian. In no way were

Christian nations required to spread their brand of "scriptural holiness" as this was the responsibility of individual Christians. Blacks, wherever in the world and whether slave or free, were neither the "noble savages" nor the "white man's burden" but worthy recipients of the Gospel of grace like any other human being depraved by sin.

Earlier we saw that Wesley felt bound by "duty to declare unto all that are willing to hear, the glad tidings of salvation." The Evangelical Revival in Great Britain during the eighteenth century was born of the desire for all the peoples of the world to experience God's grace, and Wesley's influence in that movement was monumental. The burden of evangelical obligation is tempered in Wesley's understanding by the recognition of human freedom, as the task of proclamation cannot be undertaken against the will of a person. Such religious liberty allowed one to choose his or her own religion, and to worship God according to one's own conscience. Love of neighbor was not to be construed as "desire to convert" as that would amount to a misreading of Wesley's conception of salvation. No one had the right to pronounce judgment and sentence the heathen to damnation, for it is better, says Wesley, "to leave them to him that made them, and who is 'father of all flesh'; who is the God of the Heathens as well as the Christians, and who hateth nothing that he hath made."[5] As Irv Brendlinger has observed, this was an "amazing position" to adopt for an eighteenth-century evangelical, one that transcends time almost as far as world missions are concerned.

NOW IS THE HOUR

Nearly a century after Wesley's death, another Methodist was calling Christians gathered in Edinburgh to embark on the evangelization of the same heathen world with a sense of renewed urgency. John Mott, a lay youth leader of the World Student Christian Federation, was the genius behind the World Missionary Conference, which he organized along the implicit principle that most of Europe and North America were Christian. Mott was born in 1865 and was one of the most widely traveled Christian leaders of his time. He won the Nobel Peace Prize in 1946 and was instrumental in the formation of the WCC in 1948. It is important to note that the 1910 gathering was not about world mission but rather about mission from Christendom to heathen lands. It was not concerned with mission to the whole inhabited earth, but instead with mission to those parts of the world that everybody agreed were outside the purview of Christendom. Mott's book, which appeared immediately after the conference, was called *The Decisive Hour of Christian Missions*, where he outlined a strategy to meet the missionary challenge for the twentieth century. It is worth observing here how two Methodists inspired by the same Gospel, and emerging as leaders with a universal message but living a century apart from each other, could share the same sense of urgency for God's intervention in human affairs.

Edinburgh 1910, despite Mott's best efforts, is infamously remembered for its truncated delegations that served to exclude those from the "younger" churches. It was Mott, says his able conference lieutenant, Joseph Oldham, who above all others had "insisted in the face of a good deal of conservative opposition that the younger Churches should be represented."[6] In the event, only seventeen delegates of color or "natives from mission lands" were brought to Edinburgh. The conventional view seems to have been well articulated by a London Missionary Society secretary at the time when he observed, "I do not think the time is ripe for the inclusion of delegates appointed by the Churches in non-Christian lands in any great conference such as ours."[7] Edinburgh's clock in 1910 was not one where Roman Catholic, Orthodox, or emerging forms of independent Christianity featured at all; God's decisive hour seemed to be directed to God's agents in heathen lands who were mostly white, male, and mainline Protestants only, with a small band of women helpers in attendance.

EDINBURGH 2010

To overcome the paralyzing inertia of missionary paternalism that has dominated succeeding paradigms of mission in the twentieth century, those involved in planning the centenary celebrations of the great World Missionary Conference have sought a break from the immediate past. The initial conversations in looking towards a centenary gathering called "Edinburgh 2010" have revolved around the need to articulate a theology of "mission in humility and hope." This was later modified to include the notion of "serving God's mission together" lest too much attention be given to applauding the human effort in missionary conquests. Still, the overriding considerations relate to the presence of the "other" with due recognition that the majority of Christians in the world are now no longer located in the global north. Women have exercised a profound influence on Christian missions and will no longer accept being subservient partners in the task of evangelizing the world. Pentecostalism is a relatively new phenomenon since 1910, but accounting for over 25 percent of world Christianity. In a world that has come through enormous and profound change, Christian discourse about mission is in need of a new way of speaking about God, a new language and a new "translation" of God's love for the same world of today.

Edinburgh 2010 presents itself, therefore, as an opportunity to do God's mission again, in the presence of witnesses from all parts of the world and without cultural domination by any one particular language or form of discourse. It is deliberate about the need to develop mission synergies and expand networks across the globe, provide new guidelines based on a "polycentric" study process that includes participants from all traditions sharing the same common space and responding to the one mandate. The hope is for a vision to evolve among churches that would provide fresh energy and impetus for undertaking the task of mission in ways that would not cripple existing resources or structures, nor be a burden in times of rapid decline of church memberships. World mission is often hindered by the pluralist view of world religions which, if used to undergird one's approach to mission, will effectively remove the urgency to seek the conversion of individuals. For those involved in the Edinburgh 2010 initiative, however, evangelism and conversion remain intrinsic to mission. Edinburgh 2010, like so many of its conference predecessors, is meant to be a time to reflect, rethink, and become resolute about God's mission again when all signs seem to be pointing towards ecclesiastical fracture and ecumenical fatigue.

The missionary paradigm perpetrated by John Mott and his generation, as evidenced in Edinburgh 1910, suffered severe distortions from its inability to transcend divisions of humanity into those civilized and those ostensibly waiting to be acculturated into the Western way of life. Mott, nonetheless, was an early advocate of the view that Christianity "can adapt itself to the people it seeks to save" and that it was not desirable that "the ordered life of the Christian community in Asia and Africa should follow in every respect the lines of European and American Christianity."[8] Such "inculturation" has since become a hallmark of the Christian encounter with peoples of cultures from the global south. To escape the limitations of the historical baggage, leadership in mission is increasingly being placed into the hands of leaders of the more vibrant and growing, but still younger, churches. Methodists have a helping hand in making the transition in world mission, from seeing people in distant lands as objects of God's mission, to a recognition of the world as the parish for mission. Churches that are growing the fastest seem to be those of the "stranger in our midst," in other words, the immigrant churches. Vitality is a feature of church life in the emerging churches who do not ordinarily send overseas missionaries but who are more mindful of their local and immediate surroundings.

The landscape for mission in the twenty-first century has certainly changed as, it might be said, the world becomes a smaller place where mission is from everywhere to everywhere. This, though a mantra of Edinburgh 2010 and The United Methodist Church, was not in any way near to the understanding of mission at evidence during Edinburgh 1910. It is, however, continuous with a very Wesleyan view that informed the early beginnings of the Methodist movement and poses a critical challenge to our rethinking of world mission. Those sent to do mission today in humility and hope may also wish to recall Wesley's words to fully appreciate the dynamic of mutuality, which should be a feature of every missionary encounter: "I went to America to convert the Indians; but O! who shall convert me?"

NOTES

1. Brian Stanley, "Edinburgh 1910 and the Oikoumene," in *Ecumenism and History: Studies in Honour of John H. Y. Briggs*, ed. Anthony R. Cross (Carlisle, Eng.: Paternoster, 2002), p. 90.

2. Percy L. Parker, ed., *The Journal of John Wesley* (Chicago: Moody, n.d.), p. 74.

3. Henry D. Rack, *Reasonable Enthusiast: John Wesley and the Rise of Methodism* (Philadelphia: Trinity Press International, 1989), p. 478.

4. See Wesley's "Thoughts upon Slavery" in *The Works of John Wesley*, 3rd ed., vol. XI, ed. Thomas Jackson (London: Wesleyan Conference Office, 1872), p. 74.

5. Irv A. Brendlinger, *Social Justice through the Eyes of John Wesley* (Ontario: Joshua Press, 2006), p. 71.

6. J. H. Oldham, "John R. Mott," *Ecumenical Review* 7 (1955): p. 258.

7. Letter of Ralph Thomson to J. H. Oldham, 7 February 1910. Quoted in Stanley, "Edinburgh 1910 and the Oikoumene," p. 93.

8. John R. Mott, *The Decisive Hour of Christian Missions* (Edinburgh: Foreign Mission Committee of the Church of Scotland, 1910), p. 43.

BIBLIOGRAPHY

Brendlinger, Irv A. *Social Justice through the Eyes of John Wesley.* Ontario: Joshua Press, 2006.

Clements, Keith. *Faith on the Frontier: A Life of J. H. Oldham.* Edinburgh: T & T Clark, 1999.

Hopkins, C. Howard. *John R. Mott 1865–1955.* Grand Rapids: Eerdmans, 1979.

Nuessle, John E. *Faithful Witness: United Methodist Theology of Mission.* New York: General Board of Global Ministries, United Methodist Church, 2008.

Rack, Henry D. *Reasonable Enthusiast: John Wesley and the Rise of Methodism.* Philadelphia: Trinity Press International, 1989.

Reiger, Joerg, and John Vincent, eds. *Methodist and Radical.* Nashville: Kingswood Books, 2003.

Ross, Kenneth, and David Kerr, eds. *Edinburgh 1910: Mission Then and Now.* Oxford: Regnum, 2009.

30

HARNESSING THE POWER
OF REVIVAL

LEADERSHIP TRAINING FROM A
WESLEYAN PERSPECTIVE

Norival Trindade, Jr.

In the early 1990s, David Thagana, a schoolteacher and part-time evangelist in rural Kenya, quit his career to establish a church for those who had become Christians through his ministry. Ten years later he led a team of more than twenty pastors and leaders and established Glory Outreach Assembly as a small indigenous denomination with a dozen churches in the area surrounding his original church. During the same period, Pio Carvalho left his own career as a pharmaceutical industry executive in southern Brazil to establish Abba Christian Fellowship, an independent church that began as a small home gathering of seven couples and in fewer than ten years grew to almost four thousand people and a handful of affiliated churches. On the other side of the world during the same time, as China underwent dramatic economic and social changes, the once hidden and persecuted underground house church was changing from an essentially rural network of secret churches with the emergence of urban house churches.[1] The Chinese church began to emerge as one of the largest forces in contemporary Christianity with an estimated 91 million Christians, the majority of them loosely connected in informal networks of house churches.[2]

For the Kenyans, the pressing question at that stage was how to reach beyond their particular tribal group and geographical location in the rural highlands of central Kenya. For Carvalho and his congregation, the challenge was to continue growing in a sustainable fashion and managing large numbers of conversions. For the Chinese underground church, the overwhelming challenge has been to take millions of first-generation Christians deeper in their walk with God and to reach the great multitudes of Chinese still untouched by the Gospel.

Tremendous growth, overwhelming challenges, and fascinating opportunities: this is the face of the emerging global church.[3] These are examples of a worldwide movement that emerged as the center of gravity and the axis of growth of the global church shifted south and east during the last half of the twentieth century.[4] Global research on the church shows "we are living in the time of the greatest ingathering of people into the Kingdom of God that the world has ever seen."[5] For the emerging global church, numerical growth is not a challenge. Leaders in different continents agree that there is a trend of revival, as the rapid growth of the three movements described here demonstrates. The pressing issue for these leaders is how to harness the power of this revival so that the immediate impact of the Gospel message can be translated into sustained personal and societal change.

This new reality poses new missionary challenges. Whether defined as *preaching to the heathen* or *reaching unreached people groups*, the calling for men and women to take the Good News of Christianity to those who never heard it has been the predominant missionary model of the last three centuries. Today the churches of Latin America, Asia, and Africa, formerly identified as the *mission field*, have grown in numbers, established their presence in society, and become mission partners, sharing the responsibility of the Great Commission with the Christians from the Western Hemisphere. This new reality has resulted in a new missionary challenge to sending churches, both in the West and in the emerging global church. Whereas the challenge of taking the Gospel to unreached and remote regions of the world persists, an additional calling has been issued by the emerging global church. They ask for specific training in leadership, evangelism, and mission. The great task entrusted by Christ to the church requires the multiplication of passionate and effective leaders who can effectively lead this growing community of believers in fulfilling the Great Commission.

Like Carvalho, Thagana, or the Chinese leaders, the global emerging church is not unaware of the need to train leaders. In fact the subject has become a trend in today's church, in step with a growing interest in "training and management development activities in the business world."[6] Seminary programs, leadership schools for church members, and short-term leadership seminars attempt to raise new leaders and develop existing ones. At the same time, leaders worldwide are quick to point out the existence of a crisis due to the shortage of leadership in the worldwide church, so that "the unfinished task of world evangelization still overwhelms us."[7]

John and Charles Wesley were God's instruments to bring a powerful revival to the British Isles and North America. One of the secrets of the enduring power of this movement was the ability of the Wesleys to harness the power of that revival by training and mobilizing large numbers of Christians. The training and leadership they provided was informed by their theological thinking. John and Charles Wesley themselves did not become desk theologians or write systematic theology per se. Instead, they postulated their thinking "in passing, or exemplified [it] in the process of actual theological activity."[8] This is why the main source for understanding Wesleyan theology comes from scattered writings, such as John's journal, sermons, and other publications, and Charles's hymns.[9] This essentially practical theology set the Wesleyan thinking apart from other Protestant traditions of that period and provided a framework to help the church respond to the challenge of leadership training and development.

LEADERSHIP TRAINING THAT IS OPEN AND DIVERSE

In the last two centuries many have attempted to define leadership and to understand how leaders exercise influence over followers. Today multiple theoretical formulations try to explain leadership, although it still remains "one of the most observed and least understood phenomena on Earth."[10] Today there are multiple models of leadership that are useful not only for business leadership and management, but also for Christian leadership.[11]

Wesleyan theological thinking is essentially *catholic*. Although firmly entrenched in the Church of England until his death, Wesley had an appreciation for the church at large and developed his thinking with an open mind, taking seriously other traditions, contemporary and historical. He borrowed from the church fathers, Eastern and Western theology, the early reformers, Pietism, and other expressions of the Christian faith.

Beyond religion itself, Wesley was interested in a varied array of subjects and areas of knowledge.

Leadership training inspired by Wesley's various sources of knowledge and wisdom will be open and diverse, recognizing the value of the growing body of knowledge and the theories and models of leadership developed in the last one hundred years.

In this time of rapid and global communication, leaders from the emerging global church have access to information and are aware of these resources and models. Churches like Abba Fellowship, Glory Outreach Assembly, and the Chinese house church recognize the need to be at the cutting edge of knowledge in order to become effective and relevant in today's world. A Wesleyan approach can offer a model of leadership training that considers what the world has to offer.

ONLY ONE SOURCE

In many aspects, leadership for mission within the church is not different from business, community, or political leadership. There is, however, one element in Christian leadership that is unique, and that is its spiritual nature. Christian leadership flows out of the leader's intimacy with God, a relationship that permeates all of the leader's life. The Christian leader influences others not because of personal abilities, but because of a personality that is "irradiated, penetrated, and empowered by the Holy Spirit."[12] In order to foster intimacy with God, out of which will flow spiritual leadership, training must have a solid biblical foundation.

While Wesley was open to various influences and promoted free thinking, he was steadfast in his affirmation of Scripture as the final and central tether against which all tradition, reason, and experience had to be measured. In essence, Wesley and his followers were *people of one book*.

A leadership training model inspired by Wesleyan thinking will highly value the inspiration of Scripture and the truths it proclaims, looking at leadership theories and models through the eyes of Scripture and drawing practical insight from the many powerful leadership lessons contained in biblical narratives. Such a firm biblical foundation can prevent free thinking from straying from a healthy orthodoxy and will result in training that fosters the kingdom of God as its main goal.

The high value of Scripture that characterizes much of the emerging global church aligns with biblically based leadership training. The church in the non-Western world generally takes the biblical message and meaning in much more literal ways than Western Christians.[13] Leaders in the emerging global church will greatly value and give credibility to training that is firmly founded in the truth of Scripture and draws insight from the biblical teachings.

DEVELOPED IN COMMUNITY

In an environment of revival and rapid numerical growth, the sheer numbers of people added to the church can be overwhelming. The ability to harness the power of revival for sustained growth and relevant impact depends on developing and training sufficient numbers of leaders who can help build the community and disciple individual Christians. This is the current climate in much of the emerging global church, making the multiplication of effective leaders essential.

For the Wesleys, theology was not only dealing with the divine, for true theology has an essential social component. The very fact that Wesleyan theological thinking comes out of practical living of the Christian life is evidence of the social element. There is no theology per se, but rather practical writings to be used by preachers, societies, and classes, as well as hymns that teach theology even as they usher people into the presence of God in worship.

This practical and social approach to theology can be a powerful framework for leadership training in an environment that requires the multiplication of leaders. Training with this aspect in mind happens in community and those being trained also act as teachers, as their experience comes to bear in the training process. Learners turned teachers, in turn, have the potential to multiply their training in others. To take advantage of this multiplication factor, training needs to be reproducible, designed and delivered in a way that can be passed on from one leader to another.

Leaders like Thagana or Carvalho have established teams. They believe every Christian needs to be trained for life and mission, making the multiplication of leaders a necessity. The sheer numbers and relatively young history of the Chinese underground church demands the multiplication of trainers to equip the scores of first-generation believers. This reality requires a reproducible and multipliable model of leadership training that is done in community.

RELEVANT TODAY

The pace of change in today's world is fast and rapidly increasing, with no evidence of slowing down. Globalization has allowed even those living in remote areas access to a wealth of information unimaginable decades ago. The danger is that if unchecked, globalization can become the new colonialism. Today's leadership training must recognize cultural diversity and build on a foundation of cultural sensitivity and relevance.

Precisely because it was social and practical, Wesleyan theology took its environment seriously and was dynamic, adjusting its elements to the needs and requirements of its surroundings. While grounded in Scripture, Wesleyan thinking was relevant, applied to everyday living and committed to transforming society.

Training leaders from a Wesleyan perspective will take culture seriously. Whereas biblical principles are cross-culturally applicable, their actualization in daily leadership practices are culture-specific. The dynamic aspect of Wesleyan teaching will help develop training that respects and adjusts to culture without imposing imported models.

In a dynamic and relevant approach to training, teaching must be relevant to everyday life and ministry as well. Just as Wesley didn't reflect on theology for its own sake, leadership training done from a Wesleyan perspective will provide practical and relevant teaching immediately applicable to life and ministry.

EXPERIENTIAL AND TRANSFORMATIVE

In recent years, leadership thinking has shifted from a focus on specific behavior and skills or environmental factors to greater emphasis on character issues. Leadership authors recognize the importance of integrity. According to author Peter Drucker, "they [authors] admit that the longer they study effective leaders, the more they have seen that character is the *defining* [original emphasis] issue."[14]

The training of a leader, therefore, requires more than just transfer of skills and technology. It includes identification and questioning of leadership assumptions, search for alternative practices, and ultimately personal change.

One significant aspect of Wesleyan theological thinking is the strong emphasis on experience. Although Wesley never allowed experience to be the final source of revelation, the movement that he helped initiate was only possible after his own dramatic and transformative experience at Aldersgate. For Wesley, religion is not a matter of subscribing to a particular way of thinking. "The Gospel is not a mere creed; it is a living, throbbing, dynamic experience."[15] Members of classes and societies were expected to experience religion internally and express it externally. When seen through the lens of experiential religion, effective leadership training is not only the transfer of content and skills, even as diverse, biblical, reproducible, and relevant as they may be. Learning must be personally experienced and life-changing. It must be a transformative event.

Leadership training can take great advantage of Wesley's experiential theology by creating an environment where leaders can undergo transformative changes in assumptions related to leadership, their roles, and the mission itself. Beyond learning technical skills for efficient leadership, training can help participants analyze their assumptions and challenge their perception of leadership and its practices. In the training environment, leaders can safely engage in critical reflection about their own leadership, search for alternative models, and even begin to experiment with alternative practices in a safe environment.

CONCLUSION

The growth of Abba Christian Fellowship or Glory Outreach Assembly in the first decade of their parallel paths during the 1990s is not the end of the story. In the first years of the new century, Thagana and Carvalho received training that they consider personally transformative. The training they received was biblical, widely informed, reproducible, relevant, and transformational, focusing on leadership and global mission. Both leaders passed the training on to their top leadership teams and implemented changes in their organizations. Today, as both organizations approach the completion of their second decade, they have undergone significant growth that both leaders credit to leadership training.

Glory Outreach Assembly planted more than one hundred churches since 2001, having reached three unreached ethnic groups in Kenya, and extended their influence to several East African nations. Leadership training and development is one of the denomination's core values and regular programs have been developed to equip pastors for churches and church members for mission. The denomination has recently played a significant role in the relief efforts after the 2007 post-election crisis in Kenya when thousands were displaced by political and ethnic violence.

Abba Christian Fellowship has grown to more than 6,500 active members between 2004 and 2008. Most members participate in approximately five hundred small groups. Their network of affiliated churches has extended to five Brazilian states and their influence has reached beyond national borders into Africa. Leadership training is also one of its most important areas. Abba's Ministry Training School annually trains over seven hundred leaders.

The Chinese church is only now opening itself to the outside world. The government has grown more tolerant of Christianity. The Chinese underground church is slowly showing its face and the love of Christ publicly.[16] Recently one network became openly involved in rescue efforts after the massive earthquake that devastated the Szechuan province. This and other networks of Chinese house churches are clamoring for leadership training that can equip Christians to reach their nation and the world.

After two thousand years and over sixty generations, the Great Commission is still to be completed. For the last three hundred years, missionary activity and the sovereign work of the Holy Spirit have resulted in a strong emerging global church that is already sharing in the responsibility for the completion of this Mission. Like Thagana, Carvalho, and the Chinese leaders, other leaders and churches around the world are waiting for the opportunity to thrive. These believers are asking for training that will enable their leaders to join the rest of the church. Wesleyan thinking can contribute to the process of equipping these leaders for the task. Leadership training from a Wesleyan perspective can make a unique and significant contribution by developing curriculum and strategies that are diverse and open, solidly biblical, developed in community and reproducible, dynamic and relevant, and profoundly transformative. This approach to training can multiply effective leadership for the church that can help leaders harness the power of revival and accelerate the spread of the Gospel.

NOTES

1. Rob Moll, "Great Leap Forward," *Christianity Today* (May 2008): p. 24.

2. Patrick Johnstone, *Operation World* (Carlisle, Eng.: OM Publishing, 1993), p. 160.

3. In this work I have used the term *emerging global church* in reference to the new church movements and denominations currently emerging in the non-Western world. A significant part of this segment of the church is not part of mainline denominations or even established Pentecostal churches. It is important to differentiate this group from the emerging church as described by Brian McClaren and other North American authors in reference to new church movements in the U.S.A.

4. Phillip Jenkins, *The New Christendom: The Coming of Global Christianity* (New York: Oxford University Press, 2002).

5. Johnstone, *Operation World*, p. 25.

6. Raymond A. Noe, "Trainees' Attributes and Attitudes: Neglected Influences in Training Effectiveness," *Academy of Management Review* 11, no. 4 (1986): p. 736.

7. Edgar J. Elliston, "Designing Leadership Education," *Missiology: An International Review* 16, no. 2 (April 1988): p. 204.

8. Randy L. Maddox, *Responsible Grace: John Wesley's Practical Theology* (Nashville: Kngswood Books, 1994), p. 26.

9. Kenneth J. Collins, *The Theology of John Wesley: Holy Love and the Shape of Grace* (Nashville: Abingdon Press, 2007), p. 2.

10. James MacGregor Burns, "The Crisis of Leadership" in *The Leader's Companion: Insights on Leadership through the Ages,* ed. Wren, J. Thomas (New York: Free Press, 1995), pp. 8–10.

11. Among the many leadership theories of today, probably Robert Greenleaf's Servant Leadership (see http://greenleaf.org/) and Bernard Bass and Bruce Avolio's *Developing Potential Across a Full Range of Leadership* (Mahwah, N.J.: Lawrence Erlbaum Associates, 2002) are among the most useful theoretical models for Christian leaders.

12. J. Oswald Sanders. *Spiritual Leadership: Principles of Excellence for Every Believer* (Chicago: Moody, 1994), p. 28.

13. Jenkins, *The New Christendom.* Phillip Jenkins points out in several sections of his book how Christians in the non-Western world are much more conservative in their thinking and take the Bible and the facts narrated therein much more literally than their Western counterparts.

14. Peter Drucker, *Empowered Leaders* (Nashville: Nelson, 1998), p. 178.

15. Robert E. Coleman, *Nothing to Do but to Save Souls: John Wesley's Charge to His Preachers* (Grand Rapids: Zondervan, 1991), p. 75.

16. Rob Moll, "Great Leap Forward," p. 24.

31

THE USE OF "MEANS" IN EVANGELICAL MISSIONS TODAY

Darrell L. Whiteman

William Carey's pamphlet, "An Enquiry into the Obligations of Christians to Use Means for the Conversion of the Heathens" published in 1792, the year after John Wesley died, was an important catalyst for what many missiologists have called the beginning of the modern missionary movement. In eighteenth-century Britain there had been significant breakthroughs and innovations in transportation and communication. William Carey argued that these "means" should also be used for world evangelization. My task in this chapter is to explore the various ways evangelical or independent mission agencies go about the task of mission. What are the dominant "means" by which mission is carried out today? I will then look at The Mission Society as a case study in the "use of means" in mission.

It is safe to say that evangelical mission-sending agencies tend to have evangelism and church planting as their main concerns. Among evangelicals one often hears talk of reaching unreached people groups (UPGs) and an enormous amount of time and energy is spent on developing strategies to do so. At one time the number of unreached people groups was said to be as high as 17,000 but that number has steadily declined in the past twenty-five years. In fact, in November 2008 I received a promotional piece from a large evangelical mission organization that works among Muslims, noting that my financial contribution would help them reach the remaining 247 Muslim people groups who have yet to hear the Gospel.

What is the status of evangelization in the world today? If we were to take the world's population and divide it roughly into three categories this is what we would find:

1. A third have become followers of Jesus;
2. another third have been exposed to Christianity, but have chosen not to follow Jesus;
3. and nearly a third has never heard the Gospel.

One way to describe this scene of world evangelism would be to say:

1. A third of the world's population say, "Thank you, Jesus";
2. another third say, "No thank you, Jesus";
3. but nearly two billion people say, "Who is Jesus?"

Therefore, for most evangelical mission organizations their primary objective is world evangelization and they employ multiple means to reach this goal.

In preparing to write this chapter I consulted the most recent edition of the *Mission Handbook 2007–2009* which is perhaps the best source to discover the many means that mission organizations use today.[1] The *Handbook* gives a lot of helpful data, including the number of missionaries serving more than four years, the number of shorter-term missionaries, and notes the various activities in which the agency is involved. The *Handbook* presently lists seven hundred Protestant mission organizations in the United States. Many of these agencies are very small organizations, sometimes with only a handful of missionaries. There are also some very large evangelical agencies. The *Handbook* lists the thirteen largest agencies with 500 or more missionaries. In this category the range is from The Evangelical Alliance Mission (TEAM) with 514 full-time missionaries, to the Southern Baptist Convention's International Mission Board with 4,009 full-time missionaries serving four years or more. It is notable that all thirteen of these largest agencies are evangelical or independent. The denominational conciliar mission agencies, which were the largest ones fifty to sixty years ago have all declined dramatically in the number of full-time missionaries they employ. The *Handbook* notes the following trends:

1. Although there was a drop in the number of U.S. citizens serving as missionaries through U.S. agencies from the

previous *Handbook* (42,787 in 2001 to 41,329 in the present *Handbook* with data collected in 2005), the overall trend since 1992 has been a slow but steady increase in the number of full-time missionaries.

2. The greatest increase in the number of missionaries has come from non-U.S. citizens working for U.S. agencies. This has increased dramatically. Perhaps we should expect this increase since the center of gravity for Christianity is moving from the northern hemisphere to the global south.
3. As the arena of "business as mission"[2] gains traction as a means of ministry among evangelicals, it is not surprising to see that over the past decade there has been an increase in the number of tentmakers.
4. There has also been a significant increase in the number of U.S. agency home staff.
5. While commitment to evangelism and church planting is by far the leading activity of evangelical mission agencies, a notable trend over the past decade has been an increase in the income reported for overseas ministries, which is concentrated in the largest agencies, whose primary activities focus on relief and development. For example, World Vision reported income of $752 million and MAP International received $319 million.
6. A sixth trend over the last decade reveals that there has been a decrease of activities in the category of evangelism and discipleship. There has also been a decrease in the number of agencies reporting primary activities in personal and small group evangelism, and a decreasing number of agencies reporting activities in the areas of mass evangelism and national church support. Does this mean that evangelism is falling out of favor as a primary means for evangelical mission organizations? I don't think so. Evangelism is still the primary "means" of mission. This trend may simply indicate that evangelical agencies are broadening the scope of their ministries.
7. A seventh trend shows increases in activities have been in the areas of leadership development, community development, and theological education. Also there has been an increase in the number of agencies reporting activities in the areas of

discipleship, short-term mission coordination, childcare and orphanages, and member care.

What does this mean? I think it demonstrates that evangelical mission organizations, like The Mission Society, are getting a larger vision and a more holistic understanding of evangelism that is broader than simply "saving souls."

Let us now take a closer look at the activities or the "means" of mission agencies. The *Handbook* lists fifty-nine categories of activities ranging from A (agricultural programs) to Y (youth programs). In rank order here are the top twelve activities with the corresponding number of mission agencies who are engaged in those activities. Many agencies, of course, are involved in more than one mission activity, hence the total number of agencies in this table is greater than the seven hundred listed in the *Handbook*.

RANK	NO. AGENCIES	MISSION ACTIVITY
1.	378	Church Planting
2.	221	Personal and Small Group Evangelism
3.	219	Leadership Development
4.	136	Theological Education
5.	125	National Church Nurture and Support
6.	123	Community Development
7.	120	Short-Term Programs
8.	114	Mass Evangelism
9.	114	Support of National Workers
10.	108	Discipleship
11.	101	Medical, Dental, and Public Health
12.	98	Literature Distribution

Notice the large gap between the first and second ranked activities and between the third and fourth ranked activities.

Traditional avenues of evangelical mission activity have been evangelism, education, and medicine or what are sometimes jokingly referred to as Bibles, Books, and Band Aids. Today medicine and education are no longer the growing edges of mission activity, but they have left a significant legacy of hospitals and schools all over the world. Concerns over abject poverty and the accelerating gap between the rich and the poor have led more evangelical agencies to begin to take more seriously the need for community development, for clean water, and the promotion of small-scale business ventures through micro-loans.

This has been a brief overview of evangelical mission agencies and the means they are using. We turn next to the underlying ecclesiological and missiological issues confronting these evangelical mission agencies.

ECCLESIOLOGICAL AND MISSIOLOGICAL ISSUES OF EVANGELICAL MISSION ORGANIZATIONS

Evangelical mission organizations can be divided into two major categories. The largest category is what is often called "faith missions" such as the China Inland Mission founded by James Hudson Taylor in 1865 and now known as OMF International. The other category includes evangelical denominations such as the Southern Baptist International Mission Board (4,009 missionaries serving four years or more), Assemblies of God World Missions (1,809), Christian and Missionary Alliance (761), the Church of the Nazarene World Mission Department (363), and other smaller denominational missions. The vast majority of U.S. missionaries, however, serve with faith missions and are responsible for raising their own support. This used to be one of the distinguishing contrasts between denominational missions and faith missions, but now with shrinking budgets and lean economic times many of the denominations are requiring their missionaries to raise part or sometimes all of their financial support. This can be a daunting task and certainly an exercise in faith building.

We need some reliable research to see if there is a difference between faith missions and denominational missions when it comes to the issue of working themselves out of a job and passing leadership on to nationals. Are "faith mission" missionaries or missionaries working under the auspices of a denominational mission agency doing the best job in training an indigenous leadership and passing control over to them?

Missionaries serving under evangelical denominations are no less inclined to focus on evangelism and church planting, but they also tend to be more concerned with denominational extension rather than planting indigenous churches. I have often observed that the "Book of Discipline" or the "Polity Manual" of denominational missionaries is one of the first things translated, so that the newly planted churches will look more like churches in the missionaries' homeland. This, of course, impedes contextualization.

I remember Eugene Nida, who spent a lifetime in Bible translation all over the world, telling me the following story. He would often go into a mission church worship service, make observations and take good notes, and then guess what denomination had planted this church. Because often the local church was similar in worship style, liturgy, architecture, polity, and so forth, as the North American church who sent the missionaries, he nearly always guessed correctly what denomination had planted it.

A continuing challenge for many evangelical mission agencies is to develop a more holistic and kingdom-oriented understanding of mission. Many evangelical mission agencies are still caught in the wake of the fundamentalist and modernist controversy of a century ago. That debate often drew a sharp distinction between evangelism and social justice, with the fundamentalists concerned more with saving souls and the modernists paying more attention to social ministries. A challenge for evangelical missionaries today is to focus more on the kingdom of God and to reclaim the whole Gospel that does not divide spiritual from social ministries, but holds them together as two aspects of the one Gospel. Unfortunately, there are still many evangelical missionaries who interpret ministries of social concern and justice as too liberal, and therefore they tend to avoid these ministries.

In October 2008, thirty-one missionaries and staff from The Mission Society met in Prague for five days to think about what The Mission Society should look like in twenty-five years. In 2009, The Mission Society is twenty-five years old, so we wanted to begin thinking more strategically about the next twenty-five years. It was a great exercise in thinking about the future. At the end of our five-day discussion we projected that in 2033, The Mission Society would be a member of a global association of missional communities who collaboratively send and receive cross-cultural kingdom stewards. We then noted that in order to accomplish this goal our Core Commitments and our Primary Strategies should be:

Core Commitments:
1. Living incarnationally.
2. Reaching the least reached.
3. Making disciple-makers.
4. Doing and proclaiming God's justice.

These are the key theological themes that ground us. Now what *means* will we use as an expression of these core commitments? We came up with seven, listed below, not necessarily in order of priority. We realized that in order to become the organization we want to become in 2033 we will need to employ the following avenues of ministry. Some of these we are already doing, some we need to focus on more, and some we need to begin to do now.

1. Church planting and strengthening.
2. Pastoral training and leadership development.
3. Educational ministries.
4. Business as mission.
5. Community development.
6. Church mobilization for mission.
7. Advocacy for the poor and oppressed.

One of our young staff members was looking over this list and he was amazed at the parallels between our lists and elements in the "Lausanne Covenant," which is a document that nearly all evangelical mission agencies subscribe to. Without consciously trying to be "evangelical" in our goals and our means to achieve those goals, we had articulated an approach that was thoroughly consistent with the "Lausanne Covenant." So, for example, we anticipate that in 2033 we will be a member of an association of various mission organizations collaborating with each other. Of course we are already doing this today, but in twenty-five years it will be an even more essential mode of operation. Article 7, "Cooperation in Evangelism," of the "Lausanne Covenant" states:

We affirm that the Church's visible unity in truth is God's purpose. Evangelism also summons us to unity, because our oneness strengthens our witness, just as our disunity undermines our Gospel of reconciliation. We recognize, however, that organizational unity may take many forms and does not necessarily forward evangelism. Yet we who share the same biblical faith should be closely united in fellowship, work and witness. We confess that our testimony has sometimes been marred by a sinful individualism and needless duplication. We pledge ourselves to seek a deeper unity in truth, worship, holiness and mission. We urge the development of regional and functional cooperation for the furtherance of the Church's mission, for strategic planning, for mutual encouragement, and for the sharing of resources and experience.[3]

The point I want to make is that many evangelical mission agencies have a much broader agenda today than just "saving souls." Most evangelical mission agencies will argue that evangelism is primary, but there must also be concern for the whole person, the whole of society, and so issues of justice and advocacy for the poor and the oppressed are increasingly addressed by evangelicals. This stance is also consistent with the "Lausanne Covenant." Yes, there are plenty of evangelical missionaries who fit the stereotyped caricature of missionaries concerned only with evangelism in a narrow sense, but there is a growing number who have a more holistic understanding of salvation and are focused more on the kingdom of God than on the extension of their denomination or the expansion of their mission organization.

Let us look now at The Mission Society as a case study of how an evangelical mission agency emerged from a mainline denomination and the "means" they are using in mission today.

CASE STUDY OF THE MISSION SOCIETY

The Mission Society for United Methodists was founded in 1984 by a group of concerned United Methodist pastors and others who believed that the evangelistic thrust of the United Methodist mission board had been in steep decline for the past generation. In 2005 the Mission Society for United Methodists changed its name to The Mission Society. While maintaining our Wesleyan theological orientation, we had grown beyond our Methodist constituency. Today The Mission Society works with fourteen different denominational groups in thirty-three countries.

Our founding president, H. T. Maclin, who served for thirty-one years with the General Board of Global Ministries of The United Methodist Church, notes in his book *The Faith that Compels Us* (1997),

The founding of the Mission Society for United Methodists as a voluntary agency within the church is another effort among the people called Methodists to recover our evangelical roots and once again regard missions as an opportunity to introduce Jesus Christ through a variety of means as the one and only provision God has made for our salvation.[4]

A precedent for the founding of The Mission Society was the founding of the Anglican Church Missionary Society (CMS) in 1799 when the Church of England already had two established mission agencies—the Society for the Propagation of Christian Knowledge (SPCK) founded in 1698 and the Society for the Propagation of the Gospel (SPG) founded in 1701. The founders of CMS had come to the conclusion that the older Anglican mission societies had essentially abandoned their primary task of evangelization.

The founders of the Mission Society for United Methodists believed the same phenomenon was happening within The United Methodist Church, that a social agenda was replacing evangelism, with a corresponding rapid decline in the number of missionaries being sent from North America. For example, in 1965, the Presbyterians, Methodists, and Southern Baptist mission boards each had about fifteen hundred missionaries in cross-cultural service. With the demise of political colonialism and the granting of national independence to so many nation states, it seemed to some people in the mainline churches that the era of mission should also be over. Today the United Methodists and Presbyterians have a very small number of missionaries, whereas the Southern Baptists have significantly increased their numbers.

In his book on the first decade of the Mission Society for United Methodists, H. T. Maclin cites D. Elton Trueblood from his book *The Validity of the Christian Mission*:

> The greatest danger in modern missions is not the one which existed previously, that of evangelism without service, but rather that of service without evangelism. If the service is performed as nothing but service, i.e., without being done as witness, it is bound to wither and die, for a fragmented Christianity is always close to death. Because the service which is not grounded in a message will soon cease to be even a service . . . if it stands alone it will soon cease to stand at all.[5]

This articulated what the founders of the Mission Society for United Methodists had come to believe. Gerald Anderson delivered a paper in October 1983 titled "Why We Need a Second Mission Agency" that was instrumental in serving as a catalyst to start the fledgling Mission Society for United Methodists in 1984.[6] Today The Mission Society has 216 missionaries serving in thirty-three countries using a host of means in ministry as we hold together the Great Commission *and* the Great Commandment.

CONCLUSION

Let me conclude by posing some questions that should be addressed by evangelical mission agencies as we consider the various means that are employed as we join in God's mission in the world.

1. How are you overcoming the gulf between evangelism and social concern?
2. What challenges do you face in planting indigenous churches, recognizing that God is at work in other cultures and traditions?
3. How do you deal with the tension of wanting to extend your denomination while at the same time focusing more on the kingdom of God?
4. How do you deal with the challenge of being Christocentric while at the same time having a deep appreciation for cultural and religious differences?
5. How do you make sure your board structure and membership reflects the cultural diversity where your mission agency is working?

In summary, the evangelical mission agencies are the main agents in mission from North America today. Many are defying the caricature and stereotype of previous generations of evangelical missions by their holistic use of means, combining the Great Commission with the Great Commandment to reach the whole world with the whole Gospel. "To God be the Glory."

NOTES

1. Linda J. Weber and Dotsey Welliver, eds., *Mission Handbook 2007–2009: U.S. and Canadian Protestant Ministries Overseas*, 20th ed. (Wheaton, Ill.: Evangelism and Missions Information Service [EMIS], 2007).

2. For examples of using business activities in the service of mission see Tom Steffen and Mike Barnett, eds., *Business as Mission: From Impoverished to Empowered*, Evangelical Missiological Society Series No. 14 (Pasadena, Calif.: William Carey Library, 2006); Tetsunao Yamamori and Kenneth A. Eldred, eds., *On Kingdom Business: Transforming Missions through Entrepreneurial Strategies* (Wheaton, Ill.: Crossway Books, 2003).

3. The Lausanne Covenant is a document written in 1974 calling for commitment to worldwide Christian evangelism. It has become the "gold standard" for defining evangelical involvement in mission. For the complete text of the Lausanne Covenant and papers and responses from the initial 1974 International Congress on World Evangelization in Lausanne, Switzerland, see J. D. Douglas, ed., *Let the Earth Hear His Voice* (Minneapolis: World Wide Publications, 1975). Text of the Lausanne Covenant can also be found at http://www.lausanne.org/covenant.

4. H. T. Maclin, *The Faith That Compels Us: Reflections on the Mission Society for United Methodists*; *The First Decade: 1984–1994* (Norcross, Ga: The Mission Society for United Methodists, 1997), p. 7.

5. D. Elton Trueblood, *The Validity of the Christian Message* (New York: Harper & Row, 1972), p. 101.

6. Gerald H. Anderson, "Why We Need a Second Mission Agency," *Good News* (March–April 1984): pp. 55–62.

LIST OF CONTRIBUTORS

Robert Aboagye-Mensah is the presiding Bishop of the Methodist Church Ghana. He was formerly the General Secretary of the Christian Council of Ghana.

William J. Abraham is the Albert C. Outler Professor of Wesley Studies, Perkins School of Theology, Southern Methodist University, Dallas, Texas and is actively involved in mission work in Kazakhstan and Nepal.

Gerald H. Anderson, Director Emeritus of the Overseas Ministries Study Center, New Haven, Connecticut, was formerly President of Scarritt College in Nashville, and was a United Methodist missionary on the faculty of Union Theological Seminary in the Philippines for nine years.

Daniel C. Arichea, Jr., is Bishop in residence at Duke Divinity School and Professor of Biblical Studies at Philippine Christian University and served for twenty-six years with the United Bible Societies in the Asia Pacific Region before his election to the United Methodist Episcopacy in the Philippines in 1994.

Lindy Backues is the Assistant Professor of Economic Development at Eastern University, St. Davids, Pennsylvania and served for almost nineteen years in Indonesia with Millennium Relief and Development Services.

Daryl Balia, a native of South Africa and Methodist minister, is the International Director of Edinburgh 2010, a research project related to the centenary celebrations of the 1910 World Missionary Conference and based at the University of Edinburgh in the United Kingdom.

David B. Barrett serves as an Anglican missionary priest with the Church Mission Society, undertaking research in Africa and other continents. He edited the *World Christian Encyclopedia* (1982, 2nd ed. 2001).

Paul W. Chilcote is the Professor of Historical Theology and Wesleyan Studies and Director of the Center for Applied Wesleyan Studies at Ashland Theological Seminary in Ashland, Ohio. He formerly taught at St. Paul's United Theological College in Limuru, Kenya, and was a charter member of Africa University Faculty of Theology in Old Mutare, Zimbabwe.

Luís Wesley de Souza, the Arthur J. Moore Associate Professor of Evangelism at Emory University's Candler School of Theology, Atlanta, Georgia, was the founder of and is visiting professor at South American Theological Seminary in Londrina, Brazil, where he also served as president of the board of directors of the Paul Pierson Center for Global Mission.

Ajith Fernando is a Methodist local preacher from Sri Lanka and has been National Director of Youth for Christ, Sri Lanka, since 1976. His books have been published in fourteen languages.

Dean Flemming is a lecturer of New Testament at European Nazarene College in Büsingen, Germany, and formerly taught at Asia-Pacific Nazarene Theological Seminary, Manila, Philippines.

Dean S. Gilliland is the Senior Professor of Contextualized Theology and African Studies in the School of Intercultural Studies, Fuller Theological Seminary, Pasadena, California, and was a United Methodist missionary in Nigeria from 1956 to 1977.

George G. Hunter III is the Beeson Distinguished Professor of Evangelization in Asbury Theological Seminary's E. Stanley Jones School of World Mission and Evangelism, Wilmore, Kentucky, and he formerly served as evangelism executive for the United Methodist denomination.

Arun W. Jones is the John W. and Helen Lancaster Associate Professor of Evangelism and Missions at Austin Presbyterian Theological Seminary, Austin, Texas. He was born in India of missionary parents and served as a United Methodist mission intern and short-term missionary in the Philippines.

H. T. Maclin served as a Methodist missionary in the Belgian Congo and Kenya for nearly twenty years, then was a Field Representative for Mission Development in the denomination for a decade. In 1984, he became the founding President of the Mission Society for United Methodists, now The Mission Society.

Arthur G. McPhee is the E. Stanley Jones Professor of Evangelization in the E. Stanley Jones School of World Mission and Evangelism at Asbury Theological Seminary, Wilmore, Kentucky.

W. Jay Moon is the Professor of Intercultural Studies and Director of the Wesley House of Study at Sioux Falls Seminary, South Dakota. He was a missionary with SIM among the Builsa people of Northern Ghana from 1992 to 2001.

Michael Mozley is the Africa Regional Coordinator for The Mission Society. He is based in Accra, Ghana.

Terry C. Muck is the Dean and Professor of Mission and World Religions in the E. Stanley Jones School of World Mission and Evangelism at Asbury Theological Seminary, Wilmore, Kentucky.

Sandra Richter is the Professor of Old Testament at Wesley Biblical Seminary, Jackson, Mississippi.

Dana L. Robert is the Truman Collins Professor of World Christianity and History of Mission, and Co-Director of the Center for Global Christianity and Mission at Boston University School of Theology.

Michael A. Rynkiewich is the Professor of Anthropology in the E. Stanley Jones School of World Mission and Evangelism at Asbury Theological Seminary, Wilmore, Kentucky. He served as a United Methodist missionary in Papua New Guinea from 1997 to 2002.

Howard A. Snyder is the Professor and Chair of Wesley Studies at Tyndale Seminary in Toronto, Ontario, Canada. He served as Professor of History and Theology of Mission in the E. Stanley Jones School of World Mission and Evangelism, Asbury Theological Seminary, Wilmore, Kentucky, and served for eight years in São Paulo, Brazil, as a Free Methodist missionary.

Wilbur Stone is the Program Director and Lead Faculty for Global and Contextual Studies, Bethel Seminary, St. Paul, Minnesota. He served for eleven years in cross-cultural ministry in Hong Kong and Malaysia.

Timothy C. Tennent, President of Asbury Theological Seminary, Wilmore, Kentucky, formerly served as Professor of World Mission and Indian Studies at Gordon-Conwell Theological Seminary, and has taught missions each year for the last twenty years at the Luther W. New, Jr. Theological College, Dehra Dun, India.

Norman E. Thomas is the Vera B. Blinn Professor Emeritus of World Christianity, United Theological Seminary, Dayton, Ohio. He served as a United Methodist missionary for eleven years in Rhodesia (now Zimbabwe) and four years in Zambia, and taught mission and evangelism at Yale Divinity School and Boston University School of Theology.

Norival Trinidade, Jr., is the Vice-President for Training of the International Leadership Institute, Carrolton, Georgia, has degrees both in medicine and theology, and worked in Paraguay for ten years as a medical missionary.

Robert G. Tuttle, Jr., is the Professor of World Christianity at the Florida Dunnam Campus of Asbury Theological Seminary in Orlando.

Andrew F. Walls began missionary service in West Africa in 1957, teaching in Sierra Leone and Nigeria. He was the founding Director of the Centre for the Study of Christianity in the Non-Western World at the University of Edinburgh, Scotland. Currently, he serves as Honorary Professor in the University of Edinburgh, Professor of the History of Mission at Liverpool Hope University, and Professor at the Akrofi-Christaller Institute in Ghana. He is General Editor of the (British) Methodist Missionary History Project.

Darrell Whiteman is the Vice-President for Mission Personnel and Preperation and Resident Missiologist with The Mission Society in Norcross, Georgia. Following research and mission experience in Central Africa and Melanesia, he served as Dean and Professor of Cultural Anthropology in the E. Stanley Jones School of World Mission and Evangelism at Asbury Theological Seminary, Wilmore, Kentucky.

Hwa Yung is Bishop of the Methodist Church in Malaysia and was formerly Director of the Centre for the Study of Christianity in Asia at Trinity Theological College, Singapore.

A. H. Mathias Zahniser, Emeritus Professor of Christian Mission, Asbury Theological Seminary, is Scholar in Residence at Greenville College, Greenville, Illinois. An ordained minister in the Free Methodist Church of North America, he served a brief term as a missionary in Egypt.

AMERICAN SOCIETY OF MISSIOLOGY SERIES
PREVIOUSLY PUBLISHED WORKS

The American Society of Missiology Series seeks to publish scholarly work of high merit and wide interest on numerous aspects of missiology—the study of Christian mission in its historical, social, and theological dimensions. Able proposals on new and creative approaches to the practice and understanding of mission will receive close attention from the ASM Series Committee.